The Peace Movement in America

A facsimile reprint collection

"Peace"

Jerome S. Ozer, Publisher

1972

Library of Congress Catalog Card No. 75-137559

This edition is reprinted from a copy in the
collection of The New York Public Library

Manufactured in the United States of America

REASON *vs.* THE SWORD.

REASON *vs.* THE SWORD,

A TREATISE;

IN WHICH IT IS SHOWN THAT MAN HAS NO RIGHT TO TAKE HUMAN LIFE; AND THAT WAR IS VIOLATIVE OF THE LAWS OF NATURE AND OF REVELATION,

AND DESTRUCTIVE OF

THE RIGHT OF SELF-GOVERNMENT.

By JOHN M. WASHBURN.

For the Son of Man is not come to destroy men's lives, but to save them. Luke 9: 56.
Glory to God in the highest, on earth peace, good will to men. Luke 2: 14.

NEW YORK:
PUBLISHED FOR THE PROPRIETORS,
BY G. P. PUTNAM & SONS.
W. G. HUBBARD, COLUMBUS, O.
1873.

Entered according to Act of Congress, in the year 1872, by
W. G. HUBBARD,
In the Office of the Librarian of Congress, at Washington.

172.4
W273r

TO THOSE WHO BELIEVE THAT THE
SCHEME OF GOD'S MORAL GOVERNMENT IS SO GOOD,
THAT
PERSECUTION IS UNNECESSARY
TO THE
PURITY OF THE CHURCH,
AND THAT
HIS SCHEME OF NATURAL GOVERNMENT IS SO WISE
THAT THE SWORD IS UNNECESSARY
TO THE INTERESTS OF THE STATE,

IS THIS VOLUME DEDICATED.

CONTENTS.

	PAGE.
INTRODUCTION	15

PART FIRST.

THEOLOGICAL ASPECTS OF THE SUBJECT IN GENERAL.

CHAPTER I.

THE END OF MAN'S EARTHLY LIFE AND THE NATURE OF HIS FUTURE LIFE	25

CHAPTER II.

THEOLOGICAL ASPECT OF THE SUBJECT	37
§ 1.—The supposed right to take life as derived from the laws of nature	37
§ 2.—Is there a right to take life derived from the constitution of natnre since sin introduced death into the world?..	43

CHAPTER III.

THE THEOLOGICAL ASPECT OF THE SUBJECT	47
§ 1.—The right to take life as derived from the Old Testament	47
§ 2.—The right, as derived from the Old Testament, to wage war	62
§ 3.—Inference against the principles of war from the whole teaching of the Old Testament	73

CHAPTER IV.

THE THEOLOGICAL ASPECT OF THE SUBJECT	81
§ 1.—The authority for war as derived from the New Testament	81

§ 2.—The authority for war as derived from the New Testament—Particular Texts.................................. 95
§ 3.—Argument against war from the New Testament....... 102

PART SECOND.

POLITICAL ASPECTS OF THE SUBJECT.

CHAPTER I.

THE NATURE OF HUMAN GOVERNMENT....................... 115

CHAPTER II.

THE POLITICAL PRINCIPLES AND THEORY OF GOVERNMENT..... 126
§ 1.—The basis of Civil Government—Different forms of Government.. 126
§ 2.—The United States Government the model—Axioms of Liberty... 133
§ 3.—Reflections on the axioms of Political Liberty......... 143
§ 4.—Natural wants and self-government inseparable—American colonies....................................... 148
§ 5.—State Rights, Secession, Slavery, and their Incidents.. 158
§ 6.—Other Aspects of State Rights and Secession......... 166
§ 7.—Coercion conditions right by power—The Church and War... 176
§ 8.—Other incidents of Self-Government................. 186

CHAPTER III.

§ 1.—Can Government be supported without the use of the Sword?.. 197
§ 2.—Reason unites with interest to form the "cement" of government... 205
§ 3.—The Colonial Government of Pennsylvania........... 215
§ 4.—The war spirit amongst Christians—Its cure amongst men... 227
§ 5.—Some of the means that might be used to sustain government.. 240
§ 6.—Objections to the preceding section noticed, with other incidental thoughts.................................. 257

CHAPTER IV.
VARIOUS OBJECTIONS NOTICED—INDEFINITE SECESSION 272

CHAPTER V.
PECUNIARY ASPECTS OF THE WAR-QUESTION 288

PART THIRD.

THE MORAL ASPECTS OF THE SUBJECT.

CHAPTER I.
THE REVEALED LAW OF GOD THE ULTIMATE RULE OF RIGHT .. 305

CHAPTER II.
ELEMENTARY PRINCIPLES OF CHRISTIAN MORALITY 316

CHAPTER III.
THE PRINCIPLES AND MORALITY OF WAR 324

CHAPTER IV.
BRAVERY, VALOR, COWARDICE, TREASON, AND OTHER VICES AND VIRTUES OF WAR 350

CHAPTER V.
WAR PUNISHES THE INNOCENT AND LETS THE WICKED GO FREE .. 368

CHAPTER VI.
§ 1.—Personal Self-Defence by Destroying Life 381
§ 2.—Right to defend the life of a nation 398

CHAPTER VII.
ENLIGHTENED REASON FORBIDS WAR AS THE MEANS OF PRESERVING CIVIL GOVERNMENT 408

CHAPTER VIII.
POLITICAL MORALITY.—WAR DELUSIONS.—CARE FOR NATIONAL DIVISIONS 420

CHAPTER IX.

RELATION THE CHURCH AND MINISTRY ASSUMED TO THE WAR.—
THE ASSASSINATION, ETC. 430

CHAPTER X.

RELATION OF THE CHURCH AND MINISTRY TO WAR 341

CHAPTER XI.

FINAL GENERAL REFLECTIONS ON THE SUBJECT OF WAR, ... 453

INTRODUCTION.

IT is proper that those who read the thoughts of another should, as far as possible, understand the reasons and motives which actuate the other in their expression. And this is eminently proper if the thoughts or teachings may be regarded in their tendency as suited to have an effect upon established social regulations which are esteemed valuable by men. In the teachings of this work, the author is very likely to be misunderstood, and then his motives may be impugned, and he denounced, in a manner at once untrue and unjust. For, although the teachings of this volume are mostly self-evident, yet the facts and truths employed in making up the trains of reasoning, are employed in a manner somewhat novel; and at the same time there is an application made of them which may array against both the reasoning and the author an unjust prejudice.

It is not the design to apologize for the teachings of this volume; for though very imperfect, they are honestly believed to be correct. It is only designed to have the reader realize so far as possible, the real feeling and motives of the author. The author is of the opinion that the germs of the thoughts herein were born with him, as from his earliest recollection the idea of slaying men in war, or of inflicting on them Capital Punishment filled his mind with abhorrence. Of course, at so early a period of life, it was rather matter of feeling than of thought well defined to the consciousness. Increasing years increased the feeling, till events and circumstances caused the feeling to assume the thoughts contained in this volume.

When the storm-cloud of war recently burst upon our

country, it filled the writer with amazement and confusion. The idea of fighting, to him was abhorrent; the idea of dividing the nation was painful; the institution of slavery was odious. The situation of the nation was at once complicated and delicate. The writer could not believe that war was right, and thence could not help believing that there must be some better way of settling such matters than by the cruelties of war. As the dreadful scenes of the war progressed, he sought to reflect carefully about the matter. He was appalled by the dimensions and the horrors of the war; and felt that both parties were committing not only a sad mistake but a fearful crime in carrying on the war. He was entirely satisfied that the time would come when wars would wholly cease amongst men, as the prophet Isaiah clearly foretold, and as the whole spirit and letter of Jesus and the apostles taught. He saw clearly that Jesus and the apostles forbade utterly the indulgence of the feelings and passions on which war necessarily depends, and so necessarily forbade all war. But it is not less plain that God ordains the powers that be. Thence, believing in the wisdom of God as moral Governor of the world, it must follow, from God's ordaining that there should be government, and forbidding the indulgence of the passions on which war depends, that war was not necessary either to the well-being or the permanence of government. The idea, then, was presented, that there must be some principle which, when reduced to practice, would render government permanent, and relieve the world of the scourge and horrors of war.

Reflection led him to see, as he believes, that the principle lies in the common fatherhood of God, and the consequent brotherhood of all men. This principle would involve the natural equality of men in rights and privileges, and it suggested the thoughts which are developed in the body of the book. The writer saw at once that the primary or radical principles which would be involved in the reasoning that must do away with all war, were axiomatic, and had been theoretically recognized in this country from the beginning of our present form of government. He took up these radical principles, or axioms, and employed them in the endeavor to show that the sword is not necessary to maintain government, and that its use cannot consist with the idea and fact of self-government.

In employing these axiomatic principles, it was seen at once that they had a wide scope of application, and would as readily do away with all sorts of slavery as with the sword. The assumption of the axioms brought the reasoning into harmony with the moral government of God, whose laws at once forbid all sorts of slavery, both of mind and body; and hence at once and forever forbids the use of the sword, which originates and inflicts all sorts of slavery. Indeed, the reasoning of this volume proves, if it proves anything, that all hatred, violence, war, slavery, and persecution, are as unwise in themselves as they are unnecessary to the well-being of the state and the good of mankind. They are unwise and unnecessary, because they violate man's rational nature, and come into conflict with the laws of the moral government of God. And the whole process of reasoning into which he was led by the raging of the horrid and revolting war, induced him to believe in the inalienable right of self-government in all people. Thence the theory of the reasoning of this volume was presented to the mind. Shocked at the wild storm of war raging in the country, the more he reflected on the thoughts thus presented to the mind, the clearer they became. He then began to commit his thoughts to writing without pausing to digest them into a nicely adjusted plan. Beginning to write, the details of thought were arranged as the writing progressed. The first draft had no GRAND DIVISIONS; but was written chapter after chapter, as one thought sprang out of another. And thus a considerable part of the manuscript was written, and was laid aside. But exhibiting it to a distinguished divine, he urged the writer to prepare it for publication as meeting an urgent demand in the public mind. After considering the matter for some months, and hoping that if published, it might do something to draw attention to the great subject of Peace, he decided to re-write the manuscript, that it might go to the public if circumstances favored the publication. But, in re-writing, the first careless method was abandoned, and the PLAN, as it now appears, was adopted. The change was probably unwise; for it cost considerable labor, and left other imperfections, rendering some parts a little diffusive, and involving some needless repetition, not discovered till too late to be remedied without another writing.

THE PRESENT PLAN OF THE WORK

is, it is hoped, simple and natural, involving THREE GENERAL DIVISIONS: THE THEOLOGICAL; THE POLITICAL; THE MORAL. These divisions seem to cover the whole subject. The First and Second divisions do not necessarily involve extended discussion. But Part Third opened a field vast and nearly interminable, involving the entire domain of ethical law.

THE PLAN OF THE THOUGHT

is not coincided with the FORMAL DIVISIONS of the work: But it is also three-fold: First, There is an underlying logic which, it is hoped, pervades every paragraph, teaching that rational man is a being too noble to be butchered upon the battle-field, and that God designed him for a far greater destiny. Then, secondly, It has pleased God not to bestow on man the right to take human life. This thought is more prominent in Part First; but, in dimmer outline, is implied in every section, losing prominence in passing from Part First to Part Second, but gaining fuller relief again in Part Third. THE THIRD THOUGHT is an outgrowth from the First and Second combined: Because man is a noble being, and because God does not allow his life to be taken, together with the idea, that men have urgent wants, as social and living beings, arises the Third Great

Thought, *That all people have the inalienable right to maintain self-government, free from the terrors of the sword*; and hence that all wars for coercion are immoral and criminal. Part First and Second involve the premises and reasoning which logically infer Part Third as the general conclusion. For if in searching the laws of nature and revelation there is found to be no right to take life ; and if in searching the axioms of political liberty, it is self-evident that all men have the right to sustain self-government ; it must logically follow that it is immoral to engage in war, or to inflict capital punishment. But the logical links between Parts First and Second, and the inferences of Part Third, are mostly left to be supplied in the mind of the reader. In Part Third, therefore, the processes do not so logically spring out of each other ; but the processes in that part are more particular developments of laws expressed or implied in some more general process in Parts First and Second. Therefore, the continuity of Part Third with Parts First and Second, lies in a more comprehensive underlying implication of logic, supplied by the reader's mind, the inferential connectives being omitted in the reasoning.

THE STYLE AND TEMPER OF THE WORK

may by some be regarded as severe. But it is hoped that thoughtful readers will excuse these defects, as the subject seemed to admit of nothing else. Although the style may be severe, the writer is conscious of the immeasurable distance between his expressed conceptions and the horrid realities of war. And he is conscious of no other

MOTIVE IN WRITING THE WORK

than the love of truth in itself. With no parties to the late war, as such, could he sympathize ; nor even with the Christian church so far as it took part in the conflict ; and so his own mind, without favor or disguise, has been expressed on the subject treated with feelings towards the *persons* of neither section of the country. The subject treated is one of the gravest of this or any other age, and merits the solemn consideration of all reflective men. If the views expressed are correct, their practical adoption would confer infinite blessings on our race. If they are not correct, he has no desire that mankind should embrace them. No one, therefore, will more readily accept the criticism which points out an error in the work than its author. In no respect does the volume approach his own ideal; yet the nature of the subject involves no profound reflection; no great metaphysical research elaborated by years of patient thought. As a whole, the work contains no thought that ought to be new to reflective people, and no principle that Christian people should not feel bound to reduce to practice. The radical thoughts which are used in the more rigid logical processes, are few and axiomatic, and those with which we have been familiar from childhood. The world ought to adopt the conclusions in all their practical results.

THE OBJECTIONS THAT MAY BE MADE TO THE WORK, are refuted by the logical inferences arising from the familiar and axiomatic principles mostly employed in the reasoning. Some of the reasoning will of course be misunderstood, and may elicit severe criticism. The author is prepared for anything that will bring out the truth. He has consciously written in the interests only of truth; and so will listen to whatever may bring it out. He is painfully conscious of his imperfections, and so is prepared to regard with favor suggestions for improvement, and to profit from them. For his temerity in standing face to face *with words*, before that Political Majesty, whose breath exhaled war over all the land, and calling in question the very principles on which the war was conducted, some persons of this age may denounce him; but he has full confidence in the final triumphs of human nature; and has the utmost faith that progress of thought will vindicate the substantial truth herein advocated. In the *principles of peace* his faith is full and complete, and he believes that they will finally triumph though they involve the overthrow of long cherished political philosophy and stereotyped dogmas. The suggestion of the moral right to sever this great nation into two nations, as the alternative to war, is the suggestion to which most exception will be taken. But since the principle involved in the suggestion, is that which is to take away the last plausible pretext for the use of the sword, it was felt that the point should be plainly developed; since it rested directly on the axioms of political liberty, recognized by this nation from the foundation of its existence. At all events, the writer has that undoubted confidence in the accuracy of peace-doctrines, and that hope in the progress of humanity, that he hesitates not, in their rational support, to assail the right to draw the sword even for the purpose of preventing the division of so great a nation as ours. In considering the question of the division of the nation, the painful idea was somewhat mitigated by perceiving that the reasoning which put away the use of the sword, would also banish from the world the sin and crime of personal slavery—removing from the world by the same reasoning, the two greatest of human scourges.

THAT CHRISTIANS HAVE NOT SUFFICIENTLY CONSIDERED THE SUBJECT OF WAR

must be admitted by all reflective people. All intelligent persons admit that war is wrong in its necessary principles, when tried by the teaching of the Son of God. Yet it is hard to make them see that the admission, logically concedes all that peace-men claim. But it does. For it is too plain that men are never under the necessity to do wrong. And if the moral laws of God forbid all war, morality obliges men never to engage in it; and logically infers, from God's being a wise Moral Governor, that upon the whole, men can derive no benefit from engaging in it. To urge that they must engage in it, under the circumstances in which they are placed, is to urge that God has placed them under the necessity of doing wrong. To maintain that God ordains the existence of government, and to admit that, in His revealed will, He forbids the use of the sword; and then to contend that the use of the sword is necessary to sustain government, is palpably to impeach the wisdom and benevolence of God as Moral Governor of the world. All agree that God " ordains the powers that be ;" and all must agree that God forbids the indulgence of the *necessary* principles of war. If, then, war is necessary to sustain " the powers that be," it logically follows that God ordains the existence of something, the existence of which He also forbids, by forbidding the use of the means necessary to its existence. The war-man cannot escape this dilemma—a dilemma in which the peace-man is not at all involved. War-men are involved in other difficulties not less perplexing: No reason can be urged for the use of the sword in the interests of the State, that cannot as well be urged for its use in the interests of the church. And the church has as much right to prevent men from acting with reference to their spiritual interests as the State has the right to prevent them from acting with reference to their temporal interests. And the right to prevent them from acting, implies the right to prevent them from thinking; since acting is only thinking carried into practice. If secession in act is criminal, secession in thought is criminal; and this involves the idea that the State has the right to punish the subject for thinking. The only difficulty will be in knowing how the subject thinks; the expression of the thought will make the crime complete. Thence, if the reasoning of war-men is correct, the State may forbid both free thought and free speech, when they relate to itself. And such is the result to which the coercive use of the sword logically and ethically leads. No man can show a good reason why it is not morally right to prevent men from thinking and speaking what they may not reduce to practice, since the moral quality of all action lies in the thought. So, if it is criminal to reduce a thought to practice, it is criminal to have the thought which produces the practice. Whence, if the moral right exists to prohibit the practice, the moral right exists to prohibit the thought which produces the practice. This is the mode of reasoning which persecutors have always employed; and it is the only mode that can be logically employed by the coercionist. Indeed, coercion and persecution stand on an identical ground of reason, having a diversity of application: one having reference to the State; the other, to the church.

The general principles are, it is hoped, explained in the body of this volume, If they shall be read by men, and contribute in some degree to lead them to consider the horror of war, and to see the beauties of the doctrines of Peace, the author will be grateful to God, and feel amply rewarded for the labor he has bestowed.

J. M. W.

December 25, 1872.

REASON *vs.* THE SWORD.

PART FIRST.

THEOLOGICAL ASPECTS OF THE SUBJECT IN GENERAL.

CHAPTER I.

THE END OF MAN'S EARTHLY LIFE AND THE NATURE OF HIS FUTURE LIFE.

COMPARATIVELY few persons attach just importance to human life, because comparatively few entertain distinct and impressive conceptions of its true object. And the objection which lies against the act of taking it is the most cogent objection that can lie against any act : it is that God disallows it, and that the consequence may involve the loss of the soul. There is a view in which life is of infinite value, because, in that view, it embraces infinite results. Considered as the period during which the destinies of the soul are determined, thoughtful men must admit that the finite mind can form no adequate idea of its value. In itself, however, life can hardly be regarded as valuable beyond the grasp of the mind. For, patiently considered, it is not free from doubt, whether its joys or its sorrows preponderate. Even in the case of those who seem freest from its ills, it is doubtful whether its sorrows do not outweigh its joys. But its chief importance is derived from the relation which God has appointed between it and men's future lives. And it is hence that it derives its transcendent importance ; and hence is derived the unanswerable argument against men's taking it. Studiously contemplated in this aspect, the idea of men's earthly life thrills the mind with emotions of solicitude. In every earnest mind, the anxious inquiry must arise, What shall be the issue of this brief and fleeting life in the flesh?

But impressive and awful as such an inquiry must be to the contemplative and sensitive mind, observation teaches that the masses of men are not greatly impressed by it. For it is painfully evident that the multitudes of men live and die without seriously reflecting about the true end of their earthly existence. Nay, the multitudes strive to withdraw their thoughts from dwelling upon that future on which they must so soon enter.

It is evident, too, that the large majority of the human race employ the brief period of life in the worthless follies which solicit the attractions of sense and supply the gratifications of vanity. They rarely permit serious thoughts to possess the mind, touching the relation which this life sustains to the future. Thoughts of the end of life are studiously banished as unwelcome guests.

And such is the truly sad lesson taught everywhere in the school of experience. The careful observer may take a stand-point for observation where he may—in fashionable or in humble life—in the tumultuous city or the quiet country—amongst statesmen or politicians, scholars or philosophers—in heathen or in Christian lands, everywhere and in all time, the same melancholy lesson is taught—men are anxiously and profoundly attached to this world, and regard with indifference the world to come. And here lies the root of all war—that bitter root, grown into a huge tree, which has spread its malaria, fraught with death, over the fields of earth's civilization. For it is because men care little for the world to come, and greatly for the world which is, that they forget the former, and fight and slay each other about the latter.

To the mind capable of reflection touching the susceptibilities of the soul in the future, one would think such thoughts would be invested with the highest interest. But experience teaches a lesson at variance with this inference of reason. For, while nothing is more evident than the comparative worthlessness of mere worldly attainments, nothing is more evident than the indifference with which most men regard every thing but mere worldly attainments. Nothing is more evident than the evanescence of worldly goods and worldly honors, yet nothing is sought with such arduous zeal and unremitted perseverance. And though a life spent in the attainment of them is spent in vain, the masses of men spend life in the attainment of little else.

Now, dispassionate reason, guided by enlightened conscience, surely dictates the folly of such conduct in rational mortals. Yet, by the seductions of passion and the attractions of carnal self-love, reason seems blinded and conscience hushed into silence. Still, despite the infatuation of such rashness, there are intervals in the history of all men, when reason and conscience reassert their rejected dominion, and inspire their guilty violators with apprehensions of a future and fearful doom. Nor can all the schooling of the soul to insensibility save the guilty wretches, thus arraigned and sentenced at the bar of reason and conscience, from acknowledging the justice of the sentence to future retribution. And the guilty must have occasional apprehensions of a coming fearful doom. But amid the furious storms which passion excites in the soul, the voice is unheeded. At such times, terror rules over the soul. Reason and conscience are drowned in the deluge; and rational man becomes the slave of irrational passion. Yet conscience is but hushed. In the moments of thoughtful sobriety, when the tumults of passion cease their tyranny over the deeper life, conscience reasserts its authority, and whispers to the guilty culprit that he is in danger of future wrath. And every individual, feeling at times an apprehension of coming wrath, also feels at times solicitude about his future well-being. The one feeling is as universal as the other; while each belongs to the occasional experience of all men. And these feelings are matters of fact. They cannot be mistaken. They may be thrust aside; in life they generally are. Still they are in the soul; and anon, lifting their voice above the clamors of passion, they shriek alarm to the soul, imparting a faint foretaste of what awaits it in the future.

These forebodings should teach men a lesson not to be forgotten; lest, unheeded, they inflict a doom not to be disregarded. And they ought to teach men, because they are the result of a cause which God has put into the soul: We are the inhabitants of this world for an end which surpasses the grasp of imagination or the flight of fancy. And with emotions full of solicitude, it behooves each person to inquire for himself, *Why am I in this world?* Why has God given me a mental and moral organization so exquisite in its sensibility? Why, despite all my efforts, is my soul alarmed at times, and made to long for future joy?

Questions such as these are full of argument and replete with significance. In them are involved the issue and doom of the human race. In them are involved the seminal arguments against all war. Related to them are all the properly associated thoughts of this volume, and all the interests of human life. And it is in the fact that men have souls to be saved or lost in the future, that our theme gathers its principal interests. The soul attracts about it an intense concentration of interests, and invites to a more detailed consideration of its attributes before we reach the logical burden of our thought. This consideration it is now the time to bestow.

It is assumed that all the works of God are consistent. It is then as evident that He gives us being in time for some great end, as that He gives us eyes to see and ears to hear. And it is evident that we are endued with desires of future good and fears of future ill for a final end, as that we have any faculties and senses for an end. Hence the first inquiry is, Why does God give man a probation on earth? Why has man a world-life? God could have made him complete in life, exempt from ills, and perfect as the good shall be when they are clothed in the likeness of Christ's glorified body. Why did He not so form him in his original creation?

The inquiry is intended to present the question of man's life in the flesh, with the view of ascertaining whether that life may be trifled with in the games and chances of war waged in the supposed interests of worldly good. And we repeat the question—Why does God give man existence in the world? Can a more important inquiry be started concerning the apostate race? God has revealed the fact that man is destined to survive the dissolution of death, and to live in endless duration beyond the earthly scenes; and, unless we have the temerity to charge Him with folly, reason suggests that a great purpose must belong to his earthly existence. But reason, unaided, might be inadequate to the task of learning the exact end of man's world-life. Experience teaches that such is the case. Heathens infer nearly every thing else than the true end of man's life in the flesh. It is feared that nominal Christians often commit a mistake equally great. The light of Revelation, however, presents the true end of life in this world. It tells us that the true end of life in time is to prepare for life beyond time. And all things are suited to instruct right reason in this conclusion. Every function of our being—our hopes, our fears, our joys, our sorrows, our love of life, our shrinking from death—every thing within us, and every thing without us—all the voices of reason and all the utterances of nature are suited to instruct us that God has made this life brief, uncertain and anxious, for the purpose of engaging the soul in preparation for that life which is to come. But do men learn the intended lesson of this instruction? Look at real life. What is the fact there? Do they measure and value life as God manifestly intended they should? Alas! they will plunge into the horrors of war and slaughter each other, as if a hereafter was a tradition and future life a myth. Yet, given the idea of an endless future dependent upon the behavior of this life, does not enlightened reason teach that no earthly inducement should form the lowest possible motive to send a soul unprepared into the future? And all blinding passion aside, is not this the conclusion of the dispassionate and thoughtful mind?

It subtracts nothing from the force of this conclusion, that men do not avow and act upon it. They are often grossly inconsistent, and act from lower carnal considerations, abjuring and ignoring the higher reason of the spirit and conscience. Often their convictions are in flagrant antagonism with their conduct; and it is not risking much to affirm that the convictions of all really intelligent Christian men stand in antagonism to the assent which they give to the practices of war amongst the nations of the earth. But they yield their assent under some plausible sophism—some argument of *expediency* which they do not care to examine minutely.

But it is not proposed to analyze the inconsistencies of men. They are many and great. The purpose is rather to draw the inference that the great end of men's lives is, that they may save their souls; and not that they may butcher one another upon hostile fields. And if we may confide in the conclusion that we have ascertained truly that end, another inquiry of prime importance for consideration arises: What is the nature of that future estate which it is the great end of man's life in the flesh to attain?

If it is true that our present being derives its chief importance from its relation to the future, then the importance of the present life is increased or diminished in value as it stands related to the future, in accordance with *the nature*, *the susceptibilities*, and *the duration* of the soul in the future. Accordingly, it becomes fitting to consider these in their order.

And here it is proper to observe that unaided reason is necessitated to silence. The inquiry transcends its limits. Reason unaided has its assigned office. It inquires, compares, deduces, and infers about things within its reach. But unaided, of that dark and mysterious future, it knows nothing. It may imagine and theorize, but the *future* will be as dark as the reign of chaos. The reason is, that the whole field of thought lies beyond the unaided mental vision—lies beyond the reach of the telescope of thought. It is the province of God to furnish us knowledge of the future of our being; and if we have such knowledge, we have it in both kind and degree, as God has been pleased to bestow it. Hence the question comes to be one in the nature of a fact: What does God tell us as to the nature, duration, and susceptibilities of the soul in the future?

But we have no purpose to enter largely into a Bible argument on the question now engaging attention. And in this connection it is only necessary to observe that God represents the future of the soul as endless, its nature as fearful, and its susceptibilities as greatly increased beyond their present powers. He plainly represents the future as divided into two parts or departments; and that these departments will be occupied by those who shall have contrary characters. The happy shall have joy unmingled, delight uninterrupted. But the unhappy shall never hear of the tidings of hope. Their doom is one of desolation, intense and endless. Vivid figures are employed in order to convey to our minds a conception of their suffering. It is called an endless death; and the unhappy beings are represented under the bold figure of being in a lake of fire. All the imagery descriptive of their condition, is suited to convey vivid conceptions of a doom hopeless and appalling.

As we are unable to conceive of the anguish of the lost, so are we of the happiness of the saved; yet the anguish of the lost and the happiness of the saved constitute, to the respective parties, the *nature* of their future existence.

Now, since we have thus the *nature* of the soul's destiny in the future from God himself, no deduction is to be made, unless we cannot confide in the source of our information. But that will not be questioned by those with whom we reason. For we shall not appeal to those who do not accept the Bible as true. Sceptics and unbelievers are outside our range of reasoning. If our reasoning is allowed to be correct thus far, the conclusion is reached that our conceptions are too dim and shadowy to grasp the awfulness of that future on which we must soon enter. Yet another important element must be added to the conception of the future. It is its *duration*. *God* tells us that it is simply endless. *We* can reason nothing about it. *We* are only helpless in wonder at the idea. It is one of those conceptions that belongs to the Infinite, while suited to impress our minds with the most reverent and awful of emotions.

And while the soul is endless in its duration, God tells us that its *capacities* for enjoying or suffering will experience no diminution; and whatever information we have on the subject must come from Him. For the whole subject lies beyond the reach of the human faculties. But not only will the capabilities of the soul in the future not be diminished, they will be vastly enlarged. God reveals to us many things which both teach and imply this.

Now, if this reasoning about the future life is allowed to be just, how intense and profound should be the emotions awakened whenever the mind is directed towards it! The pen is impotent to portray the interest which must ever attach to the idea of the soul's endless future. Life itself is a mystery of awful significance. But an endless life God only can understand.

Having briefly considered some of the elements of a future life, there still remains one other thought of the general subject to be considered: *What is the relation which the present life sustains to the future?* It has been briefly said that, in the appointment of God, life in this world is man's probationary period, decisive of his allotment in the future world. The frame and temper of the soul at the moment it leaves the body, will fix the condition of the soul itself, in the future, forever. God has revealed this as His unchangeable appointment. Why this is the appointment of God, lies beyond the sphere of our inquiry. We do learn, however, that the preparation for the endless future must be acquired during the life in the flesh. This is the clear teaching of God. There is no work nor device in the grave. The preparation for the future must be made *before* the soul is cited hence, or it will be endlessly lost. God so tells us, and He alone understands the whole of the subject. Man can know nothing on the subject by the use of his own faculties. He must learn from God all that he knows. The whole is a grave and awful subject to the reflective mind. And it is from the consideration of it, and the relation of this life to the future, that life derives its chief value ; and, aside from the inherent cruelty and repulsiveness of war, here is derived a general argument against it, which can find a show of reply only by abandoning, really or practically, the whole idea of Christianity. By divine appointment, eternal life has its birthplace upon the earth, while the soul is in the body. Hence if the future is lost, life loses a large portion of its value. If the soul is doomed by sin to perdition, it is hardly doubtful that the quicker the person goes to his place the better ; because, after the doom is fixed by unrepented sins, he but treasures wrath for the day of wrath. And it was on this account, undoubtedly, so far as we have the means of knowing, that God appointed destruction to the inhabitants of Canaan. The cup of their iniquity was full. Their sins had outlawed them from God's covenants of grace ; and as there remained to them no hope, God ordered their destruction. The destruction was executed by dreadful war; but executed by the *certain* command of God ; and God had the right to make the command. The possibility of future life lost by sin, the present life was ordered to be destroyed. This distinguishes the Jewish wars forever from all other wars. So long as there is a possibility of future life remaining, for *us*, upon our own motion, to destroy the present life, can be sin only, sin aggravated and revolting. And since we can never know when the possibility of future life is gone, war, by our motion, must ever be only sin, aggravated and revolting. For, from the human side of the question, under the gospel, preparation for the future may be made at any moment while the soul remains in the body. And, as we understand the matter, the *great* object of life is that preparation for the future may be made. Such preparation, therefore, is as priceless as the soul. Without it the soul must be lost. And should the soul be lost, all will be lost. For it would be better that it had not been at all than to be lost. Now, if we believe God, no price can be put upon the soul; and if we believe Him, the soul will be lost if not prepared to be saved while in the flesh. Life is chiefly given, that, during its continuance, the soul may be saved; and it may be saved at any moment during life. We have, then, a strong case made. For it follows that the act of taking life may cause the loss of the soul. Dreadful and appalling, then, to the reflecting mind must be the idea of war, which is but the idea of the wholesale butchery of men! Should anything but the unmistakable command of God induce the condition of war? And are men at liberty to engage in the wholesale slaughter of each other about the perishable things of this world—may they destroy each other's bodies, and thence each other's souls about the phantom of human government, or that impalpable thing styled national honor? The soul must be of priceless value—of infinite value. Think then of the loss of life and of the consequent loss of souls by means of war! The bare idea benumbs thought and paralyzes the mind. Yet the primary and professed business of war is to destroy human life; and as a necessary consequence, it destroys souls. For war finds its existence in violence. Therein consist its fierce glory and bloody triumph. Therefore, war cannot do less than inflict on mankind infinite wrongs. Destroying both the bodies and the souls of men, how can its wrongs be less than infinite? Look at the matter for a moment. Concede a fact or two in themselves axiomatic, and then mark the conclusion. 1. Souls are of infinite value. 2. War destroys souls. Now, apply the logic: Whatever destroys the souls of men inflicts on them infinite wrongs. War destroys the souls of men. Therefore war inflicts on them infinite wrongs. Again, the loss of souls is an infinite loss.

War involves the loss of souls. War, therefore, involves infinite losses. Hence, since no number of the finite can constitute the infinite, so no number of finite causes added can justify a war that may involve infinite losses. Wherefore, if we follow war to those logical and necessary sequences which include loss of lives and souls, no number of causes combined can afford a justification for it. And hence, by this process of reasoning, the force of which cannot be avoided this side of atheism, the conclusion is attained, that war is no less than an infinite wrong—loss, and sin committed against mankind. Whence it must follow that no number of causes combined can justify it. And to the presentation and elaboration of these fundamental thoughts, shall the following pages be devoted. But before finishing this quasi-introductory chapter, it seems proper to notice an objection which has been urged to this mode of reasoning: "The decrees of God," it is urged, "stand in opposition" to this reasoning. Perhaps. But, since no man knows what the decrees of God are, the affirmation is more reckless than logical. We know what God's decrees are only as God tells us; and as God has told us nothing about His decrees on this subject, we know nothing about them; and so, to affirm this or that about them, is to violate that *known* decree which requires the utterance of truth.

God tells us in His revealed word that we *shall not kill;* then, if He tells us in His decrees that we *shall kill*, His story contradicts itself, and is unworthy of belief. The *supposed* decree is false, then, or the *known* word is false. It seems to us that all war-men act upon the latter supposition; and that, practically, they substitute some imagined conception of God or His laws for His clearly revealed will; and so engage in war under the influence of this imaginary conception, rather than by authority from Him. Men engage in war under the influence of their wicked passions, just as they steal, rob, murder, and commit adultery under their impulse; and God's decrees justify all these precisely as they do war. The persecutor also might, with equal justice, allege the decrees of God in support of his conduct. Alexander VI. and Leo X. might, with the same logic, urge the decrees of God in justification of what they did in their lifetime. Expanded and varied, to suit the selfish and wicked passions of men, such reasoning would indeed form an excuse, if not a justification, for every crime and iniquity that has polluted and disgraced the human race. And God's decrees can be urged on one side of a question as well as on the other. Like His providence, men can construe His decrees to suit their purposes, and no one can prove them or disprove them; for men, in no just sense, can reason at all on the subject. To talk of God's providence, as a means of learning duty, understanding by it His mode of administering government over this world, is to talk folly, if not insanity; and a duty so learned is likely to be about as near the truth as the feeling which induces theft comes to the fulfillment of the Golden Rule. Such processes of reasoning are a sheer delusion, and the practices growing out of them will be unalloyed wickedness. War, slavery, and oppression have always been inferred from the decrees or providences of God; and so long as men learn their duty from such modes of reasoning, we must expect the continuance of just such crimes. Duty, real duty, must be learned from the revealed will of God, made clear and intelligible to the mind by the illuminating and sanctifying offices of the Holy Spirit; and duty so learned will lead to acts of love, and not to those of wholesale slaughter on hostile fields.

CHAPTER II.

THEOLOGICAL ASPECT OF THE SUBJECT.

§ 1.—*The supposed right to take life as derived from the laws of nature.*

IN approaching the burden of our thought, the first consideration inviting attention, is, *If man has the right to take life, whence does he derive it?* If man has such right, upon a little sober reflection it is clear that he must have obtained it from God, as God is the source of all life. But God, having the right to take life, might, it is conceived, grant the right to take it in a diversity of ways. 1. The right might have formed a part of the original constitution of nature, and its existence might have been learned by intuition or the inferences of reason. 2. It might have formed no part of the original constitution of nature, but might have resulted from man's transgression and fall, and been learned by intuition or the inferences of reason. 3. It might have formed a law in the constitution of nature, not discoverable by the offices of human reason, but might have been revealed to man by God. And, in the last case, it might be revealed in either the Old or the New Testament, or in both. 4. And there is still another method in which it might be derived: God might have entrusted every person with the right over his own life, with the right to alienate it to others. In all these cases, and in any case of which we can conceive, it is self-evident that the right must primarily proceed from God, who is the source of all life. In the discussion of the general question, therefore, the investigation will always become an inquiry for something in the NATURE OF A FACT. If the right *to take life* formed a law in the original constitution of nature, it is a fact to be learned as a fact. If the right did not exist till *after* the fall, but then became a law of nature, that is a *fact* to be sought as such. So, if the right comes to man through the revealed will of God in either Testament, the record of that will must contain the fact, and it must be sought accordingly. Now, passing through these several inquiries and their related incidents, will complete the inquiry in its theological aspects. Hence, the first question under this division of the subject, is, *Is there a right to take life derived from the constitution of nature?* This more general question is naturally divided into two parts,—the one including the constitution of nature *before*, and the other, including that constitution, *after* the fall. The former part of the inquiry invites the first attention.

But here a preliminary question of grave importance presents itself for consideration: What shall be the character of the evidence necessary to establish the right to take life? Is it sufficient to justify it, *That there appears to be a sort of necessity, just as we find men? Or that it seems reasonable in given circumstances to engage in war?* These are the great popular arguments of our day. So we are told that, from certain passages of Scripture, it is *reasonable* to infer that God intended to bestow the right on man, in all time, to take life. But we insist that, to satisfy the demands of sober reason, " *The grant of authority must be clear beyond reasonable doubt*"—as was the command to Abraham to offer Isaac, or the command to the Jews to destroy the Canaanites,—or as plain, from the laws of nature, as the necessity of the sexes, or the law of social life, which itself forbids all war. But if the right can be derived from the laws of nature only through the impulses of carnal passion; or if it shall come through the cunning processes of metaphysics, all shaped and modified by self-love ånd cupidity of worldly gain; or if it can be deduced from revelation only by the processes of subtle interpretation which put to the torture a few texts of rather ambiguous meaning, ignoring the whole tenor of God's revelation to us, while nearly innumerable unambiguous texts stand on the other side—in all these cases the easily assumed right must, by all sober-minded men, be regarded as wholly insufficient. Nor can it be conceived that this demand is at all unreasonable. For let us look at the matter a little. Life is peculiar. It is the direct gift of God. It is the great gift of God. All other gifts are incidents. Without life, other gifts have no value. Compared with it, all other gifts are as nothing. They are as dust in the balance. And though uttered by false lips, it is true that "All that a man hath will he give for his life." It stands on a higher and more sacred eminence than any or all other gifts; while it is utterly false that the privileges conferred by the State are superior to it; for the State can confer nothing. It only secures what God confers. It is, therefore, but reasonable and just to demand the kind and degree of evidence which will leave the mind without a rational doubt.

This demand is the more reasonable, too, because the act is the most fearful as well as the most revolting exercise of power; while the consequence to those who lose life is irreparable in this world, and may be irreparable in the world to come—may be at once infinite and eternal. And once done, the act—it may be the cruel and unjust wrong—is beyond remedy. Life gone, no mistake can be rectified; no wrong repaired; and no compensatory means employed to alleviate or mitigate the injury. The sufferer disappears from the body, goes before God, and enters upon his final rewards.

For a moment let us contemplate, in practice, the authority supposed in war. Let the mind, which is a little experienced in the selfishness which attaches to human affairs, ponder the authority for war *as derived from* God, as it passes through the boisterous and murderous passions of men till it finds expression upon the actual battle-field. Let the mind now note, with a realizing sense, the practical effects of authority to wage war. Hear the infernal enginery of death, and behold the work of infuriated passion! Now attend to the shrieks of the dying! Listen to the piteous moans of the mutilated and mangled, erst in health, hope and joy! Gaze on the eye, dim, glassy, and wandering, as the spirit struggles in the agony of a cold and hopeless death! Then, from beholding human creatures mangled and torn in the horrid forms witnessed only upon the hostile field, where heaps upon heaps, the wounded, the dying, and the dead, are found trampled in the mire in *all* horrid and sickening forms, let the sensitive beholder incline his ear and listen to the wail of wives made widows, the cries of children made orphans; let him contemplate wasted countries and conflagrated cities—districts ravaged and happy homes consumed—fruitful fields converted into noxious burial places, and cultivated ones into wasted deserts—the morals of the people corrupted, and the religion of the Cross despised;—let him turn next to an exhausted treasury and a tax-oppressed people, while he beholds the scrambling of the ambitious for power and the struggling of the covetous for gain—Judge of all the earth! what duplicity! what fraud! what foul slanders! Is pandemonium turned upside down, emptying its inhabitants upon the earth? Oh! deluging horrors! What means all this wild inversion? Ah! it is nothing but the natural fruit of war—the legitimate consequence of God's authority to wage war. Necessity has been laid upon men to convert this fair world, intended as a dwelling place for brethren, into a cage of unclean birds, into a den of devouring serpents. Is this picture too boldly sketched? If not, but if it comes immeasurably short of the truth, shall it be thought unreasonable that we demand clear and undoubted evidence for authority, whose necessary and intended results produce such shocking horrors? And should not authority, whose consequences are so terrible, be plain beyond all possible question? But is the authority claimed supported, in point of fact, by more than plausible arguments?—have the best war-arguments a foundation more solid than avarice, passion, ambition, and selfishness? Nay, tried by the word of God and by the teachings of enlightened reason, the best argument—outside of the wars waged by the command of God—ever urged in support of war—is merely plausible—is no more than a sort of respectable sophistry addressed to selfishness and cupidity. As we proceed to investigate the authority to take life, we shall find, if we do not greatly err, that the argument urged in support of it is invested at every point in great and substantial doubt—shall nowhere find the legitimate demands of reason met and satisfied. And, as a concluding remark, it is hardly necessary to state that the burden of the proof lies on those who assert the authority. The state of the argument on both sides admits this.

And with so much premised, we may proceed to consider, *Whether the right to take life could be derived from the constitution of nature before man's transgression?*

If the argument under this head is short, it has the advantage of being conclusive—to the real Christian or to the man who but believes the Bible, it is preclusive of rational doubt. For, if we believe in the teaching of the Bible, there existed in the original constitution of nature, only the possibility of death—to rational creatures, at least. *Before* the actual transgression of our primitive ancestors, so far as our race is concerned, death had no existence in the empire of God. For, though prior to man's sin, Satan may have revolted against God and sustained some kind of loss, we have no means of knowing the nature of it, nor that, in any respect, it resembles death to man. And while Milton and other persons of genius and brilliant imaginations, have attempted to portray wherein Satan and his associates in guilt suffered loss by their revolt, we should regard the attempt rather as the work of the imagination to please than as matter of information to instruct. God has not revealed to us the nature of the loss sustained by the rebellious angels; and, especially, He has not informed us that they incurred anything resembling bodily death to our race, incurred by the sin and fall from his favor.

But we are informed both *how* and *when* death, as known to our race, was introduced. In Genesis, ii: 16-17, God tells us, "And the Lord God commanded the man, saying, Of every tree of the garden thou mayest freely eat; but of the tree of knowledge of good and evil, thou shalt not eat; for in the day that thou eatest thereof thou shalt surely die." Here it is stated that death would flow as a sequence of the violation of an appointed law. In the third chapter we are told of the happening of the contingency on which the sequence was suspended, and how the inexperienced pair were seduced into the revolt which introduced death into our world. In the 12th verse of the 5th chapter of Romans, the Apostle informs us that "by one man sin entered into the world, and *death* by sin." Whence we learn from God himself that *man* was not liable to death before he transgressed the divine command—learn that prior to the event of sin, there was no death in the world. And if, prior to the event of sin there existed no death, whence could the authority for man to inflict it be derived from the original constitution of nature? If we believe what God says on the subject, before the fact of sin occurred death had no existence for our race. For as death came by sin, before the existence of sin there could be no death. Sin came by man, and death came by sin. Where, then, till sin became a fact, was the law of death to be found? The Bible tells us of the creation of the world, of the formation of the original constitution of nature, with all its laws and capabilities, and that all were arranged prior to the events of sin and death. Whence it surely must follow, that, prior to those events death had no place in that constitution—it existed only in the incidental capabilities as a contingent possibility. And it follows, of course, that authority to inflict death could not be derived from a constitution in which the law of death found no place. And the proof of the non-existence of death in the original constitution of nature, though negative, borders closely upon demonstration, and is exhaustive of the subject. For if death to our race existed in no form in the original constitution of nature, it surpasses the powers of the mind to imagine how man could derive from that consitution the right to inflict it. If no law of death existed, he could not legally take his own life, and could grant no authority to others to take it. Wherefore it must follow, and demonstrably, that if man has any right to take life, he must obtain it from some new law or authority introduced into the constitution of nature since sin introduced death into the world. Hence, we come to the second inquiry :

§ 2.—*Is there a right to take life derived from the constitution of nature since sin introduced death into the world?*

There is no doubt that sin introduced great changes into the moral government and administration of God. This is clearly taught in the Bible, and is scarcely less plainly taught in the world of outward nature. But whether sin produced changes in the essential laws of nature, or only necessitated the different administration of a system which continued essentially unchanged, we can determine with no certainty, and such determination seems unnecessary to the argument before us.

If the sinful act of man did bestow upon himself a new and potent power for mischief, it legitimately rests on those who claim it, to exhibit the authority on which it reposes. For it is not obvious to the mind how the commission of a wrongful act would invest the wrongdoer with a new and efficient power, which might be wielded with immeasurable destruction to human virtue and happiness ; and wielded, too, in the interests of the wrong through which the power is claimed to be derived. And if before man sinned there was no death in the world, it escapes the wariest research to discover how the sinful act could invest the sinner with the prerogative of inflicting death upon another sinner !

Where, then, is the new power bestowed on the sinner to inflict death? And where is the law which bestows on the self-complacent Mably such authority that he "may take the life of him who lifts his hand" against himself? And from what mysterious law of Providence does it arise, that "the excess of male children over females" may be slaughtered in the pens of horrible war? May Mably, upon his own *ipse dixit*, snatch away the life of him who lifts his hand against his own? and may the State, in its wantonness, slaughter the excess of males over females? If so, why not go further and say with Filangieri, "If I have the right to kill another man, he has no right to live?" And then, why not advance another step, and say with Rousseau, that, in consequence of the social contract which we make with the Sovereign on entering into society, "Life is the conditional grant of the State?" This language, of intensely selfish and scoffing infidelity has not been wholly unfamiliar to American ears for the last decade. We have seen the opposite and belligerent contestants for power act upon just those principles. We have heard it said that "traitors had no right to life or property," on the one side; while the other side have said that "traitors to their cause deserved to be shot and hung." And thus, have not we returned, in spirit, to that reign of atheism which deluged France in blood?

But is it true, indeed, that "Life is the conditional grant of the State?" Does the citizen retain his life at the pleasure of the State? Is he the State's tenant at will? and has he the right to keep his soul and body together at the State's pleasure? If we seek language more reckless and revolting than this, it can only be found in the horrible declaration of the Rev. Dr. Breckinridge, who said, "The blood of traitors is the cement of government." But whence is authority derived thus to trifle with the lives of men? We have seen that it did not exist in the original constitution of nature; nor can we perceive how it could come to the sinner by the wrong which brought death into the world.

Life, we have seen, was held upon a condition that was violated. But when the condition was violated, to whom would the forfeited life pass—would it pass to the cunning accomplice who procured the violation of the condition? That supposition does violence to our whole sense of justice, and destroys the vindication of law and government. Or would the forfeited life pass to another sinner, sustaining similar relations to the violated law? That conclusion, too, is absurd and unreasonable. Or, again, upon the forfeiture, did the power over life pass silently as a *new* law into the constitution of nature, there to remain, *in trust*, till man, in other years, should form the State, and then, by the contract with the Sovereign, did it ever rest with him to be employed in the games and chances of war, or sported with " to beguile the tedious hours of royal pleasure?" And thus does it prove true, as Rousseau assures us, that " Life is the conditional grant of the State?" and is it thence true, as we are again told, that " the blood of traitors is the cement of government?" If these " horrid doctrines " are true, we labor under the misfortune of having no spark of evidence of their truth. No such authority as a trust in the constitution of nature can be discovered. Nor can its transmission to the State be perceived. The conclusion is therefore lodged in the mind, that all such mental modes may be delusive—the offspring of arrogance and ambition.

The intuitions of reason teach us that life forfeited would revest in God, who gave it. In giving life He had the right to prescribe the condition on which it should be held; when, on violation of the condition, it is matter of intuitive logic, that the life forfeited would immediately revest in the Giver. Whence the ado we hear about the *laws* and *constitution* of nature, the *State* and the *sovereign*, is simply vain and idle. *We* know little about the constitution of nature, either before or since the fall of man; and as to " States and sovereigns," they have done little but play the tyrant since the world began, sporting with the lives and happiness of the people; while we have had infinitely too many proud and selfish men to support their cruel and murderous demands of usurped power. Millions of men have been mangled in death, to appease the avarice and ambition of such empirical reasoners—hundreds of thousands but too recently in our own country.

And thus, as the claim of authority from the constitution of nature to take life, is preposterous and absurd, so some able moralists and publicists, as Wayland and Blackstone, have conceded this in express terms. Wherefore, we may conclude that such authority cannot be derived from either the laws or the constitution of nature.

CHAPTER III.

THE THEOLOGICAL ASPECTS OF THE SUBJECT.

§ 1.—*The right to take life as derived from the Old Testament.*

IF, then, as has been seen, no authority can be derived from the constitution of nature to take life, either before or after the fall of man, the next inquiry is: Has God, in the Revelation of His will, conferred on man the authority to take it?

This question naturally divides into two parts, the one relating to authority from the Old Testament, the other to authority from the New. The general question of the Old Testament, also divides into two parts, the one relating to the right to inflict CAPITAL PUNISHMENT, the other to the authority to engage in war. The question of Capital Punishment demands the first consideration. We are aware that there are persons who think God disallows men to wage or engage in war, who yet believe that He grants the right to inflict Capital Punishment. But we think the *principle* is the same in both, and that the right for the one may be derived from the other, if either exists.

It has already been seen that the law of death had no existence in the *original* constitution of nature; and that, in the constitution of nature *since the fall*, there is no law discoverable by human reason, granting the right to take life. We have also seen that, upon the forfeiture of life by the act of sin, the right to take it would revest in God. And since, upon that forfeiture, the right to the forfeited life reverted to God, it is consistent with reason and justice, for God, if He should see proper to delegate the right to take life to man. Hence the question directly arises, *Has God, in fact, delegated to man the authority to take life by inflicting Capital Punishment?* For if God has delegated such authority, man may use it according to the true meaning of the delegation. And there are two ways in which such authority could be delegated: the one by the laws of nature; the other, by those of revelation. We have already seen that the laws of nature contain no such delegation of authority. Hence the inquiry remains, *Do the laws of revelation contain the delegation of authority?*

There is a branch of the general subject of the right to take life, involving a strong *a priori* argument against the idea that God would grant to man a *general* authority to take it, worthy of a passing notice: When man sinned and forfeited life, we *know* that God respited the execution of the sentence of death, in view of provisions made by himself, through which the sinner might be restored to the favor of God; and thereby escape the more fatal part of the death sentence incurred by his sin. And we know that provision has been made, at infinite expense, for the restoration of men to the favor of God, if they will, in the earnestness and simplicity of their souls, accept the provision made and offered. Now, humanly speaking, the grant of a *general* authority to man, to take life, would, in many instances, actually defeat the object which induced the suspension of the death-sentence, and frustrate the end for which God had made the infinite outlay. For, without rash presumption, can any one suppose that of the thousands of millions that have been cut off in the midst of life and in their sins, many, many would not have repented and been saved, if they had not died of violence? Would not thousands who were slain in their sins in our own unhappy country, in the late conflict, have repented and enjoyed eternal life, if they had not fallen on hostile fields?

Therefore, we begin the discussion with very strong probabilities against the idea that a *general* authority would be conferred to take life; while the grant of *special* authority to take it, *in a few cases*, would by no means overcome the strong probabilities against a general grant *upon principles;* since the reasons on which the probabilities against the *general right* would stand, might not exist in the instances of the special grant. And so far as Revelation gives us information on the subject, it tells us that the destruction of the Canaanites was commanded, *because* their "iniquity was full." Gen. xv. 16. That is, God ordered their destruction, because, through their iniquity, all hope of their becoming reconciled to Him was gone. It may even be believed that God would not have given their country to the Israelites, had not their iniquity and idolatry cut off all hope of repentance and reconciliation. But since it is plain that *we* can never know when the iniquity of a people is full, it is plain that *we* may never destroy a people but by the direct command of God. Hence, we come directly to the question: *Do the Scriptures confer on man the right to take life?*

Sir William Blackstone and Francis Wayland contend that authority for CAPITAL PUNISHMENT is contained in Genesis IX: 6; while the latter maintains that the Bible bestows no authority for waging war. The moralist, Laurens P. Hickock, cites no authority for either war or Capital Punishment, but seems to base the right for both upon *custom* and the *Constitution of the country.* The celebrated Paley tells us that "The objects of *just* wars are precaution, defence, or reparation;" and says, "Every *just* war supposes an injury perpetrated, attempted, or feared." And so Paley, too, derives his morality from the customs of society and the practices of governments. And it is from such reasoners that men have derived the accepted interpretations of the Scriptures in favor of the right to take life. The conclusion of the mind *precedes* the argument; and the argument is adjusted to the end of sustaining the conclusion. And it is evident that the argument is composed of loose and ill-considered dicta—not from the teaching of God, but from the laws of nations and the customs of society.

So far as we know, Gen. IX: 6 is the only text in the

Bible *relied upon* as authority for inflicting capital punishment. We know of no text cited from the New Testament, and no other one from the Old. It is true that others are cited by the advocates of war; but they shall be considered hereafter. We shall attend now to Gen. ix : 6, which reads, " *Whoso* sheddeth man's blood, by man shall his blood be shed."

Now, the first pertinent remark to be made upon this text is, that if it admits several interpretations, each just as reasonable as the one put on it by the advocates of capital punishment, all thinking and fair minds will regard it as insufficient to authorize taking life. And there are two views, at least, of this text, more reasonable than the one which derives from it the authority to inflict capital punishment. Indeed, assuming the accommodated and accepted interpretation of it, some of the learned interpreters of the Scriptures have frankly admitted that they do not understand what the passage means. And, just in this connection, it is pertinent to observe, that, in the analysis of this text, our opponents employ a little rhetorical legerdemain. They assure us that the text is a *command* given to *Noah*. Thence they tell us that, being given to Noah, it is not limited to the Jews, since it was given anterior to the separation of the Jews as a distinct people. And being thus given to Noah, they urge that its authority passed to all the Gentile nations.

Now, this view is plausible, sufficiently so to impose on millions from age to age. For it is lamentably true that few persons pause to question what is plausible, especially if it has been familiar to them from infancy, and accords with their wishes and supposed interests. Accordingly, for ages, the great majority of men have accepted this ambiguous text as conferring authority to take life. But let us examine the text and the context, that we may see with how many difficulties it is surrounded, if we would force from it the right to take life.

It is said to be a *command*. If it is, to whom is it given?

Is it indeed to Noah, and, through him, to all people for all time? Is it to man as man? If so, is it to him as an individual or as a body politic? If to him individually, what individual shall obey the injunction in shedding blood? Shall the brother, the father, the son, or the neighbor of him whose blood has been shed? And how shall it be ascertained *who* has shed blood, and *how* the shedder shall have his shed in turn? If the first blood is shed *without* intention, shall the shedder die notwithstanding? But are we told that the text provides against *wilful murder*? We reply that it says nothing about *wilful* or *unwilful* murder. It speaks simply of shedding blood. Therefore, we may pertinently ask, How it is known that it provides against *wilful* murder, or any other kind of murder as distinguished from " shedding blood." Is it said that all these things shall be provided for by law? The reply is, the text giving the right for no such provision, the interpretation adds to the word of God, and will necessarily impose on the scriptures a political interpretation. But is it said that the right to shed blood is a delegation of authority *to* human government? The answer again is, The interpretation adds to the revealed will of God; since the text says nothing of the kind. Is it then said, that the the text is hard to be understood? We reply that able commentators, attempting to coerce from it authority to take life, have reached the same conclusion; and we think it cannot be understood, if it is insisted that it confers the right to take life.

If it is urged that the sixth verse bestows on *man* authority to take life, what shall be said of the fifth? It reads, "And surely your blood of your lives will I require; at the hand of every beast will I require it, and at the hand of man; at the hand of every man's brother will I require the life of a man." What is the teaching of this verse? Surely, in itself, it is obscure. Yet, the expression, " at the hand of every beast will I require your blood," is, indeed, emphatic—is as emphatic as that other expression. " by man shall his blood be shed." Is each a delegation of authority, the one to man, and the other to the beast? It cannot be so regarded. Reason rejects the idea. And viewed as conferring the right to take life, both the text and the context are obscure and difficult. Hence we must seek another interpretation. And does not the difficulty arise from the attempt to impose a forced and unnatural interpretation on the language?—an interpretation suited to the prejudices and passions of men? We must think that the moral code of such interpreters is first adopted, and that then ingenuity is employed to cut and trim the word of God so as to meet the demands of an adopted mode of social life or human government. It is manifest that Paley, Hickok, and others, wrote an *accommodated* morality; while it is no less manifest that multitudes of Divines write and teach morality in the same manner in this day. They make morality and the scriptures mean what they wish they did mean. Not reverent of the sacred word, they criticise, modify, and shape it, till it fits their preconceived notions. And to some extent this mode of understanding the revealed word may be a necessary incident of the human mind. Still, it may be pressed beyond the necessity of the case, and thence become the source of needless error. It has been so, in the manner of interpreting Gen. IX: 6. Obscure till the proper clue is obtained, ingenuity can impose upon it a plausible construction inferring the right to take life. Yet such a construction is neither necessary nor natural, and was probably adopted through the wish of ecclesiastic courtiers to find authority for the princes to sport with the lives of their subjects.

Granting that the character and degree of the evidence necessary to establish the right to take life, are, as we have stated, reasonable and just, we might properly dismiss the text under consideration as too doubtful in its significance to establish a right of so fearful nature as all experience shows the right to trifle with life to be. Indeed, having shown that the interpretation which derives from it authority to take life, is surrounded by a multitude of perplexities, we might, according to the established rules of disputation, dismiss the subject without further discussion. Yet it is proposed to show that the text admits of two views, either of which agrees better with enlightened reason and the general teaching and spirit of the Christian revelation, than that which derives from it the right to take life.

The first of these views regards the text simply as a *prediction*—as telling in advance what would be the cruel conduct of men towards each other. Viewed in this light, the text does not state whether God did or did not approve the conduct of those to whom the language related. As impartial pre-written history, it simply stated that "whoso sheddeth man's blood, by man shall his blood be shed." And regarding this as the correct view of the passage, there is abundant Scriptural usage to support it. As an example of such usage, Genesis IX: 25 may be cited: "Cursed be Canaan; a servant of servants shall he be unto his brethren.". The curse here is written in present time; but the statement that the posterity of Canaan should, for generations, remain in bondage, is a prediction. It is *as if* the history of Canaan's descendants was written at the time of the utterance; and written without a word's being said as to whether the conduct of the brethren would be right or wrong. But as the Divine Eye glances down the cycles of time all events are beheld by it. And so, what God, by the mouth of Noah, foretold *would be* the condition of Canaan's degraded and enslaved children, actual history shows *has been* their condition. They have been servants of servants to their brethren.

"So, in the expression, "Whoso sheddeth man's blood, by man shall his blood be shed," was contained an exceedingly brief statement of the future history of men. In this view, it was history drawn in brief, but graphic terms. Knowing what the history would be, God revealed the fact to Noah. And if the intimation was dismal, the fact has been dismal. Blood and slaughter form the burden of man's woful history. From the utterance to this moment, there has been a wild wail of anguish, caused by themselves, amongst the children of men. The inhumanity of man to man has been great! Could all the cruelties of men be written, it would, indeed, be a bloody tale! In sobs, cries, and wild anguish would the whole story be told. Shedding blood has formed a large portion of the business of Noah's children. Thousands of millions have been slaughtered, tortured, and destroyed, in all conceivable forms of cruelty, till the prediction has been more than abundantly verified. Kings and statesmen, orators and scholars, Christians and infidels, have vied with each other in fulfilling the declaration, till history would have to be carefully collated, to determine whether more blood had flowed from Christian pulpits or Pagan altars. Indeed, at best, the tender mercies of men have been cruel. In the brief, dark prediction, how much was contained! And had its intimation been heeded by Noah's descendants, what wretchedness, sin, and misery, would have been avoided! Dark as was the intimation, it was enough to turn men from the streams of blood which they have caused to flow. But, delighting to revel in blood, and to banquet on tears, the descendants of Noah still verify the ancient prediction.

The foregoing view of the text is both rational and consistent. The language is the language of prediction. The style is terse and obscure, admitting, apparently, of several constructions; while the facts of history accord well with it as a prediction. It seems that the distinguished and benevolent Thomas Dick, whose soul revolted at the scenes of blood in every age of the world, regarded this text as a prediction.

But the second method, which we prefer, regards Gen. IX: 5-6, *as the germ of the Mosaic Code.* A careful inspection of the fifth and sixth verses, and their comparison with the provisions of the Code of Moses, will leave the mind without doubt, and reduce the two verses, hitherto so difficult of interpretation, into harmony with the general teaching of the Scriptures. And there are strong reasons, both rational and scriptural, for regarding these verses as containing the germ of the Law of Moses. First, this view accords with the usage of Scripture in revealing truth. Thus, the promise, *that the Seed of the woman should bruise the serpent's head*, contains the germ of the gospel. The method of instructing, by giving the germs of truth, which were afterwards greatly expanded, prevails throughout the Old Testament economy. And doubtless the New Testament contains the same kind of germs, which will be expanded in the light of providential developments, or in the higher light still, of the soul's introduction into the world of blessedness.

Secondly, While the method of *germinally* teaching conforms to Scripture usage, it allows these obscure texts ultimately to be reduced into harmony with the teaching of the gospel. It also harmonizes them with the visions of prophecy, when men shall learn war no more. But that interpretation, which is generally accepted, places these texts in antagonism with many of the utterances of prophecy, and many of the teachings of Christ and the apostles. If the 6th verse is a *command*, it must ever bind the church; and so the church must ever act according to the age and spirit of Moses—must ever continue under the schoolmaster, and never come to Christ. For, manifestly, the *spirit* of this interpretation belongs to the shadows of another age. On the contrary, regard the fifth and sixth verses as foreshadowing Moses' Law, and as passing by development into it, and harmony at once ensues. The *germ of Genesis* then becomes the *Law of Moses*. The germ is dark and obscure; but the development is plain and free from doubt.

Let us pass now from the *seminal* intimation in Genesis to the *expasion* in Exodus. In Exodus XXI: 11, read: " He that smiteth a man, so that he die, shall surely be put to death." *Here* is the blood required at the hand of man, in the sixth of Genesis ninth. Other parts of the code define the incidents connected with the legal provisions—define who shall compose the judicial tribunal—the evidence required to convict, the manner of executing the sentence, etc., without courting the aid of the imagination to frame an interpretation which will suit the vanity of princes or governments. Then in the twenty-eighth verse of the same chapter we read: "If an ox gore a man or a woman that they die; then the ox shall surely be stoned." Here is the blood required at the hand of the beast, in Gen. IX: 5, and plainly means that the beast which had gored to death should be stoned or slain. Now there is no mystery. The IX: 5-6 of Genesis become very plain. The mystery and difficulty come from an attempt to accommodate the teaching to the wants of a state of society which is false and unnatural. Whence the difficulty is not in the texts, but in the forced interpretations. Obtain the correct clue, follow the plain teachings of the word, by the true mode of interpretation, and the obscurity and perplexity will disappear.

And now, passing Genesis 9: 5-6, into the Code of Sinai, we may behold their full force and office. They adumbrated to the mind of those who preceded Moses, as the laws of Moses adumbrated the things which were made plainer under the fuller light of the Gospel. But if any one, with the view of claiming the right to take life, should contend that "the judgments which" Moses "set before the people" are still in force, it could hardly be esteemed a duty to argue with him; for he will probably do, as some have been heard to do—will select such parts of the Law of Moses as suit his purpose, and contend for their binding force, and reject the next verse or clause that may chance not to suit his purpose. Charity may not bind us to the obligation of regarding such person as candid.

But, long schooled in the idea of the right to take life, men are very pertinacious about it; and we may justly spend a little time in considering other phases of the question. The question is generally asked, "Did not the law of Moses authorize life to be taken;" and, when answered in the affirmative, it is asked with confidence, "If it was right to take life then, is it not right now?"

Now, it is exceedingly difficult to reason with such a

mind. The whole force of its intelligence is composed of mere prejudices; and to it there is little difference between what is *new* and what is *false*. It can draw no distinction between what is wrong in itself, and what is wrong in the circumstances—cannot perceive that what may be right in God, may be wrong in men.

It is freely admitted that the Mosaic Code authorized Capital Punishment; and as freely admitted that, since God gave the Mosaic Code, the punishment inflicted by its authority was right. What then? Does it follow that Capital Punishment is *still* right, though the Mosaic Code is abrogated? Capital Punishment was then right, *because* the law of Moses made it right. Without the law of Moses, it would have been wrong then. But the law of Moses having been fulfilled by Christ, *we* have no authority from it—no more than if it had never been enacted. By the authority of God, Moses was the law-giver to the Hebrew nation; and the right to take life depended upon the law made by him. Without the law authorized by God, the act of taking life would have been murder then; and without a law authorized by God, the act of taking life is murder now. Had Moses made a law, without authority from God, allowing life to be taken, the execution of the law would have been murder—would have been murder because life was taken without authority. So, if men make a law now without authority from God, allowing life to be taken, the execution of the law is murder, because it is taking life without authority. As God alone has the right to dispose of life, so God alone has the right to make a law authorizing it to be taken. In the law of Moses God did authorize life to be taken; and when taken by authority of that law, the act was right. But we are not under Moses, but under Christ; and Christ abrogated the law of Moses by fulfilling it. In Matthew v: 38, 39, Christ says: "Ye have heard that it hath been said, An eye for an eye, and a tooth for a tooth. But I say unto you, that ye resist not evil." Since Christ uttered these words, the law of Moses, as such, has had no more binding obligation upon men than if it had never been enacted. It may be matter of information to mankind, but cannot be matter of religious or civil obligation. Wherefore, the fact that God authorized Capital Punishment under Moses, no more authorizes it now, than the fact that He authorized the Jews to hold slaves, would authorize us to hold them.

It seems improper to pass from this part of the subject without adverting still to other matters. Men tell us that " We do not need authority from God to take life ; that *human reason and a sense of justice* afford sufficient authority." But, alas! such reasoners deserve pity! One can better answer the follies of ignorance than the bigotry of self-sufficiency. And there is more hope in a Gentile than there is in a Pharisee—more in an Infidel than in a self-satisfied believer. The Jews rejected Christ, the Gentiles received Him. The former were bigoted, the latter ignorant. But what shall be said to the man who, having come to mature years, lives under the light of the Gospel, has studied the history of our race written in blood, and yet coolly and earnestly affirms "that human reason and a sense of justice afford sufficient authority" to sport and trifle with human life? We have witnessed that sense of justice in practical operation in our own country. In the North, in the South, it was conspicuous. In the treatment of the black by the white race, it was conspicuous in the years of our past history. In bringing on the late war in this country, it was seen. Then it was seen during the war. In the State, in the Church it appeared. It was little different in all localities, or by whomsoever exercised. It always conceived in sin, and brought forth iniquity, whether in Church or State. And so far as history informs us, the story told of " human reason and a sense of justice " in our country, is the story told of them in all countries. In short, as now educated, the "justice" of mankind is the right which results from *might*. Away, then, with this "human reason and sense of justice." It is the genius of wrong and cruelty. Witchcraft, persecution, and war, have come of them.

The whole idea is a specious delusion—the deceitful song of the siren. Tell not of man's sense of justice! The dream of it is utopian. Faith in it is blind insanity. The surging waves of passion roll over it, and it is drowned beneath them. In our day military courts are drunk with blood, while we have heard the very pulpit utter wild screams for human victims. But recently all was trembling before the tornado of wild passion; and one was hardly secure against its onward and vehement surge. But we forbear. The story of cruelties, done by the counsel of "human reason and a sense of justice," is long, and too revolting to be told. The atrocities committed by them shall be known only in eternity.

Now this argument properly stops here; for, if the foregoing observations are at all correct, there is no need of Capital Punishment, simply because God bestows no right to inflict it. For we reason upon the basis, THAT GOD HAS GRANTED TO MAN ALL THE AUTHORITY THAT IS NECESSARY FOR THE WELL-BEING OF SOCIETY UNDER GOVERNMENT; it being evident that God designed men to live in society, and being equally evident that government is necessary for the protection and development of society.

We think it has been shown that no right to inflict Capital Punishment can be derived from the laws of nature; and that God has bestowed none in the laws of Revelation: and, therefore, there is no right in man to inflict it. Whence we argue that the right to inflict it is not necessary to the well-being of society under government. We are aware that men have long argued that crimes against society can be lessened and prevented *only* by severe penalties; and that even the terror of losing life does not fully prevent the commission of high crimes against the lives of men and the well-being of society. The assumption is admitted: the terrors of Capital Punishment do not prevent great and revolting crimes. And history shows that the fears of being punished capitally, will not prevent the commission of the most trivial and insignificant offenses against the prejudices of a community. When it was a capital crime to associate with a Gypsy in England, the offense was repeatedly committed. And so men would kill hares in the sport, at the peril of their lives. If the State should make it a capital crime for men to chew tobacco, and spit the vile juice upon the streets, they would occasionally commit the outrage. All men know this to be true, as it is true that men have suffered death, in other days, for the most trivial acts. What then? Simply this: It is a great mistake to suppose that men are prevented from committing crime by the severity of penalties. To the people of this generation, that is a hereditary idea. They have not considered it as they should. They have taken the philosophy implied in penal sanctions for granted, forgetting that our ancestors of a few generations ago were exceedingly deficient in knowledge of the laws of mind. And those generations seemed to think that man was to attain all the ends of civilization, and even morality and religion, by means of penal sanctions. Hence they punished, punished, punished. They punished for civil offenses, for moral offenses, for religious offenses, for offenses against their prejudices, passions, and narrow customs. But did their punishments secure the ends desired? By no means. The more punishments inflicted, the more crimes seemed to be perpetrated. Why? Because the whole system was erroneous—was founded upon false philosophy, upon a misconception of the laws of the mind. For the real means of preventing crime are within the mind itself. Penalties never have prevented crime and never will. The pages of Statute-books may glitter with penalties as the blades of grass with the dew-drops, but they will not prevent the perpetration of crime. They are impotent upon the mind. There must be an energy in the mind itself. The mind must be educated. Intellectual cognitions must be awakened in the soul, and a moral energy put into the heart. All the passions of the mind are necessary, for God made them; but they must be educated and guided in the right direction. The understanding must be developed; the reasoning faculties enlarged; the passions guided; and the conscience enlight-

bition and lust of power, with no kind of authority from God save what they gathered from a *mysterious providence*, interpreted through the medium of a blind selfishness, what would have been the moral character of them? Would their wars have been other than immoral and murderous? But what other authority did any war, not commanded by God, ever have than avarice and ambition? " Whence come wars and fightings " amongst men? " Come they not of the lusts that war in their members?" *All* wars that have not the command of God for their sanction, must come of the "lusts" of men's hearts. And are such wars justified by the Jewish wars, founded on the command of God as established by miracle? Wars based on ambition and love of power are often eulogized by selfishness, as involving the best interests of mankind. The Crusades were called The Holy Wars. And were they not waged for the possession of pious relics! Was there ever a war, however ambitious and selfish the object, which was not thought by those who waged it, to possess some singular excellence? Cæsar speaks of his ambitious enterprises and campaigns as if they sustained important relations to the welfare of mankind. Bonaparte inspired his blind adherents with the conviction that the liberties and happiness of the world depended on the success of his career of conquest; while he did little else than achieve selfish ends, by leading millions of men to the embrace of bloody graves. The founders of our own government precipitated a bloody revolution; and, according to the popular theory of the day, committed treason in establishing the Constitution; and when established, it had in it the torpedo of slavery, whose explosion caused the late dreadful war. Were any of these wars founded in principles essentially different from those of Alexander, Charlemagne, or other military captains? They all came from the lusts which war in men's members. And will Christian men say that any one of them stood upon the command given to the Jews by God, to possess Canaan by destroying the people? But if none of them stood upon that authority, since God gave no other authority, they had authority from Him; and if they had no authority from *Him*, they had no authority at all. But having no authority from God, all the men killed were men murdered; for, killing men without authority from God, is murdering them.

But it is time to attend a little more specifically to the examples of the Jewish wars. We can conceive of two ways in which these examples may be thought to afford authority to mankind to engage in war. The one is, *To regard the command to the Jews as including all the Gentiles, and as being unrepealed.* The other is, *To engage in war from the identical reasons which induced God to make the command.*

Now, not even the advocates of war pretend that the command to the Jews to make wars, was intended to apply to any but the Jews. Then, since, if the command was still in force, it would be confined to the Jews, we need not consider that branch of the argument. Still, while the Gentile nations think the command expired, the Jews, more Christian than Christians, *believe all wars to be wrong*.

It thence remains to consider the other condition—*To engage in war from the identical reasons which induced God to make the command.*

The advocate of war assumes here a severe task. For, since God has not revealed the reasons for the command, the task involves the examination of the mind of the Infinite. The learned John says, the only reasons revealed for expelling the inhabitants from Palestine, are found in Geneis xv.: 16. It reads, "But in the fourth generation they shall come hither again; for the iniquity of the Amorites is not yet full." Another writer, quoted in Upham's translation of John, says: "Moses writes histories, and records laws; but the war-manifesto against the Canaanites, from whence we might deduce its justice, has not been furnished us by him. And as he mentions no reasons for the war, we are not entitled, from his silence, to form conclusions against any particular cause to which it may be ascribed."

God gave command to expel the Canaanites when their iniquity was full, and He said when that event should be. But beyond that information, revelation is silent. We have not the "war-manifesto against the Canaanites," from which we may deduce *God's reasons* for commanding their expulsion. How, then, is the war-advocate to learn *those reasons?* Suppose God's reason was, that "their iniquity was full;" are we able to determine when the iniquity of a people is full; and, consequently, when they are ripe for destruction? But, suppose we could imagine a man so insane as to reason himself into such a notion, how could he learn whose duty it was to destroy the iniquitous people. Had God told the Jews that the iniquity of the Amorites was already full, but had given no authority to destroy them; would the Hebrews have had the right to do it? In that case, would not their destruction have been murder? When, in this country, men contend for war, from the example of the Jewish wars, it is not easy to credit their sincerity; because, if you apply their own argument in vindication of *slavery*, they become indignant, and rudely and scornfully turn from you, as if an insult had been offered to their reason. And true it is that the argument for war is as strong from the Jewish wars as the argument is for slavery from Jewish slavery. Yet it is a test of the fairness and candor of those who contend for the right to engage in war from the example of the Jewish wars. The argument is conclusive in favor of war; but exactly the same argument is detestable in favor of slavery. With these reasoners, the Jews were right in engaging in war, because *they* wanted to engage in it; but when the Jews practised slavery, it was abominable, because they wanted to destroy slavery by war.

In another part of the country, the argument ran upon a different parallel. There the people wanted slavery. They, therefore, exalted those Jewish laws which authorized slavery. But they also wanted to engage in war. Therefore, they ungraciously modified the war argument, contending that "*it should be kept out of the churches and pulpit,*" though they neglected to practise the distinction. Upon the whole, it requires the exercise of large charity to believe there is much candor in any war. But Robert Hall says, " War is the temporary repeal of all the rules of morality." And it certainly does repeal all the rules of justice, truth, and candor.

But if the subject was not solemn, one could not repress derision to see on what slender grounds men cleave to the relics of a barbarous age, and seek to find justification for them in the benign code of Christian morality. And thus they seek to bring war, with its unutterable enormities, into harmony with the sublime morality of Jesus Christ. They seek to do this by a shallow and glaring sophism—by that shallow and glaring sophism, which would persuade us that we could know the reasons for God's conduct, where God had not revealed them. Yet this absurd and glaring sophism is quite in harmony with that other sophism and delusion, which lately assured us that " God's providence had brought on us war, and made it our duty to sustain it by our money and lives." Strange reasoning! Wonderful delusion! God's providence established slavery in the country. God's providence brought about the rebellion to perpetuate slavery. God's providence brought on war to suppress the rebellion. God's providence brought about the assassination of President Lincoln. God's providence brought about the crucifixion of God's Son. And, perhaps, not many events have happened since God began to rule the world, that did not occur under God's providence. It happens that men do not know much about God's providence, and may not always innocently engage in what God's providence causes to take place. Our blind and perverted notions of God's providence, do not form the rule of duty to us. For, then, all could construe God's providence—as very many do—to signify just what selfish interest urges. Accordingly, one part of the country, lately, construed God's providence to mean "rebellion," and to that end war; while the other construed the same providence to mean they should "put down rebellion," and to that end war. And so each part of the country went to war under the pressure of God's providence. Such processes of reasoning are selfish delusions. But let the supposed authority from the Jewish wars be viewed in another light. As stated, as nearly as we can gather, the argument for war from the Jewish wars, is: Men may now engage in war from the reasons which influenced God to command the Jewish wars; and God has nowhere revealed those reasons. And here is the task of the advocate of war: He proposes to engage in war wherever he finds the same reasons to exist, that caused God to command the Jewish wars. And God has not told what those reasons were. And this is a just statement of the argument as derived from the Jewish wars. For it is evident that the force of the argument lies in the identity of the reasons between a justifiable war now and those commanded by God formerly; since the war-argument is professedly based on that identity. Destroy the identity, therefore, in any given case, and the authority of example for that case will be destroyed. If a new reason is added, or one reason subtracted, the identity of reasons would be destroyed, and the authority changed; that is, the authority becomes no authority. Hence, according to the war-argument itself, in no case could a war be waged or engaged in by authority of the Jewish wars, only when, and so long as, the reasons were identical with those of the Jewish wars. But that this identity might be ascertained, all God's reasons for ordering the Canaanites to be destroyed, would have to be learned. Not one reason could remain unlearned, because the unlearned reason might modify the other reasons, and so modify the general result. Every reason would also be necessary, in order to ascertain the identity aforesaid, in any instance in which it might be thought proper to wage war; for upon that identity the whole war-argument rests.

Now, contemplate the task. It involves nothing else than a thorough examination of the mind of God. For where God does not reveal his reasons, they remain in His Infinite Mind; and hence they can be learned only by exploring that mind. But that Mind occupies eternity past and eternity to come. The examination would, therefore, have to extend through eternity past and eternity to come, in order to learn God's reasons for destroying the Canaanites. And so, wherever war might be thought necessary, before it could be commenced, eternity past and eternity to come would have to be examined, for the purpose of ascertaining the presence of the identical reasons which induced God to order the Canaanites to be destroyed. But observe, that the validity of the argument depends upon the identity of reasons in any case. If in passing the domains of eternity, and in exploring the Mind of the infinite, there is want of perfect coincidence in the reasons, the idea of a contemplated war must be abandoned; for, knowing the exact reasons that induced God to destroy the Canaanites, we do not know that He would have destroyed them, had one reason been different. Unless, therefore, the coincidence is perfect, in any case. with the wars commanded by God, war could not be undertaken by authority from those wars; and, if commenced with that coincidence, it could continue only so long as the coincidence should continue. Hence, at every moment of its progress, it would be necessary for those who carry it on by authority of the Jewish wars, to have eternity past and eternity to come before the mind, in order to note the continuance in or departure from the identity, at every moment.

And, imperfectly drawn out, such is this branch of the war-argument, when followed to its logical conclusions. The measure of its absurdity is the difference between the finite and the infinite; for its logical results involve the comprehension of the mind of God by the mind of man. And little less absurd than this argument, is every argument that can be urged for war—except the command of God alone.

Let us illustrate the question under consideration, by a

supposed case. There is an assembly of *true* statesmen. They have met to declare war, but have decided to proceed on the principle of identity as presented in the foregoing pages. In real earnest, they turn to the record of the Jewish wars, and make honest search. With solicitude they turn from record to record. The naked command to make war, they find, but the war-manifesto, and the reason for the war, they find not. With diligence and solicitude quickened, they turn again and examine. They find the promise to the Patriarch that he shall have Palestine,—and the command to expel the inhabitants. But the reasons lie hidden in the divine mind. At length, this sentence only is found: "But in the fourth generation they shall come hither again; for the iniquity of the Amorites is not yet full." They would learn here " *fulness of iniquity* had something to do with the strange events. But there the inquiry would end. "The iniquity of the Amorites is full," they might repeat; and strange questions would rise in their minds. "How shall *we know* what *God means* by fullness of iniquity?" they would ask. "Can we know otherwise than by having God's mind and thoughts? Surely, we cannot. Yet, who, by searching, can find out God?—who can find out the Almighty unto perfection?" Then they would ask again, What is meant by saying, "they should come hither again in the fourth generation, the iniquity of the Amorites" then being full? Again honest men would pause, and inquire, "What are we to understand by this language? Does God mean to tell us that *His reason* for destroying the Amorites, was the fullness of their iniquity, or does He intend only to inform us that their expulsion should take place when their iniquity should be full?" After honest inquiry and reflection, earnest men would be compelled to say in despair: "Thy way is in the sea, and Thy paths in the great waters, and Thy footsteps are not known." "Nor," they would say, "are our thoughts as Thy thoughts, neither are our ways as Thy ways. For as the heavens are higher than the earth, so are Thy ways higher than our ways, and Thy thoughts than our thoughts."

Since God has not given man an account of His doings, such an assemblage would perceive that no progress whatever could be made in discovering the principle of identity which they sought. The naked command they could find; but a reason for the command they could not find. They would perceive that the right of expulsion by war stood nakedly upon the command; and that without the command, the expulsion would be illegal; thence the persons killed in the wars would have been persons murdered. They would reason as we have, that all life having been forfeited by sin and having reverted to God, *He* might dispose of it as He chose, without assigning a reason for His conduct; and hence that God's command is sufficient authority for a creation, without the right in him to demand a reason. They would also reflect, *that it would be an easy thing for God to bestow a general authority to make war, if He intended man to have it*—would be just as easy as to give command for the Hebrew wars; and that in the absence of such general authority, it would be great presumption to infer anything beyond the literal command. They would discover also, upon reflection, that a general inference in favor of waging war from reasons known only to God, would prove too much for their purpose, unless it was the intention to make war in the interests of religion as well as in those of the State; for at every step of their investigation they would see that the Jewish wars had quite as much regard to religion as politics, to the interests of the Church as to those of the State. Thence there would be just as strong an inference that men might fight *now* for the defence of the Church as for the defence of the State. At this point such an assembly would close its labors, satisfied that the *right to make war belonged to God;* while with them the vanity, pride, and ambition of the human mind, would be humbled. And, guided by meekness, and realizing something of the fearful responsibility that attaches to the act of declaring war, by which human hearts are wrung with anguish, and souls are sent into eternity; remembering how ambition vaults, avarice yearns, passions burn, and hearts bleed; how fields are desolated, homes are conflagrated, women are insulted and outraged; how the people's morals are corrupted, and the name of God is blasphemed,—every such assembly would adjourn without issuing a war-manifesto presuming to embody the *identical reasons that induced God to order the destruction of the Canaanites.*

It is evident that any earnest man, that will lay aside passion and self-love, and devote himself to the investigation of the subject, must reach the same conclusion. Indeed, since all wars originate in lust and undue self-love, to lay passion and self-love aside, is itself more than half the task of investigation. To satisfy the mind of this, let one take the pains to learn the exact shape of this branch of the war-argument in the minds of the most intelligent war men. The result of the inquiry will amaze him! Like all the elements in chaos, he will find the argument "without form and void," while "darkness is upon the deep" of the soul's rational processes. He will not be able to avoid the conclusion that people's zeal may be in the inverse ratio of the well-defined views of their minds; which is the precise state of mind which constitutes true fanaticism. It may, therefore, well be questioned whether the condition of war does not produce a temporary repeal of all the laws of reason, as well as a temporary repeal of those of morality.

§ 3.—*Inference against the principles of War from the whole teaching of the Old Testament.*

No mind having a clear perception of distinctions in truth, can reflect attentively, read the word of God attentively, or take a comprehensive view of the scheme of things as constituted by God Himself, without seeing that the act of taking human life is not *per se* a sin; for if the act was *per se* a sin, God could not do it without sin. But what right and wrong are in their own essence, finite beings may never know. Whether they consist in the nature of things, or depend upon the will of God, or are a part of the essence of God's own nature, *we* do not know. And perhaps no amount of speculative reasoning could make all the distinctions of right and wrong clear to a fallen mind. Yet no amount of argument could create the belief in the enlightened Christian mind, that God could do wrong. Whence it follows that when God takes life, or commands others to take it, the act must be right; and if right, then reasonable. For the acts of God must always be reasonable; since the Divine Mind is pure reason. The reason may not be discoverable by our reason—may not always be discoverable by the highest form of angelic reason, because all created reason is finite, and finite reason cannot always comprehend the acts of infinite reason. But the highest energies of human reason are justly employed in believing that all the acts of the Infinite and the Infallible are in themselves reasonable and just, and would be seen to be so, could that reason fully comprehend them.

Now, it is from the fact that the act of taking life is not *per se* a sin, and from our conviction that the acts and commands of God are reasonable, that we regard the Jewish wars, waged by the command and miraculous aid of God, as right. But because God may do a thing, it does not follow that man may do it. God is a sovereign. To suppose that man may do a thing because God does it, is a fatal blunder. And this mode of reasoning is the fatal blunder of the advocate of war, when he infers authority to engage in war from the Jewish wars. God may ever take life, while man may never, except by the command of God made known by miracle; made known by miracle, because God being a Spirit, man could only be assured of His command by miracle.

The records of the Jewish wars show plainly that the Jews were simply instruments in the hands of God to destroy—instruments as pestilence and famine may become His instruments to destroy. Whence *His* act in destroying the Canaanites, by the hands of the Jews, would no more authorize one people to destroy another now, than *His* sending cholera on the people of Constantinople, would authorize England to declare war against France. Nor, from the command to destroy the Canaanites, can we infer the general authority to make war, more logically than we can infer, from his sending cholera on the people of Constantinople, that the cholera shall ever after prevail over all the nations of the earth.

It is an act of mercy for God to take the life of the aged Christian, and introduce him into the joys of heaven. But for the ruffian to take it, would be murder. We bless God for the act. But language cannot express our indignation towards the execrable ruffian. Nay, strange as it may appear, God Himself seems to have disliked the persons who executed His judgments on the doomed people. Even in the times of the Old Testament war was the exception, not the rule. The rule then was, *Thou shalt not kill.* God's finger wrote it on the table of stone, as he had before written it on the constitution of nature. *Thou shalt not kill*, is the command of God to our race—delivered to each individual of the race. A part of the original law of nature, it is republished in the decalogue—stands plainly as the law of the gospel—is nowhere repealed—and to-day is the law binding upon all human consciences.

Here, then, is the general law, addressed in the singular number to every individual of the human race, because it is the republication of a law of nature. And it is evident that a *single command*, given to a particular people, would suspend the *general* law only as to the particular people; and to them, only in respect to the end for which the single command is given. And though the command might continue in force for centuries, because the end for which it was given continued for centuries; yet no utterance of reason is more free from doubt than that a single command to a particular people, for a special end, could revoke a general law, only in respect to the particular people and for the special end. As to all other people, the general law would remain in force; and the general law would remain in force as to the particular people, beyond the limits of the single command. Whence, the single command to make war upon the Canaanites, gave the Jews no right to make war upon any other people, unless the other people stood in the way of securing the end of the single command; and, with respect to all other people, as with respect to the Canaanites themselves outside of the single command, the Jews were obliged by the general law. So, if a Jew had slain a Canaanite, the act would have violated the general law; and had the Jews waged war against the Amorites ere their iniquity became full, that being the time when the special command should take effect, the war would have been in violation of the general law. If any people but the Jews had waged war against the Amorites at the time their iniquity became full, the killing would have violated the general law. And, thus, under the Old Testament economy, the authority to make war, or to take life, was limited and exceptional; for the same principle of reasoning as the foregoing will apply in reference to the special cases where capital punishment might be inflicted under the law of Moses.

Now, no Christian believes that there is inconsistency in the teachings of the Old Testament and the New; for such belief would destroy one or both as a revelation from God. The two Testaments must, therefore, be consistent, though it does not follow that our minds are able to trace out the consistency. We have confidence in God, and that His teachings are all consistent, though our minds may not always perceive the consistency. Hence, although there might be an *apparent* inconsistency in the teachings of the Old and New Testament on the subject of war, it would not follow that there is a real one. And there is an apparent discrepancy; but it is not difficult to reconcile. The principles of reconciliation are involved in the reasoning heretofore, but may be more briefly presented. It is involved in the attributes of God. God has all right over life, and cannot err. His will is the measure of duty to man. Hence to learn our duty, we have only to learn His will, knowing that he cannot will wrong. But *we* can only certainly learn His will from revelation. His commands form our only unerring rule of duty. So soon as we learn what He commands, inquiry ceases, and obedience begins. As a faculty of inquiry, reason is exhausted when we learn what God teaches; but, having learned what God teaches, it is an office of reason higher than inquiry, to accept what He teaches as true. The teaching of God is the highest reason. And, thus, the command of God to destroy the Canaanites by war, was no more in conflict with the sixth command, which is the teaching of the New Testament, than their destruction by famine or pestilence would have come in conflict with it. And the command to the Jews to destroy them, no more conflicts with the law that the Christian shall not resist evil, the law of the New Testament, than the act of God in destroying the Canaanites by earthquake, would have come in conflict with the law of love as the duty of Christians. Why men do not see these distinctions is amazing. If they did not consider it their interest not to see them, they surely could. For it is evident that the whole scope of the teaching in the OLD Testament, lays *mankind* under obligations to desist from wars and the sinful tempers in which they originate; and if men did not consider that it accords with their interests to engage in war, they would see such teaching. For certainly it is true, that the teachings of the Old Testament, altogether, are opposed to the spirit and practice of all modern wars; while the spirit and practice of the Jewish wars were not, necessarily. Not originating in lust and passion, but from the command of God, the Jews might perform the office of executing the command, simply in obedience to God, without mingling malice or hatred with their acts, just as Abraham might have sacrificed Isaac in obedience to the command of God. No malice, no hatred, only love and obedience in the executive act, the act would be an act of pious obedience, though a just and fatal judgment on the people destroyed. And the record of the Hebrew wars supplies just this inference. Whenever the victors mingled avarice, lust, or malice with their victories, they incurred the displeasure of God. We see this principle in the conduct of Saul, in the war with the Amalekites. When "the people took of the spoil, sheep and oxen, the chief of the things which should have been utterly destroyed," though reserved for religious service, "to sacrifice unto the Lord," the prophet assured Saul, by authority of the Lord, that God delighted not in burnt offerings, but in obedience to the voice of the Lord. 1 Samuel, 15 chapter. In the 7th chapter of Joshua, the same principle is brought out in the affair of Achan. The avarice of one man incurred the displeasure of God, as it defeated the principle of obedience, and so exposed the people to divine wrath. The same principle runs through all the wars approved by God, in the Old Testament. The Lord God went before and did the fighting, so long as the people were obedient to do all the Lord commanded. But so soon as they "went presumptuously," they "were smitten before their enemies," and were "chased and destroyed." Deut. 1. The principle is too plain to be mistaken, that the Jewish wars were approved by God, only so long as they were carried on without intermixture with those sinful lusts and passions which constitute the essence of all wars of human origin. When those wars ceased to be acts of obedience, when the selfish agency of the instruments came into activity, the wars became disobedience, God refused to do the fighting, and the people fell before their enemies. The Jewish wars, therefore, had no element of "lust" in them, so long as they accorded with the divine Mind; and the instant "lust" became an element of conduct, the wars became criminal. So long as the spirit of the command was kept, the wars were the will of God—and were carried on by God; and hence they form no precedent for any wars now-a-days, because God now commands no wars. The people *then* constituted the mere instruments with which God conducted the wars. No other wars are, therefore, like the Jewish wars; and hence no others can be justified on their principles. And since the Jewish wars stood on the command of God, their *necessary* principle did not violate the 6th command,—did no more violate it than the judgment of God, in taking the lives of the people by pestilence, would violate it.

When, therefore, the Jews executed the command of God upon the doomed people, they did right; but when they executed their own command, they were murderers. In the former case, their example can be no authority to us, because the act was the act of God, the Jews being only His instruments. In the latter case, their act, having no authority, was sin to them, and so could be no authority to us.

Therefore, upon the whole, the will of God, as recorded in the Old Testament, stands opposed to the right to make war. And this inference, general and clear, arising from a careful inspection of the Jewish wars, is confirmed by some special considerations. We are told that the Lord hates bloody men. "The Lord will abhor the bloody and deceitful man." The Psalmist prays, "Gather not my soul with sinners, nor my life with bloody men." " But Thou, O God, shalt bring them down to the pit of destruction; bloody and deceitful men shall not live out half their days." " Deliver me from the workers of iniquity, and save me from bloody men." Who could not join in this prayer? We have a significant expression of God's hatred of war, in His refusing to allow David to build " an house of rest for the ark of the covenant of the Lord." David had cherished the idea: "As for me," he says "I had in mine heart to build an house" unto the Lord. "But God said unto me," he continues, "Thou shalt not build a house for my name; because thou hast been a man of war, and hast shed blood." 1 Chron., 28: 2-3. Warfare and bloodshed are not in harmony with Christian character; and it is not fitting for bloody hands to build " houses for the name " of the Prince of Peace. And the very ideas of carnal wars and Christian purity seem contradictory and mutually destructive. But it may be that David, who was not a faultless man, had shed blood and made war outside of divine authority; or he may have acted through motives other than those of pious obedience. In either case, since the acts would be without authority, his guilt would be plain.

That the *spirit* of the Old Testament is against all war, can be no longer doubted, when we contemplate the visions and promises of prophecy. These are full, grand, and unmistakable. They fill the heart with hope, -and plainly adumbrate the spirit of the Old as well as that of the New Testament. Isaiah tells us that the people "shall beat their swords into plow-shares and their spears into pruning-hooks;" and that the nations shall learn war no more. And surely the real teachings of the Old Testament must accord with the sublime foreshowings of the prophet; and hence they are substantially and essentially peaceful and opposed to war. About all the teachings of God, as well in nature as in revelation, there must be some mystery; but few things are more free from doubt than that the teachings of the Old Testament, as a whole, are in opposition to the principles and practices of war, and in harmony with the teachings of the New Testament.

CHAPTER IV.

THE THEOLOGICAL ASPECT OF THE SUBJECT.

§ 1.—The authority for war as derived from the New Testament.

OUR argument passes now from the Old Testament to the New, and, therefore, from a darker to a brighter dispensation; from the ages of types and shadows to the time of more literal reality. All along we have been under the schoolmaster, but now come to Christ. And as we come to His period, there would seem to be natural presumptions; but what are they? The multitude of the heavenly host announced the coming of Him who should rule in this new and brighter period, amid acclamations of joy and rejoicing, saying, "Glory to God in the highest, and on earth peace, good will toward men." Hitherto the sword, as the emblem of warfare, had destroyed the peace of mankind, filling the earth with tears and sorrow. The personage whose birth was now announced, who was to rule over men, was styled by way of emphasis, The Prince of Peace. Peace should characterize his teaching and precepts; and if men would observe them, peace should attend them in all the walks and duties of life. The coming of this Ruler was long looked for by the church, and the anticipation filled the minds of "good men of old" with delight. The prophetic vision inspired the poet with new fire and the bard of Zion with sweeter strain. There was to be a new empire, a new kingdom, a novel condition of things. Over this new empire was to reign that Prince, appearing then in prophetic vision, now born in Bethlehem. Now what should we expect in the reign under the Prince of Peace? By His authority should we expect a rule of war, bloodshed, and desolation? To suppose so, is to suppose that God's prophets, poets, and bards, were inspired with a delusion—is to suppose that God's prophets were filled with delight in contemplating a reign of peace when men should learn war no more ; while the Prince came in fact, not to teach men to learn war no more, but to teach them to learn war evermore.

And such is the inconsistency of the Christian who contends for authority from Christ to make or engage in war. For if Christ allows war, there is a manifest conflict between His teachings and the visions of prophecy. And if, on the contrary, Christ does not teach that men should learn war no more, there is inconsistency between His teaching and the visions of prophecy. Whether there is such inconsistency, is the general question now to be considered. And it shall be the purpose to discuss the question of war with reference to the cases in which the right to make it has been the least doubted.

However, before we come to consider the question soliciting attention, it is desirable to notice the aspect of the war-argument in general, as it is transferred from the field of the Old Testament to that of the New.

Now, from the Old Testament, there can be cited no text, that, in the least degree, winks at *general* authority for war ; while some aspects of the Old Dispensation may be claimed as countenancing authority for war. Therefore, from the Old Testament, the war-argument is inferred from the general aspect. But, in the New Testament, the general aspect and the whole spirit are so overwhelmingly against the whole spirit of war, that expertness itself can deduce no shadow of support therefrom for war. On the contrary, in the New Testament there may be found a few isolated texts, which, employed by ingenuity of construction, may be made to lend a seeming countenance to the military profession. Therefore, the general tone and spirit of the New Testament are ignored, as if they had neither existence nor significance, while the isolated texts are drafted and pressed into the service of the war-argument with more than becoming zeal. And he who will consider this little manœuvre in the tactics of the war-argument, will discover that it is not without significance. In argument, as in war, men maneuver only when they are pressed by the forces brought against them. Even to *war*-men the *war*-argument is not wholly satisfactory.

As it is proposed to discuss the war-question in the aspects which most favor the cause of war, our line of argument will, in its general scope, embrace a question something like this : *May Christians, under any circumstances, engage in war, for the end of maintaining government ?*

We propose the question thus, because we conceive the whole war-question as finally narrowed to this. It is hoped that considerations of chivalry, of honor, of conquest, etc., as justifications for war, belong to the past. Let the dead bury the dead. Christ's kingdom is not of this world ; and so, as such, it has nothing to do with this world. And while Christ's real children are *in* the world, they are not *of* the world. They may, perhaps, take part in the things which belong to the world, but they must not act as if this world was their all.* And what part Christians may take in a government upheld by violence of the sword, is not a matter easy of solution to the thoughtful mind. By a new spiritual birth called into a kingdom not of this world, nothing could seem more inconsistent than for them to engage in the scrambles of avarice, selfishness, and ambition, by which the *men of this world* seek and obtain place and influence in the *kingdoms* of this world. For them to slaughter each other about worldly kingdoms, must be the height of folly and the fullness of infatuation.

Upon slight reflection it will be evident that men will decide the foregoing question according to the standards of judgment which they adopt. Having no absolute ideas, men measure all their notions by the standards which they accept as true. In what he conceives to be religion, the Jesuit will prevaricate and deceive ; by his standard, the Romanist will persecute and torture ; while amongst Protestants, the Churchman hates the non-conformist, and both despise the Quaker. Each judges truth by the standard he adopts; and, if consistent and intelligent, carries his notions into practice. And, Christianity being the true measure of truth, the distance that each one's practice is removed from genuine Christianity, will be the measure of *his* removal from the true teachings of Christ. So in all the thoughts and acts of men. If they idolize government, and esteem life as a sport with which ambition, caprice, and avarice, may play hilariously, herein will be found a measure of truth to them; and their conceptions and practice will agree with their standard. If their standard of duty require them to bow in compliance with the behests of imperious rulers, at the cost of truth and conscience, they will practise accordingly. And if, to retain the *form* of a government, because their fathers made it, they feel justified in slaughtering men who have undying souls, they will adopt notions and practices consistent with the standard accepted.

And it is thus that men ever act. Some have one measure of truth, and some another. Some measure it by the maxims and customs of Greece and Rome; and some by the customs of their own country. The standard may be essentially heathenish and cruel; still, the proposition is true, that man's thoughts and practice will be of the nature of the standard which they adopt. There can be but one unerring standard of truth, if God is the author of truth, and all truth is consistent and related. And as the notions and actions of men conform to this standard, their practice will produce peace and happiness amongst mankind; and conversely. In measuring the thoughts and actions of men, it becomes necessary to ascertain a FINAL STANDARD OF TRUTH. Where shall we find it? We accept God's revealed will, as contained in the Scriptures, as that FINAL STANDARD. Not pausing now to give the reason for adopting it, in any case involving truth or duty, the question is, *What do the Scriptures teach?*

And do THEY teach that *Christians may engage in war, for the end of maintaining government?* The advocate of war answers, Yes. The peace-man says, No. Thus the issue is formed. In proof of his position, the war-advocate quotes certain passages of Scripture; and the peace-man insists that they do not sustain the proposition.

The text most relied upon by the war-advocate is Rom. XIII: 1, 7. The text is too long to be quoted, as those to whom our argument is addressed are supposed to be familiar with the Scriptures.

And, now, the simple question is, *Does this passage* NECESSARILY *authorize war for the end of maintaining government?* It is thought not. Neither the necessary nor the natural construction of it deduces such authority. But how is it to be understood? What is the mind of God, as contained in it? Is there in it a delegation of power, absolute and unlimited? If not, where is the limit? At the time Paul wrote the passage, the godless Nero was emperor of Rome. Might he, by virtue of the authority in the text, act according to his cruel caprice? He saturated the garments of Christians with inflammable materials, and, in the courts of the palace, set them on fire, that the blaze might illuminate the Halls in which he reveled. Are we to understand that such was the legitimate use of the authority bestowed by God? Nero has aptly been styled "Rome's omnipotent tyrant." And if no limit is imposed on the text, he was the "omnipotent tyrant" by divine investiture; and hence he did the will of God, when he had Christians put to death for TREASON, in preaching a novel religion in the empire. But does the text admit of such an interpretation? Must it not be limited? Can the accepted interpretation bear the scrutiny of reason? Is it not an accommodation to the cruel customs of war? Surely, such an interpretation places this text in antagonism with the whole spirit of Christ's teaching, and in conflict with hundreds of other texts.

In seeking the meaning of the text, we may be aided by bringing about us the facts which surrounded Paul when he wrote the letter. Let us briefly recall them. The letter was written, then, about A. D. 58 or 59, to the Christians at Rome. There the Church was composed of Jews and Gentiles. Some of the Jews were wealthy, influential, and consumed by zeal in maintaining the Law of Moses, about which there were great strifes in some of the early churches. These zealous persons imparted their factious spirit to others. Inflamed by the contagious spirit, the unbelieving Jews engaged warmly in the contests; and created such excitements and tumults, that, about the year 52, the Emperor Claudius banished the tumultuous parties from the city. Two persons, unjustly ranked with the factious parties thus banished, took their abode at Corinth. Meeting Paul there, they took lodging with him. Living under the same roof, they were engaged with him in one calling. From them Paul learned the situation of affairs in the Church at Rome.

In about two years after Claudius banished the Jews, he died, when the order of banishment became invalid. Upon the death of Claudius, Nero ascended the imperial throne. At first, he was mild and forbearing; and several years expiring from the time the Jews were banished till Paul wrote the epistle, a large part of the Jews had returned to Rome. But their banishment did not cure the spirit of faction. A few years of quietude under a lenient prince, sufficed to restore the contentious and factious spirit which had recently procured their banishment.

Added to the specific spirit of faction and tumult, was a general and permanent impatience in the Jews to the yoke of their heathenish governors. They affected great contempt for the government itself. This spirit of restlessness and impatience had attracted the attention of the Roman authorities; and, in turn, had imparted feelings of suspicion towards the new sect of religionists, whom they regarded as a band of superstitious fanatics. Thence were generated mutual jealousies and hatreds. The Jews were clamorous and seditious. The Roman authorities were suspicious and supercilious.—Aquilla and Priscilla, severe sufferers from the order of Claudius and the unchristian conduct of the Jews, and desiring a more pacific state of things, would feel solicitous that Paul, who had great renown in the churches, should do what lay in his power, to preserve the church from scandal on account of the ill conduct of the Jews.

Speaking of the disposition among the professing Christians at Rome, a celebrated writer says: "Some, both of the Jewish and Gentile believers, reckoning it disgraceful to obey constitutions made by idolaters, had, in several instances, contemned the wholesome laws of the state, and were in danger of being punished as evil doers, to the great scandal of the Christian name."

This contempt for the government of idolaters was the product of pride and arrogance. The Jews conceived that they were the special favorites of God, and argued themselves into the belief that they were not required to submit, unless, like the Theocracy, the constitution was made by God himself.

Aware of the condition of affairs, the Apostle takes occasion to address an epistle to the church at Rome. He rebukes their haughty and seditious spirit, laying before them the character and spirit required by the gospel of Christ. He enters upon a vigorous and piercing strain of logic, and passes under hasty review the doctrines and conduct of both Jew and Gentile, ranking both in the category of sinners; hurling just denunciations upon both, as grossly and shamefully coming short of what *they* urged to be the duty of others. He arraigns the Jews in their complacent self-sufficiency, and rebukes the Gentiles in their imperious reliance upon their vain and foolish philosophy; and graphically presentis to their minds the system of true religion as revealed by God. At length, in the thirteenth chapter, he very briefly speaks of the nature of human constitutions, and of the duty of those who live under them. At once, he touches the subject with a vigorous hand, cleaving it wide open, and dealing a fatal blow to that Jewish bigotry which caused the trouble in the church at Rome. In the second verse he declares the general truth which forms the basis of all governments and puts them on the same level, making God the author of the Theocracy and of the Constitution of the idolatrous Nero. In dealing with the subject he displays superior wisdom—wisdom which the ages since have overlooked and neglected; yet just what the calm reason and common sense of mankind ought to teach to all men—that the thing which God ordains is *that there should be civil government*—ordains what has been called *abstract sovereignty;* and by abstract sovereignty is meant, that *general authority* made in the nature of things, in the use of which men form civil government. This general authority *God* ordains; but, in the history of the world, He reduced this authority to the form of a constitution and government only once. In all other cases, He has left men to form their civil governments as their wants and wishes suggest, imposing on them the single limitation, that they shall not violate His revealed laws, nor the dictates of justice. And there is a clear distinction between *abstract* and *concrete sovereignty*—between the *authority* for government appointed by God in the nature of things, and that authority formed by man into civil government. The apostle recognizes this distinction, calling the former *exousia*, and the latter *archōn*—the one represents the authority for making government in the abstract, the other represents that authority as vested in the rulers. The one is God's ordination; the other is man's ordination. The one exists wholly by divine ordination. The other is the divine ordination employed by human agency, and reduced to practice. Paul calls the one the *ordinance* of God; and the other the *minister* of God. Those who oppose the ordinance of God array themselves against the divine constitution; while men have no right to oppose the latter so long as it ministers to the subject *for good*, that being the limitation fixed by divine authority.

Hence we must observe a distinction between God's ordinance and man's use of it. We are obliged to observe

God's ordinance; but submission to His ordinance may oblige us to refuse submission to *men's use* of it. Paul himself acted upon this distinction, after he wrote the letter to the Roman Christians. He refused submission to Nero. So long as Nero was "not a terror to good works," but was "the minister of God for good," Paul continued an obedient subject. But when the "use" Nero made of God's "ordinance," required of Paul what the law of God disallowed, Paul obeyed God rather than man. The "ruler" then became "a terror to good works," and so, ceasing to be "the minister of God for good," his authority over Paul as a subject ceased. Hence Paul continued to preach the gospel in Nero's empire, though, by the laws of the empire, the act was treason punishable by death. Nero's "use" of God's "ordinance" was illegitimate, and therefore void; and so Paul ceased not to act in defiance of the laws of the empire till martyrdom terminated his earthly career.

The conclusion is therefore inevitable that the language of Paul itself implies a limitation on the authority of the ruler. He may employ the "power ordained" only "for the good" of the ruled. He is *God's* minister for that purpose. He does not rule in his own right. God ordains the *power*, men form it into such government as they think suited to their wants, and then appoint their rulers, who, when appointed, become the ministers of God "for the good" of those whom they rule. And ruling thus for God, they cease to be His rulers so soon as they cease to rule *for good*, and become "a terror to good works."

For this view of the subject we have both the precept and example of Paul, who is so often quoted to prove that conduct like his own violates the ordinance of God. The precept declares that rulers are *God's* ministers to the people "for good," and it follows by inevitable conclusion, that they *cease* to be *God's* ministers so soon as they cease to rule *for good*. Paul did not enjoin the Roman Christians to surrender the rights of conscience in blind obedience to earthly rulers. For he utterly refused to do this himself.

And did he *teach* one thing and *practise* another? It was his object to instruct and rebuke the restless Roman Christians, and to repress their *unjust* impatience towards their idolatrous rulers. They had despised *wholesome* laws, and had factiously and wickedly denied to their idolatrous rulers *any* authority from God to rule over them. This *arrogance* the apostle encounters and demolishes, declaring that their governors, though idolaters, are the ministers of God to them; and assures them that, if they were not *evil doers*, their rulers would not be a terror to them. "For rulers," he says, "are not a terror to good works, but to evil"— your rulers are imposing on you only such laws as "the powers that be" may impose. And if "thou wilt not be afraid" of the "powers," do that which is good—cease your national pride and arrogance, become orderly citizens, by obeying your *just* laws.

But let it be carefully observed, that, as has been said, there is imposed upon the *archon*, or ruler, a limit. He is the *minister of God* "for good"—not for tyranny, or selfishness—but "for good." And he ministers not for self, but for God. God ordained the power for the good of the subject; and the ruler is invested with it for that end only. The ruler's power is a trust, created by God and put into his hands by God through the agency of the ruled,—a trust which shall not be used as "a terror to good works," but a trust which the ruler as the minister of God shall use for the good of the ruled. The trust may not be used for the ruler's wantonness and luxury, nor for sporting with the lives and happiness of his subjects, but only *for their good*. And refusing so to use the trust, he ceases to act by authority of God; and though he may continue in the place of God's minister, the ministration is not God's, and the subject may innocently refuse obedience, as Paul did.

As the *good* contemplated is only *natural* good, even a heathen ruler may understand and minister it. The law written on the heart is such that Nero, "the omnipotent tyrant," might have known how to rule for *good*. The natural intelligence of the soul, guided by conscience and the "light which hath appeared unto all men," leaves the heathen "without excuse."

But the question may arise in the mind, *Who shall judge when the subject may refuse obedience?* This may often be a nice question. But the general answer must be, *The subject must be the judge.* This grows out of the nature of things; and, like all human relations, is liable to abuse. But in morals, the subject of moral government must decide for himself, because on him rests the responsibility. And in matters of mere "good," in matters of temporal government, the subject is the sufferer; and so *he* must be the judge. The principle is plain and free from doubt; the application may sometimes be difficult. The minds of men are perverted by pernicious education; and, in consequence, the subject may sometimes have to obey, not only for conscience' but for wrath's sake. This was the case with the Christians at Rome. Nero came to be a bloody tyrant; and, under such a wretch, it would be better to submit, than "resist unto blood."

Whence, let us directly consider the authority claimed from God to use the sword. In the fourth verse it is said, "For he beareth not the sword in vain." What does this mean? Does it delegate authority to rulers to employ the sword at pleasure? Nero was a vile and bloody ruler. His name is a disgrace to humanity. Under the symbol of the sword, did Paul sanction his unwonted cruelties? Or, under it, does Paul sanction the Roman Criminal Law, as some have hastily concluded? To all these questions an emphatic negative must be given. Paul's teaching and example, and the whole teaching of the gospel, contradict the interpretation. And every time Paul preached in the Roman Empire, he violated the *criminal law* by committing *treason.* For *treason* he was finally executed. Did Paul sanction the law which put himself to death for obeying God's command? Are not men gone far in extremity when they resort to such expedients for authority to use the sword? Paul declares that Nero "beareth not the sword in vain." Does the statement either necessarily or naturally imply a sanction to take life? Claudius thought banishment punishment severe enough for tumult and sedition. Did Paul go beyond Claudius and tell Nero that *God* authorized *him* to add *death* to Claudius' punishment? —tell him that God authorized him to destroy His own children, because they were proud of their descent from Abraham, and restless under his idolatrous rule? Yet the popular interpretation of the passage involves all these absurd and cruel conclusions.

But, from the language, does the conclusion necessarily follow, *that authority is conferred to take life at all?* In the known facts of the case, nothing is found to warrant such a belief. According to the laws of the Empire, the Christians had committed no offence punishable by death. Hence, nothing called for the grant of authority to take life. And, without occasion, did Paul go out of the way to confer on the bloody Nero a needless power? Such a conclusion is simply without reason, and the work of an over-anxious imagination.

It is a fact well known, that, when Paul wrote, the *sword* was the symbol of the *punishing power*. It did not necessarily imply capital punishment; and only implied it, when the nature of the case precluded any other punishment. The factious arrogance of the Jews was not punishable by death; and that was what Paul talked about. The conduct of the Jews was punishable, and Claudius had punished it by banishment. That kind of punishment was included under the symbol of the sword. Why say, then, that Paul meant to confirm the cruel criminal law of Rome, or grant the right to the "omnipotent tyrant" to revel in the blood of the restless Christians? Such pretences are sheer assumptions, the work of imagination and fancy. And the most natural and rational mode of understanding the language of Paul, is also the most easy and simple mode. We must surround ourselves with the facts in the case; and then bear in mind the writer and his object in writing. The facts in the case have been given. The apostle was instructing, admonishing, and rebuking. Many things that he said were simply facts. What he said about the powers and ordinances of God were facts—divine facts, and divine and human facts connected and mixed. A fact is a thing done. Hence, it is a divine fact that God constituted the *exousia*, or that condition in the natural constitution of things, from which civil government results. It is a fact that human agency employs the *exousia*, and from it forms civil government, concreting the abstract power, by vesting it in the rulers of the government. Then it is a fact that the *exousia* and the *archōn* become blended in a sense, and when so blended they constitute the *archōn*, or ruler, " the minister of God?" It is a fact that God's providence—which is God's method of conducting the affairs of the world—often calls bad men into civil office, and makes them His ministers. It is a fact that Nero was the *archōn* of the Roman Empire when Paul wrote the letter to the Roman Christians. It is a fact that the Roman law invested Nero with the sword, or the power to inflict punishment. It is a fact that the power to punish was not vested in Nero in vain. He used it greedily. Claudius had recently used it to banish the turbulent Jews and professing Christians at Rome. Read in the light of the facts and of reason, the apostle says in substance: " How recent since Claudius banished you! And how both you and the cause of the Lord Jesus Christ suffered from your conduct so unbecoming His followers! Let down your pride and false notions of a Theocracy, and live peaceably under the constitution of idolators; for even idolators may be the ministers of God in conducting the affairs of this world. You have been factious, and have contemned wholesome laws of the State; and thereby brought on yourselves suffering, and on the cause of Christ shame and scandal. This is wrong and ought not to be so. For the love you have for the Lord Jesus Christ, and to avoid scandal, you ought to submit to your rulers. Conscience ought to induce you to submit to wrong rather than to bring shame upon yourselves and the cause and name of Christ. These things are said in earnestness, but in love. And if such considerations fail to bring you to right conduct, be admonished and forewarned of the fact, the like of which is recent and must be bitter in your experience: *The law of the Empire invests the ruler with the authority to punish you.* And he is not invested for nothing. His is not a vain authority. He will use it. You will be punished, unless you submit. It is not necessary to say whether he holds the authority rightfully or wrongfully. He holds the power, and in his hands it will not be a vain power. He beareth not the sword, or power of punishment in vain, but he will surely employ it, unless you submit. Be admonished, therefore, to pursue that peaceable conduct which is so becoming to the followers of Christ."

We understand this to be the scope of the apostle's argument. There is a presentation of the foundation and nature of all civil government, with the extent of the power and the limitation of the authority of the ruler. God ordains the principles of all governments, and men constitute them into governments. The distinction is clearly drawn between the ordinance of God and the use that man may make of it. Here is a very important point in the argument. War-men wholly overlook or forget it. Government is complex in its formation. God ordains the existence of its principles, and man forms those principles into actual government. And when so formed, man appoints the rulers, while God limits their authority; man appoints the rulers, who, when appointed, are God's ministers—God's ministers with the expressed limitation that they rule *for the good* of their subjects. Nothing could be plainer than this, but nothing will probably be harder for the reader to understand. Men have been so long familiar with the sound of war, and the use of the sword, as the symbol of the authority to take life, that it will be hard for them to understand that the ruler ceases to be the minister of God so soon as he ceases to rule in the interests of the subject. Yet this is just the doctrine taught by Paul, and his practice correspond with his teaching.

A careful inspection of the xiiith chapter of Romans, the great text of the war-man, is far from sustaining his pretentious claims. It rather rebukes them, and imposes a clear limit on the rulers in civil government. Let those rulers observe the limit which Paul prescribes, let them minister *for the good* of the subject only, and civil wars will cease forever.

And thus, a close analysis of the apostle's teaching instructs us largely in relation to civil government; and instructs us that civil government ought to be popular government conducted in the interests and *for the good* of the people. The authority of the ruler is clearly limited to the *good* of the subject; and the duties of the subject are not less clearly defined. Upon the whole, a strong proof is herein found of the divine inspiration of the Scriptures, and for the theory of government exhibited in these pages.

§ 5.—*The authority for war as derived from the New Testament—Particular Texts.*

In the preceding section, we noticed from the xiiith chapter of Romans, the text most confidently relied on as a justification for war. But, carefully considered, it is conceived that it utterly fails to support the conclusion. Thence we come to bestow a passing notice on the texts which have been cited as authority for war. It is not proposed, however, to quote all that have been employed for that purpose. A few of the strongest ones may suffice, as they involve the argument. Luke iii: 14, has often been cited by the advocate of war. It reads: "And the soldiers likewise demanded of Him, saying, And what shall we do? And He said unto them, Do violence to no man, neither accuse any falsely; and be content with your wages."

Had not men of learning and position gravely cited this

text to prove the legality of war, its citation, for that purpose, might properly be dismissed by bestowing on it an innocent smile. Yet, invoked by theologians, moralists, and statesmen, it must not be lightly or ludicrously passed by. The gist of the text is regarded as lying in the clause, be content with your wages." This, it will be remembered, is the language of John. It was spoken to restless and avaricious soldiers, who appear to have been dissatisfied with their wages. In those days John was a new character. Possessing a rare and eccentric genius, burning enthusiasm, a vehement oratory, he came as a voice in the wilderness, under the expiring auspices of the Old Dispensation, preaching the baptism of repentance. Having more light in regard to the Messianic Kingdom, he was greater than the prophets of old, yet he was less than the least one that had been initiated into that Kingdom. Still his wild enthusiasm, eccentric dress, manner of tongue and impetuous oratory, created excitement and drew attention. In the general uproar of restless human nature, one excited by one hope and another by another, dissatisfied with their wages, doing much violence, and accusing many falsely, the avaricious soldiery, hoping in some way ill-defined to their own minds, to obtain advancement, came to John, asking what they should do. The reply of John was singularly befitting the occasion and characteristic of his impetuous and penetrating mind. "Do violence to no man, neither accuse any falsely; and be content with your wages." Singular authority for war! Rapid is the logic which thence infers authority for the science of human butchery! It is only defective because it ties two ends together regardless of the middle. And it would be difficult to say what such logic *could not* prove from the Scriptures! However, the whole answer is the utterance of John and the language of Scripture. Therefore, what does the war-man say of the words, "*Do violence to no man?*" Does that language comport with his rapid logic? Does the sentiment accord with the business of war? The vocabulary of war is, *Do all the vio-*

lence you can: kill, maim, burn, desolate. By chicanery, fraud, and falsehood, make all manner of false accusations, and inflict all forms of violence. Let the soldier comply with John's injunction, and do violence to no man, utter no falsehoods, and he will do well. He may then be content with his wages, and remain in the military profession.

What would be that kind of war, wherein neither violence nor falsehood should be employed? Violence and falsehood are as necessary to war as hatred and malice, powder and bullets. It is amazing that such language should be quoted as authority for war, whose essence consists in violence and falsehood. But why dwell on this passage? Idolatry, cruelty, and the right to compel Paul to fight wild beasts, can be supported by such logic.

Again, Matt. VIII: 10 is cited as authority for war: "When Jesus heard it, He marvelled, and said to them that followed, Verily I say unto you, I have not found so great faith, no, not in Israel." The mode of influence here is much the same as in Luke III: 14. The *point* lies in that part of the verse in which Jesus approved the *faith* of the centurion, but condemned not his business. It is *hence* inferred that he did not *dis*approve his business; and thence that he *approved* war. But if anything could be more wild in logic, or extravagant in dealing with the word of God, it would be interesting, if not instructing, to witness it. Jesus said nothing against his being a soldier! But he was a Roman soldier; and therefore an idolator. Jesus said nothing against his idolatry. Let us then employ the logic of the war advocate, and infer that Jesus approves idolatry. The principles of influence are identical in the two cases. But such uses of the rational faculties are simply vain and foolish. Jesus confined not His benevolence to the *good*, nor to the *souls* of men. He bestowed it on the good and the bad; relieved both the souls and the bodies of men. The Roman centurion believed that He had power miraculously to heal disease, and importuned Him to exert it in behalf of his diseased servant. Jesus complied with the request, and commended the faith he exercised in Himself as having divine power, which faith may have been necessary to the end importuned. But Jesus said nothing about his being a soldier, an idolator, a saint or a sinner. And from nothing, nothing can be logically inferred.

The centurion probably had no idea of Jesus as a Saviour, and not unlikely continued a soldier and an idolator. There are many now-a-days, who believe that Jesus wrought miracles, and continue idolators and in the business of war.

We are told that it is not said that the centurion abandoned his employment; and hence it is inferred that Jesus did not condemn it. But we are not told that he did not abandon it; and so nothing is said on the subject. Therefore, from nothing, nothing can be logically inferred. Nothing being said about a change, the natural inference is that all continued unchanged. And the centurion being a soldier, and probably an idolator, continued a soldier and an idolator; thence inferring nothing as to whether Jesus approved or disapproved war. *Silence* cannot support an affirmative argument.

However, we do learn a wise lesson from the centurion. He was sensitive about being a soldier. He said, "Lord, I am not worthy that thou shouldest come under my roof," and he assigned as a reason, "For I am a man in authority, having soldiers under me." In these days, soldiers are in no way noted for sensibility and modesty. But there are professed ministers of Jesus who show less sensibility, though they have assumed to reverse the order of God, in employing carnal weapons instead of spiritual ones. The modest conduct of an idolatrous soldier might properly be commended to their imitation.

In Acts, x: 1-2, we read, "There was a certain man in Cesarea, called Cornelius, a centurion of the band called the Italian band, a devout man, and one that feared God with all his house, which gave much alms to the people, and prayed to God always." From this text the sanction for war is inferred. The supposed argument is inferred from the circumstance that "Cornelius, a centurion," is styled "a devout man, and one that feared God." Hence, the mode of argument is identical with that in the foregoing texts. The inference is based on the idea that the business in which "a devout man" engages, must be proper and have the sanction of God. If this is not the basis of the argument, the question has no pertinence. If it is the basis, it is difficult to treat such manner of argument and inference with seriousness. It looks like trifling with the Word of Life. It is futile—appears like irony; and seems little less than mockery. But grave men introduce such arguments into works on which they bestow thought; and quote in good faith such texts in proof that Christian people may, upon their authority, plunge into the horrors of war. We have Paleys, Breckenridges, Hickocks, and the whole array of fashionable Christians, clad in carnal armor, and relying on such texts and arguments, to confront. It is true that they are not profuse nor cogent in argument, but they are bold, and some of them reckless, compelling attention. They are great in name, if not in argument, suggesting to our minds the fact, that the force of an argument does not lie in the fact that great names use it, or great men invoke and misapply such texts. Quite the opposite inference arises. For the argument for a cause must be feeble, when the *masters* are necessitated to support it by bad logic. And the weight of argument lies not, as we have said, in the fact that distinguished men employ it; for such men have advocated all sorts of follies. But the real weight of an argument lies in its conformity to truth and the nature of things.

And tried by this test, attention is asked to the argument inferred from this last text. Let us look at the *argument*. The point is, *That the business in which a devout man engages must have the sanction of God.*

If the quotation is pertinent, the proposition is fair and just. But thus stated, the proposition is worse than futile; it is both absurd and silly: it imputes infallibility to all devout men, and implies a oneness between their business and the law of God; while we know that devout men have committed all sorts of crimes against law and morality. Look at the devout men of the Spanish Inquisition; at the devout world in Luther's time; at devout persecutors, and Puritans; at the devout praying Jesuit in the early history of our country, as, in the face of danger and death, he went to the Savages to make them more savage still. Look at the devout people of any country during the storms of war; and if devotion implies oneness with the laws of God, those laws make no distinction between right and wrong. For what a picture have devout men painted! Blood and tears have been the materials with which it has been drawn. The foreground has been sorrow, and the background wickedness. Yet for thousands of years, devout men have been blotching its hideous outlines on the pages of history. And while the forbidding work has progressed, the devout men have done much in giving alms to the people, and prayed to God always.

But, employing the logic of the war-advocate, it is not said that the "devout centurion" *was born of God by a new spiritual birth.* And, therefore, it is not said that he was a *real disciple of Jesus.* Devout he might have been, and much in almsgiving and prayer; but all that does not necessarily constitute him a true Christian. Hence, in that respect, his example is nothing to us. Nor, if a true Christian, could his example be anything to us, unless Jesus Christ enjoined the example. A *man* may be saved, and his *works* burned. The *example* of the *apostles* bind us, only so far as they accord with the *law* of Christ; and then it is not the example, but the law, that binds us. When they quarrelled, they did not leave an example to bind us. The example of the impetuous Peter in cutting off the servant's ear challenges not the approbation of our mind, as it did not that of the Master's. Nor are we required to copy his example in denying the Lord with an oath. Surely, a cause must be weak, when grave and *devout* men seek its defence by logic so inherently impotent.

It is freely admitted that *devout* men now engage in the business of war. But does that prove the *business* to be right? If it does, it proves the business to be right on both sides of any war; for, where large numbers are engaged, equally devout men are on both sides. But such modes of reasoning are all futile and absurd—unworthy a great cause or a clear and logical mind.

Observe that the argument of the war-man consists in inferences from the fact, that some one engaged in the profession of arms, is named as being devout or exercising faith, in a general way; and thence inferring that the *profession* has the sanction of Jesus Christ. Now, what were the alleged facts during the late war in this country? Each party claimed that it had revivals of religion in its army, at the moment each charged the other with being engaged in committing atrocious sins and crimes. Now, by a process of reasoning less faulty than that of the war-advocate, it might be urged that such revivals show that God approves the cause and business in which those who are converted are engaged. And in tones of self-complacent triumph, it could be asked: *Is it possible that God would convict and convert men while they are engaged in sinful and criminal business?* Indeed, the Southern leaders did affect to construe the revivals into tokens of God's favor to their cause. And the argument is plausible to the unthinking. Yet a moment's serious reflection dispels the plausible delusion. For, if it proves anything, it proves that both parties were right, since both had revivals. In that case, the parties had each the sanction of God, for the slaughters committed.

But whatever may have been the fact about the revivals, whether they were genuine or spurious, all such modes of reasoning are deceptive. They may be plausible but they are delusive, and mischievous and dangerous, because they *are* plausible. Where the affections are fondly centred, a mere appearance satisfies the mind already determined to believe. And such is the case with the war-argument.

But the examination of special texts need not be pursued. The ones we have considered give the clue to all others. A text cannot be adduced which can supply more than a plausible sophism for war; and the ingenuity which educes the sophistical construction, will place the text in antagonism with hundreds of texts as plain as human language can express thought. The texts which we have presented have been regarded as the strongest ones in support of war. But examination shows the strength of such proof. If examined, others would stand on no better ground. And here, satisfied that no text from the New Testament affords any just argument for the revolting practices of war, we shall pass to another branch of the general question.

§ 3.—*Argument against war from the New Testament.*

We have just seen what the New Testament does *not* teach; and now come to consider what it does teach. In so doing, we observe that the religion of Jesus Christ is an affair of the *affections*, and is not at all dependent on the *mere notions* men may hold respecting any question of worldly interest. Nor is the relation created by the new birth, affected by their notions of philosophy, or their speculative opinions on *any* subject. Nor can the views they have of political government, as the means of attaining worldly good, affect in any respect their Christian character, unless they lead to injustice or to the violation of Christian charity. Whether a person has accurate conceptions of astronomy—believes the days mentioned in Genesis were sun-marked or vast indefinite periods—believes the United States Government confederate or consolidated—whether he is a secessionist or an abolitionist—is pro-slavery or anti-slavery—or whatever may be his speculative notions of those things not practical, whose reason lies in a region beyond the reach of the mind's faculties,—can have not the least to do with Christian character. Equally good men and Christians are found on all sides of such questions;

and so far as they are worldly questions, they are sinful or not, as they are used and loved. Christian character depends on relations and conditions different from all these. The grace of God distilled into the soul, creating it anew in the image of God, filling the soul with fervid love, and leading it away from the things of the world, and fixing the ardent affections on the Lord Jesus, and filling the soul with love to men, are the things which make Christians. And a saving relation formed between the soul and God, men's notions may be diversified about their worldly interests—quite as diversified as their countenances and personal habits—and will affect as little their Christian characters.

In relation to the subject before us, the troublesome question is, *not how men think, but how they act*—is not in their *thinking*, but in their *killing*. God has given us no measure for determining the accuracy of *speculative opinions*. But He has given us rules to regulate our *conduct* about them. At best, worldly interests are short-lived, and ought not greatly to engage our affections. Surely, reason suggests that we should not *butcher* each other about them.

Yet the fact is sorrowful and lamentable, that so-called good men and bad men have about alike been engaged in crimes abhorrent and atrocious—have waged and engaged in war about the things of this world, with about equal zest.

And here, for a time, we shall pursue rather a desultory line of argument. Many thoughts demand a passing notice, and will fit one place nearly as well as another; while the difference in the position would not compensate the trouble of adjusting them nicely in the argument. Moreover, if our argument is occasionally desultory, it may find some apology in the fact, that we have to meet one which, as yet, lies in the outlines of chaos. For it would be hard to find a well-sustained argument in favor of war; or a logical development of the subject, or science of human butchery. Wild outbursts of passion, extravagant declamation, fulsome panegyrics upon the "best government in the world," have been cheap material for years past; but a temperate, rational development of an *argument* in favor of war, is still a literary desideratum. Such a thing was never heard on American soil. As yet, neither statesman, divine, nor politician, has given us more than a tissue of passion, or a thunder-burst of furious oratory. But, indeed, is not the idea of a war-sermon a contradiction in terms?—nay, a contradiction in moral essence? A war-sermon! War, the fruit of essential lust, served up in the form of a sermon! Godless passion in the pulpit! It were a monster! May not the fact be thus accounted for, that war-sermons are never founded on the teachings of the *New* Testament? War-sermons are appeals to passion; and men only appeal to passion when reason fails; and only attempt to scowl to silence what they cannot overthrow by argument. And that distinguished divine before alluded to must have acted upon this principle when he said, " The blood of traitors is the cement of government;" because the sentiment is as false in political science as it is foul in Christian morality. How deep is the tinge of heathenish cruelty in the sentiment! It smacks of Nero and Herod; and is not becoming a venerable professor in a school of Christian theology. But in this connection we need not, by direct argument, encounter every passage of Scripture to which fertile ingenuity can attach a plausible showing in favor of war. Assuming that the Bible is a revelation from God, we must also assume that it is consistent in all its teachings. Thence, adopting this simple principle, the mind can be satisfied in many conclusions that might otherwise be unattainable. Some parts of Scripture are confessedly hard to understand, because the nature of the subject treated falls quite without the range of the mind's faculties. But God has not engaged to clear all subjects of revelation from doubt and difficulty to our minds. Our religion is one of *faith*, not one of *knowledge*. Yet availing ourselves of the conception that, by a *just* interpretation, all parts of the Bible harmonize, and we may remove a large portion of the obscurity, by reading the dark texts by the light of the plain ones. And, employing this method, it is not absolutely necessary that we compare those which have been regarded as parallel. Even the opposite course may often be properly employed. In regard to the question before us, this principle may be fittingly used. Sad experience teaches that, by the use of a subtile ingenuity, there are texts, which, by critical torture, may lend a seeming countenance to war. Yet strip war of the apparel with which passion, ingenuity, and imagination, have clothed it, and, calling things by plain English names, it is simply a system of wholesale murder, decorated with fraud, cunning, cruelty, and such other appendages of crime as have been added.

But, returning to the subject of interpretation, how shall we read those tortured texts so as to learn our duty? Shall we attend them on the rack of criticism, as they are tortured into an unwilling testimony for war? Or shall we employ a more just method of dealing with the oracles of truth, and understand obscure or doubtful texts by the aid of plain ones? And we may ask, whether the most plausible ingenuity has been able to force from the teaching of Revelation, more than a plausible showing for war? Yet, is not the whole teaching of the gospel eminently peaceful in its character? Does it not beyond question condemn the entire spirit of war? From the New Testament can there be cited a single utterance which does not condemn the indulgence of the passions and lusts on which war necessarily depends? And do not unlawful feelings and volitions always precede powder and bullets; and are not deceit, treachery, and cruelty of the very essence of war? Nay, avarice and lust, two most godless passions, are more necessary to war than powder and lead; and a man must lose a large portion of his virtue before he is fitted for a great captain or warrior. For do not wars come of the lusts that war in men's members? And by the laws of Christ may such warring lusts be indulged? Peter says these lusts "war against the soul," And may men indulge in lusts which seek the life of the soul? Now, if the life of war is in those lusts and passions which are utterly forbidden by the law of Christ, does that law still allow war? If the law of God totally disallows the means to an end, may the end still be lawful? And does not the law of Christ forbid utterly the use of the means necessary to carry on war? If wars come, as James says, of lust, and lust gendereth death, are the wars themselves not under the malediction of God?

It is precisely at this point that the law of Christ displays its supernatural wisdom for correcting the sinful practices of men. Human law-givers divide crimes into classes and grades, attaching sanctions according to their apprehended aggravation. But this is not the mode of the Divine Legislator. He analyzes the human character, and seeing the various streams of corruption, He traces them to their origin in the affections of the soul. Then, by a single command, negatively or positively given, all the practical duties of man are made plain. And, since the source of all conduct is in the affections of the soul, whatever regulates the affections, gives character to the life. If *love* rules them, the life meets the demands of Christ's law, for love is the fulfilling of the law. But if lust rules in them, it produces the fruits of the carnal mind, amongst which are the wars and fightings of men. This is a wise provision proving the superiority of Christ over all other law-givers. Looking into the source whence feeling is born, He fixes virtue and vice in the qualities of the initial thought. It is by virtue of this constitution of the mind, that the whole duty of man consists in the two fundamental provisions of *love to God and love to man.*

If no other law of Christ condemned the practices of war, *the law of love* must place it forever under God's unqualified malediction. To love God with all the heart, and one's neighbor as himself, is forever to put away war. And one's neighbor is not one who lives near by, or belongs to the same political party or district of country. It includes all fellow-beings, all heirs expectant of eternity. Nor is the love which is to be exercised that mere passive feeling which lets one live or die as chance or fate may befall. For the word which the translators have rendered *love* is a strong one, signifying *to entertain*, *to make welcome*, *to delight in*. Whence the clear import of the law of love is, that Christ obliges all men *to love* or *delight in* the happiness and prosperity of every being of our race wherever he may have his habitation on the globe. And is not such a precept like God, who stretches out the heavens and suspends their grandeur over *all mankind*, and makes it to rain on the just and the unjust? But how unlike the selfish maxims and practices of men! How infinitely unlike that foul sentiment, radiant all over with the poison of hatred, "that the blood of traitors is the cement of government."

If but a partial application of the two great commands was reduced to daily practice amongst mankind, the multiplied horrors of war would disappear from the world, as the mists and fogs of the night disappear before the bright rising sun.

And no painful doubts linger about the teachings of Christ. There is no necessity of passing His sayings through the moulding processes of subtile ingenuity, to force from them a dubious testimony. They stand out in their own significance, and he that runs may read; while he that runs *knows* that *to love* a man, does not mean *to kill* him; that *to entertain* him, does not mean *to bayonet* him; *to make* him *welcome*, does not mean *to burn* his home and *lay waste* his possessions; and *to delight in* him, does not mean *to cast* him *into a military prison*. Men of plain judgment may be lost in the mazes of ingenious criticism; but it would be hard to convince them, if their minds are not all perverted by false education, that *to love their neighbor* as they *love themselves*, means the cruel and horrid desolations of war. And the injunction *to love a neighbor as one loves himself*, needs no interpretation.

Now, contrast Christ's teachings with the stammering utterances of war begging a pitiable support from the voice of *silence*, from remote and constrained influence, and cold and far-fetched interpretations of the sacred text. And what are the utterances and oracles of war, the ethics taught by the *bloody science?* For the oracles of war are as unmistakable as the oracles of the gospel. Each has a vocabulary of well-defined words. Their dictionaries are not books of synonyms; but they contain words of contrast. Their terms are always terms of antithesis. Representing differences which arise in the birth-place of thought and feeling, their first activities are activities in contrariety. Their first words are, therefore, uttered in the accents of contrast, in dialects as different as those of the fallen and the unfallen angels. As illustrative of their dialects and learning, we may present a few of their oracles in contrast. The one says, Love your fellow as you love yourself. The other says, Hate your fellow as you hate a viper. The one says, Love your enemies. The other says, Stab, bayonet, and shoot your enemies. The one says, Forgive him that offends you. The other says, Hang him that offends you. The one says, Pray for your enemy. The other says, Put your enemy to the gibbet. The one says, If thine enemy hunger, feed him. The other says, If thine enemy hath plenty to eat, take it from him that he may starve. The one says, Clothe the naked. The other says, Rob the clothed, that he may become naked. The one says, Bind the broken in heart. The other says, Break the heart that is bound. The one says, Heal the wounded. The other says, Wound the healed. The one says, Suffer all things. The other says, Resent all things. The one says, Resist not evil. The other says, Let no evil be unresisted. The one says, Vengeance belongs to God. The other says, Vengeance belongs to man. The one says, When smitten on one cheek, turn the other. The other says, When smitten on one cheek, return the blow with the bayonet. The one says, Be merciful. The other says, Be unmerciful. The one says, Return not evil for evil. The other says, Return every evil, adding as much as possible. The one says, No murderer hath eternal life in him. The other says, The hero and wholesale murderer hath eternal life in him. In short, all the oracles of war are the contrasts of the oracles of the gospel. The natures of the two things are essentially different. The fish of the one is the scorpion of the other; the bread of the one, the stone of the other. The tender mercies of the one soothe sorrow, remove wrinkles from the brow, and yearn in compassion over suffering humanity. The tender mercies of the other desolate homes, lay waste lands, and add all possible sorrows; buffet, insult, drag to prison, torture, and, in the end, put to death. Between the two, there is a great gulf fixed—a gulf beyond which there issues from all tongues, kindreds, nations, and people, a low, wild wail of despair, the voice from the thousands of millions of souls sent into the eternal world as the victims to the God of War.

Let men not tell us that the gospel of love gives sanction to bloody war, whose tenderest voice is the wildest wail that can rend a widow's heart or desolate her home! No, no. The peaceful gospel and bloody war never utter the same language. The language of the gospel is pure, simple, honest; free from guile, and far from iniquity. The language of war is impure, full of passion, deception, and death. The gospel makes its subjects free. War is the tyrant of tyrants. And thus is the contrast complete throughout. Light and darkness, good and evil, sin and holiness, are not more unlike.

Now, by the side of the plain teachings of the gospel, lay again those ambiguous texts which dark theology has tortured into reluctant testimony for war, such as, "*I have not found so great faith, no, not in Israel.*" And how true it is that Israel had not faith enough to cure *its* malady, while the soldier did have enough to cure *his*. Yet there is doubt whether the inference justly follows, that the Captain of salvation has commissioned the Generals and Heroes of earth to spread dismay and death over the world's civilization. There is some doubt about this text. But what doubt attaches to the following: *The Son of man is not come to destroy men's lives, but to save them. Lay aside all malice. Avenge not yourselves. If thine enemy hunger, feed him; if he thirst, give him drink. Recompense no man evil for evil. Put off anger, wrath, malice.* These texts, with hundreds of others throughout the New Testament, are unmistakably plain. If in the midst of a battle, the true principles of the gospel should suddenly possess the belligerents, they would throw down their arms and rush to the relief of the sufferings mutually inflicted. And there is no mistake in this. To put away wrath, malice, and anger, would be to cease to stay in the midst of the fiercest battle. To lay *these* aside, is to lay war aside. They are the necessary condition of its existence at every moment in anticipation, in preparation, in the fierce conflict. Separate the soul from the body and the latter is dead; separate wrath, malice, anger, the soul of war, from it, and war is dead—is dead the instant of separation.

Look now at all the texts of Scripture that have been cited as giving authority for war; and so construed, they come into conflict with hundreds of others which are as plain as language can make them. How, then, must the few doubtful or ambiguous texts be read? Shall the hundreds, too plain to be mistaken against war, be construed by the light of the few doubtful ones, or shall the few doubtful ones be understood by the aid of the hundreds of plain ones? For centuries men have acted on the doubtful ones, and have plunged into the horrors of war, without satisfying the reflective mind that war has ever brought to humanity, upon the whole, any desirable result. If men would keep in view the rule of interpretation which has been presented, and read doubtful texts by plain ones, they could not go astray on this subject.

Whether men do or do not rightly understand, "He beareth not the sword in vain, Be content with your wages,

Let him sell his raiment and buy a sword," and the like, so as to learn their duty from them, no skill can render doubtful such utterances as, " Love your neighbor as yourself, Pray for your enemy, If thine enemy hunger, feed him, Return not evil for evil, Put aside malice, anger, wrath, Avenge not yourself;" for human genius can not gloss such teachings so as to render them doubtful, or hide from the mind the obligations arising from them. For, *to love* your neighbor, does not mean *to bayonet* him ; *to pray* for an enemy, does not mean *to run him through with a sword*; *to lay aside* malice, anger, wrath, does not mean *to burn and lay waste the property of others;* for we cannot recognize as Christian the habit of religionists, formerly so prevalent, of holding the fire-brand in one hand, and the prayer-book in the other—of burning heretics, commending their souls to God.

As the question of the right to engage in war and of the duty of Christian people in relation to the whole subject, depends upon the construction of the Scriptures, it seems pertinent, at this point, to combine the prophecies of the Old Testament and the teachings of the New, as a means of reaching a just interpretation of the latter, and of inferring the duties of Christians therefrom. And we need not again quote the prophecies relating to the reign of peace which many think shall at length prevail on the earth. It will suffice to call the attention of the reader to the places where some of them may be found. Hence see Ps. XLVI: 9, Isa. II: 2, 4, Ez. XXXIX: 9, 10, Hos. II: 18, Zech. IX: 10; and there are some in the New Testament regarded as relating to the millenium period.

Now, whatever else men may doubt, Christians cannot doubt that these texts teach that the time will be when men will cease to engage in carnal wars. The early fathers of the church thought the time had come in their day. But, since the reign of peace *amongst Christians* lasted only a little over three centuries, the scope of the prophecies does not seem to be met ; and we may rationally expect a permanent rule of peace over the whole earth. And this is the view generally held by those Christians who themselves, with the last degree of inconsistency, unhesitatingly engage in war. But accepting the common opinion—which may be the correct one—that the predicted reign of peace is in the future, or more signally in the future; and the very pertinent question arises—*How and by what instrumentality are the visions of prophecy to be realized, by the introduction of the general reign of peace upon the earth?*

Most people hold the canon of Scripture to be complete, though some hold that revelation to men has not ceased. But the latter notion is too vague to be employed in an argument for or against the question of war. In our argument, we assume that the canon of Scripture is complete; so that whatever we *shall know* from God in this world, we *may now learn* by the true interpretation of the Scriptures, our minds, hearts, and lives being in harmony with their teachings.

If these assumptions are correct, whatever we shall know or practise in the millennium, we may know and ought to practise now. For how shall the visions of prophecy touching the reign of peace, be realized, except through compliance with the teaching of the Scriptures in relation to that reign? Christians accept the Scriptures as the perfect standard of both truth and duty. Hence, the reduction of their teachings to practice amongst the nations of the earth, will bring to pass the visions of prophecy, and introduce the millennium. Hence, it must follow also, that the teachings of the New Testament, if the teachings of God, must agree with the visions of prophecy in regard to the millennium, if those visions are the teaching of God. The laws of our rationality compel us to reach this conclusion. Whence, if the conduct of mankind *will be* peaceful in the millennium, because it will agree with the visions of prophecy and the teaching of the New Testament, the conduct of Christians must now, to be consistent, be peaceful, because the New Testament requires such conduct. Let the idea be stated in language more easily understood: The prophecies of the Old Testament and the teachings of the New, are in harmony in relation to war, and require of men the same conduct and course of life. The New Testament teaches the principles and exhibits the means necessary to bring about the visions of prophecy, and the practical observance of the teachings of the New Testament. Whence, whatever conduct will be practised in the millennium, ought now to be practised by Christians, because the teachings of Christ realized in the hearts and lives of men will introduce the millennium. For how is the millennium to be introduced? Is it not by Christians' reducing perfectly to practice the teaching of Christ as contained in the perfected canon of Scripture? The millennium will be the absence of war and the reign of peace. But if Christ's teachings are not opposed to war, then Christians may forever practise the customs of war. Why is it desirable, then, that the visions of prophecy should be realized? And if the practices of war accord with the teachings of Christ, why may they not continue in the millennium? But if they are contrary to the teachings of Christ, how can Christians justify themselves in violating those teachings by engaging in war? For it is plain, that, if the teachings of Christ contain the whole duty of Christians, whatever *will be* required of them in relation to war, is now required of them; and in the millennium, they will be obliged by the same laws that now oblige them. Hence, if they will be *then* required to practise perfect peace, they are *now* required to practise it.

How Christians can avoid these obvious conclusions, it is not easy to discover. Yet, it is easy to see how they can and do render them practically nugatory: it is done by alleging that Christians are not obliged by the teachings of Christ, because *wicked men* refuse to observe them; by alleging that the teachings of Christ are *impractical* in a wicked world. For Christians say that the laws of Christ forbid war, and that *they* are only justifiable in engaging in war, because all men will not observe the laws of Christ. If all men were peace-men, they tell us that peace doctrines would be beautiful; but that is not so, and men must take the world as it is. But such reasoning is pitiable. The logic and morality are the same as to say, The laws of Christ forbid stealing, but so long as wicked men steal, Christians may, too; for we must take the world as it is. *Our practical* men are the teachers of this doctrine. *But are not Christians to let their* LIGHT SHINE AMONGST WICKED MEN for an example? Christians really *teach more* by example than by precept. But there is no force in their example if they act as the world acts, and urge that they must so act, in order to compete with the world. The wicked do fight and kill about government, patriotism, and national honor, may Christians, therefore, do the same things for the same ends? Low indeed must be the standard of Christian morality, when Christians thus reason! Under such maxims of conduct, how are the visions of prophecy to be realized? May Christians wait till the wicked "learn war no more," before they begin to practise what they admit Christ teaches? Must the wicked lead the righteous into the ways of peace? Strange logic, but true, if the war-Christian's mode of reasoning is good. But have we so learned of Christ?

PART SECOND.

POLITICAL ASPECTS OF THE SUBJECT.

CHAPTER I.

THE NATURE OF HUMAN GOVERNMENT.

The intimate and often blending relations of the various phases of the war-question, render the task difficult, if not impossible, to keep the closely-allied parts from running into each other, occasionally. Nor is the task less easy to say sometimes, whether a given aspect of the subject more properly belongs to the general theological, political, or moral division of the subject. In these particulars, precision of analysis is not aimed at, as the general thought is more esteemed than strict adherence to any well-studied plan. Accordingly, we shall attend to the consideration of civil government as it relates to the word of God, under the general POLITICAL division of the subject.

Up to this point in the argument, we have examined somewhat the nature and end of man's life in this world, touching slightly on the nature of that endless future on which all shall soon enter. Thence we turned to nature herself, and besought her to disclose to us from which of her laws man had the right to exact a fellow's life, and send him into that future; and finding no clear and satisfactory response, we turned to the revelation of God, as given to Noah, to the Jews in war-commands, and as presented in the general teachings of the Old Testament. Thence, passing to the less shadowy utterances of the New Testament, we sought the true import of Paul's teachings to the Roman Christians, and of Christ's teachings in their own light and in the light of the whole scheme of the gospel and as in harmony with the visions of Jewish prophecy. In none of these could we find authority for taking life or engaging in war. By natural progress, we come thence to inquire for the right to engage in it for the support of civil government. In latter times the wars which have commanded the approbation of the better classes of mankind, have had relation to the supposed permanency, interests, or honor of human governments; and thence are derived the plausible arguments for war. Hence, it becomes necessary to inquire a little carefully into the nature of civil government.

The purpose which we have in view makes it necessary to scrutinize a theory or two, which men have, with more or less distinctness of conception and language, advocated in relation to government. The one may be called *The Political Theory;* the other, *The Politico-Theological Theory.* The abettors of the former tell us that CIVIL GOVERNMENT was originally formed in *contract by agreement.* They tell us that the contract is made and entered into by those who constitute the subjects of the government where it is formed. Each subject contracts with all the others, rendering the government a matter mutual amongst all the members of society. The consideration which imparts validity to the contract, consists in the agreements made mutual between each individual, as one party, and the residue of the subjects, as the other party. Even the more precise terms of the contract are exhibited by these theorists. They assure us that, before the contract is formed, each individual is, as they style it, in a state of nature. In this state, no one is obliged by law except as God imposes it. For, in that state, there are no superiors and no inferiors, neither rulers nor subjects; hence no restraints from human law, because God's is the only power superior to the individual.

Thus situated, with no restraints from human power, each being "his own lord in creation," the theory supposes a congress of the people, for the purpose of forming civil government. At this congress the contract is made, from which civil government results. By the contract each individual is supposed to yield certain rights, which it is agreed belonged to him in his state of nature. The aggregate of the rights so yielded, constitutes the whole legitimate power of the government.

In thus forming the government, each individual is adjudged to retain all rights not expressly granted by the contract. Then further stipulations are made as to the mode of carrying the granted rights into practical execution. The whole general method of accomplishing the result gives the *form* and *style* of the constitution and government. The *government* itself consists in the act of reducing to practice the rights which constitute the aggregate power as ceded by all the individuals who compose the government. The right in the individuals who compose the government, to concede power to the government, is limited by the laws of God only.

Such is the Political Theory. In itself it is beautiful—beautiful amounting to the sublime. Viewed through it, the field of political government is luminous as light. Complied with in practice, the confusion and crimes of war would at once disappear from the world. Reduced fully to practice, the visions of prophecy would be immediately realized, when men would learn war no more.

As based on the axioms of the Declaration of Independence, this is the THEORY of the United States Government, the most beautiful and desirable form of government in the world. It is the theory of self-government—the theory of free government—the theory that all just power in government is derived from the consent of the governed. We shall have occasion hereafter to dwell at some little length on this branch of the subject, when it shall be our endeavor to show that the assumption of power to wage war in order to preserve a government from division into more than one government, forever strikes down the principles of free self-government, as well as this beautiful theory.

The Politico-Theological Theory is neither so easy to understand nor to explain. It is undefined, recondite, and, lying in doubt and darkness, clouds and gloom hover about it. Its abettors express it in language, general, vague, and mystical. The whole subject appears to be in their minds veiled in chaos, without form and void. Taking their language as the symbol of thought, a single conception seems clearly defined to their mental apprehension. They thus utter that apprehension—" The powers that be are ordained of God."

It is not denied that this utterance is a truth, even a truth of divine inspiration. Yet, like *many* truths of inspiration, it is very general, and is susceptible of a more specific conception of the mind. But our theorists tell us little beyond the naked utterance. Now, since it seems evident that God intends us to employ our rational faculties in ascertaining the more specific nature of His truth revealed in general terms, when the nature of the case is level to our apprehension, and the case before us being so, the pertinent inquiry arises, *In what sense is the mind to apprehend the utterance—" The powers that be are ordaiued of God."*

Although this is the utterance of inspiration, it is the embodiment of a thought which lies within the grasp of the mind's apprehension. In other words, there is a *true and proper sense* in which the mind may comprehend *how* it is that God *ordains the powers that be.* This would seem to be the rational conception of the subject; and the *true sense* of the inspired utterance must consist with the *facts* which we *know* attach to human government. What then is that true and proper sense? Here lies the vexed question, which our vague theorists do not answer. They make the utterance the basis of war, but not the basis of a clear and rational judgment. When it is solemnly protested that war is wrong, a cruel, needless, monstrous wrong, disallowed by the laws of God even to support civil government, the reply flaunted into the face is—The powers that be are ordained of God. But we ask, *Where is the logical connective between the ordination of God and the use of the sword ?* If the utterance is attentively analyzed, it is feared that the rational *nexus* is scarcely better discovered by those who flippantly use the quotation than by those who fail to see in it the power of the sword. For the church is ordained of God ; and may men link it with the terrors of the sword, and, fancying that theirs is the only notion, may they begin about it the work of slaughter and devastation ? How long since this was the notion of the church ; and how long since the fires of persecution went out ? Where is the land in which they did not burn; and with what earnestness of zeal were they not kindled ? And what sort of a heretic would he have been thought, who had urged that fire and fagot were not necessary to preserve both the existence and the purity of the church ? Leo X. regarded the extermination of Luther, his heresy, and his adherents, as of first importance to the church, and calling for the full force of the State. And many of the mitred and crowned heads of Europe combined to crush the heretical monk, lest his success should prove the overthrow of *all religion.* And what reason can be urged for using the sword in the interests of the State, which may not with equal force be urged in the interests of the church ? For centuries it was as zealously and plausibly urged for the destruction of *religious heresy*, as it is now used for the destruction of *political heresy*. In both cases and equally, when stripped of the gauze of sophistry, the use of the sword is simply persecution—is the denial of the use of the rational faculties, the deprivation of judgment and conscience, and the substitution in their stead, of fire and fagot, powder and lead. Still, often as the voice of protest is raised against the use of powder and lead, it is deemed sufficient to echo—*The powers that be are ordained of God.* And is there indeed no limit to political power ? When government inflicts wanton cruelty and takes life, that it may expand ambitiously over large territory, when objection is made, is it enough ever to flaunt back—The powers that be are ordained of God ? And who that had a heart to feel, did not become sick of the meaningless changes rung on this phrase, when recently hundreds of thousands were monthly dying in the slaughter pens of war?

But let us proceed more directly to the subject, and lay before the mind the axioms and principles which show *how* it is that God ordains political government.

We may discriminate two senses in which God ordains things: the one, *immediately;* the other, *mediately*. And in one or the other of these senses, He ordains the existence of *all things*,—even of moral evil. Both of these modes are involved in the ordination of civil government. God *immediately* ordained the nature and constitution of things, and the *un*fallen nature of man. Then civil government results from this *immediate* ordination of God in combined action with the *fallen* nature of man. Let the idea be expanded. God, by *immediate* creation, made man holy. In that state he needed no civil government, and had he maintained that state, he would never have formed a political constitution. He would have had God's law, and by keeping it would have lived. Deu. XXVII: 26, Gal. III: 10. But by sin man fell from the favor of God, and lost ability to live by keeping His law. Thence he was thrust from the presence of God upon the barren earth, among thorns and thistles which, to curse him, sprang thick and rank over all the earth. Thus thrust out, he stood a trembling, fainting creature of wants, nameless and touching in both kind and degree. He was destined to subdue the earth, and from it to extract whatever of good he could cause it to yield; thus, partially alleviating his wants, till, yielding up the ghost, the spirit should return to God that gave it. Forlorn and hopeless without the protecting presence of God, urgent and numberless wants became incentives to activity. Lapsed from his primitive condition, the soul tainted and darkened by the revolt, the poison of sin transfused through the whole being rendering the person sensitive to every chilling blast, and to thousands of painful wants, he retained still a rational mind capable of comprehending something of his own nature and constitution, and something of the nature and constitution of things about him. And God, determining to grant a respite to the sentence of death which attached to the revolt, and which all nature now seemed disposed to execute on the victim, reserved to Himself the general providence of the system which He had appointed and into which sin had introduced derangement by reason of the curse which justice had written in the laws of nature, to be executed on the introduction of sin.

In view of man's sin and fall, God provided and appointed a merciful and remedial system tendering to man the means of escaping the consequences of his revolt from God. And thus there are two distinct systems of law appointed by God over the world: the one is a system founded in justice; the other, in grace. Owing to his sin, man was thrust from the presence of God and put under the laws of justice, now disposed, as we have seen, to execute on him the sentence of the violated law. And as his sin produced derangement in his mental and moral faculties, so the curse pronounced on account of his sin, seems to have deranged the whole system of laws in nature.

God still presides over both of these systems of laws, but in a manner too mysterious for the dark and disordered mind of man to comprehend to any considerable extent. Still, we know He presides, because the sun continues to rise and set, and souls continue to be converted from a state of sin to one of holiness.

We know too that man's sin produced derangement in the mental and moral faculties, darkening the mental and stupefying the moral faculties; and we also know that God pronounced a curse on nature, on account of his sin. Now, it is from this double condition of things,—the derangement of man's mental and moral faculties, and the curse pronounced on nature—that there results what the Apostle, in Romans XIII: 1 calls *exousia, the power, means,* or *authority* for establishing civil government. Whence we see plainly the basis of civil government. It is laid in the WANTS of man as a fallen being. For man, fallen and sinful, was thrust from the presence of God, and because pressed and importuned by *ceaseless* WANTS; and *these wants*, appealing to the rational soul for gratification, suggested the idea of civil government. And thus the foundation for civil government being laid in man's constitution as deep as his ceaseless wants, man himself, more or less guided by the hand of a mysterious Providence, was, in the exercise of his rational agency, to build upon that foundation the superstructure of civil government.

It is easy to see that, in his fallen condition, such were man's wants, that necessity was laid upon him to employ the *exousia*, or *authority* appointed by God, in the formation of civil government. The "*power*," or *authority* was ordained by God, but *its construction into government* is the work of man. The wants resulted from derangement caused by sin, and the "power" *(exousia)* to form government resulted from sin and the curse pronounced on nature; and government became a necessity from the twofold influence of sin. God knew, of course, *what* the wants of man would be, and knew that, from the foundation laid, he would institute government. And it is thus, by God's *mediate* and *immediate* ordination, that government is formed; by His *immediate* constitution given man since the fall, and by His *mediate* formation of government through the rational agency of man under the fall: man's wants demand what government promises to supply, and to this end and in this mode, God ordains "the powers that be."

In no other sense can we conceive of the institution of government, in consistency with the facts which surround its existence. It is true that God is the author of the powers that be, but is the author through the agency of man. The agency acts in virtue of the activity which God gave, operating on the laws of nature and those of self-preservation, forming civil constitutions and governments. And thus it is plain, as we have already said, and may properly repeat, that civil government results from the combined *mediate* and *immediate* ordination of God: *immediate*, by that Creative Energy which made the laws and constitution of nature, and the laws, constitution, and wants of man; *mediate*, by that agency of man which, employing the laws and constitution of nature, and the laws and constitution of man, combines them and forms government as a means of supplying man's wants.

A little sober reflection will satisfy the mind that the foregoing is just the way in which God ordains the powers that be, and that He ordains them in no other way. Government was by no means either the first or most pressing of man's necessities. In the nature of things, it could not exist for some generations; and when the necessity for it did come, its *value* would be *measured* by its *ability to gratify the wants* which suggested its formation. It could be regarded as the means only of procuring those wants. And this is the true nature of all civil government. In its own nature, to *many* of the wants of man, it must be subordinate; and it mainly contemplates the attainment of worldly interests, though it may incidentally produce moral discipline.

And thus we may behold the first principles and the simple nature and offices of government. But men of this age have attached to it many other conceptions. Borrowing the notions of heathen nations, they have exalted it as a means of national fame and splendor, bowing before it in the homage of idolatry. But stripping it of the bewildering ideas which idolatrous homage has attached, and looking at the *thing itself*, we are enabled to see *how* "the powers that be are ordained of God," while, at the same time, we behold the reason, nature, and necessity of the thing itself. And thus viewing the matter in the light of reason, the whole subject of government becomes plain and simple. The *common* sense of men can lay hold of and appreciate it.

But to affirm that God ordains government in a different

sense, is to affirm what is destitute of proof and inconceivable by the mind. And first to exalt government to the place which God does not intend it to occupy, and then to support it by the horrors of war, cannot be less than idolatry attended by human sacrifice. While God ordains, therefore, that there shall be government, He leaves all people free to choose the forms of it which they deem best suited to answer its end. And *His ordination* sustains the same relation *to all* forms of it—kingdoms, monarchies, democracies, republics. This view of the subject accords with natural justice, the truths of the Declaration of Independence, and the axioms which show the equality of all men before the laws of nature as contained therein. And since God *ordains as we have seen*, we have reason to believe that He ordained the government of Nero just as he did the government of Washington; and the government under the Articles of Confederation just as the Provisional Government under Jefferson Davis. For the latter were both governments, in popular language, under rebellion; and how can *we* say that God ordained one in a sense different from the other? In *principle* no man can perceive a difference; and if the act of one, apart from *fighting*, was a sin against God, the other was. But in both cases, the real sin consisted in the *fighting*. This shall be more fully shown in future chapters.

In sober reason there is no special sacredness attaching to civil government. It is but a means to a worldly end. Why, therefore, enthrone in it a bloody god, and keep red before it the altar of human sacrifice? Or let any sense that men please be attached to the utterance, that *the powers are ordained by God;* and *how* is the right *thence* derived to keep the altar wet with the blood of human victims?

Thus have we endeavored to exhibit the sense in which God ordains the existence of civil government; and in so doing, we have seen also the nature and office of government itself. In the exhibition we have been enabled to attach intelligible and rational conceptions to the teaching of inspiration on the subject of government; and are hence prepared to consider other branches of the subject.

CHAPTER II.

THE POLITICAL THEORY AND PRINCIPLES OF GOVERNMENT.

§ 1.—*The Basis of Civil Government—Different forms of Government.*

THE last chapter was devoted principally to the consideration of the general nature of civil government as symbolized to us in the inspired language which declares that the "powers" are ordained of God. In presenting that aspect of the question we were induced, in connection with it, to speak of the *wants* of men as forming a sort of counterpart, or complement of the *exousia*, or "power," and the power and wants together we regarded as constituting the elements of all civil governments. Under the "powers ordained," however, the inspired writer probably includes the *wants* of men, regarding the *wants* as a part of the "ordained" elements out of which governments are formed. And having dwelt somewhat upon one aspect of the "powers," it is now fitting to dwell a little more fully on the nature of those *wants*, as they form an important element in the composition of government, and the other aspect of the "powers ordained."

Human government itself certainly results from the *depravity* of man. Had he not sinned and lapsed from his state of favor with God, he would have needed, for his government, nothing but the law of God, without human law. His mind unclouded, and his heart unselfish, he would have perceived and observed all the requirements and obligations of the perfect laws of God. By these he would have seen that all men sustain the same relations to God and to the world; and that from these relations arise the obligations of men towards each other. From these relations it would have been perceived that each man owed to his neighbor the same obligations that he owed to himself; and, being unselfish, each would have discharged the obligations perceived. In that case, there could have been collision of neither interest nor feeling, because there would have been no self-preference. All the wants of men would have been supplied by the bountiful hand of God, without anxious care to His just and rational creature; and selfishness excluded and love prevailing, God's law alone would have been the rule of man's conduct. There would consequently have been no foundation or need of human law or government. Hence, we see that the law of love is the law of nature.

Upon the sin and fall of man, *a host of painful wants pressed upon him.* The ground was cursed; the elements were cursed; man was cursed. Upon the commission of sin, he immediately found himself naked; and then, the earth cursed, the elements disordered, reason darkened and passion rampant, he was thrust from the presence and protection of God, to experience the keenness of the chilling blast and the gnawing of the voracious appetite. He now found all things in disorder and ruin. His numerous wants taunted and tortured him in all directions. He could only flee from his *wants* by fleeing from himself. The inseparable incidents of his earthly existence, they pressed and importuned him at every turn of life. Hence they became the ground of ceaseless solicitude, the basis of restless activity. Reaching up through the lower appetites and passions, they demanded in their interests the best efforts of reason. They engaged also the sympathy and action of his social nature.

But, not attempting to develop all the effects of his clamorous wants upon him, we may pass to the point at which they would suggest the idea of civil government. At that point, we shall have gone beyond the *patriarchal* form of government; for that is not the natural form for mankind. The ongoings of *wants* would soon imperatively demand things which that form could not supply; and humanity would thence exact a government on a larger scale. And it is evident that the required government might assume *any one* of the *many* different forms. We need not attempt to state them all. The "powers" might assume whatever form the PEOPLE should choose to give them. The authority might be absolutely lodged in the hands of one man ; or a limited power might be conferred on one as a kind of head, and be assisted by aids and advisers. The chief officer might hold his position for a term of years or for life, by election, at first, and then by descent. Or the "power" might be given to the few, for the purpose of working the machinery of government ; and they might hold their places by election and inheritance, for years, for life, or during good behavior. Or the *people* whose *wants* were to be met, so far as possible, through the instrumentality of government, might meet in person and decide as to the *form* in which their own government should be conducted. The *possible* forms in which the *people's* wants could be supplied by government, would constitute the measure of the forms into which the "powers" might be moulded. Any of the possible forms would have the sanction of God ; and one as much as the other. He ordains the "powers" and man's agency ; and man's *wants* prompt to the formation of the government.

Which of the possible forms of government would be best, it would be difficult to decide. One form would be better for one people, and another for another, depending on their circumstances and civilization. For our purpose this branch of the subject needs not be pursued at length. We need to notice only, that the *wants* which form the true basis and bond of government, are the wants of the *people ;* and, hence, that the government ought to be formed with *direct reference* to *their* wants. But *how* that end could be best attained, is a question difficult of solution. For one people, one form would be best ; for another people, another would be best. Mixed forms would often be best suited to reach the end. Nearly all the governments that have existed, have been more or less mixed in their forms. The great defects of governments have been in their *administration*. They have not been administered with reference to the "good" of the masses so much as with reference to the aggrandizement and luxury of the few. And when Paul says the "ruler is the minister of God for good," he alludes to the idea that government ought to be *formed* and *administered* for the "good" of the *people*. And the allegiance of the subject depends on the faithfulness of the ruler or the competency of the government "to minister" to the "good" of the subject. Yet, in all Europe, as a whole, and in nearly all the governments of the earth, civil constitutions are instituted and administered on the idea that the *people* are but the incidents and appendages of the rulers. And as the *people* are ruled now, so have they been in times past. Even when the government has been *called free*, it has been little less than an oligarchy, administered by the few for their own ends. Ancient Sparta was little more than a military camp in which the *people* were schooled for the slaughter-pens of war. Greece and Rome were scarcely any better. The *people* were largely *slaves* and *soldiers*. The end of their governments seemed to be ambition, conquest, and military glory. And, indeed, the *nations* of antiquity were little else than pirates, thieves, and conquerors; and their influence and example have largely given character to the nations which sprang from the downfall of the Roman Empire, and to all the civilizations of modern times. For, although, at first, barbarians conquered the Romans, finally the Romans conquered the barbarians, giving them their character and civilization. And a disregard of the *wants* of the people is a characteristic of the constitutions of modern Europe. Nothing is more offensive to the mind imbued with a just conception of the true end of government, than the semi-idolatrous awe with which the people are taught to reverence their imperious rulers. Proper respect and obedience are due to them, not as haughty masters but as their own chosen agents, in theory at least, to conduct the interests of the people; and the people owe respect and obedience because the rulers minister for the good of their good. And a people are guilty of no moral wrong, in throwing off allegiance to a rule that fails to promote *their good.* It is for their good that all legitimate government is instituted. Their *wants* are the basis of all such government; and when government disregards their wants, it ceases to be *their* government; hence they may justly and innocently repudiate all allegiance to it. *And the people are forever the judges when their wants are regarded and their interests protected.*

Hence the nature of POLITICAL GOVERNMENT becomes plain. *Human wants are the basis of it, and human interests secured, are the bonds of it.* So, in this connection, *wants* and *interests* are co-related terms. Our *wants*, as has been shown, are inseparable incidents of our depravity. Hence, they are as wide-spread as that depravity; and so lay the foundation for all government. It is *interests* which supply the *wants*, and gratify their demands; and it is through the instrumentality of government, that the interests are secured. It is interests, therefore, that bind men to government; while it is for the security of their interests, that they form government. Whence, their obligation to obedience to government arises solely out of the fact that it secures and promotes their interests.

Thus we see, in the plainest manner, that the basis of government is laid in the *wants* of men. Reflection suggests the great variety of wants which men inherit by the fall. Yet we must carefully bear in mind that government refers only to " good " for men. The ruler is " the minister of God *for good.*" Government is the source of *good* and *happiness* to man; its blessings belong to man as man belongs to *this* world. *It* has nothing to do with him, directly, as a *spiritual* or *moral* being. Its duty is to aid in securing and promoting the *interests* which gratify *bodily* and *mental wants;* and with these its direct duty terminates. Its whole positive duty lies within the province of *moral indifference.* With *moral* qualities, as such, it has nothing to do. As incidental to the attainment of the *interests* which it is instituted to promote, it may *recommend* morality, perhaps religion, but exceeding recommendation, it exceeds its legitimate province. It is man's *moral nature* which constitutes him the subject of *moral government,* and the Lord Jesus reserves to Himself the sole prerogative of ruling therein. That emphatically constitutes *His* Kingdom, and His Kingdom belongs not to this world.

Because morality and religion make good citizens and *tend* to secure *worldly* good, the State may *encourage* them, but may not punish the disregard of either, as such, because both relate to conscience, and conscience comes under the sanctions of God's moral government. Careful reflection will generally enable us to separate readily between moral and civil government, so as justly to limit the functions of the latter. The former always has reference to duty and obligation ; the latter, to the wants and interests of the people. The distinction is clear in principle, but may sometimes be difficult in practice. For an act may be compounded of *moral* and *political* elements ; and so may be liable to the action of political government, while it is under the moral government of God. Such act may be restrained by government, not as a violation of moral law, but as a violation of political rights. To illustrate. Drunkenness is a moral crime punishable by the moral law. But it is also a political crime, because of its evil example, and its inevitable tendency to violate positive political law. It may, therefore, justly be punished, not as a crime against moral law, but as a crime against civil law. Many other crimes come under the same principle, and may be punished for the same reason.

Still, the great principle remains, that the province of civil government lies *within the territory which has no moral qualities,* and consists in securing to the subject those *interests* which gratify the *wants* of man as a being of this world. What a man thinks, what is his philosophy, what are his notions of religion, science, society, or of civil government, are matters beyond the rightful cognizance of the *powers that be*. Men form civil government for no such ends, and were such ends proclaimed, rational men would refuse to form it, preferring to forego their *bodily interests*, rather than surrender the freedom of thought and the liberty of conscience.

We will do well, then, carefully to remember that the end of civil government is to secure the interests which relate to the wants of man as a sinful being of this world; for, by so doing, we escape entanglement in those errors which have led to the suppression of free thought and speech, to persecution and war, and the hundreds of ills which have grown out of the abuse of the just powers of civil government. With the end of government intelligently fixed in the mind, the ship of state may steer so as to avoid the breakers on which the nations have heretofore wrecked their hopes and murdered their people. And reflect as long and closely as we may, we can find no *just* basis for government but men's *wants*, and no *righteous* bond but their *interests*. Take from man bodily wants, or supply the interests which gratify them, and he would have no use for government. It is in seeking the interests which gratify wants, in an illegal way, that most crimes are committed against both individuals and society. "The love of money is the root of evil." If the wants were removed, no scrambles would arise for *money*, which, in the foregoing sentence, is the representative of all human interests. Wars, frauds, slanders, brawls, bickerings, and challenges; ambitious struggles for power and place, generally grow out of avarice and the various forms in which worldly interests are sought. And nearly the whole direct object of civil government is to regulate and restrain the scrambles of men in their pursuit of those interests; while the wants which underlie the interests prompt its formation and constitute the bond of its continuance. Hence, *wants and in-*

terests, and not "the blood of traitors," are "the cement of government."

This is the teaching of right reason; and, hence, the teaching of the gospel. But "lust" has a teaching different from this. That teaching was stated by Doctor Breckenridge in a celebrated speech in which he put off the gown and put on the shoulder-strap. Ignoring enlightened reason and Christian morality, he uttered the false and foul sentiment, that "the blood of traitors is the cement of government." His is strange cement, and stranger morality! "Blood," the bond of government! "*The blood* of traitors" its "cement!" Few more execrable sentiments have escaped human lips; and foul, false, and malignant, it is to be hoped that no more may be uttered while the world stands.

Disregarding the wants and interests of men, it is monstrous to hold them in allegiance to government by "the cement of blood." No government ever stood on a foundation more hateful and tyrannical. It brings vividly before the mind a Nero, Herod, and Caligula. But it is a *fitting cement* for tyrants, bigots, and persecutors; and they have largely employed it since the world began. Indeed, where reason and Christianity have been laid aside, and lust has taken their place, *blood* has generally been employed by the numerous disciples of Cain, the illustrious inventor of that kind of "cement." Doctor Breckenridge announced but a popular truism. Its announcement at the time required less genius than worldly mindedness; and at the time of its announcement, it had the recommendation of popularity, if not that of truth in moral or political science.

§. 2.—*The United States Government the model—Axioms of Liberty.*

Having briefly considered the nature of government in the three-fold relations, 1st., as to the *exousia* or *power* in the nature and constitution of things as made by God: 2dly, as to the wants of man consequent upon his depravity: and 3d., as to those interests which co-relate to those wants, and form the just bonds of allegiance to civil government,—we now pass to the further development of these elementary principles and to consider other questions embraced in the scope of the general argument. For the purpose of educing the argument and presenting it in its proper light, we prefer to conduct it, in its whole length, in connection with the *theory* of free government. Indeed, no part of our reasoning would be applicable to any but a free government; since it can have no relation to a government in which intelligence and free thought are ignored and rejected. Where "blood is the cement of government;" our reasoning has no pertinence. For, indeed, one cannot reason with .powder and lead, and our endeavor is to employ reason; and so our processes are impertinent, where the government is based on physical force or the right that is founded on might.

Our own government is the form—in theory—which we take as the model; and it is the form which is utterly inconsistent with the use of the sword as the bond between itself and the citizen. This last idea is self-evident if we bear in mind the principles exhibited in the last two or three sections. But the general conception demands elucidation. Let us then begin with the theory of United States Government. That theory is based upon the truths stated in the Declaration of Independence; and those truths are declared to be self-evident. We accept them as political axioms. So soon as the terms in which they are expressed are understood and the truths are apprehended in their relations to God and to men, they become as self-evident as the axioms of Geometry. Their self-evident character necessarily results from the view which has been exhibited of the *basis* and *bond* of civil government. Men's *wants* are inseparable from them wherever they may be upon the earth; and we hold it to be self-evident that wherever they may be upon the earth, they have the right to seek the *interests* which God intends as the means of supplying the wants: and

God everywhere bestows on them the right, as inalienable as their *wants*, of employing civil government as the instrument to that end. The wants being the inalienable attendants of humanity, so is the right to self-government, as the appointed medium of supplying the interests demanded by the wants. The wants, the interests which correspond to them, and the right of self-government, are at once and equally the inalienable attendants of humanity. *No act of men can separate from them their wants—no contract, no constitution, no form of government, can do it; so no act of theirs, no contract, no agreement can deprive them of the right to seek the interests which answer to the wants, or of the right of that self-government which God has appointed as the means of securing the interests which answer to them.* These three propositions, then, are self-evident : 1.—*Man is a creature of wants.* 2.—*God has appointed in nature certain interests suited to relieve those wants.* 3.—*God has appointed self-government as the medium of obtaining the interests which relieve those wants.* These are inalienable from man by man himself. It is impossible for himself or others to separate his wants from him. But his co-related interests *may* be separated from him ; and the right of-self-government, as the means attaining the interests, may be separated from him ; but both will be acts of wrong and tyranny.

We, thus and for these reasons, hold that ALL MEN are endowed by their Creator with the inalienable right of instituting and maintaining self-government. And we readily perceive the basis of the right in the three propositions just stated. The axioms of the Declaration of Independence begin with the *third* of the foregoing propositions, as the author of it satisfied himself by *beginning* with the *political* axiom, without exhibiting the two antecedent ones on which that one rested. But the presentation of the two antecedent ones strengthens the one with which he began— showing *why* self-government is an inalienable right—showing that it is inalienable because the " ordination" of God for the mitigation of the ills of human life. From this stand-point, we are also unable to vindicate another axiom of that instrument, lately questioned and assailed, namely, "that all men are created equal." Man never uttered a truth more clearly self-evident than this, if it is regarded with a single eye and mixed with no foreign ingredient. Just as Mr. Jefferson stated it is axiomatic; but not as others have caricatured it. It is not self-evident because stated to be so by a distinguished man, but because it is so in the nature of things. It is *not* true "that all men are created equal" in natural strength or endowments, or in the social distinctions made in the world. It is *not* true that all men are created in the line of kings, nobles, or aristocrats—it is a pity that any are. It is not true that all are born equal in moral endowments, or in earthly wealth. Had Jefferson said these or a thousand other things that ingenuity or unfairness could attribute, the affirmation would have been false within the common experience of men. But the easy and natural reply to all such objections is, that the axiom ceases to be an axiom so soon as there is included in it something not included by its author. In all such cases, what the author *said* is still an axiom; but what others *say he said* is not an axiom. But did he say what special pleading has often attributed to him? Did he, a slaveholder at the time, say that, under the perverted notions and laws of men, the slave was created the political equal of the master? Such an utterance would have exhibited surpassing stupidity rather than great sagacity. Did he say that the son of the humble artisan was created the equal in privilege with the son of wealth and station? He uttered the language of no such folly.

But what did he say? He was speaking of *political* government, and dealing with first principles. Man can go back no further than to the creation of men. And how are they equal in that creation? 1. *They are all equal in having wants.* 2. *They are equal in having the right to seek the interests which answer to the wants.* 3. *They are equal in having the inalienable right to maintain self-government in the interests which answer to the wants.*

It is self-evident that all men are *created* equal in these respects. In these respects the slave of Mr. Jefferson was the full equal of Mr. Jefferson himself. He had *wants*, and they attracted the right to seek the *interests* answering to them; while the *interests* involved the right to personal and political self-government. That Mr. Jefferson opposed his slave's carrying into practice a self-evident truth, cannot invalidate the truth: *it proves only* HIS *inconsistency.* The principle is still true within the intuitions of reason. And to deny it, is to blind reason by passion and self-love. Mr. Jefferson might think the capacity of the slave disabled him from employing a self-evident right; but even that incapacity could only suspend and could not destroy the right. *Capacity* is not the measure of rights. *Rights* belong to, and are inseparable from, *wants* and *interests;* and belong to *slaves* and negroes as well as to freemen and white men. The *slave* has inalienable *wants*, and these are *interests* which inseparably attach to them, and these attract the right of self-government. And the *rights* of the slave are the same, though they may be withheld from him, or he may be incapacitated properly to use them. The rights are self-evident, though they may have been withheld for centuries, and thereby may have taken away the capacity wisely to use them. The people of all Europe and Asia have for centuries been deprived of the right to maintain self-government, and are thereby doubtless incapacitated to maintain it rationally; but their right is thereby in no respect impaired. It is self-evident that they are created with the right, whether they have the capacity or not to make rational use of it. It is self-evident that the slave is created with his equal rights, though he may ever be deprived of them. *Rights* and the *privilege of using them* are two distinct conceptions. Nay, men are created equal in a sense broader than that stated in the Declaration of Independence. In all the *essential* relations which they sustain to God, and to one another, they are equal. Men are the common offspring of God, and sustain the relations of a common brotherhood. The little earthly distinctions which *they* create are unworthy of notice. They are below the follies of childhood. In a great conception, " *all* men are created equal," though by the follies of men, there are many inequalities in earthly allotments. There is still another sense of the created equality of all men, and it is probably that which was intended by Mr. Jefferson. As a historical fact, we know that the truths of the Declaration of Independence, were alleged as the grounds on which the Revolutionists justified themselves in committing rebellion against England, by repudiating their allegiance, and instituting self-government. And these truths constituted at once the justification, and contained in themselves the first principles, on which the new government was founded. And Mr. Jefferson probably generalized the truths which we have exhibited as the rights of individuals, and applied them to a collective number of men. In this case, the truths are axiomatic in relation to the multitude, because they are axiomatic in relation to the individuals composing the multitude. In its application to the case, and as read in the light of historical facts, the axiom would then assume this expression : *It is a truth self-evident that all men are created equal in the sense, that a multitude of men amounting to two or three millions, may at all times, when they think their incerests are not secured, repudiate their allegiance to the government under which they live and institute for themselves a new one.*

If this *is* the kind of equality intended by Jefferson and our ancestors as applicable to *all* men, it is self-evidently true, because it is the general expression of a truth, which is true of all the individuals that compose the generalization. And if it is self-evident that the slave has the right of freedom, it is self-evident that any *large* multitude of men have the right to renounce their allegiance to one government, and institute another. For the principle is essentially the same in the two cases. The slave has the right to seek the *interests* which meet his *wants*, as he may think best. To prevent this, is to retain him in slavery. It is the same with the multitude of men. If they may not change their allegiance and seek their interests in their own way, by instituting a new government, they are not freemen but governmental slaves. But we shall recur to this part of the subject hereafter.

From the pen of John H. Hopkins, D.D., a worthy Bishop of the Protestant Episcopal Church, we recently read a piquant attack on the truth of the Declaration of Independence, in relation to the natural equality of all men. He arraigns the supposed axiom in terms of indignant confidence; and regards it as false within the ordinary experience of men. But we suspect that the good Bishop misconceived the import of the axiom, or else he was not enamored of free government, or it is possible that his episcopal modes of reasoning unfitted him to embrace so democratic an idea. Yet it is exceedingly clear that Bishop Hopkins rather arraigns his own conception of what Mr. Jefferson might have said, than the truth of what he did say. For Mr. Jefferson affirms not a proposition that the Bishop encounters; and the Bishop encounters not a proposition that Mr. Jefferson affirms. The facts of history and the acts of those who signed the Declaration of Independence, prove that both they and Mr. Jefferson understood that axiom in the light which we have stated it, and not in the light in which it is presented by those who contemplated bringing objections against it.

We hold it to be an axiomatic truth, that the people on this side of the Atlantic had, by virtue of the laws of nature, the right to renounce their allegiance to the English Crown, and to institute for themselves such a government as they deemed best suited to secure and promote their own interests. They were born possessed of that right inalienably; and held it equally with all other nations of the earth. Their right to do so is as unquestionable by the laws of nature, as the right of England at the moment to retain her own government. The reason in both cases would be the same. Each people had wants, and each, through the instrumentality of government, had the right to seek the interests which answered to them.

If the Bishop holds that they are not endowed by the Creator with that kind of equality, he holds that men have not the right to institute and maintain self-government. For that is the practical proposition which our ancestors asserted and maintained. In this sense, all men that believe in the inalienable right of self-government, believe that the thought objected to is indeed an axiom. And unperverted by false education and the traditions of the past, it is perceived to result from the natural appointments of God—is a clear revelation to us through our intuitions. Nay, all the axioms of political liberty are deducible from the constitution of man and of nature ; and are true, as stated in the Declaration of Independence, because they are true in nature. Those stated by Mr. Jefferson had been substantially educed from the laws of nature and of human consciousness long before he made the forcible summary of them.

Since these axioms are constituted *by God*, they are true at all times and in all parts of the earth. It is true at all times, and in all parts of the earth, that the slave has the right to be free, because the reasons why he should be free exist everywhere and at all times. And these axioms are everywhere and at all times true, because the reasons always exist. Just so long as men have wants and there are interests answering to them, which may be secured and promoted through the instrumentality of government, they have the right to renounce their allegiance to one government and institute for themselves another ; and the moment they cease to have that right, they may be made political slaves.

As we hold the axioms of the Declaration of Independence to be axioms, because they exist in the constitution and laws of nature, we regard them as having value apart from their relation to the theory of our government, and as constituting the first principles of political liberty for all people. It is therefore pertinent to quote in this connection a paragraph from that justly celebrated instrument: " We hold these truths to be self-evident—that all men are created equal ; that they are endowed by their Creator with certain inalienable rights ; that amongst these are life, liberty, and the right to pursue happiness ; that to secure these rights, governments are instituted amongst men, deriving their just powers from the consent of the governed ; that whenever any form of government becomes destructive of these ends, it is the right of the people to alter or to abolish it, and to institute a new government, laying its foundation on such principles and organizing its powers in such form, as to them shall seem most likely to effect their safety and happiness."

These are, indeed, truths of our intuition. No reasoning can make them clearer than they are so soon as the terms in which they are expressed are understood. For, comprehended in themselves and in their relations, as forming a part of the laws of God, the intelligence appointed by the same God, must perceive their truth by its own activity. Still, there is advantage to be derived in employing them in reasoning. Like the axioms of Geometry, they are capable of a variety of applications, and their employment presents them and other truths in new and striking combinations.

Now, the truth of the axioms of freedom is not more self-evident than that their just application is utterly inconsistent with the use of the sword to coerce a multitude of subjects into unwilling obedience. For there is no intellect sufficiently acute to reconcile self-government with a coerced allegiance. The two things are at once irreconcilable and mutually destructive. If a people are coerced, they are not free. If they are free, they are not coerced. Coercion necessitates the absence of freedom. Freedom necessitates the absence of coercion. Their co-existence in a people is a logical and natural contradiction, and an impossibility. Like the qualities of sin and holiness, they are necessarily contraries. The presence of either implies the absence of the other.

In the light of history and of what has been said in this section, let us analyze and enumerate the axioms of political freedom as contained in the Declaration of Independence, that we may see how utterly they are all disregarded in war and in coercing allegiance by the sword. Notice, then, carefully:

1. All men are created equal, in the sense that any large multitude of people may withdraw their allegiance from one government, and institute a new one for themselves.

2. All men are endowed by their Creator with certain inalienable rights: among which are,

3. The inalienable right to life: never justly taken except by command of God.

4. The inalienable right to liberty: only forfeited by personal crime inconsistent with liberty in others.

5. The inalienable right to pursue happiness or to acquire the interests that gratify inalienable wants.

6. The inalienable right to maintain self-government, as the means of pursuing happiness.

7. Government derives its just power from the consent of the governed.

8. Whenever the government becomes destructive of its own ends, the governed or any large body of them have the inalienable right to alter or abolish it—the governed having the right to decide when the government has become destructive of its own ends: When,

9. The governed have the inalienable right to institute a new government. And then,

10. The governed have the inalienable right of establishing the new government on such principles as shall seem to them most likely to effect their safety and happiness.

§ 3.—*Reflections on the axioms of Political Liberty.*

We may now pertinently append some reflections on the axioms of political liberty as affected by the coercion of the sword. And let it be carefully noted that the rights just enumerated belong to *all men,* and are *in*alienable. Whence it matters not as to the form of the government or by whom made, *these rights* belong still to the governed. It matters not what agreement the governed may have made about them, *these rights* belong still to the governed. No matter that the governed may have attempted to grant them to the government, they still retain them. No matter that words, attempting to grant them, are written with all possible plainness, in the constitution, *these inalienable rights* remain in the governed. *These rights* remain inalienable in the governed, because their *wants* remain inalienable in them. God has made them a part of the laws of nature, and the correlative of human wants. *He* has placed them beyond all acts of precipitancy or folly in their possessors; related to the inalienable natural wants and interests of men, and indirectly related to the allegiance due to Himself. He has put them beyond all interference by any earthly power, potentate, ruler, king, or government, and beyond the alienable prerogatives of the governed themselves. It is, indeed, a constitution of admirable wisdom, suited to moderate the presumptions and usurpations of rulers and governments.

Life, a singular and unique endowment of the Creator, belongs to all men by a right which is inalienable. It is exempt from all rightful interference, except by *certain* authority from Him who gave it. The right to take it cannot be alienated, because it is a crime for the governed to take it from themselves; and, therefore, they can grant to others no rightful authority to take it. To take it without authority, is to murder.

Like the first truths of all science, the axioms of political liberty are few and simple, though they are further divisible than as stated in the Declaration of Independence. Life, liberty, and the right to pursue happiness, are specified. For the purpose in view, this specification sufficed But, as *abstract* rights, these are valueless. They, therefore, attract to themselves other rights such as are requisite to their enjoyment in practice. One of the rights attracted is that of altering, abolishing, or instituting civil government. The right of *instituting* government alone would be insufficient. There must be the right of *altering* and *abolishing* governments already instituted. But this is not sufficient. The idea of government implies a division of the people into governors and the governed. The former compose a small part of the people ; the latter, a large part. Therefore, lest life, liberty, and the right to pursue happiness, should be imperiled, the axioms of freedom declare that all the *just power* of the government is obtained from the *consent of the governed*. Hence, life, liberty, and the right to pursue happiness, may be regarded as the *primary* inalienable rights of all men. The right to institute, alter, and abolish government, may be regarded as the *auxiliary* inalienable rights of all men.

Although these rights are all bestowed by the Creator, and are inalienable, it does not follow that they are all held by an equally solemn tenure. *Life* clearly stands out from the rest. It is the chief right. All the others are secondary, greatly inferior. Therefore, its termination extinguishes the possibility of enjoying any of the others. And a wrong done to *life*, is irreparable forever. To deprive one's self of it, is a high crime ; for the state or another to take it, can be no less than murder.

In connection with the axioms of political liberty, life possesses another noticeable property. It is declared to be an axiom that governments derive their *just* powers from the *consent of the governed*. And this is the *theory* of our government. But how do governments derive power over the lives of their governed? The governed have no power over their own lives. How, then, can the government derive the just power from *their* consent? Is any axiom plainer than that the governed cannot grant to the government a power which *they* do not possess? And is it not as plain as an axiom that the governed have not the power to take their own lives? Would it not be a crime against God for them to take their own lives? And would it not be equally a crime for the government to take their lives, under a power which had no validity? How, then, we repeat, can government derive just power from the consent of the governed to take life?

In the late war in this country, the government took hundreds of thousands of lives. Where did it derive the *just* power to do it? Did it derive it from the consent of the governed? But the governed had no power to take their own lives; and how could they grant such power to the government? If the governed could not grant the power, the government could not justly possess it. And if the government could not justly possess the power, it could not possess it at all; for unjust power is properly no power. Hence, if it took hundreds of thousands of lives without just power, it murdered hundreds of thousands. It may be said, however, that the late war was carried on by authority of the Constitution of the United States. Then the pertinent question rises, *Whence was the authority of the Constitution derived?* If the self-evident truths of political liberty are not self-evident lies, all the just authority of the Constitution is derived from the *consent* of the governed. And we have just seen that the governed have no such authority to grant to the Constitution. Still, it may be urged that the government derived authority for the war from God. But if this view is correct, the self-evident truth, that government derives its just authority from the *consent of the governed*, is a self-evident lie. So, it is a self-evident lie that the late war was carried on by just power in the government, if it derived its power from the consent of the governed. And it is a self-evident lie that government derives its just power from the consent of the governed, if it derives it from God. But the self-evident truth is that the government had no just power to carry on the war. It did not derive the power from God; it could not from the consent of the governed. So, the axioms of political liberty remain true, while the murderous usurpations of the government become plain.

But it may be still further asked, Had the government no *just power* to suppress the revolt by war? We answer frankly, It had not, unless the self-evident truths of political liberty are self-evident lies; and ours is *not* a *free* government founded on the *consent* of the governed. For it is a natural contradiction to say that a free people are coerced by the sword. War and coercion are one thing; and government founded on the consent of the governed, is another thing. And if the axioms of political liberty are right, coercion by the sword is wrong. If coercion by the sword is right, the axioms of political liberty are wrong. For the two things are natural contradictories, and cannot both be true.

Therefore, the clear logical conclusion follows, that the Constitution of the United States could give no authority for the late war. If it contained authority in its letter, the letter violated the axioms on which it professes to be founded, and is in violation of the natural appointments of God. It could therefore give no just authority, for it could itself have no just authority. For if the axioms of political liberty are true, it could have no just authority; and if those axioms are not true, there is no such thing as political liberty, and men have no right to maintain self-government. In that case, the United States Government is a lie and a cheat—founded in wrong and injustice; and the governed ought to return in their allegiance to England,— they ought to return in their allegiance, because its transfer was wrong in the beginning; and a wrong, however long continued, cannot justify the continuance a moment longer.

Another obvious reflection growing out of the axioms of liberty, is that they contain the *first truths* of all free government, and would, in their full practical application, banish from the world both WAR and SLAVERY, the twin relics of barbarism. They agree also, *in theory*, with our government; and based upon our intuitions, because they accord with the natural laws of God, their perfect application would exactly fit government to the expanding wants of men, render it permanent and progressive, with the sword sheathed forever; while slavery, personal and political, would be driven from the earth.

But, founded on a true theory, the United States Government is far from having a true practice. The practice repudiates and violates every principle of its theory. And the history of mankind records no more flagrant inconsistency than the conduct of the government, when a part of the States lately attempted to change their allegiance. Ignoring all its former history and professions, it scouted and trampled in the dust the axioms of liberty from which it derived its own existence. Professing to believe that *all* men have the inalienable right to maintain self-government, it called to arms millions of men that the right might be smitten into the dust. All slavery is odious, political no less than personal; and the government set free four and a half millions of personal and made twice the number of political slaves. It did a great right, and perpetrated a great wrong: it gave freedom to a few millions of slaves; but in doing it, it slew more than half a million of its own citizens, and in slaying them it procured the death of nearly as many more, and put a mortgage on the nerves and sinews of the whole nation for generations to come. Professing to slay men for the preservation of the constitution, it violated every principle and axiom out of which the constitution was formed. Smiting with the sword an odious personal slavery, it inflicted an odious political slavery. Snapping the manacles of the one, it forged the chains of the other.

Now, the whole gross inconsistency grew out of the fact that the government usurped power—the power to make war. There being no such just power, its employment must produce slavery; and if it destroys one kind of slavery, it *must* create another. As water, emptying one place, must fill another; so unjust power, breaking the chains of slavery in one place, must forge them in another. So our government did in the late war, and so, in the nature of things, *all* war must do.

§ 4.—*National wants and self-government inseparable—American Colonies.*

Many of the governments of Europe and of the Old World, originated in a period where we have little reliable history. When the hordes of Northern barbarians overran and destroyed the Roman Empire, they introduced a night of darkness and ignorance such as precludes the eye of history from penetrating it; and the events of the period are lost in myths and romances. As the night of myths and romances covers a period of some centuries, the history of those centuries is lost in legends and superstitions.

It was during these dark ages, that many of the European governments had, in a sense, their origin. We have therefore little history or knowledge of the facts in which they began their career. By the time they emerge into the light of reliable history, they come environed with those idolatrous conceptions which still attend them, and which have so often deluged the world in blood and the horrors of war. England stands amongst the government idolators; and from her the people of the United States principally derived their civilization and conceptions of government. And while those people have rejected the *theory* of the English government, they have retained much of its *practice*. For it is certain that they have not followed the beneficent theory of their own government to its logical and practical results. In *theory*, the government of the United States is free, and conforms to the requirements of reason and the laws of nature. In *practice*, it is not free, but is despotic—abjuring its theory. And our national inconsistencies lie in the fact, that we have adopted the *theory* of a *free* government, and the *practices* of despotic governments. The truth of the statement may be shown in various ways. A careful inspection of the axioms of political liberty proves that the practices of our government are those of despotisms. Despotism claims that nothing need stand between the government and the governed but the power of the sword. Our *theory* is, that the *consent* of the governed, based on the pursuit of happiness, is the bond between the subject and the government. But, in practice, there is no difference in our government and the rankest despotism. Each, with equal facility, appeals to the sword, and each maintains a coerced allegiance. A coerced allegiance is consistent with the assumptions of despotism, but most inconsistent with the axioms of political liberty.

We will reach the same conclusion in relation to the despotic practices of the government, if we study the facts and principles connected with the early history of our national existence. And the general argument which we seek to develope, finds an apt and forcible illustration in that early history; so that we may properly consider the subject, for a time, in that connection. We may begin in the history at the time when the several Colonies had gained some strength and were meditating the propriety of renouncing their allegiance to the British Crown.

Now, it is evident that the Colonies would incline to adhere to, or repudiate their allegiance, as they would be prompted by *interest*. And it is just as evident that they were *bound* in their allegiauce by no considerations apart from *interest*. Government is necessarily a worldly institution. It stands on a foundation wholly distinct from that of the church. The church stand on a moral and spiritual foundation. Government stands on worldly interests, regulated by moral law. Government is established in the pursuit of happiness, or in pursuit of the *interests* which supply our wants, as beings of this world; but in the pursuit, our actions must be regulated by moral law.

This principle is true in respect to those who *instituted* our government. The colonization of this country by English people, formed no reason for the people's paying allegiance to the British Crown. This country was made by God, and did not belong to an English king. Nor were the people, because they were born on English soil, obliged to stay on that soil a moment beyond their pleasure. By all the laws of reason and right, they had the privilege of leaving their native land, and of migrating hither. God, natural right, and reason, all permitted it. And bringing to this country their natural wants, they brought also the natural right to use all the means that God allows to relieve those wants. Amongst the means thus allowed, was the right to institute and maintain self-government. The assumption of power by the government of Great Britain, placed the people under no obligation to the British Throne; because they had the inalienable right to seek their own interests by forming their own government. Nor did the fact that they chose, during a century or two, to pay allegiance to that Throne, place them under obligation to continue it a moment beyond their pleasure. Subject alone to the law of God, they had as all people have at all times, the right to institute such government as *they* thought best fitted to attain the interest which co-related to their wants. Allegiance to the British crown did not alienate their natural wants, nor could it alienate the natural right to institute government as a means of supplying them. Wants and the just means of relieving them are forever inseparable. And as *God* nowhere forbids people to maintain self-government, it was a just means for our ancestors to relieve their wants, by repudiating the British crown, and establishing self-government. In doing so, they violated no principle of moral obligation. The *means* they employed we are not considering. We speak of the moral principles involved in changing allegiance from one government to another. *And people are bound in their allegiance simply by what they conceive to be their inter-*

ests. This is both the law of reason and the law of nature. And since the ruler is the minister of *God* to the subject *for good*, his rule over the subject can justly continue so long only as he ministers *for that good*. If the *subject* may not decide *when* the rule ceases to be for his good, the rule is of no force ; since a tyrant would never agree that he ruled contrary to the interests of the subject.

It is difficult to see how men can dissent from these doctrines, and yet profess to believe that the people have the right to govern themselves. The masses of men would not dissent, if their minds were not perverted by false education or undue self-love. In this country the people heartily agree to them as between themselves and England, because, in that case, their interests are promoted. But as among themselves, they scorn them and smite them with the sword. Yet, if the principles are *right* in the one case why are they not in all cases ? If the principles are axiomatic in one case, they must be in all cases. Correct, axiomatic principles must always lead to correct practice. If the *principles* of self-government are good, the *practice* must be good. If the principles are axioms in the laws of nature, they have universal application, and would be beneficent if universally adopted. This proposition is self-evident, if the laws of God are wise and suited to men's wants. That this nation recently prevented the application of these axiomatic principles, by the terrors of the sword, no more affects their force in reason, nor proves that their application would be unbeneficial, than the persecutions of other days prove that the principles of toleration are not right and beneficial in their application.

Our opposition to the general application of them grows out of the following considerations : 1st. National ambition. 2nd. The fact that the national mind is imbued with the usages and customs of despotic governments. But 3d. and mainly, Because, through perverted education and a want of clear apprehension of the principles of government, men cannot see how it can be supported without the power of the sword. There are thousands of honest men all over the country, who believe all government would be destroyed and society resolved into anarchy, without the conservative influence of the sword. Such persons are simply ignorant of the whole nature of civil government, and of the ligaments by which it is properly kept together. They need education and to be toned up to a higher civilization, when they will be led to see that *force* is not the bond of law and order.

The late war in this country was conducted on a misconception of the whole nature of government, and in violation of the axioms of political liberty. The mass of the people were honest,—so far as people can be honest when borne away by a whirlwind of passion—but wholly mistaken. Upon the theory and axiomatic principles of our government, several millions of the people would have the inalienable right to renounce allegiance to the government and *quietly* to institute another. And no reason can be alleged against those axiomatic truths on which the principles of universal self-government repose. Men do not reason against the *principles*. They reason against their *application*. They have in their minds certain traditional prejudices, notions of ambition, and usages of despotic governments, against which they think the application of the axioms of political liberty would militate. And it is with reference to these that they fight. They also have in their minds indefinite feelings of idolatry for government, by which they are deceived and misled.

It was through the influence of such principles as these, that the government conducted the late war. The South had never, upon the whole, been of pecuniary benefit to the North; and for years the two sections had been violently quarreling. The South had bought and paid for their lands. The South, in those material improvements so highly prized by the nations, was half a eentury behind the North. It was suffering under the blight and curse of negro slavery, in every department. It had, by slave-tillage, impoverished the soil—had retarded invention, had degraded the lower classes of white people—had built up an insolent, offensive aristocracy—had fostered some of the odious customs of the middle ages. The civilizations of the two sections were nearly antipodal, and wholly conflicting. Why, then, did the North call from their homes more than three million men to subjugate the South and prevent the reduction of the axioms of political liberty to practice? The answer is, the North was actuated by a motive compounded of ambition and ignorance. It wanted the flag to wave over large territory. Here was ambition. It misconceived the true bond of allegiance and the nature of the axioms of political liberty. Here was ignorance. Hence, it totally disregarded the central axiom of our national existence, and forgot that our constitution and government are founded in the exact conception in which the South repudiated its allegiance, and for which the North flew to arms. It also forgot that the axiom which it smote is the hope of political liberty for the world—the axiom that *all* people have the inalienable right in " the pursuit of happiness," to " abolish" an existing government, and to institute another founded on such principles as *they* deem suited to promote their safety and happiness. In this our government acted the part of a despotism, repudiating totally its own theory and axioms. There is a show of reason in despotism's drawing the sword. It eschews and ignores rights in the people. Hence, it may, consistently with its theory and principles, appeal to the sword—may smite the axioms of liberty, and by force prevent the people from maintaining self-government. The self-evident truths of a free government are the assumed lies of a despotic government. The " cement " of free government is the right to pursue happiness. The " cement " of despotic government is force—the argument of powder and lead The theory of free government is, that the *governed* may alter or abolish the old and institute for themselves a new government. The theory of despotism is that the governed may be *forced* and *held* to allegiance by the coercion of the sword. It is evident therefore, that the government prosecuted the late war on the theory of despotism, and employed its usages and customs.

But let us return to the Colonies of this country. They are about to form a confederate government. What is the inducement to form it? Is there any *moral* obligation to do it? Do the laws of nature oblige them? Does religion oblige them? Nothing of the kind affects them. Nothing but simple worldly interest affects them. They may confederate or let it alone as they think their interests demand. Thirteen colonies did finally unite. In a moral point of view, they might have remained thirteen colonies to this day; or they might have united two and two, three and three, or in any other combination. There is simply no *moral* question in the case. The whole business was purely a transaction of *interest.* God ordained the *power, exousia*—and the colonies had the right to employ it in the form *they* thought best suited to secure their interests, restrained only by the *moral* laws of God.

The limits of their ingenuity would fix the limits of the forms after which our ancestors had the *right* to construct their government, with the approval of moral law. Suppose the majority of the colonies had united in a confederation, and the others had refused to come into it. What means might the majority use to bring the minority into it? It is evident that the majority would have been actuated by considerations of *interest.* How might they then deal with the minority? Might they use other means than arguments drawn from considerations of interest? Might they menace—coerce with the sword? Might they lay waste the territory of the minority, burn their houses, slaughter the people? Could Goths, vandals, or bandits, do worse? The RIGHTS of the majority would extend simply to *arguments* drawn from motives of *interest.* And the minority would be obliged by no other considerations. If they deemed it their *interest* not to come into the confederation, their right was perfect to stay out. Force employed would be tyranny and oppression. To make war upon them, would be barbarity. To kill them, would be cold-blooded murder.

As *interest* would be the cause for repudiating allegiance to the British crown, so it would be the only cause for uniting in the confederation. No element but interest would enter into the question. By the rules of morality no other element needs enter into it. *But the foundation might be laid for compromises.* The interests of the colonies to enter it might be unequal; the interests of some might be great, and those of others small. Hence, those having the great interests might offer to divide their interests with the less interested ones, as an inducement to the latter, to enter into the project. This act would constitute a *compromise;* and the colonies would have the right to do it to any extent, not forbidden by moral law. Still, in all this, interest would be the only proper inducement. If the colonies should think it to their interest to enter a combination on equal terms, their right to do it would be perfect. But such an argument as the last would bring into action an element not controlled by mere interested considerations. A *moral* principle would arise. Concessions by compromise would oblige the parties making them, though they should be detrimental to interest. If the parties making the compromise should be mistaken as to its effect upon their interests, moral law would still bind them to faithfulness, so long as the government to which the compromise attached, should continue. And the refusal to observe the terms of the compromise, would release the other parties from their agreement to enter the government. For the consideration inducing the formation of the government being violated, the ground for forming it would be taken away. To hold the injured parties afterwards, would be tyrannical and oppressive. And we must bear in mind that there is a line of broad distinction between the *compromises* of government and government itself. The *principles of government* lie in the nature and constitution of things. They may forever be used by men in reference to mere interests. They are made by God, are alike for the use of all, and are inalienable. Properly, they are detached from moral qualities. But a compromise is an agreement personal in character, and attracts the sanction of moral obligation. Therefore, compromises oblige by moral considerations; while government influences only by interested ones. Yet compromises, as we are considering them, are but the *incidents* of government. Governments themselves are always *formed* in view of the axiom that those who form them, or any that may come under them, have the inalienable right of altering or abolishing them. As compromises are the incidents, they cannot affect the inalienable right of altering or abolishing that to which they attach. All parties are *morally* obliged by compromises so long as the government to which they attach, continues. But compromises cannot continue the government, when the interests which bind to the government cease to be secured. That would make the incidental control the principal thing, and defeat, in many instances, the right of self-government.

Government being a mere business transaction, the interested parties may make among themselves all such compromises as do not violate moral law. The interested may therefore continue to buy the governed to allegiance, so long as they may offer inducements regarded as an equivalent for the allegiance given. And so long as the allegiance shall be paid, the compromises bind by moral obligation. And all experience teaches that no government can extend over considerable territory without oppression or the free use, in some form, of the principle of compromises. Whatever theories men may espouse, they will abide by a government only so long as it abides by them by securing their interests. Beyond this their allegiance is coerced and tyrannical. Beyond their *interests* they ought not to abide by it. And, in the nature of things, conflicts of interest must arise to a people who are spread over territory of different soils and climates. In these cases, coerce the people from pursuing their interests, and they cease to be freemen: coerce them by the sword under the government, and they become political slaves, when the government does not secure their interests. Where conflicting interests thus arise, one of three results must follow: 1. The injured interests must be secured by compromise. 2. The people must be coerced in defiance of their interests. Or, 3. The people must withdraw from their government and form another suited to secure their interests. The first method of securing interests may justly and properly be employed, so long as the government is worth more than the compromise. But the second remedy must always be illegitimate, because violative of natural right and justice, and productive of tyranny. The third remedy may justly be employed when the interests lost are worth more than the government, of which the governed shall be the judge.

We have spoken several times of the *moral* obligation of compromises. The question may rise in the mind whether *moral* obligation does not attach to obedience under government. The question is quite free from doubt. Moral obligation has little to do directly with government. Government deals legitimately with interests only; and moral obligation simply restrains from seeking interests improperly. The principle runs through the details of every-day life. Every man may seek his own interests, only he may not do it in violation of moral law. He may innocently quit one employment and begin another—may quit one country and go to another. But he may never violate moral law in pursuing his interests. It is the same in reference to government. There is no wrong in renouncing allegiance to one government and adopting or instituting another, if done without violating moral law. And all just government is adopted with the axiom before the mind and understood, that the governed agree to abide by the government only so long as it secures and promotes their interests. This right is inalienably in the governed. God placed it there, and man cannot remove it. Government itself must ever be formed with the axiom before it, that the governed are to pay allegiance only so long as their interests are secured. Interests subsisting are the price of allegiance; and the interests ceasing, the allegiance may cease. And withdrawing allegiance without war, strife, or bitterness, can involve no wrong to other parties, because the axiom of liberty always stands to notify them that interests secured are the condition of continued allegiance.

§ 5.—*State Rights, Secession, Slavery, and their Incidents.*

Having considered, to some extent, the general nature of free government, it seems fitting to look a little at an established government, as related to the axioms of political liberty. And this seems to lay on us the task of considering the relation of our government *to these axioms, to coercion and war,*—a task we would fain avoid as one is likely to be misunderstood and to array against himself men's unreasoning passions. Nevertheless, it is the desire to probe the question, to see if there is not a better way than war; and if the consequence is, that one arrays against himself the passions of men, though not pleasant, he must bear in mind that novel things, though true, have generally had this result in all the years of the past. It is our deep conviction, that the *axioms of political liberty* can in no way be reconciled with *allegiance coerced by the sword;* and to make that idea appear, is a part of our task.

In developing this part of the subject, it becomes pertinent to confine the mind to a brief consideration of some questions local to our country. We shall therefore have occasion to look at the questions of STATE RIGHTS, SECESSION, and SLAVERY, as connected with our late war.

In the minds of those who precipitated the late war, State-Rights and secession seem closely blended. In their minds the right of secession depended on State-Rights. They regarded secession as the means of securing State-Rights.

From the origin of our government, different opinions have obtained touching the nature of the Federal Constitution. It was not enthusiastically adopted by all the States which finally came under it. Some men, esteemed able, regarded it with suspicion. The history of the times shows it, and especially the papers of the Federalist. By some of the States the constitution was accepted with watchful reluctance. And the perusal of *The Federalist* will show that a conflict between the States and the Federal Government was always regarded as amongst the contingencies. In relation to the subject, ours is a bitter experience. Blood has freely flowed.

State-Rights men argue that the Federal Government was created by the States of the Union, and not by the people of the whole country; and hence they urge that the Federal is subsidiary to the State Governments; and that the latter may throw off the former at pleasure. Whence arises the right of secession, as the means of securing State-Rights. The opponents of this view regard State-Rights as political heresy, and secession as treason justly demanding fire and sword. Even some divinity-doctors have regarded the whole thing as arrant heresy as tested by the *teachings of the gospel!*

The opponents of State-Rights regard the Federal Government, not as made by the States as such, but as made by the people, acting through the States as their agents for the purpose. This view regards the Federal Constitution as acting on the people directly, and not on the States as organized political bodies. It regards our system of government as complex—as two governments operating at once on the people.

As nearly as we can understand the matter, it was to settle this difference in political opinion, that the parties appealed to the argument of the sword. The *interests of personal slavery* were the occasion of the South's attempt to assert secession. *Interest* induced its conduct—interest of a singular kind. It asserted an axiom of political liberty, that it might perpetually destroy an axiom of personal liberty. It asserted the inalienability of political liberty, that it might destroy the inalienability of personal liberty. It had the right to be actuated by interest; and interest was the bond and measure of its allegiance: but not immoral interest. The South had the right to be free from the control of the North, by virtue of the axioms of political liberty; but it would be grossly illegitimate and immoral to employ political liberty for the purpose of destroying personal liberty. Personal liberty is more valuable than political liberty, and the latter is founded on the former, and both on human wants. All men's rights to personal liberty are, justly, as inseparable from them as their wants; and the color of their skin can no more affect their rights than it can their wants. Whence it follows, by the axioms of liberty, first, That the Southern whites had the right to be free from the control of the North, by virtue of the self-evident rights of political liberty; and secondly, That the Southern blacks had the right to be free from the control of the Southern whites, by virtue of the self-evident rights of personal liberty. Now, employ the principles herein advocated and note the result: 1. There will be no quarreling nor fighting about liberties. 2. All personal slaves will be set free. 3. All people will be allowed to employ their political liberty in securing their worldly interests. These results would be infinitely better than the horrors of war and the butcheries of the battle-field.

It was to save the institution of slavery, founded on the continued violation of the axioms of personal freedom, that the South sought the ends of State-Rights through secession. Imperiousness is the natural result to those who take from others the rights of liberty, whether political or personal. A continued course of injustice destroys both the sense and the feeling of right and wrong. And this course had been so long pursued by the South, in depriving the slave of personal liberty, that the master had become blind to the feelings of wrong which he was fostering and developing. Chivalry and daring had been united to imperiousness, giving the Southern people the style and feelings of feudal aristocracy. They, therefore, precipitated the war in the interests of slavery, with a fiery zeal which made the world stand aghast in amazement. Reason was blinded by the terrific onset, so that even the rational precautions of war were not observed. The result was, that they lost in the conflict their cherished all—State-rights, secession, and slavery.

A careful examination of the questions of State Rights and Secession, as questions growing out of the construction of the Federal Constitution, shows that they have only a plausible foundation. There is nothing solid in the argument. The history of the Constitution as well as the Constitution itself, can leave little doubt in the premises. It was the purpose of those who framed the Constitution, to obviate the very defect implied in the teaching of State Rights and Secession. The Articles of Confederation possessed the exact qualities which State Rights impute to the Federal Constitution. Many of the arguments in the *Federalist*, employed to persuade the people to adopt the Federal Constitution, are able arguments in refutation of State Rights and Secession. As questions of war, there is little argument in favor of State Rights and Secession; and *they* have a place in our general argument, only incidentally and very lightly. It is our business less to consider what human law is, than what it ought to be. Secession is doubtless a grave political heresy, tried by the standards and maxims of men; and when attempted to be carried into practice by force and war, it becomes a grave moral crime. Our argument takes sides with neither of the belligerents in the late war. Tried by it, they were alike criminals; and tried by their own axioms, they were both grossly inconsistent. We deal with both belligerents in their criminality and inconsistency. Both violated the axioms of liberty and the natural rights of men. Both committed cruel acts against moral law and natural justice. Their conduct is historical, and we shall freely deal with it. They both violated, too, the Federal Constitution, in plunging into the war, as we shall clearly see hereafter. Neither one, therefore, deserves either the admiration of the head or the sympathies of the heart.

True peace-doctrines have no accord with the South in the late conflict. But had the South dealt fairly by its own people—had it given them a just expression of opinion as to whether they would or would not continue under the Federal Government; and then had the people—not the leaders—pursued their own choice, calmly, firmly, without the use of fiery zeal and the bloody sword, their conduct must have challenged the respect and admiration of all true lovers of political liberty. However, it acted no fair part in any respect. Claiming the right to withdraw from the Federal Government and denying the right of coercion to the Federal Government, it scorned the voice of the people, jeered its own principle as amongst the Southern States, and had no hesitancy to enforce, with the iron hand of a relentless despotism, the odious doctrine of coercion. If, in the career of self-government, it set out with fixed principles of action, it did not advance far till it scorned and spit on them, being as remorseless to its own principles and people as the North was remorseless in spurning all the axioms of political liberty, and in cruelly coercing the South into obedience to a government which it professed to despise. Here was a three-fold violation of the axioms of liberty: 1. The South violated personal liberty, renouncing its allegiance that it might render it more complete and enduring. 2. The North violated political liberty in attempting to coerce the South to a continued allegiance to a government which it hated. 3. The South violated political liberty in attempting to coerce a part of itself to a continued allegiance to a provisional government which the part hated.

Had the Southern people held primary elections over the country, giving all the opportunity to hear the questions involved discussed, with no terrors from the slave oligarchy which came into existence; and then had the South, with persistency and with elevation of purpose, rejecting studiously all appeals to the sword and force, insisted upon the RIGHT of separating from the North and instituting such a government as it deemed better suited to secure and promote the interests of its people, nothing could have withstood the appeal. Had such magnanimity characterized the Southern conduct, the people of the North, out of constraint and love for political liberty, would have voluntarily consented to a final separation. But its bantering braggadocio, its unjustifiable invective and violence, its avaricious adherence to the institution of personal slavery, and the positive dishonesty of the disposition it made of the armory of the General Government, so aroused the belligerent passions of the North, that it too became blind to a sense of justice and decency; and spurning all claims of the South, even those rights heretofore regarded as axiomatic, it would be content with nothing but subjugation. It was indeed a conflict of passion against passion, cruelty against cruelty, murderous war against murderous war. Lost to reason, justice, and Christian morality, both parties were fiercely whirled about by the tornado of wild passion.

But aside from the violent means employed and from the motives of perpetuating personal slavery, and on principles more fundamental than the sophisms of State-Rights and Secession, the axiomatic right lay with the South — the inalienable prerogative of maintaining free government. Had it, by a sublime magnanimity, risen above the mists and lowering storms of blind passion, to assert that inalienable prerogative by fairness and the force of reason, the flow of time is no more certain than that it would have secured its national independence. It may be said, however, that *such* magnanimity would have broken the shackles of personal slavery, and so have removed both the necessity and desire for a separate government.

That may be true, and it is the very end for which we are arguing. The peace-doctrines require exemption from all forms of slavery; and seek to develope the way and means of securing that end. The writer sees the end through the axioms of liberty, made universal and practical, respecting both individuals, nations, and parts of nations. Peace-doctrines have no sympathy with the negro-slavery of the South, with personal slavery of any kind; and they have as little sympathy with the political slavery the North inflicted on the South, in destroying the South's personal slavery. Rejecting all deadly force, appealing to man's best reason, they perceive no consistency in exchanging one form of slavery for another. And the peace-man clearly perceives that the doctrines of war and the policy of the North did that. So far as the degradation of generations of slavery would allow, the black race are free from personal slavery; but for years, already, the former master of the personal slave has been a political slave, coerced by the sword to yield obedience to belligerent masters, and he may thus remain for long years to come. The peace-man perceives the two kinds of slavery and rejects both. Because personal slavery is the more odious of the two,—apart from the direct horrors of the sword—he cannot choose for a time the political, because it may destroy the personal, slavery. He sees no need of either, and rejects both. He perceives that the axioms of personal liberty will destroy personal slavery; and those of political liberty will destroy political slavery. Therefore, the consistent peace-man is in harmony with the North in wishing the personal slavery of the South removed, but he can have no sympathy with the means it employed to secure the desired result. So he is in harmony with the South in its desire to employ the axioms of political liberty in establishing for its people *such* a government as *suits* them; but he can have no sympathy with the means it employed, nor with the purpose of rendering perpetual the bonds of personal slavery. Therefore, during the four years of mortal combat, *he* could have little sympathy with either belligerent as such. He could see cruelty, injustice, and outrage on both sides, with probable results of perpetual slavery, political or personal, as the one or the other belligerent should conquer. For should the South conquer in the axioms of political liberty, he perceived its great inconsistency in rendering permanent personal slavery. And should the North conquer in the axioms of personal liberty, he perceived its great inconsistency in rendering permanent political slavery. He now sees the result, and is not surprised. War cannot exist without slavery; for war means slavery. It is brute-force prevailing instead of reason, and the consequence must be some kind of slavery.

A candid man will not deny that the Southern whites have been ruled, since the close of the war, by military power; nor will an intelligent man deny that such rule implies political slavery. And so long as the South or any people remain under an allegiance coerced by the sword, they remain political slaves. Therefore, the whole effect of the late war is the exchange of one kind of slavery for another—is the release of four and a half million blacks from personal slavery, and the subjugation of twice the number of whites to political slavery.—But a voice is heard, saying, "It is but just that the master who lorded it so long over the slave, should himself feel the smart of slavery." That may be true. But it is for God to deal in justice. We have no right to deal in kind. God has reserved judgment to Himself. The sentiment involves the principles of war, and the rights of retaliation and counter-crime. It would give the South the right, if it had the power, to conquer the North and reduce it to political slavery. Axiomatic and inalienable rights can only be withheld by means of injustice and wrong; and, *in principle*, it is as unjust and wrong for the North to hold the South in political slavery for five years, as for the South to hold the negro in personal slavery for more than two centuries. A wrong by the South cannot justify a wrong by the North.

§ 6.—*Other Aspects of State-Rights and Secession.*

It is not difficult to dispose of the questions of State-Rights and Secession as legal questions. If we consider the Constitution out of which they grow, and the facts and history in which *it* had its origin, and the end which it proposes to compass, the reason and the argument are with the North and against the South. Were an intelligent peace-man sitting as Judge to decide the questions on judicial principles, he could have no hesitancy in concurring with the North as to the proper construction to be put upon the Federal Constitution. In this aspect of the subject, State-Rights and Secession must be regarded as erroneous. Let the meaning be made plain.

Let us regard the Federal Constitution as a *legal instrument* between two parties, brought before a court for judicial construction. The South is the plantiff, and the North, the defendant; while the question to be decided is, *State-Rights and Secession in the interests of slavery.* The form of the question would be, *By virtue of the provisions of the Federal Constitution, has the South the right to secede from the Union, institute a new government, and render slavery under it perpetual?*

Now, it must be observed that this general question involves three distinct questions: 1. Has the South the right to secede from the Union? 2. Has it the right to institute a new government? 3. Under a new government, has it the right to make slavery perpetual? The simple answer that an intelligent court must give in the premises, would be, That the Federal Constitution says nothing on the subject. It says nothing about Secession, nothing about State-Rights, nothing about instituting a new government, and nothing about perpetual slavery. The court would conclude, therefore, that the question could have no light from the Constitution.

But if the question is presented to the peace-man, not

as a Judge, but as a Philosopher, seeking the solution of political questions on the principles of reason without the desolations of the sword, he will find a solution in the axioms of liberty which lie behind the Constitution and form the ground and reason of it. As the Constitution says nothing about State-Rights and Secession, he readily concludes that they are not derived from it. And so far the Judge and the Philosopher would agree, and the Judge, being bound by the law *as it is*, would find on the whole question, for the defendant. The Philosopher could go beyond the Judge. He, going beyond the law and Constitution, could reason about the laws and axioms of liberty, on which the Constitution itself is founded. And from this stand-point the peace-philosopher must dissent, in part, from the decision of the Judge. He must argue that the axioms of political liberty are superior to the provisions of the Constitution, because the former are made by God, and the latter by man. Therefore, while the Judge would decide the *whole* question for the North, because the instrument out of which it grew is silent on the subject, the philosopher and peace-man would decide two of the foregoing questions for the South and one against it: He would decide that the South has the right by the axioms of liberty, first, to secede or withdraw from the Union in the interests of self-government; and, secondly, by virtue of the same axioms and in the same interests, it has the right to institute a new government. But, thirdly, he would decide that, under the new government, it has no right to make slavery perpetual, because that would be employing the axioms of political liberty to destroy those of personal liberty. He would hold that the third question—the right to make slavery perpetual—has no necessary or logical connection with the right to withdraw from the Union, or the right to institute a new government. On the contrary, he would argue that the act of making slavery perpetual, would be a flagrant violation of the axioms of liberty, by virtue of which the withdrawal and the institution of the new government justly took place.

It is precisely in this manner that we reason on the whole subject. We contend that, by virtue of the axioms of liberty, the South had the right to withdraw from the Union and the right to institute another government; but deny that it had the right to establish or perpetuate slavery under the new government. The right to withdraw is an axiomatic right, by the laws of nature made known to us by the intuitions of reason; and the right is inalienable, because it is the correlative of man's inalienable wants. But the whole force of the argument in favor of the right to withdraw and institute a new government, applies against the right to perpetuate slavery. And it is a remarkable fact that the Federal Constitution contains no provision allowing either secession or coercion; so that the conduct of both the South and the North in the late belligerent conflict, was without authority from that instrument. There is clearly no authority for secession in the Constitution; and, *in terms*, there is none for coercing a State into allegiance to the general government.

In the Federal Constitution, we find but three provisions which could, by rational construction, be regarded as having reference to the right to coerce. They are the following: " To provide for the common defence and general welfare of the United States: To provide for calling forth the militia to execute the laws of the union, suppress insurrections, and repel invasions." These are in section eight of the first article of the Constitution. In section three of the third article we have the following: " Treason against the United States shall consist only in levying war against them, or in adhering to their enemies, giving them aid and comfort." Reading the words, " to provide for the common defence," in the light of history and of the origin of the Federal Constitution, at once settles the question, that " the common defence " meant the defence of the United States against foreign enemies. To construe it to mean the defence of one part of the States against another, is to pervert plain language and not to construe difficult. Nor can the provision " to execute the laws of the Union," give the right to coerce the allegiance of a State. The execution of the laws, by the militia, is a different thing from coercing whole States into subordination to a Constitution which the people profess to despise ; and such a construction is far-fetched and irrational. " To suppress insurrections " is a provision. Was the act of the South an insurrection ? If it was, the *act* of those who gave us the Federal Constitution, was an insurrection. For the principles involved in the two cases are identical, and neither was an insurrection. Both were acts of *throwing off allegiance* to established governments,—acts of abolishing existing governments. And whatever, in a legal point of view, the act of our ancestors was, the act of the South was in its late conduct. The simple question, then, is, whether the framers of the Federal Constitution were defining themselves to be " insurrectionists." For, if the Southern people *were* insurrectionists, those who framed the Constitution were. We deny that either committed insurrection. Both were simply acts repudiating allegiance—acts which the people had the inalienable right to do.

But was the act of the South an act of treason ? If so, the act of our ancestors was, and our constitution is founded in treason ; and then, if treason is a crime, they were all criminals, and living under that constitution, we are all living in the fruits of crime. But it is no easy task, always to say whether a given act is or is not treason : for treason itself is not a very specific and definite thing as defined by law; and it frequently stands upon passion and caprice, more than on well-defined law. It has long been the catch word of tyrants, and has murdered thousands of victims. It is certain, if the act of the South was treasonable and criminal, that the framers of the Constitution defined themselves to be traitors and criminals ; for we repeat, the act of the South was but a repetition of the act of the framers of the Federal Constitution. But the truth is, neither was an act of treason. Each was an attempt to transfer allegiance from one government to another; one having the glory of success, and the other the infamy of defeat. And thus, none of the provisions of the Constitution applying to the acts of the South, the conclusion follows, that the Constitution contains no authority for coercing States to an unwilling allegiance.

The plain fact is, the Constitution, as we have seen, makes no provision for Secession, on the one hand, nor for coercion of States, on the other hand. Had it been the design of the framers of the Constitution to create coercive authority, it would have been specifically provided for. They were familiar with the idea. It may be that the framers thought such a provision would be so flagrant a violation of the political axioms out of which the government was formed, that they designedly *omitted* to make it. Indeed, there are strong reasons for thinking such was the case. Such provision would have been a direct and stupid violation of the principle of self-government, in which the Federal Government was founded; and would have involved the framers of it in a worse than stupid inconsistency. Though this question itself is not discussed in *The Federalist* it contains such discussions as implicitly confirm our view of the subject. It argues that a union such as the PLAN of the constitution contemplates, would " be essential to the security of the people of America against *foreign* danger," and " essential to their security against contentions and wars amongst the different states." *Federalist* No. 45. But we find nothing said about the National Government's coercing, by the sword, a part of the States into an involuntary allegiance to the Federal authority. Indeed the authors of the *Federalist* appear to reject the idea of State-coercion. They use the words *coerce* and *coercion*, but not with reference to *States*. Alluding to the enforcement of legislative enactments upon the States, as organized bodies under the Articles of Confederation, it is said

"This exceptionable principle may, as truly as emphatically be styled the parent of anarchy; it has been seen, that the delinquencies in the members of the union, are its natural and necessary offspring; and that whenever they happen, the only constitutional remedy is force, and the immediate effect of the use of it civil war. It remains to inquire how far so *odious an engine of government, in its application to us, would even be capable of answering the end.*" Fed. 16. If the remedy of " force " could not safely be employed to enforce a legislative enactment upon a state, could " so odious an engine " safely be employed continuously to hold a state to an unwilling allegiance? If Hamilton, Madison, and Jay, thought it dangerous to enforce a law upon a state, could it be thought proper for the Constitution to provide, that states should be perpetually coerced to allegiance by " civil war."

On the 31st of May, 1787, in the Convention, we hear Madison say, "the use of force against a state would be more like a declaration of war, than the infliction of punishment, and would probably be considered by the party attacked, as a dissolution of all previous compacts; a union of states containing such ingredients seemed to provide for its own destruction." In the New York State Convention, Hamilton said : " To coerce a State would be one of the maddest projects ever devised." Now, add all these things together, and bear in mind that the Constitution itself contains no coercive provision, and the conviction is unavoidably fixed in the mind, that the Constitution never contemplated the coercion of states. Whence, we reach the conclusion, that the South seceded in violation of the Constitution, and that the North coerced the South back, in violation of the constitution. But—

Had the South the right on any principle to separate from the Federal Government? Upon the principles of peace and of liberty, we answer in the affirmative. These two fundamental propositions are true under all circumstances :

1. *Men have no just authority to make or engage in war.*
2. *All people have the right to maintain self-government.*

The grand errors of mankind have consisted in denying these two propositions, and in acting on their contraries. All nations have denied the first, in both theory and practice. But this nation admits the second in theory, but denies it in practice. Admitting the theory of the second proposition, and the truth of the first, the practice of self-government would follow; since it is by the use of the sword that the right of self-government is withheld. The great blunder and fearful sin of the South lay, not in the act of separating, but in the act of making war. Had it asserted the truth of both these propositions, and labored to realize the second in the teaching of the first, during the four years of its bloody war, the result must have been in its favor. Ignoring the shallow sophisms of State Rights and Secession, it should have taken a firm and peaceable stand upon the axioms of political liberty, and the self evident right to maintain self-government.

Distinctly repudiating the right or the intention of appealing to force, and denying and deprecating the right and act of the North's doing so, it should, appealing to the axioms of liberty, have pursued its purpose with a just and temperate magnanimity. The result is not doubtful. The influence of blinding passion aside, it is not extravagant to affirm that our people could not, with their history and axioms of liberty before them, have withstood the appeal. Refusing the appeal to force, would have unarmed the North of force; and the magnanimity would have aroused its complement in the mind of the North, deploring deeply as they might the division of the government, when a result in favor of peace and political liberty must have taken place. Had the South thus acted, how could the North have resisted? It could not. Sheer consistency would have been compulsory. For the nation had, during three-quarters of a century, admitted the right of self-government to be inalienable. And could the whole conduct of the nation from its birth have been ignored and despised? If appealed to, with a sublime magnanimity, could twenty million people have stultified and scorned the facts and pride of all their former history? Would not the Sewards, McCullochs, Raymonds, Henry Ward Beechers, and even Lincolns, have espoused the right of self-government? And what would have been the conduct of the *many* Greeleys? Did not Greeley, during the war, fervently deplore the war as the greatest of calamities, and steadfastly urge the right of self-government? He counseled peace, and urged that the South should be allowed to separate, rather than appeal to the sword. The ages to come will vindicate the wisdom of his advice. After the war, he was of the same opinion. When assailed by Doolittle, for being willing to let the South separate, he frankly admitted the fact, and justified himself by appealing to the authority of such apostles of liberty as John Milton, John Locke, Algernon Sidney, James Otis, Patrick Henry, George Washington, and even Abraham Lincoln. Hence, such names are authority for the peace-view of the subject as we are endeavoring to conduct it. For we are the advocate of neither party to the war.

Instead of acting as the South did, suppose, in good faith and in its convictions of securing its own just interests, it had acted the ingenuous and magnanimious part we have indicated, what course would have been taken by scores of the leading journals in the North? They would surely have advocated peaceable separation. Their doctrine would have been ours—the peaceable adjustment of all such questions, by acknowledging to all people the axioms of political liberty. And such an adjustment would have formed the most remarkable and influential precedent in human history—the most potent for good. Let not the reader imagine that the writer has any sympathy for the division of these States apart from its being the alternative of war. He is not talking about his sympathies, but is seeking upon principles of reason, to show how war may be avoided when the alternative of war or division must come; and to show that the application of the principles exhibited would obviate the necessity for war over the whole world. Believing that the late war in this country could have been avoided, he seeks to exhibit the manner in which it might have been done, and ought to have been done. In exhibiting this, it appears that both the belligerents were partly right and partly wrong *in principle*. It happens that the traditions of the past and the assumptions of the governments, stand against the truth as he conceived it to lie with the South, and the labor necessary to remove these out of the way of the argument, gives him the appearance of advocating the cause of the South. But he abjures the idea, and denies that he is the advocate of either party or its cause. He seeks the sole end of showing that war is wrong; and, as a most important incident thereto, attempts to show that the axioms of political liberty forbid war as a process of compelling allegiance to government. Thence, reason and the exigencies of the argument required him to show how the political difficulties of his own country ought to have been settled. This he attempts to do, discovering, at the same time, that the arguments and reasons apply with all their force to the situations of all nations; and thence become the arguments and reasons of universal principles. Therefore, the parties began the war by assuming the false and deadly proposition, that men may slay each other about their worldly interests. Then both violated the Federal Constitution—one by *fighting* to repudiate allegiance to it; the other by *fighting* to prevent the repudiation. Hence, both were wrong in their motive, wrong in their action, and wrong, from the beginning to the end, in their conduct. Constitutionally, morally, and religiously, both were wrong from the beginning to the end of the conflict.

The writer could never see one cogent or justifiable reason for the conduct of either belligerent. The reasons urged for the war, during its progress, were shallow and sophistical on both sides. They were rather tissues of passion than arguments or reasons. As has been hinted, and will be more fully shown in another place, the reasoning of the North was not against the axioms of liberty, so much as against the supposed consequences of the application of the general right of the States to secede from the general government. Even this reasoning is based upon the false principle, that force may be used to hold a free people to their alegiance. And the latter idea is as absurd as to argue that force may be used to hold a free people to their allegiance. And the latter is as absurd as to argue that force may be used to hold a free-man in slavery. Force and freedom, in this relation, are contradictories. The South forced personal liberty from the negroes and they became slaves; and they could not be free while the force lasted. So, a people whose allegiance is forced, are not a free people, and cannot be free, while the force lasts. Yet, during the war and still, the Northern people did not and do not seem to perceive the shallowness of the arguments for the war. But we shall have occasion to notice this shallow sophism more at length hereafter, and need not dwell longer on it here.

It is a circumstance worthy of notice that many of the wars of mankind have drawn their inspiration, not from the inductions of calm reason, but from senseless shibboleths. The late war in this country was no exception to the rule. Each party had its inspiring shibboleth. If one sent forth the wild scream of "abolition;" the other shrieked in no less piercing tones, "The last man and the last dollar!" And around these catch-words of heated passion, the respective parties gathered as if they were the symbols of ideas, reason, or sense. Now, after the lapse of several years, as one looks back and reflects upon what he witnessed—the wild tossings of passion, the irrational conduct of men, he wonders if the nation was not spell-bound under the influence of some deadly hallucination! He nearly loses confidence in the rationality of human nature. And did he not feel that God reigns, he would be possessed by the feelings of a cold and cheerless despair.

§ 7.—*Coercion conditions right by power. The Church and war.*

The question of the right of self-government is a distinct question from that of State-Rights and Secession. We reject the latter as cut off by the Federal Constitution; but hold to the former as unaffected by it. The latter relates to the construction of the Federal Constitution; but the former is independent of the Constitution itself. The right of self-government is the gift of God, and belongs to all people at all times, regardless of Constitutions or existing governments. This right does not come from any human appointment or government. It is more fundamental than human constitutions, and incapable of being affected by them. It comes from the constitution of God, and subsists in the laws of nature and the relations of things. It is the counterpart of men's wants, and, rightly, as inseparable from them. In all lands and under all forms of government, the right of the people to it is, at the bar of reason, unquestionable and should be unquestioned.

Although we have repeatedly alluded to the North and South in the late conflict in this country, by way of bringing out and illustrating the argument, the substantial logical idea, which we have wished to keep before the mind, is, THAT ALL WARS ARE WRONG AND CRIMINAL; and that, granting to all people the peaceable right of personal and political liberty would be a great step towards doing away with all war. As force, which is but another name for war, is the traditionary means of sustaining government, in opposing it, or all war, we felt that it justly devolved upon us to exhibit some *principle*, on which government could be supported, while war should be totally repudiated. And to us that *principle* seems exceedingly clear: *It consists in granting to all people the right to maintain self-government without coercion from the sword.* For let us dwell a little longer upon this branch of the subject, treating of *principle*, not the usages and customs of the nations, for these usages and customs should be tested by principle. Suppose

it had been understood among the States which formed the
Federal Government, that, upon entering the Federal relations, they should, without regard to change of interest,
remain in those relations forever, can rational men believe
the Federal Government would ever have been formed?
As it was, with the axiom declaring "that whenever the
form of government becomes destructive of" the end of it,
" it is the right of the people to alter or abolish it, and to
institute a new government, laying its foundation on such
principles, and organizing its powers in such form as " to
the governed " shall seem most likely to effect their safety
and happiness," they gave wary and cautious adherence to
the Federal Government. Rhode Island withheld its allegiance for some three years after the other States had
transferred theirs. But suppose it had been announced,
contrary to the axiom of political liberty, that once transferred, without regard to circumstances or changes of
interest, the allegiance remained forever, what would have
become of the "*plan*" of the Federal Constitution? It is
risking nothing to say that not one of the thirteen original
States would have adopted the "plan." Wary as they were,
they would have rejected it without exception. It is true
that no provision was made for changing allegiance. But
why make such provision? It was an axiom that all people
have the reserved right " to alter or abolish " the government, " and to institute a new " one when the existing one
becomes " destructive of the ends " of government. And
the people and the States regard this axiom as more sacred
than any form of government. Our ancestors had had
trying experience with their governments, and it is irrational
to suppose that they would transfer their allegiance without
reserved rights. To suppose that they did, is to regard them
as dotards rather than as tried and wise men—is to regard
them as forging their possible manacles, rather than as
erecting the bulwarks of freedom. If we may believe anything recorded in history, we must believe that the men of
the Revolution believed on the subject of political liberty

as we have argued. Otis, Henry, Jefferson, Washington, Hamilton, Madison, the signers of the Declaration of Independence, the Congress of the United States, and the intelligent men of the age, either believed as we have argued, or there is no such thing as consistency amongst men, and they were all dupes and dotards ; for they asserted an identical belief over and over, and staked upon it their property and lives. *They* did believe it as certainly as *this generation* does not, though it was certainly believed till within a few years. For on the 12th of January, 1848, the late President Lincoln, then a member of Congress, used, on the floor of Congress, these words : " Any people, any where, being inclined and having the power, have the *right* to rise up and shake off the existing government, and form a new one that suits them better. This is a most valuable, a most sacred right—a right which, we hope and believe, is to liberate the world. Nor is this right confined to cases in which the *whole* people of any existing government may choose to exercise it. *Any portion* of such people that *can*, *may* revolutionize, and make their own of so much of the territory as they inhabit." This is the exact *principle* for which we contend in all these pages. The point with the late President was, that he opposed in *practice* the *principle* of his theory. He believed in war ; and thence his mind became confused. He held the right of self-government as a mental conception, but denied the right to reduce it to practice. It is easy to see the confusion of his mind at the time he uttered this language so fitting to our argument. " Any people, being inclined *and having the power*, have the right." Here was his confusion. He made *right* dependent on *power*. According to his reasoning, " the *right* to shake off the existing government" depended on the "*power*" to do it. There was no *right* without the *power* to assert it.

Now, if the *rights* of a people do depend on their *power* to assert them, the whole reasoning of the writer herein is unsound. But if all people have the *rights*, as the late President declares, and those *rights* do *not* depend on *pow-*

er, the reasoning of the writer herein is sound. Take away the President's idea that *right* is conditioned on *power*, and the conceptions of the President are exactly those of the writer. Will the reader please recur to the quotation, and read it, omitting the four words "*and having the power.*" Here is just the doctrine advocated in these pages, leaving out, "and having the power," which words mean war and bloodshed; and this doctrine constitutes the *principle* on which the "world *is* to be liberated." For, truly, the world is now in bondage, and through this "most valuable, most sacred right," not depending on *power*, but on men's "inclinations," founded on their interests, "we hope" to see it "liberated." And all thoughtful men must deplore to the end of time, that President Lincoln, when in the presidential chair, adhered to the idea that *rights* depend on *power*.

Notwithstanding the fearful conflict of the recent war—founded on Mr. Lincoln's idea that *right* depends on *power*—whose funeral notes have not yet died away on the ear, and with hundreds of thousands in bloody graves, we cannot but believe that the calm reflection of the American people, if not in this generation, then in the next, will decide that the world's liberation depends upon the *right* which is *un*conditional by *power*. Perhaps, we are not rationally to expect this generation to decide in favor of rational or even axiomatic principles. The dark insinuations of passion have spread a deep pall over the minds of the men of this generation. But the development of progressive events will dispel the gloom, and prove to the thinking world, that *rights* are not dependent on *power*. Men but need the clue. Time will ultimately, though it may be long, work out the result. The struggle for religious liberty was long deferred, but finally it came. It will be so, with political liberty. Charles V. and Leo X. thought *religious rights* were conditioned by *power;* but *we* have learned better. Other generations will be wiser than our late President was about political *rights*, standing on *power*. For the law which inclines the needle to the pole is not more invariable than the law which attaches men to whatever secures their temporal interests ; and, through these interests, they will finally work out the idea, that they have *rights* which do not stand on the *power* to assert them.

Suppose that the right of self-government be denied to " *any* people, any where," and the denial be sustained by the " power " of the sword. Suppose the South affirms that the general government does not secure and promote its interests. Then several important questions will arise. First, the affirmation may be denied. The South may affirm that its interests are not secured ; and the North may affirm that they are secured. How is this issue of fact to be settled? There is no tribunal to decide it. Shall the affirmation of the South or that of the North be proof in the case ? The question ought to involve no difficulty, on the late President's *principle*. The party alleging the grievance, must decide the question ; otherwise tyranny and oppression may be practised. The governor may never, but the governed must ever, decide it. For the oppressor would never decide in favor of the oppressed. However oppressive the yoke, *he* would decide his rule to be lenient and beneficent. The singularly infatuated House of Stuart ever thought its rule in the interests of the *ungrateful people*. And the British Government contended that it had nourished, with parental tenderness and solicitude, the American colonies, even when its policy was odious and oppressive. And when the wrongs and outrages had driven the people to despair, even to the sword, England had the effrontery to declare before the world, that the colonies had been nurtured into greatness by protection of the crown. It were vain to acknowledge the right of free government, unless the governed have the prerogative of deciding *when* their interests are not promoted. The interests are the interests of the governed, and their decision on the subject is conclusive. We do not hold the decision of the governed conclusive, because they will never err ; but because, in the nature of things, that is the only just mode of decision.

Those whose interests are imperiled must decide for themselves, because there is no just tribunal to decide for them, and tyrants would always decide for themselves. Such is the principle that must obtain in the recent conflict in our country. It needs not be said that the North was oppressive. It was not. Still, principle awards the sole judgment of the occasion and the time when the South would withdraw to itself. Whether the occasion was sufficient or the time opportune, was for the South alone to determine. The North had nothing to do with it. To meddle with it would be against right. It mattered not that Mr. Lincoln had done no act injurious to the South. It mattered not that the South *unjustly* despised the new President, and, saying that he *would be* a tyrant, on that pretext, withdrew from the Federal Government, *before* Mr. Lincoln was inaugurated. The right of self-government being axiomatic and inalienable, the right was perfect at every moment for the South "to rise up and shake off the existing government, and form a new one that suited" the people " better." So the late President said in 1848, and so he ought to have said in 1861. By not saying so, the nation lost more than half a million of its citizens, with the lamented President himself.

But, secondly, suppose the North decides that the existing government secures the interests of the South, and draws the sword and coerces allegiance. In that case, the South will not be the judge of its own interests; but the North will judge of the South's interests. And since, by the supposition, the South is coerced by the sword, and is disallowed to pursue what it conceives to be its own interests, its subjects cease to be free men, and cease to have self-government. And since the South is coerced and disallowed the right to pursue what it conceives to be its own interests, but comes under the coerced control of the North, the condition of the South may assume two forms: The North may govern the South, not in what it conceives to be its own interests, but in what the North conceives to be its interests. Or, 2d, the North may govern the South, without regard to its interests, wholly in the interests of the North. In the first case, since the North governs the South, and not the South itself, the people of the South cease to be free, and cease to have self-government. They are subjects under the North, coerced and conquered by " power." They have not " the right to shake off the existing government," though " inclined," because they have not " the power," and " *the right* " sinks and is lost in the want of " power." They would have " the right," if they only had the *might;* for, by the keen logic of the late President, *the right* is conditioned by *the might.* And, by the necessities of our rational modes, that must be the logic of all coercionists and war-men.

But, in the second case, since the North governs the South, not in its own but in the interests of the North, the South not only cease to be free men and to have self-government, but the people become slaves. For these are the conditions of slavery. Slavery is simply " right" conditioned by " power." The slave is governed, not by what he, but by what the master, conceives to be the slave's interests, or by what the master conceives to be the master's interests. The slave is deprived of the rights of free men, and of the right to pursue his own interests. In principle, his is the second of the foregoing cases, his being personal, and the other political, slavery. For if the South is, by " power," deprived of the right to pursue what it conceives to be its own interests, but is coerced to pursue what the North regards as the North's interests, the South can be nothing but the slave of the North. Deprived of choice, *right* conditioned by *might*, coerced by "power" of the sword, directed in opposition to its own interests, what are, or what can be, the Southern people but vassals and slaves, constrained and manacled ? Yet, our late President tells us that " the right to shake off the existing government" depends on " the power" to do it. By that logic, why has the slave *any* " right" apart from the *might* to assert it ? And if " right" is co-related to and conditioned by *might*, why is it not *right* for the *mighty* to subject the *weak*, and forever to subordinate them in their toil to the gratification of the *powerful*? If the argument of the late President and his practice are correct, that result logically follows. Such confusion of conceptions must lead to deplorable results—to oppression, to slavery, and to conflict of arms.

It seems unjust to impute to President Lincoln what his language fairly signifies. Yet, as President, he acted in accordance with it. The "people" were "inclined," and "rose up" to "shake off the existing government" with the view to "form a new one that should suit them better," but the President denied "the right" till tested by "power." Therefore, in waging the war, the part the President acted was, to test "the right" by the use of "power." If the South had the "power" to *rise up* and *and shake off the government*, it had the *right* to do it; but if it had *not* the *power*, it had *not* the *right*. And it was to test this question by belligerent gladiatorship, that the President called for nearly four million soldiers; and to test it, more than half a million lives were sacrificed.

This is the logical result from the President's reasoning; and is the logical result of the assumption that *power* is the bond of allegiance. It would be vain to dwell on what the President said, if it was not the necessary logic of all coercionists. For all coerced allegiance is simply slavery. The difficulty of the President is the difficulty of all coercionists. It is the confusion of holding at once two conceptions, whose co-existence is an impossibility—the conception of self-government and that of coerced allegiance. The President attempted to hold both conceptions; and hence he conditioned *right* by *power*—tested the *freedom* of a people by their *power* to assert it by the sword. He had accepted the axioms of liberty, the right to have self-government, and, at the same time, the contradictory idea, that men might fight about them. He had assumed the harmony of two propositions, which no genius can reconcile—that men can be free and yet be coerced. He was right in his conception of liberty, but wrong in those which allowed liberty to be conditioned by "power." The conceptions of liberty he had considered; and they found a full theoretical lodgment in his mind. But the right to engage in war he had not considered. He took that for granted. He never laid the axioms of liberty side by side with the idea of war and coercion, to see that the latter necessarily destroys the former. Hence arose his confusion; of conditioning "right" by "power," generally. Warmly embracing the *theory* of *free government*, his confusion led him to embrace also the *practice of a despotic government;* for the ideas of free government and coerced allegiance are logical and natural contradictions. His theory reduced to practice, would have abjured coercion, and rejected the idea that *right* depended on *power.* And here is the fatal rock of war-men.

With the President the masses of the North fatally erred. Thousands, who, for party purposes, opposed his war policy were in favor of a war policy of some kind. This showed that their minds were confused, and that the *people* had no intelligent conceptions on the subject. For intelligent people cannot fight about liberty, personal or political.

In their ecclesiastic relations and actions, the churches were under the same influence. Taking an intelligent survey of the actions and resolutions of the various religious sects, in relation to the war, and that conclusion is unavoidable. For judging from their actions and resolutions, it is impossible to believe that they were based on intelligent conceptions of the subject. They were just as inconsistent as the President, for they stood with him. Therefore, they placed *right* upon *power;* and did it while acting in the name of Christ and professing to act by His authority. In passing resolutions to support war, they declared it as their conviction, that men might justly be killed for asserting a "right" which they could not sustain by "*power.*" For, unless they deny the axioms of liberty, and the right of self-government in allowing the people "to rise up and shake off an existing government," they will not deny that the South had the "right," quietly and without force, to separate from the Union. The *right*, then, being questioned, it was only a question, as the South resorted to force, of *power;* and by their resolutions, they affirmed that "rights" might be tested by "power."

But as, during the war, the churches simply went with the world, their action was simply the action of the world. Therefore, when they resolved in favor of the war, their relation to it was simply that of any worldly body—the same as that of a State or County convention of politicians. Hence the resolutions of the church were as the resolutions of any political body. But, during the war, political bodies stood by the President in declaring that "any people, any where, being inclined and having the power, have the right to raise up and shake off the existing government;" and they and the President went to war to test the question of "power." The "right" was never questioned; it was the "power." The war had relation, not to the "*right*," but to the "*power*." And the churches took sides in the war, and passed resolutions, declaring, in substance, that the war was in accordance with the laws and will of God; and hence that it was in accordance with the laws and will of God, to condition *right* by *power*.

It is conceded that such view of the subject renders the matter absurd and ridiculous. But closely scrutinized, nothing could be more absurd than war and the use of the sword to coerce the allegiance of a people called free. And while we have the right to deal with the reasonings and conduct of Presidents and governments, when absurd and ridiculous, we claim the same right to scrutinize the acts and behavior of the churches, when they willingly transcend the bounds and limits of their just province. That the necessity should occur for scrutinizing and ridiculing the behavior of the church, in regard to the doctrine of war, so fundamentally antagonistic to the teachings of

Christ, is humiliating to our rational nature, but more humiliating to our moral conduct. Still, in the judgment of reason, it ′is better to ridicule its errors than to let them pass unnoticed and be taken for granted as correct.

§ 8.—*Other incidents of Self-Government.*

Upon the *theory* and *supposition* that government is formed by *contract*, men have raised the pretext for war, or the coercive use of the sword. It is argued that *the contract* to form government imparts *moral* obligation, and makes it the perpetual duty of the governed to submit to it; and, upon refusal to submit voluntarily, it is claimed that the sword may justly be employed compulsorily. The question has different aspects, varying with the change of stand-point. When the American Colonies desired to cast off their allegiance to the British crown, the moral obligation of the contract was disregarded, without compunction, and without conceding the right to employ the sword, to bring them back or to hold them. But when a part of our own country, proceeding on the *same principle*, casts off its allegiance to the Federal Government, there is said to supervene the bond of *moral obligation*, imparting authority to employ the sword. The distinction in the two cases is more attenuated than war-men are accustomed to make —is more refined than that between "rights" and "power." How comes the distinction to be so nicely made? Does not *interest* render the vision acute in the one case, and dull in the other? Is not the whole a supple contrivance, fitted to the ends of selfishness? Recently, the act of a part of the people, in asserting the right of self-government, was regarded as a heinous crime. Yet in a short time after they became conquered, the conquerors thought it heroic virtue in Ireland, to act on the same *principle* with the conquered. The cloud•that was a pillar of darkness when turned towards the South, became a pillar of light when turned towards Ireland. And do *right* and *wrong* fluctuate with the varying stand-point of selfishness?

But *does* moral obligation spring from the contract of government? If so, whence does it arise? If the axioms of liberty are true, there is no such obligation; because those axioms declare the right of self-government to be inalienable; and no moral obligation can arise in a contract *conveying inalienable* rights! If one should agree to allow another to take his life, no moral obligation would arise; because the right to life is inalienable. So, if a people should attempt to bind themselves to remain forever under a government, they would not be *morally* obliged a moment beyond their pleasure, because the right attempted to be conveyed, is inalienable, and the act is of no force beyond the *pleasure* of the people. Let the idea be illustrated by reference to our government. The framers made it with the axioms of liberty before them, which must forever leave the right of self-government unimpaired to all parts of the people—leaving the right in " any people, anywhere, to rise up and shake off the existing government, and form a new one that suits them better." And if the contract of government was made with the understanding that the axioms of liberty should remain unimpaired, it could not bind by moral obligation to obedience beyond pleasure. If the North and South made the contract of government with the understanding that neither should be bound, only so long as its interests were secured, where is the moral obligation so binding each as to give the other the moral right of coercion into perpetual observance of it? Indeed, by the terms of such contract, where is the violation of *any* obligation, in withdrawing from the government?

And—apart from the immoral purpose of making slavery perpetual, and from the force employed—such was the case of the South, recently. The simple act of withdrawing allegiance from the Federal Constitution, violated no right of the North. It was not under, moral, legal, or political obligation to remain longer than it conceived it to be to its own interests to remain. For, at the formation of the contract, it was understood and expressed in an axiom, that either party might "shake off the existing government" at any moment, and form a new one. So that the act of withdrawing by either party, could give the other no right to resort to the coercive power of the sword.

Suppose, however, that moral obligation did spring from the contract, whom would it bind? The *present* generation did not make it. Our *ancestors* made it. And can the people of one generation bind those of another, beyond their pleasure? On what principle are *we* obliged by what our *ancestors* did? They had their wants and responsibilities; and we have ours; and we are not bound by what they did before we were born. There is no sort of force in the rigmarole about *our* being obliged by acts of our ancestors. They had their government, and pursued their interests under it. And we may have ours, and pursue our interests under it. It is impossible for them to oblige us. However, if we prefer it, we may take their government, or we may repudiate it, in whole or in part. We may do our pleasure, as they did theirs. Therefore, whatever may be the obligation of government on those who make it, it cannot bind generations unborn.

But admit that the contract of government is covered all over with the most solemn of moral obligations, how is the right to use the sword derived therefrom? How is it that men may be killed for refusing to observe moral obligations? Is the sword the sanction of moral obligation? If it is not, why may it be used to enforce moral, more than any other, obligations? Again there is confusion in the conceptions of war-men. For *why* should *moral* obligations involve the use of the sword? The blunder is similar to that which conditions "rights" by "power."

And if allegiance imposes pure moral obligation, how, therefrom, arises more right to kill than if the obligation was wholly secular and political? What is the privity of relation, or the logical connection, between *moral* obligation and the *edge* of the sword? And why draw the sword and plunge people into war about moral obligations? But how true it is that no solid reason can be given for war! And whether the reasons for it are given by the politician, the statesman, or the theologian, they are wholly wanting in soundness and cogency. Grasp them where you may, and they are based on selfishness, passion, or confusion of mental conception.

During the late war, much was said about the people's fighting for the government, because it had bestowed on them its protection and benefits. And thence it was declared, that a man ought not to be permitted to live under it, unless he would *fight* for it. But that was as bad reasoning as it was odious tyranny. It assumed that fighting is the best mode of saving government, whereas it is the worst mode of destroying it. The tyranny, the anarchy, the persecution, and a large part of the ills, which have afflicted mankind, have been produced by the sword. And, perhaps, the happy days of our country are in the past. Oppressed by taxation, the public mind corrupted, the peace of society disturbed, passion let loose, our future is not brilliant in hope. And if the sword destroys the interests of men and violates the laws of God, it is an act scarcely less odious than persecution, to urge that those who live under government should be compelled to fight for it or be banished. The reasoning is pernicious, the act would be tyrannical. And at best, war is based on the monstrous doctrine that *we may do evil that good may come;* and on that other impious conception, *that men are made for governments and not governments for men.* For thousands of years, these profligate and detestable conceptions have made the world red with blood. They are the favorite notions of tyrants and oppressors, and the argument from them is valued by the heartless and selfish. Yet how the changes were rung on the argument during the recent reign of passion. It was urged that living under the government obliged all to sustain it even at the cost of life. But look at such logic! The place of birth is not subject to choice; and so men are compelled to fight by a circumstance beyond their control. Because they are born under a government, they must fight for it! It is tyranny added to injustice. It is oppression, outrage; and none but tyrants do so argue.

It is a sound principle, that the means which may justly be employed to induce men *to form* government, are the only means which may justly be employed to induce them to continue it. If the sword may be employed justly to induce its formation, it may for its continuation. If the sword might justly have been employed to induce Rhode Island to come under the Federal Constitution, it might be employed to compel it to continue under it. For the same general reason might exist to continue the government under the Federal Constitution, that existed to form it; or, to express it better, the same reason might exist for forming a government, as for continuing it when formed. A strong general inducement existed for forming the Federal government. But that constituted no reason for using the sword to coerce some of the States into it. A part of the States might have remained out, notwithstanding the strong inducement. It was for the States themselves to consider what they would do. And if a part of the States have the right now to hold another part under the Federal government by the sword, why would they not have had the right —the like reason existing—to compel them by the sword, to come under the Federal government at first? In the two cases, what is the difference in principle? *Interest* is the principle in both cases. Without interest there would be no desire to continue the Federal government; and without interest there would have been no desire to form it. Interest, interest is the balancing power in all government. Without it, government will not be formed; and without it it will not be continued. And if the same reason exists for forming it as for continuing it, why may not the sword be as justly employed for forming it as for continuing it? If the North may now justly coerce the South to remain under the government, the South might justly have coerced the North to come under it. If allegiance may be continued by the use of the sword, it may be formed by it. If the belligerent legions of the States which wished to continue under the Federal Constitution, might justly be hurled against South Carolina because she did not desire to receive the interest which the Federal government had to bestow in 1861, why might not the same legions have justly been hurled against Rhode Island because she did not desire to receive the interest which the Federal government had to bestow in 1789? Who can perceive the refinement of causistry, which allows war in the one case and not in the other?

But ignore the idea that the Federal Constitution did *not* affect the axioms of liberty, and admit that it takes from men the right of self-government, and does the right to employ the sword follow? What is the process of logic or casuistry which evinces that conclusion? That simply allows the *contract of government* to be in force. But is the right to use the sword derived from the violation of a contract? The contract of government is inferior to the aggregate of men's ordinary contracts. Government is the general means of securing secular interests, and has or has not value in proportion as it secures particular interests. And the end of a special personal contract is of the same nature as the end of the general governmental contract. Both have the same general nature, and both are made to attain the same general ends. Both look to human wants, and are intended to secure the interests which gratify them. But the ordinary contracts are more interesting to men, because they are the more immediate means of supplying their wants. And disregarding the idea that self-government is an inalienable right, and there is no distinction in the principle of personal and governmental contracts.

If the principles of ordinary and governmental contracts are the same, with the limitation specified, why may not the same means be employed to enforce them? If it is right to slaughter men for refusing to abide by the one kind, why is it not right to slaughter them for refusing to abide by the other kind? Indeed, the right is as good in the one case as in the other; for no man can show a principle in the one case that is not in the other, with the exception specified. But that exception makes the widest difference in the cases, and makes it against the contract of government. For special contracts, as distinguished from the contract of government, are made, as they may justly be, without reference to a law of God making them *conditional;* while the contract of government is always made with reference to the laws of God which render the right of self-government inalienable. Therefore, the personal contract is binding after it ceases to promote the interests of the party obliged by it; but the governmental contract ceases to oblige so soon as it ceases to promote the interests of those who made it. Hence, the right to slay men for refusing to keep the contract of government is less cogent than the right to slay them for refusing to keep their personal contracts. Nay, there is more reason for killing men about the principles of religion than about those of government; and the act of persecuting them and bringing them to the stake for religious heresy, is less irrational than the act of slaying them for political heresy,—for secession, and State-Rights, which are political heresies. The reason is as obvious as demonstration. With those who accept the Bible as the revealed law of God, there is a fixed standard of truth. So that as to the *essential doctrines of religion* there can be no dispute, and as to them there can be no variety of opinion in genuine religion. Hence, we have a fixed standard. But the highest welfare of government is attainable only in compliance with the demands of this fixed standard, because it is only in such compliance that men take just views of the offices of government, and act accordingly. On the other hand, there is no standard of truth in politics, or government. A man *cannot know* that his doctrines, concerning the policy of government, are true. And a despotism, administered on Christian principles, is better than a republic, administered on despotic principles. The government of Nero, administered on the teaching of Paul in the thirteenth of Romans, would be preferable to the government of the United States, administered on the war-policy of the last few years. A heathen government with a Christian practice, would be better than a Christian government with a heathen practice. God has not revealed the standard of political truth; and so, in any mere political contest, no man can *know* who is right and who is wrong; and so, no man can know how God regards what *we* may think *political heresy*.

In matters of religion, we have a *fixed measure* of truth; but not so, in state-policy. But true religion is more necessary to the welfare of the state than true state policy. And since there is no fixed measure of state-policy, but there is of religious truth, it follows *a fortiori*, that it would be more reasonable to kill men for their principles and practices in matters of religion than in those of state-policy. Imbuing the mind with the first principles of religion and the first principles of state-policy, a man cannot reflect logically without perceiving more force in the argument for using the sword in favor of religion than for using it in any assumed line of state-policy. And the reasons urged against the reformation of Luther, were as rational and cogent as those urged against the division of a nation into two nations. Those who opposed Luther reasoned on the same basis with those who lately reasoned against State-Rights and Secession, with *force* and *carnage*. The mode of Luther's asserting his doctrines was correct, as he believed in *secession without violence*. And the same mode of asserting political doctrines is correct. Thus asserted, political secession is the remedy for evils in the state, as it is conceded to be, by protestants, the remedy for evils in the church. And the antagonists of Luther reasoned just as war-men in this country reason. They did not attack his doctrines with either the force of reason or the authority of Scripture; they dwelt on the *practical* results of them if they should be accepted and practised by the people. They said, "What will become of the church, if such things shall be allowed? If Luther and his followers may go off, others may go off, and the whole church will be utterly ruined by indefinite secession." The papists said of Luther: "If Christian peace has vanished from the earth; if the world is full of discord, rebellion, robbery, murder, and conflagration; if the cry of war is heard from east to west; if a universal conflict is at hand: it is thou—thou who art the author of all these things." To justify putting down the Reformation, Jerome Wehe, the able lawyer and chancellor of Baden, said to Luther, "If we did not uphold the decrees of our fathers, there would be nothing but confusion in the church."

How familiar are such modes of reasoning to us of this day! It is exactly analogous to the reasoning against political secession as a manner of asserting self-government. The right of secession, *as a mode of asserting self-government*, is not attacked with either the force of reason or the axioms of liberty; but the results are paraded, if the people should accept and practise it. Wehe said, "There would be nothing but confusion in the church," unless Luther's rebellion was put down. Our political Wehes say, "There would be nothing but confusion in the state," unless all political rebellion is put down. The papists of Luther's time said, "If the world is full of discord, rebellion, robbery, murder, and conflagration," Luther's rebellion caused it. The political papists of our day say, "If the land is full of discord, rebellion, robbery, murder, and conflagration," the South's rebellion caused it. The papists thought *the peace* of society could be preserved, only by "upholding the decrees of the fathers" in relation to the church. Our political papists argue that *the peace* of society can be secured, only by "upholding the decrees of the fathers" in relation to the state. And, thus, the papists of Luther's time, denying the rights of free conscience, fought in the interests of the church, while the political papists of our time, denying the rights of free government, fight in the interests of the state. Were not the religious papists of Luther's time as honest in their convictions as the political papists of our time? And did they not reason as cogently? Nay, did they not reason better? For may not better reasons be given for fighting about the interests of the church, than can be given for fighting about those of the state? It *appears* absurd and cruel that men should be slaughtered because they seek the rights of free conscience; but it surely *is* absurd and cruel that they should be slaughtered because they seek the rights of free government. And as we contemplate with horror the conduct of those who opposed the rights of free conscience; so will future generations contemplate with horror the conduct of those who oppose the rights of free government. For the principle of using the sword in the interests of the church is less absurd than the principle of using it in the interests of the state; and time will as surely relieve the world of the barbarism of the latter, as it has of the former. And the sword is no more necessary to secure the ends of the state than those of the church. It *was* bigotry and intolerance, veiled by principles of false reasoning, which suggested the use of the sword in the interests of the church. It *is* ambition and selfishness, veiled by false reasoning, which suggest and retain the use of the sword in the interests of the state. In both cases, its use is heathenish and barbarous, as needless for the security of the state as for the purity of the church. And, in the true sense of the term, it can no more make a *good subject* than a good Christian. In both cases, it may make compliant hypocrites. But in neither, can it convince the mind nor change the life and inward feelings. In Italy, the one may make outward religious hypocrites, by breaking the spirit of religious freedom. In this country, the other may make outward political hypocrites, by breaking the spirit of political freedom. But the Catholic in Italy will, by no means, be a good Christian; and the subject in this country will, by no means be a good patriot. Genuine obedience, in both church and state, is a voluntary offering, and not an outward compliance secured at the point of the bayonet: it is the obedience of conviction, the generous offerings of the heart, and not the coercive constraint of the two-edged sword.

Coercion, therefore, in both politics and religion, must be regarded, at once, as unwise and unnecessary. And the arguments which justify it in the one case are so analogous to those which justify it in the other, that it is amazing that it has not been totally abandoned in both. With hundreds of thousands of our countrymen lately consigned to bloody graves, it is time that we were seriously considering the sophistical and absurd grounds on which men continue the ravages of the sword in the interests of the state, seeing that its use is no less sophistical and absurd in the interests of the state than in those of the church.

CHAPTER III.

§ 1.—*Can government be supported without the use of the Sword?*

HE who assails an existing state of things, generally received by men, is, perhaps, bound by the law of reasoning, to exhibit another state such as may rationally take the place of it. All through this work, we impartially reason upon that conception in relation to war and the means of justly sustaining government. In assailing *war*, as suited to that end, we have substituted *right, interest,* and *reason*. But it seems proper to bestow on this phase of the argument more special attention, and to exhibit a more formal plan for sustaining it, aside from the violence of the sword.

This branch of the argument may be considered under the following interrogatory: *Can government be supported without the use of the sword?* Under this general proposition, several subordinate ones, demanding a passing notice, arise. *The interests which supply men's wants,* frequently alluded to heretofore, form one of these. As these *interests* constitute the only just bond of civil government, the question arises, *Are these interests a bond of sufficient strength to keep together the fabric of civil government?*

In considering this branch of the argument, it is important to remember that civil government, being an institution of God, has an appointed fitness between itself and the minds of men. Hence, men over the whole world are naturally inclined to form and maintain it. So strong is this inclination, that no people, whatever may be their intellectual or moral condition, have been found on the globe, without some kind of civil polity. It is well known that the Indian tribes which inhabited this continent when it was discovered by Europeans, all had their civil polities or tribal governments; while some of them were quite rational and wise in their constitutions. So, of all the inhabitants of oriental and southern countries. However degraded they may be in ignorance, or besotted in idolatry and superstition, they have their governments. Even where humanity wears its lowest aspects, where the people seem hardly distinguishable from the higher orders of the inferior animals, we find the wretched beings possessed of some ideas of government, which they reduce to practice. Hence we infer that the tendency to form government is native to the human mind; and the question is not, whether fire, sword, and devastation, are necessary as a bond of civil government. That is a foregone conclusion. Men of all degrees of civilization as certainly have government as they propagate their species. The true question, therefore, is, *What is the natural and rational bond of it?*

We contend that the natural INTERESTS of men, as depraved beings of this world, constitute the only just ligaments to bind them to government. By the term *interests* we meant to include *every form of worldly good that men may innocently seek, and in the attainment of which government is suited to be an aid;*—including physical, moral, intellectual, and even spiritual good, so far as government may be the means suited to these ends. And are these diversified and complex interests a sufficient bond between men and civil government? Or must the coercive and desolating sword ever be uplifted to smite and destroy men, that they may be induced to pursue one of their strongest inclinations?

Were the sword flung away and left to savages and barbarians where it more justly belongs, the fabric of government would be no more imperiled thereby, than would trade and commerce be imperiled in the heart of England, Germany, or America, because the sword is not used to coerce men to form corporations, partnerships, engage in general commerce, or plant and cultivate their fields. For the same general reason that induces all the latter acts, will induce the formation and support of government. The attainment of worldly interest is the inducement to act in relation to them all. And does not experience, the least fallible method of human instruction, teach us that the attainment of worldly interest is one of the most powerful of the motives that operate on men? What will they not hazard for it? Is it not the general incentive that *moves* the masses? and the most enterprising passion in the human breast? Does not the love of gain underlie the act of engaging in war itself? And does not lucre outweigh, by a hundred-fold, all other motives to engage in it? Perhaps it needs not be said that interest, in the sense of rapine and plunder, is always, though it generally is, the inducement to war ; but in the sense, only less criminal, that, upon the whole, it will enhance the interest of those who wage or engage in it. It is not said that war secures the ends for which it is waged. This it *never* does. It is only affirmed, that to the masses, interest is the master motive ; while a *large* proportion of men are nearly impervious to a higher motive. They are scarcely anxious about the nobler qualities of being. What they desire is interest—that which answers to want. They study about it. They imagine about it. They plan and labor for it. They strive after it. They lie awake late and open their eyes early, that they may mature methods for compassing it. All experience establishes the enterprising character of the passion of gain. Yet, the love of gain is not in itself vicious. The vice lies in its love in excess. Still it is urgent and wakeful in its solicitude. It is sleepless, vigilant—begetting anxiety till it attains. In the multitude, a sense of guilt before God, creates small solicitude, compared with the anxiety about worldly interest. Ever-abiding, all-powerful, it is the spur to activity in the heart of humanity. Attaining or failing to attain, activity is not lost. Against hope, it hopes on; against obstacles, it strives still. Baffled, disappointed, brought to the dust, it rises aloft on buoyant wing, and arming anew from hope revived, more alert and wary, it goes forth to renew the conflict. Higher passions may droop, be drowsy, but this is never dull, never nods. Death, the judgment, eternity, may forsake the thoughts for days or months. But early and late, in pain and in health—possessed of many-told thousands, or the recipients of charity—morality, religion, and the soul, scarcely so engross the minds of men, as the ever-moving, all-potent love of worldly gain.

Here clusters the sum of hope ; here culminates the cynosure of earthly expectations. To compass the desired end, perils are disregarded, and dangers despised ; the ties of affection are forgotten, and the wails of infancy unnoticed ; the swelling hearts and the flowing tears of devoted and loved wives are unheeded ; the shrieking of the elements and the howling of the ocean-waves are unheard ; and the ferocity of wild animals and the terrors of plague and pestilence, are alike impotent to intimidate in the pursuit of earthly interests. And this love of gain is in all realms, in all ages, and in all people. In all relations of life, it sways the sceptre ; it is the earthly king of kings, the earthly lord of lords. Its waving wand charms alike the maid and the matron ; the stripling, fervent in youth, and the sire, trembling in feebleness ; everywhere, the love of gain is the master-spirit, the ruling genius. In the sanctuary, where the finite should commune with the Infinite, its voice is heard, soft and soothing as that of the siren. And, having an earthly ubiquity at least, could we take the wings of the morning and fly to the isles of the sea, there should we still behold its presence. In short, pervasive as is humanity, so are the importuning WANTS of men ; and responsive and re-echoing to them, are the urgency and the craving, the watching and the grasping of men for the INTERESTS corelating thereto.

And it is upon the basis of these *wants* and *interests*, that God intended men to erect the structure of government,—that structure being, in a sense, their inseparable correlative, because the appointed means of their proper gratification. These *wants* and *interests* constitute *its* ligaments, ligaments at once potent as the love of gain, pervasive as humanity, and as touching and tender as the wants are ceaseless and the interests insatiable.

Thus, we have the true foundation of government—a foundation as steadfast as the permanency of men's wants, and the certainty that particular interests secured by government will gratify them. The solicitations of these interests are the all-sufficient inducement to the formation of government, and the only just means that can be urged for its continuance. The attainment of the interests is the sufficient reward for its non-formation or non-continuance. *And just here lies the grand puzzle of humanity:* MEN CANNOT UNDERSTAND THAT GOD HAS APPOINTED INTERESTS UNDER THE GUIDANCE OF REASON, INSTEAD OF THE SWORD UNDER THE GUIDANCE OF BRUTE-FORCE, AS THE BOND OF ALL JUST ALLEGIANCE. And the story of humanity's puzzle is told, by stripping government of the robes of sanctity with which it is invested by superstition and idolatry, by taking from it the awe which ignorance and credility have attached to it, and regarding it as the means of gratifying men's innocent worldly wants; while liberty and self-government consist in the right of the people to seek the gratification of their wants in the attainment of their interests, by that form of government which *they* think best suited to the end. Employing their reason and self-agency, limited by the provisions of moral law and unterrified by the sword, in securing what they esteem their own interests, solves the intricate puzzle. The pomp and pageantry thrown around civil government, are a kind of barbaric idolatry, inherited by us from the traditions of the past, with which are still associated in mind and practice, the hatchet and the club, refined into the sword and the bayonet. Unrobed of the idolatrous trappings, there is no mystery about civil government. As the simple means of securing wo ldly interests, the services of pomp and the sanctions of superstition are unnecessary; there is no need of sacrificing victims before its altars; no need of bowing before some ideal divinity, supposed to preside over it in blood. This bond of government practically acknowledged, there would be no use of the "blood of traitors" to make "cement," as the occasion would not arise for more to become traitors.

With the view of illustrating the subject a little farther, let us suppose the existence of a so-called free government, embracing a variety of soil and climate, and, consequently, a variety of interest to the people. Such a government, if really free, would not be formed for the monarch, nor for the privileged few, but for the people. But the moment the *interests of the people* cease to be protected by the government, they have the right to form another government such as they think will protect their interests, or they cease to be free men. And the proposition is self-evident that the moment the sword leaps from the scabbard and coerces a people, is the moment that marks their subjugation; for force and freedom are logical antagonisms and natural contradictions. It is no more absurd to call slaves freemen than to call a people conquered to allegiance freemen. The whole idea of a conquered allegiance is the idea of despotism. If, during what is called the Revolution, England had conquered the Colonies and subjugated them to the British Crown, would the people still have been a free people? Would the people of these States be now a free people, if they were bound in their allegiance to the English Throne, by the argument of powder and lead? If Canada should declare that the interests of her people were not protected by the government of England, would she not have the right to assert self-government, and would the people be free though conquered and subjugated by standing armies and mounted cannon? And if Canada thinks the interests of her people would be promoted by adopting another form of government, has she not, by the laws of reason and nature, the inalienable right to adopt it? If she has not the right, the people have not the right to be free, but of right they are made slaves. In that case, England is justly the master, and Canada is justly the slave. And if Canada possessed not the right to say *when* she will be free, she must continue a slave *by* right, till England decides that she may be free. In that event, she must remain a slave of right, till her master sees proper to set her free. And if she is bound a moment in the future, because she has been held indefinitely in the past, the fact of slavery becomes the just cause of it; and the longer it has existed, the longer it justly may exist. On that supposition, oppression and wrong become their own justification by the fact of their existence; and by that mode of reasoning, slavery, tyranny, or oppression, need only exist for a moment, to obtain the right to exist forever.

If, in order to hold Canada to her allegiance, England has the right to employ other means than those which show that her interests will be promoted, then England has the right to demand her allegiance in defiance of her interests. But if England has the right to demand it, Canada has not the right to refuse it; for the two rights cannot exist at the same time. If Canada may not dictate her own policy, but if England may dictate it for her, the condition of Canada is the condition of servitude. England, then, has the right to demand that the policy of Canada shall be ordered, not with reference to the interests of Canada, but with reference to those of England. In that case, the condition of Canada is the condition of a slave. If Canada wavers in allegiance, because she thinks her interests are not promoted, England may draw the sword and force her back. But is not the moment that allegiance is forced, the moment that liberty is gone? Allegiance extorted by force, is the allegiance of fear. That is essential slavery. Slavery is right ruled over by might. It is the use of so much liberty as power may choose to bestow. Whether one human being or a hundred millions hold liberty by such tenure, affects not the servitude; and whenever, wherever, or however such a condition may occur, there is essential slavery. The right to pursue interest, without the counter right to deter from it, alone constitutes the condition of freedom.

If, in pursuing what they conceive to be their interests, a people mistake, they must suffer the loss of the mistake, and thus endure the proper punishment. The interests are their own, the fault is their own, and the loss of the mistake is their own. The principle here exhibited applies alike to all nations and parts of nations, over all the earth and in all situations. If part of a nation has not the right to judge of its own interests and pursue them, but another part has the right to dictate its policy; then the one part that is under the dominion of the other, may be required to toil for it; and thus may be created the condition of slavery. Those who have not the right to pursue their interests in their own way, may be required to pursue them in the way dictated by others, when they cease to be freemen; or they may be required to pursue, not their own but the interests of others, when they become slaves. And those who claim that others have not the right to dictate their own policy, deny the right of self-government; and so claim that one part of mankind have the right to determine what are the interests of another part of mankind. And what is that but slavery? Freedom consists alone in freedom of thought, freedom of speech, and freedom of action—each limited by the laws of God. And these belong to all people in virtue of their natural manhood. Reduce these to practice, and they will shatter all the manacles of personal slavery, cast off the galling yoke of political slavery, relieve the nations from the vassalage of the sword, enfranchise the race in the liberties of a rational freedom, put aside the horrors of war, and render government the measure of men's interests just as knowledge and civilization progress.

§ 2.—*Reason unites with interest to form the "cement" of government.*

Another consideration which now demands attention is, that reason, uniting with interests, gives their proper cohesive power in the maintenance of government. And God gave reason to man for the very end of his being won and held to his best interests by appealing to it. If his worldly interests are not to be determined by himself, as a rational being, by the amount not so determined he ceases to be rational. And if God ordains the existence of government intended for man as a rational being, and it cannot be supported by appealing to him as a rational being; then God has been mistaken in supposing that man could be governed as man has ascertained he cannot.

Wild-beasts maintain dominion by their strength, the ferocity of their nature, and their ability to tear and destroy other wild-beasts, daring to contest for dominion. Reason is left out of the question. But where is the difference in gaining and holding dominion by sharp claws and teeth, or by sharp swords and bayonets? The one method is as rational as the other. And can the rational mind believe that God intended that His rational creatures should be governed by brute force—governed as the bear and the tiger are, by the lion? Are the glittering cimetar and the whetted sword, directed by might, the motives proper to offer to thought and reason? If so, as all history shows, men will act the part of wild-beasts. So long as the sword hangs over their heads, fencing them off from their interests, with no hope of success from a rencounter, they will sullenly submit to what they cannot avoid. But remove the quelling fear, so that there may be a gleam of hope, and the oppressed will leap on the oppressor with the ferocity of a wild-beast. War has many times proved that men, reduced to the level of beasts, will act the part of beasts; while experience shows that they will act as becomes reason, if they are treated as reasonable beings. In a struggle of brute force, they must act like brute creatures, when reason can only be employed to give more fatal energy to the brute momentum. Irrational animals cannot invent enginery to give a refined torture and a more deadly fatality to their destructiveness. They use only natural weapons. And if men will ignore reason, and appeal to force, it is matter of regret that they are, in this respect, superior to the irrational animals. If they had been only equal, millions of lives would have been spared the horrors of war, without diminishing the happiness of mankind. For while the essential principles of a belligerent contest amongst men and a contest amongst wild-beasts for mastery, are the same, the inventive genius of man enables him greatly to surpass the wild-beast in the torturing and destructive effects of his contest. Knowledge here is power—power of the nature of animal ferocity, but more torturing and deadly, because it is under the guidance of reason. So if men are to be governed by force instead of reason, it is a pity that, in the way of inventing enginery to kill, they did not stand on the level with wild-beasts. For rational men have destroyed more of their kind than wild beasts have of their kind. Whence in this respect, reason is a curse. Men have converted into a great curse what God intended for a great blessing. And to argue that men cannot be governed by reason, is to argue them on a level with the unreasoning beasts. To urge that government cannot be sustained by considerations of interest addressed to reason, is equivalent to urging that men cannot be influenced by reason ; and what is that but putting them on a level with irrational beasts ? If all history establishes anything, it establishes these facts : First, That the sword has always been used to sustain government. Secondly, That its use has failed to attain the desired end. Thirdly, That up to this time small liberty has existed among men.

In the long and tearful history of the past, the colony of Pennsylvania is the only instance in which rational men were sought to be governed by rational means. And how happy must have been those people! The blessings of peace were disseminated even among the savages. In all other instances reason and interest have been ignored, and the terrors of the sword substituted. The natural consequences have followed: The terrors of the sword, in the form of tax, oppression, or desolation, have been men's portion. Their real interests, their worldly comforts, even their lives, have been made the sport of the proud, the selfish, and the ambitious. That which is good, amiable, and lovely, has been swept away, as by the besom of destruction. And this has all occurred in accordance with the Divine warning—"That they who take the sword shall perish with the sword." Millions of times in the history of both nations and individuals, has the Divine utterance been fulfilled. Men draw the sword from the scabbard, but, in His providence, God points it to their own throats. For centuries, the nations have taken the sword, and for centuries they have perished by it. In the nature of things there is a mystery, by which, up to a given point, wrong as well as right may *seem* to produce the same result; and then the wrong becomes destructive of that which it seemed to preserve. It is so with the sword as the preserver of government. For a while and up to a point, it may hold to allegiance and save government; but destruction well armed lies in ambush, and at the moment when preservation is thought perfect, destruction is imminent. For dreary thousands of years, experience bears a uniform testimony on this subject. And just so long as God continues the moral governor of the world, and through the administration of providence, fulfils His revealed laws, we may expect, "That those who take the sword, shall perish by it." In the Old World, the rulers of the nations are tottering on their thrones. The swords which they have taken gleam in no dubious terms over their own fated heads; while we can find no rational ground of hope for our political institutions but in the utter abandonment of the sword. True, we hear much boasting about them. But it is idle, unless the tyranny of the sword is wholly abandoned. It is only the short-lived growth of self-complacency. Scouting the laws of reason, ignoring those of interest, denying self-government, and relying on the sword, the fate of the nation is sealed—it must perish by the sword. For a while and in blood it may write a history; but at length, with its own blood, will its history be written. The veracity of Deity is pledged to the uniformity of the law, and the testimony of centuries is in invariable conformity with the pledged veracity. And we may confidently announce our own national doom—we must perish. Any hope the nation may indulge that its preservation will be a happy exception to the rule, can be only the hope of delusion. For it requires neither great foresight nor depth of philosophical research, to perceive that we are generating the means of our overthrow. Cause and effect have uniform and fixed relations; and nothing much short of miracle can save this nation from destruction. Men's deadly passions uncaged, the principles of moral integrity deeply shaken, the avarice and ambition which are the inseparable attendants of war, aroused to activity and made honorable by a war-morality, only the progress of time is needed to insure our national ruin. Natural causes fulfil revealed predictions because those predictions have relation to natural laws. Indeed, such predictions intimate what the natural laws are, so as to warn us against their violation. And Jesus only more clearly announced a law of natural providence, when He declared that, "All they that take the sword shall perish by the sword"—announced a law that will be fulfilled till the end of time. All experience shows it to be a law of natural providence, of universal application, though not inclusive of every individual case. But one part of this nation has imposed an arbitrary and irrational limitation upon it, by saying that those who *first* take the sword shall perish by it. But Christ says no such thing. That is the utterance of men. Jesus no more allows *defensive* than offensive wrong—the defensive than the offensive use of the sword. The other is a human gloss.

Jesus simply says, "Put up again thy sword into his place; for all they that take the sword shall perish with the sword." And the text and context clearly reject the limitation to the *offensive* use of it. The sword was drawn to defend the Master from attack by a band of ruffians; and was forbidden for that purpose. It is said that "*all* that take the sword shall perish with it," without a word uttered about "the responsibility's resting on those who begin the fight." If Jesus is to be believed, the responsibility rests on *all* that take the sword; and *all* that take it shall perish by it.

The South *has* already perished; its glozing Confederacy is in ruins; its fathers and sons in bloody graves; its territories laid waste; its virtue evaporated: while the fate of the North is but delayed, the uplifted hand of avenging justice holding already the destroying blade. The North has taken the sword, and it must perish with the sword. The attempt to preserve the nation by the sword, though a seeming success, will prove a final failure.

The corollary from this is, that real freedom cannot consist with the use of the sword. The sword is nothing but the ferocious beast of unreasoning power. And there can be no freedom in the presence of the uncaged lion lashed to fury. Can reason struggle in thought where infuriated power frowns, and the gleaming blade is uplifted to deal the fatal blow, the instant intelligence urges that interest lies in a direction different from that fixed by blind power? When interest stands, not in the right of the interested, but in the power of the unthinking sword, can rational freedom exist? And in all the past, have not governments stood on the blind might of the sword? Does not our government so stand still? To-day have the people of the United States rational, practical freedom? Are not the South the conquered slaves of the North, vassals under a military despotism? It is idle to talk of freedom, while eight or ten million people are suffering from the desolations of war, and bowing their necks under the iron heel of an unrelenting despotism.

Nearly sixty centuries have been devoted to working out the problem of governing men by the sword, with little regard to reason or interest, and the result is a failure. Would it not be a worthy experiment to devote ten or twenty centuries to working out the same problem, through reason and interest, without regard to the sword? If, in the end, the latter should also prove a failure, there would be a great gain in the loss of lives and the destruction of morality and material interests. But how is the problem to be worked out, if blind power is ever to suppress the investigation and practice which are necessary to test the problem, *that interest and reason*, instead of the sword, are the true bond of civil government? And are men permitted, in the United States, the right fairly to investigate the nature of government, and to show that the subject is oppressed by political slavery? For a third of a century men dare not, at the peril of life, discuss in the South, the nature of the institution of negro slavery. On the other hand, in the North, it is considered a crime worthy to forfeit personal liberty, and has sometimes gained the prison, to maintain the right of self-government, in the exact principle in which our government took its existence. And yet all real freedom must stand upon reason and full discussion. Indeed, with rational beings all worldly interests should stand in reason; and so far as they are truly rational, they will stand in it. Just so far as they do not stand in reason, they stand as if men were not rational. If human government cannot stand upon reason, it is evidently not suited for rational beings. If it must stand upon power, it is suited only for beings of power. If it must stand upon brute-force, it must be suited only for brute-creatures. And this is just the conclusion to which war-doctrines lead.

If it is true that the bond of government stands in interest; then it is highly proper that reason should constantly be employed about it; and highly improper that force should ever be employed. Reason should be employed, because the mind does not apprehend its best interests without the most careful use of reason. Force should never be employed, because war destroys but never develops interest. But the use of reason implies freedom from constraint—the right to question every principle on which government is supposed to rest. And it is certain that men can be governed only in accordance with their mental and moral constitutions. It is equally certain that they are naturally endowed with reason and those wants which crave the interests that government is suited to supply. Hence, if government cannot be sustained through the medium of reason and interest, it will not, in any other manner. Mind is properly influenced by motive only, and it is both offended and degraded when brought under the dominion of force or fear. So, where government is founded on the sword, the tendency, according to the laws of mind, is to degrade and debase the subject. Experience and facts confirm this statement. Since men are rational beings, can we rationally expect to govern them, not as rational but as brute-beings? When a difference of opinion about interests shall arise, shall force or reason be employed to determine who is right? When reason alone can determine the question, shall reason be abjured and force employed? When reason is most needed and force least needed, shall rational men cease to use reason and employ force? In resorting to war, is that not what they do? Yes, they ignore reason when reason is most needed; and employ force when force is least needed.

Men assume that a given form of government accords with reason and interest, when all really free discussion is prohibited either by menace of bodily harm or the odium of public opinion. And the one method of prohibition is about as successful as the other; for few men have the courage to face a storm of hatred and scorn in the maintenance of an opinion less interesting, it may be, to themselves, than to those who scorn them. This odious habit of hating and scorning what is new to the thoughts of men, involves the horrors of persecution, and is itself the essence of a refined tyranny. Formerly, it kindled fires and made martyrs. Now, it despises reason and makes wars. In politics or in religion, the spirit is simply the spirit of persecution. Each country assumes that its form of government is the true form, when all practical questioning is disallowed at the perils and horrors of war. England, France, the United States, the despotic governments of the world—all act just alike. The sword is uplifted. Reason is laid aside. Brute-force is employed. Suffering *people* have little to say. They scarcely dare to claim reason as their own, lest their souls shall cease to stay in their bodies. What *they* regard as *their* best interests, is nothing. They receive what the haughty government chooses to bestow, with reason and interest out of the question. In such cases, there can be, of course, but the semblance of real freedom. And not one government, perhaps, in Europe, conforms to a model of reason. Irrational, unjust, heathenish, many of them having their spirit from a period antedating Christianity, they are sustained by practices and usages which are heathenish in both origin and nature. The *reason* to which they appeal for support is the sword, and the *interests* which they sustain are the luxuries of the few.

Our own government differs from these in theory, but conforms to them in practice. We have a free government if boasting makes it. Yet, if men think, they must not think aloud; and *to act* upon a novel thought, is high treason. The eye must ever rest upon the uplifted sword of coercion, or the heated engine of public hatred. Yet, men call this freedom, and vaunt loud about it. But it is a sham and a fraud. Freedom is no more than a name. Indeed, in the name of freedom, it is freedom wearing the chains of slavery. It is freedom lying a victim bleeding on its own altar. It is intelligence bowing obeisance to the sword. It is manhood supplicating a smile from brute-power; the brute-man wielding dominion over the rational man. It is blind might extorting homage from reason and intelligence at the point of the bayonet. Interest, volition, reason, intelligence, are ignored and scorned; man is unmanned; God, nature, and God's laws, are flouted and repudiated; the rational man is arrested, cast into chains, and reduced to slavery; while the dumb-brute of irrational power sits enthroned as the stupid symbol of civil government. It is the grandest farce of the world.

Such to-day is the condition of the people in the Old World; and such the condition of the people of the United States. Freedom is an idle name—a sham, a fraud. In the South, in the North, the name of liberty is an idle sound. One must hold certain types of ideas, or he is scorned and esteemed as a criminal. He is mocked with a trial before the tribunal of public opinion,—a tribunal which often reminds one of the Star Chamber and Jeffreys —and is there condemned to outlawry, without justice, mercy, or charity. And in free America, such has been liberty in church and state during the last several years.

It seems unnecessary to mention, that, in such a state of society, progress is impossible beyond a limited point. For, looking abroad a little over the world, we shall find that advancement in intelligence and in all the arts of civilized life, is in the ratio which is measured by the degree of freedom the people enjoy. No exception to the rule can be found. We may begin with slaves, such as we had recently in this country, and pass through all grades of personal and political slavery, without finding an exception. With increased freedom, there is an increase in intelligence and all the interests that gratify human wants. And were the sword banished to the lands of barbarism, where it rightly belongs, the nations banishing it would speedily reap incalculable blessings. They would rise in intelligence, morality, religion, and in all things suited to afford comforts to human existence. Nor can there be doubt to the reflecting mind, that anything which requires continued force to support it, is unworthy to be supported. If government cannot be supported without the horrors of the sword, it were infinitely better to abandon it altogether; and it were infinitely better to have as many separate governments on our territory as we have States, than to have such another deluge of passion, crime, sin, and blasphemy as we have just passed through. *For what is not better than war?*

However, we need only reflect a little to see that the abandonment of the sword would have no such decisive results; but would herald an era of progress and prosperity hitherto unknown in the world's history. Instead of society's being dissolved and thrown into anarchy, the potent ligament of interest, arranged, tied, and adjusted by reason and judgment, instead of being deranged and cut by the sword, would bring all the nations and parts of the nations into much firmer and more enduring alliance. Bigotry, ambition, and cruelty, would scarcely have a foothold in which to entrench themselves. Whence then could come strifes and divisions? War, planting itself in the base and sinful passions of men, produces a large portion of the strifes and divisions which occur in relation to the governments of the earth. Ambition lay at the foundation of the late war in this country, and ambition produced the late war among the German States. Indeed, States and nations themselves, as such, are but close, selfish, illiberal corporations—finding little support in reason or an enlarged morality. The Christian idea is, that mankind is a brotherhood as a whole; and so their intercourse should not be restricted by the narrow lines of mere nationality. The sword should not be used to build up one corporation at the expense of another. All nations as such are equals, and all parts of nations as such have the right to form a separate corporation in their own peculiar interest—interests resulting from God's natural appointments. And on true peace-principles all these results would follow. They regard mankind as one great brotherhood of equals in rights. Nations they regard as equals, having no right of imperious dictation, no right to use the sword to create distinctions, no right to overawe each other by fear of life or desolation. And if upon these principles, interest suggests the division of a nation, it is made with neither strife nor bloodshed, as an overgrown church or family may divide without disturbance of the fraternal relations.

Peace-doctrines are based on the idea that men are rational beings, and may hence be induced to pursue their worldly interests by motives presented to reason. They regard government as a general means of securing these interests; and that men may hence be induced to support government by motives presented to reason. The idea of "indefinite secession," of which we heard so much during the late war, the peace-man regards as a myth, because wholly unfounded in reason. And, upon peace-principles, an occasional secession can produce no harm. There will be no war, no angry passion; but all parties will still be friendly, pursue the cultivation of the soil, and maintain trade and commerce. All the ills will therefore be seen to arise from the principles of war, and not from those of peace. Let the sword be abandoned forever, and the nations will not be destroyed by the doctrines of peace.

§ 3.—*The Colonial Government of Pennsylvania.*

So far as we have been able to learn, in all the long and bloody history of the past, there has been but a solitary attempt made to rule men and regulate international interests without the use of the sword. That attempt is found in the case of the Pennsylvania Colony, under the celebrated William Penn. But, the question naturally arises, was that attempt attended by success?

We have already stated that most of the governments of Europe had their origin prior to the era of Christianity; and, hence, are founded rather in heathen than rational or Christian ideas. When Christianity appeared, it was introduced amongst the heathen governments but did not supplant their principles. The most that can be said of the best government, is that, in the progress of time, the modes of legislation became relieved of some barbarous customs, while some of the customs themselves were laid aside. But to this day not a European government is founded or administered upon Christian principles. And the codes are a strange medley of Jewish, Papal, and heathen conceptions, modified, after a manner, by the influence of Christianity. But nothing like a substantial conformity to the spirit of a true Christianity is found in all the codes of Europe; while the *practice* of the people is further removed from the spirit of Christianity than their *theory*. Indeed, to this day the people practise very much as they did before Christ appeared in the world. It is relieved of a little of its barbarity, as men do not now destroy with the cruel torments which they formerly employed. They are not now converted into torch-lights as Nero once converted them; they are not ground up and built into walls as they were by Tamerlane; they are not broken on the wheel, tied to the tails of horses, or quartered, as they were by our barbarous ancestors. Still, the nations do *substantially* the same things that the heathens and barbarians of other ages did, though our *manner* may be a little more civilized. The nations still butcher and slaughter, burn and lay waste, but do it in the polite courteous way required by modern civilization. *We* have powder and lead, polished swords and bristling bayonets, and do not kill people by the use of unpolished stones or poisoned darts. We can kill a mile off, and so need not stir the lower passions by personal contact—only *occasionally* in a bayonet charge.—Now, the one of these methods is the civilized, *Christian* method of attaining the end; and the other is the uncivilized, barbarous method of compassing the same result. The substance is the same; the shadow is different. The people of the United States adopt the substance, reject the shadow.

The origin of the English government dates prior to the age of Julius Cæsar; and England governs substantially to-day as she did in Cæsar's day. And the United States have adopted England's mode of government; and so they have, in substance, the practices and usages of the age when Cæsar invaded England prior to the Christian era. Those practices and usages are only changed by making them conform to the Christian mode of killing and destroying. We have quite rejected the governmental theories of the dark ages, but still retained the cruel customs and practices of them. Our theory is one thing, our practice quite another. William Penn was far more consistent than we are. He rejected at once the theories and practices of the European governments. His religion made him a peace-man; and he acted out his religion in life. Therefore, Penn was a peace-man from deep conviction and a sense of duty to God and man. Hence, he carried his principles into practice,—impressed them upon his proprietary government, and was a legislator on Christian principles, far different from some in our day, who are fervid peace-men in times of peace and ardent war-men in times of war.

Penn's biographer calls him " the Christian legislator," and tells us that he means by that designation " one who models his public actions and founds his laws, so far as his abilities permit, on the letter and spirit of the Gospel, having but one end in view throughout, the happiness of the governed, which happiness is to be produced only by means strictly moral, and by the improvement of their moral condition, and adopting, as it relates to aliens or foreigners, principles of action pure in themselves, founded in justice, of the same tendency with those established for the governed, and promotive of the same end."

We have here the first great principles of his colonial government. The end it had in view throughout, was THE HAPPINESS OF THE GOVERNED. That end being the grand key-stone, shaped the whole arch; it led to morality, justice, generosity, and magnanimity, the component elements of true peace doctrines. Nor could the influence of that great central conception be confined to the *governed*: it could not but extend " to aliens and foreigners," and have shed its golden influence to bless them. Administering a government so benign, with a single view to "the happiness of the governed," must of necessity disarm "aliens and foreigners," of all actual hostility; because so true a conception of the office of government, guided by the magnanimity to reduce it to practice, and really reduced to practice by an earnest soul feeling its responsibility to God, must not only disarm of hostility, but must attract the warmest affection. And so it was with Penn. He won the affection of the very savages; who, nevertheless, seemed less savage than the Christians who finally defeated his plans of government. For nearly three quarters of a century, Penn's policy prevailed, extending through a period of hostilities between the Christian nations of France and England. During these hostilities some of the Indian tribes formed alliances with the French, the latter agreeing to *pay the savages* for English scalps. But so effectually had the Christian conduct of Penn and his followers disarmed and won the Indians, that not *Christian* bribes could buy savage men to acts of barbarity. Penn said, "Do not abuse the Indians, but let them have justice, and you win them, where there is such a knowledge of good and evil." Penn believed that a course of justice and kindness would find response in the bosom of savages, and he steadily acted towards them on that principle. The sequel proved that he was not mistaken in the general law of human nature. In this connection his biographer says: "It is pleasing to record what return the Indians made him for all the care and kindness he had bestowed upon them; and this will appear so great, I may say so unexampled, that either his munificence must have been of much larger dimensions than we are accustomed to see, or their hearts must have beaten with the pulse which has seldom vibrated in the human heart." "I may observe then," continues the writer, "that the first result of his treatment of them showed itself in a grateful return on their part by kind and friendly offices both to himself and followers. They became indeed the benefactors of the colonists. When the latter were scattered abroad in 1682, and without houses or food, the Indians were remarkably kind and attentive to them. They hunted for them frequently, doing their utmost to feed them. They considered them all as the children of William Penn, and so treated them as brothers."

Speaking of Penn, Richard Townsend says: "As our worthy Proprietor treated the Indians with extraordinary humanity, they became very civil and loving to us, and brought us an abundance of venison." The Indians said of Penn, "Having now such an one as he, we will never do him any wrong;" and never did any people keep their word better.

" A second result," says the biography, " was manifested in their peaceful and affectionate conduct towards the settlers; so that the latter had no fear, though in a defenseless state, for their personal safety, but lived among them, though reputed savages, as among their best friends and protectors." And Richard Townsend continues, "As in other countries the Indians were exasperated by hard treatment, which hath been the foundation of much bloodshed, so the contrary treatment of our worthy proprietor hath produced their love and affection." In the manuscript of a passenger in one of the vessels that brought the first Colonists to Penn's settlement, is found the following: " A providential Hand was very conspicuous and remarkable in many instances which might be mentioned. The Indians were even rendered our benefactors and protectors. Without any carnal weapon we entered the land, and inhabited therein as safe as if there had been thousands of garrisons." And Oldmixon, speaking of the Colony of Pennsylvania, says, " This little state subsisted in the midst of six Indian nations without so much as a militia for its defence." Proud testifies that this peaceable State " was never interrupted for more than seventy years, or so long as the Quakers retained power in the government sufficient to influence a friendly and just conduct towards them, and to prevent or redress such misunderstandings and grievances as occasionally happened between them and any of the inhabitants of the Province." And between genuine Quakers and the Indians, "the Great Treaty *was* never violated," a good understanding "ever subsisting between their respective descendants, the Indians reverencing the name and memory of Penn for generations," and they declaring "that they *should never forget the counsel which William Penn gave them;* and that, though they could not write as the English did, yet they could keep in their memory what was said in their councils." The Red Men called Penn, Brother Onas, saying, " The covenant chain between us shall be as clear and lasting as the sun and the stars in heaven, that the lustre thereof may never be obscured by any clouds or darkness, but may shine as clear and last as long as the sun in the firmament." In his biography of Penn, Clarkson has collected numerous testimonies, in which the various Indian tribes have expressed their lasting love of Penn. In 1742 a treaty was made with the Governor of Pennsylvania by the six nations, when the chief of the Onondagoes said : " We are all very sensible of the kind regard which that good man, William Penn, had for all the Indians."

We have before us the speeches made by the Indians on numerous occasions of treaties with the different tribes. These speeches glow with the ardor of feeling which the Indians seemed ever to have towards Penn and his followers. And, indeed, Penn was ever the true and kind friend of the Indian. For the conduct of Penn how did the Indians act in return? Much is said about the *necessity* of fighting, and, especially, in self-defense. These settlers, in a wilderness-country, had neither militia, nor garrisons, nor armory; and were surrounded by so-called savages who yelled their war-whoops all round them, and shot, tomahawked, and scalped the inhabitants in all the other settlements. What was their demeanor towards true peace-men?

Let them tell their own story. In the year 1704, Thomas Clarkley, "an eminent minister of the gospel among the Quakers," making a visit to another part of the country thus testifies : " About this time the Indians were very barbarous in the destruction of the English inhabitants, and knocking out the brains of others (men, women, and children), by which the country was greatly alarmed both night and day; but the great Lord of all was pleased wonderfully *to preserve our Friends, especially those who kept faithful to their peaceable principles*, according to the doctrines of Christ in the Holy Scriptures." "A neighbor of the aforesaid people," continues the writer, "told me that, as he was at work in the field, the Indians saw and called to him, and he went to them. They told him that they had no quarrel with the Quakers, for they were quiet, peaceable people, and hurt nobody, and that therefore none should hurt them. Those Indians began about this time to shoot people down as they rode along the road, and to knock them on the head in their beds, and very barbarously murdered many ; but we travelled the country and had large meetings, and the presence of God was with us abundantly, and we had great inward joy in our outward jeopardy. The people generally rode and went to their worship armed ; but Friends went to their meetings without either sword or gun, having their trust and confidence in God." John Fothergill, another eminent Quaker minister, writes : " It was then a very exercising time with Friends, by reason of the bloody incursions that the Indians frequently made upon the English, being hired by the French about Quebeck, * * * so that many of the English inhabitants were murdered in their houses, or shot, or knocked down on the road or in the fields. * * * Those whom they killed they cut with great knives around the head about the skirt of the hair, and pulled the skin off the head ; and for every such skin, * * * they received a sum of money. These barbarities caused many people * * * to retire into garrisons, * * * built in many places for greater security. Yet, * * * it was sorrowful to observe that few * * * seemed to be affected with due consideration, so as to be awakened to think rightly of the cause of this heavy chastisement, and be induced to seek the Almighty's favor as they ought. But it was a profitable, humbling time to many of our Friends, who generally stood in the faith, and kept at their usual places of abode, though at the daily hazard of their lives ; and it is very remarkable that scarcely any that thus kept their habitations in the faith, were suffered to fall by the Indians, though few days passed but we heard of some of their cruel murders and destroying vengeance. We were in these parts backwards and forwards a considerable time, having many meetings before we could be clear to leave them. * * * * We were all graciously preserved, though in the open country, and we lodged several times at a Friend's house at some distance from the garrison ; and we had reason to believe a party of Indians were for some time about it, the marks of their feet being plainly to be seen in the morning ; but they went away, doing us no harm."

From these extracts it would seem that the best garrisons in the Colony of Pennsylvania were constructed from the principles of peace. We are told however, of three persons who lost life by violence, having first lost their peace-principles by apostasy. Thomas Chalkly records the fact of their death with the circumstances. One of the parties was a woman, the other two were men. The men were accustomed to go to their work unarmed, trusting the protective Providence of God ; but a spirit of distrust possessing them, "they took weapons of war to defend themselves; and the Indians who had seen them several times without them, let them alone, saying they were peaceable men and hurt nobody, therefore they would not hurt them ; but now seeing them have guns, and supposing they designed to kill the Indians, they therefore shot them dead." The woman, abandoning that protection of Providence implied in peace-principles, took refuge in a garrison. But while there, reflection making her uneasy, she left the garrison, and the Indians seeing her leave the fort, and supposing she belonged to it, waylaid and killed her. Thomas Story mentions the case of another young Friend, who was killed by the Indians through mistake. Too young men were going to their work; one had a gun, the other had not. The Indians shot the one that had the gun, without injuring the other. When told that the one they killed "was a Friend, they seemed sorry for it, but blamed him for carrying a gun," because by carrying a gun, they took him for an enemy."

All the other Colonies of this country acted on war-principles. The first thing they did, on landing, was to erect forts, make military display, and present themselves as a warlike people. And having, in this manner, secured themselves, they took advantage of the natives, would outwit, cheat and defraud them. That they might the more successfully accomplish dishonest purposes, they introduced amongst the natives intoxicating liquors. The general policy of the settlers was, in short, that of both fraud and violence. And rather than feel *proud* of our ancestors, our cheeks should tingle with shame. Both Christianity and humanity blush to think of their conduct.

As the kindness and justice of Penn begat kindness and justice; so the barbarous conduct of our ancestors begat barbarous conduct in return. When abandoned to its own principles, this is the law of fallen human nature. Accordingly, while there was peace in the Colony of Pennsylvania, the Indians of Virginia, Carolina, Massachusetts, and Maryland, so depredated and murdered the Colonists that they felt obliged to maintain a strong militia. For a generation or more, the settlers in these Provinces were hardly able to cultivate their fields, or travel in their ordinary business; and they were frequently obliged to retire and live within their forts. Even the Colony of the liberal minded Lord Baltimore, was not free from Indian depredations, though his conduct towards the Indians of Maryland was kind and humane. For Lord Baltimore was not a true peace man ; but acted on the war-policy of having forts and garrisons, and making a military show. And the savage instinct *felt* the difference between the worldly policy of the liberal Catholic, and the Christian policy of the amiable Quaker. Hence they ravaged the territory of the former, but remained the steadfast friends of the latter. In the order and moral constitution of things, who can affirm that God does not, in a *special* manner, care for those who seek protection in Him. If a man's ways please the Lord, He makes his enemies to be at peace with him.

The policy of William Penn did more than disarm the savage heart of revenge and the hand of outrage ;—it imparted to that heart a feeling of love, and to the hand the coming of a dawning civilization. For through the benevolent efforts of Penn and his co-laborers, the light of both civilization and Christianity were offered to, and partially accepted by the Senecas, the Shawanese, the Cayugas, the Oneidas, Onondagoes, Wyandotts, Delawares, Cherokees, Chocktaws, Chickasaws, the Creeks, Tuscaroras, the Miamis, and others. But the benevolent work was much interrupted by the malign spirit of war, and the actual wars which continually agitated the people of Europe. For the early Colonial interests were very sensitive to the influence of European agitation. And the reason why the Indians did not yield to the offers of Christianity and a higher civilization, was not for want of mind and heart, but because it was offered with such a mixture of savage ferocity, that even barbarians refused to accept it. In the early settlement of this country, the Jesuit missionaries who prosecuted their labors with such intrepid zeal, did little else, if we may credit history, than to impart to the Indians a different form of savage life. They even added *to* the cunning and cruelty of the savages, imparting to their minds not an element of true Christianity. And much of the Protestant teaching was little better suited to afford a just notion of Gospel truth. The minds of uncultivated people are more influenced by actions than by teachings ;

and so the actions of the missionaries being little different in character from those of the barbarians, had little influence over the lives of the barbarians. The great majority of the Christians would plunge into war, steal in war, use deceit, employ intrigue, intoxicate the Indians in order to facilitate their schemes of imposition; and often excelled the savages in acts of cruelties and treachery. How then could it be rationally expected that the savages would be willing to change one form of savage life for another? True Christianity rests mainly on spiritual influence, and such influence attends only the truth; but there being little real truth in the lives of those who missionated among the Indians, on the whole, little good was done to them. Had the spirit and policy of Penn been employed, there can be little doubt that the Indian tribes would largely have embraced Christianity. War and a war-spirit, assuming the form of avarice and selfishness, defeated the offer of Christianity to the North American Indians. To attribute the want of success to an extraordinary ferocity in the Indian character, is as superficial as it is false, as the conduct of William Penn with the Indians clearly shows. Just so far as his influence extended, William Penn proved that both civilized and savage men could be governed without the use of the sword.

While we earnestly commend the life of Penn to the attention of the reader, a single other quotation shall conclude these extracts: "He," says his biographer, "has exhibited to the world the singular spectacle, or has shown the possibility, of a nation's maintaining its own internal police amidst a mixture of persons of different nations and different civil and religious opinions, and of maintaining its foreign relations also, without the aid of a soldier or a man in arms. The constable's staff was the only instrument of authority in Pennsylvania for the greater part of a century; and always while the government was in the hands of Quakers; and never was the government, as it related to the governed, maintained with more harmony or less internal disturbance; and, as it related to foreigners, with more harmony; for, though he was situated among barbarous nations, never, during his administration or that of his proper successors, was there —a quarrel—or a war."

This is in precise accordance with what we are endeavoring to teach on the subject, while our whole object has been, and will be, to exhibit the reasons for our conceptions of the general subject. And it is no less noteworthy than amazing that thousands of years have come and gone, without the occurrence of one other such example as that of Pennsylvania, though the principle is clearly taught by Christ, and must be little less plain to the mind that thinks, than the demonstrations of Euclid. Never was a conception clearer to the mind, than the whole idea of ruling great nations without the use of the sword,—without employing an "instrument of authority" more severe than "the constable's staff." In Penn's Colony this was done for three quarters of a century, among elements as unruly as are likely ever to be thrown together. And that "staff," guided by reason and Christian principle, not only ruled men of different nations and different religious and civil notions, but, stretching its beguiling authority beyond, it exorcised savages of their ferocity, and charmed them into the love of peace. And thus we have it demonstrated that *interest* and *reason* are the proper ligament of government; while all experience proves the insufficiency of the sword to produce the same result. It is a great error to suppose that *fear* and *terror* are the ligaments of government or the preventive of crime. The wars and capital punishments of men prove the falsity of the whole idea of fear and terror; for experience establishes that one is incompetent to preserve government and the other to prevent crime. And that men adopt the one and the other can only amaze the mind which will carefully and intelligently survey the whole field of thought.

§ 4.—*The war spirit amongst Christians.   Its cure amongst men.*

In the abstract, few men will deny that the tenor of the reasoning herein is correct. Even military men admit that it is correct. But in this respect, as in respect to the axioms of freedom, men are wholly inconsistent. They assent to a theory, as a mental conception, but totally deny it as matter of practice. They *act* the same way in relation to war. They admit that war is wrong in principle, wrong in theory, — and many admit that it cannot be reconciled with the morality of Christ and the Apostles; yet they do not, at the same time, hesitate to engage in it. The departure in practice from their recognized principle, they justify, by alleging that, in the present condition of human society, war is a necessity. But in this assertion there has always seemed to be a want of moral principle. Conscience, losing its tone as a monitor, nearly loses its dominion. To reason with such persons, is a task as difficult as useless; because the trouble is less in the errors of the head than in the delinquencies of the heart. The head does not so much need instruction as the heart does purification. To concede that Christ and the Apostles forbid war in its spirit and practice, and yet zealously to engage in it, implies little else than the renunciation of all morality. and such men can be better controlled by external than by internal considerations; can be controlled more by the rules of society than by those of morality. And is it uncharitable to say that the masses of men are controlled more by habit, custom, and tradition than by moral principle? In the masses, the degree of intelligence is low, and the action of conscience feeble. The possibility of war amongst beings destined to live endlessly in a state of happiness or misery dependent on their behavior in this life, is a demonstration of the statement. But think of the idea of such beings killing each other in the horrors of war!

With the teachings of men on the subject of war, and

taking mankind as we find them on the earth, it is less wonderful that men do fight than it would be if they did not. And this consideration demands a passing attention. Let us look at two phases of this branch of the subject. 1. The probable way in which the minds of men have strayed so far from the teaching of Christ. 2. The way in which the minds of men may return to the teaching of Christ. The general argument, showing the manner in which the minds of men have so far departed from the teaching of Christ on the subject of war, may be found in all that is said in these pages. But the subject deserves, in some respects, a little more special attention, and we shall scarcely be able to keep within the political aspects of the subject. It has been stated that the European governments, mostly, and in a sense, ante-date the time of our Saviour, and the introduction of Christianity amongst men. It has also been hinted that the introduction of Christianity among the nations, neither superseded their governments, nor destroyed the principles on which they were founded. The Saviour, and finally the Apostles, did not entertain the conceptions of government which prevailed in their age. For the nations had "changed the truth of God into a lie, and worshipped and served the creature more than the Creator. For this cause God gave them up to vile affections." And "because that, when they knew God, they glorified Him not as God, neither were thankful, God also gave them up to uncleanness through the lusts of their own hearts: and as they did not like to retain God in their knowledge, God gave them over to a reprobate mind, to do those things which are not convenient." And, "being filled with all unrighteousness, fornication, wickedness, covetousness, maliciousness; full of envy, murder, deceit, malignity;" and being "haters of God, proud, and boasters"—all elements entering into the compound of war—God withdrew from them, and left them to establish governments under the dominion of such morals. When Christianity was published, the morals of the heathen world corresponded with the things here named by the apostle. Even the cultivated men yielded assent to the abominable morals of the times. Plato, Socrates, Demosthenes, Cicero, the poets, statesmen, philosophers, orators, and religionists of the heathens, *practised* similar morals. The learned Horne says : " While some philosophers asserted the being of a God, others openly denied it : others, again, embraced, or pretended to embrace, the notion of a multiplicity of gods, celestial, aërial, terrestrial, and infernal, while others represented the Deity as a corporeal being united to matter by a necessary connexion, and subject to an immutable fate. As every country had its peculiar deities, the philosophers (whatever might be their private sentiments) sanctioned and defended the religion of the State ; and urged a conformity to be the duty of every citizen. They dilligently practiced the ceremonies of their fathers ; devoutly frequented the temples of the gods ; and sometimes, condescending to act a part on the theatre of superstition, they concealed the sentiments of the atheist under sacerdotal robes." *

Such morals and sentiments as these prevailed when

* The observant mind cannot fail to notice the striking analogy in the conduct here described and that recently witnessed in this country. And substitute Government for Deity, and we shall have quite an exact description of the nations in our day. Every country has its peculiar governments ; and the philosophers, and we may add, the theologians, whatever may be their private sentiments, sanction and defend them as a sort of religious institutions, and urge a conformity to be the duty of every citizen. They diligently practise the ceremonies of the fathers as to the governments ; devoutly frequent the temples of war ; and sometimes, condescending to act a part on the theatre of superstition, the theologians conceal the sentiments of atheists under sacerdotal robes. For it is not possible, in the nature of things, for a philosopher or theologian to counsel the destruction of men about worldly interests, without being *practically* atheistic. And atheism may exist under sacerdotal robes ; may outwardly sing, pray, and preach, with a consuming faith and a furious zeal, as all ages of the world and the church have witnessed. Goods may be given to feed the poor, and the body to be burned.

Christianity was first published. And governments were formed and sustained by principles according with such morals and sentiments. And though the Founder of Christianity was the Maker and Upholder of the world, He was content quietly to teach principles which, fully taught and practised by mankind, would renovate the world of its horrid superstitions and practices. *As if He feared* the rulers of the nations, He chose to teach a few seed-truths, and to leave them to leaven all human society; and yet at His nod nature would have convulsed, and the stars have wandered in wild confusion. Depositing these seed-truths, He permitted them to be buried beneath the debris and rubbish of vast accumulations of idolatry, superstition, and ethnicism. And it appeared hard even for Divinity to acquaint the *Apostles* with the true nature of His kingdom as distinguished from the kingdoms of the world. Their minds were captivated by ambitious hopes of worldly distinction. Jewish and heathenish conceptions held them in captivity. Government idolatry found place in the deep recesses of their hearts. It was long before they were cured of their ambitious and idolatrous hopes. Finally, however, they caught the idea and spirit of the Master, that His kingdom is not of this world; and ever afterwards they realized that "the weapons of their warfare were not carnal" but spiritual, mighty only through God to the pulling down of the strongholds of the idolatrous nations and governments, by overturning and overturning the kingdoms, crowns, governments, and hierarchies of men. But once imbued, the Apostles imbued in turn the minds of all the early converts to Christianity. And not an early follower of the Master could be induced to use carnal weapons, to take arms, or to fight in war, though it cost life, or brought chains and imprisonment. And it was not till after Constantine the Great, idolatrously so-called, ascended the imperial throne, and the Council of Nice declared the Christian to be the religion of the empire, that Christians began to engage in the carnal conflicts of men. At that time the church apostatized from the Christian faith, and nominal Christianity, imbued with the sentiments of heathenism, permitted its professors to engage in war as the Jews and heathens did. Thence, the principles of Christianity and of heathenism became closely intermingled; so much so, that " natural men " could not separate them. Thence forward to this day, the principles of heathenism and those of Christianity have remained deeply intermingled amongst the so-called Christian nations. And it was but a few centuries after the Nicene Council till the hierarchy of Rome obtained more than imperial sway; and assumed intimate relation with the idolatrous foundation and practices of secular government. The hierarchy and secular government, having the common end of attaining power and personal aggrandizement, readily united and sought the attainment of the common end. Occasionally, however, the two would come into conflict, and for a time floundered as to which should have ascendency.

Finally, the flow of time shattered, somewhat, the shackles of barbarism and loosed the fetters of superstition, releasing intelligence from the iron grasp of tradition. Yet, it must stand as the amazement to the thoughtful, That all the fetters and manacles with which horrid war had bound its victims in the benighted revelries of superstition, still remained in their force and strength. Defying the teachings of Christ, the dictates of enlightened reason, the true principles of wòrldly interest, " the horrors of the sword " have survived the celebrated nations which they have destroyed, and still live in vigor as we approach the twentieth century of the Christian era. Not a heathenism that Christianity encountered, was in more flagrant and evident violation of its every principle and precept, than the " wars and fightings " which come from the lusts of men. Yet, changed a little in form, the church has sanctioned such wars, from the time of the illicit and spiritual harlotry of church and state under Constantine, till this hour. Like the fetters of the down-trodden slave, no flow of time, no change of circumstances, no phase of civilization, no progress of Christianity, has broken the oppressive tyranny of the sword. Whether Heathenism, Romanism, or Protestantism, ruled —whether under the iron yoke of Nero, the absolute tyranny of Constantine, the ravages of Charlemagne, the ambitious sway of the heartless Napoleon—whether under the mock republic of Rome, a hinted monarchy, an absolute despotism, the democratic republic of the United States,— whether Roman Catholics, Episcopalians, Puritans, Presbyterians, Heathens, or North American Savages, shall be at the head of government—there results no change from the " bloody and barbarous tyranny of the sword." In the United States to-day the unthinking disposition of the sword sways a dominion as complete as, and only a little less relentless than, it held before the Gospel was published to our race. With our boasted freedom and self-complacent Christianity, we adhere with the death-grasp, to the veriest heathenism ever practised by our race. "And diligently do our people practise the ceremonies of their fathers ; devoutly frequenting the temple of the bloody gods ; statesmen, philosophers, and theologians sometimes condescending to act upon the theatre of superstition, conceal the sentiments of the atheist under the thin gauze of " expediency." Meanwhile they sanction and defend the semi-idolatrous and quasi-religious policy of the state, by the teachings of a kingdom declared emphatically to be not of this world.

Such, then, is the probable way in which the minds of men have been led so far away from the teaching of Christ on the subject of war. When we come to notice, secondly, The way in which the minds of men may return to the teaching of Christ.

If one will open his eyes to the facts daily transpiring about him, he will be little surprised at the presence of a

pervasive war-spirit. Human nature as it is, the surprise
would be greater, if such a spirit was not pervasive. For
a hero-worship, pervading every department of life,
breathes its foul breath into the heart of every pure thought
and noble sentiment, and sends its poison over every
human interest. The thoughtless mother soothes the sensibility of her infant to repose at the earliest dawn of reason, by arousing in the little bosom the early devotions of
hero-worship; and before it can lisp the "Lord's Prayer,"
the seeds of hero-worship are sown broadcast in the soil of
its naturally idolatrous heart. And thus early commenced,
the training is assiduously continued during the period of
boyhood and youth. The boy has a miniature drum and
wooden sword. He hears of war, reads of war, and thinks
of war. He drafts other boys into the army; deploys
them on the plain; fights mock-battles; and becomes the
hero of well earned fame. In training the tiny soldiery,
he mimics the airs of a real training officer, assuming the
same commanding tones and breathing the same confident
spirit. About the infant nursery, it may be he hears a
Christian father, with more zeal than knowledge, utter in
prayer the language of hero-adoration—witnesses the pro-
fanation of the altar consecrated to religion. The accident
of birth may make enemies; and against these he hears
deadly maledictions breathed to the audience of God at the
altars of devotion, while divine vengeance is invoked to accomplish deeds of death too slowly accomplished to suit the
worshipper, by armies, guns, swords, and the munitions of
war.

And thus, instead of teaching the mind in its impressi-
ble period, that war is a horrible and soul and body destroying crime, it is taught to mingle the incense of devotion to
God with the cruel devotion of some hero-god. When he
is able to read, the opening and susceptible mind is attracted by fascinating and exaggerated accounts of the love which
Napoleon or some other scourge of men, had, when a boy,

for military achievements and glory. His mind inexperienced and seduced by the fascinations of such exaggerations, the boy inquires of the hero-worshipping father for further information than the "juvenile book" gives. In compliance with the request, the thoughtless father exhausts the vocabulary of redundant adjectives in praise of the " brave and brilliant" chieftain, whose real message to mankind had been one of sorrow-only. The young mind filled thus with the virus of war, and the strong desire for the glory of heroism, the boy again rushes forth to summon his diminutive warriors to the drill, the battle field, and the campaign. He apes the veteran warrior, by addressing his brave soldiery touching the early military taste and final glory of the hero, whose fame history and the father had alike exaggerated and perverted. Ere long this boy will come to manhood; and, it may be, without being sufficiently thoughtful to expel from the mind the poisonous seed thus early sown in it. And why wonder if then he shall thirst for a real field and actual occasion, that he may win the crown of the warrior's glory? And what wonder, if amid *his* prayers and devotions to God, mingled with " horrid blasphemy and murderous ambition," himself having wickedly made the occasion, he would wade to position and fame through the blood and tears of anguished millions?

But why pursue this thought? The training we know— the result we know. The one follows the other by the laws of human nature. For while it is true that, a child trained as he should go, is not likely when old to depart from it; it is also true that, trained in the way he should not go, he is not likely when old to depart from it. Till the same pains shall be taken to support government by peaceable and rational considerations, that have been taken to support it by the sword, we shall not cease to have faith in the former, and to abhor the latter. For we know by actual experience, that both communities and nations may be assimilated to a given spirit of life, manner of feel'ng, mode of speech, and habit of action. In this respect, the capability of human nature has been repeatedly witnessed. It is a strong law of human nature. The wide prevalence of the war-spirit is itself an example of the law. The most abhorrent of the practices of men, essentially heathenish and barbarous, by adopting false and wicked tests of virtue, it has spread its malign and deleterous spirit into the very web and woof of Christian thought and feeling, till professed Christians regard the occasional mind which rejects the spirit and practice of it as of doubtful sanity. And in many instances, it is certainly true, that as men are now educated, they cannot distinguish the murderous principles of war from the peaceful teachings of Christ. But this only demonstrates, *that men may be trained to hate as utterly as they now appear to love war.* And nothing is more potent than this capability of assimilation. Examples are found throughout history. The prevalance of a war-spirit is as we have said, a forcible example of it. Other examples are abundant. Look at the furious Cromwell and his fanatical followers. The same spirit, in detail, seemed to pervade him and them. They snuffed their breath alike ; whined their prayers alike ; indulged their religious vengeance alike ; and sanctimoniously turned up the white of the eye alike. And, so far as human nature seems capable, that cruel and inexorable saintly warrior appears to have assimilated his followers to a common model. And the example is found in the Pilgrim Fathers, who only fled from persecution, after their assimilation to their persecutors. The Moravians, the Waldenses, and the Quakers, are examples in a better sense. But every religious sect and strong organization is an example in proof of the law. The Masons, the Odd-Fellows, political and commercial combinations and associations, have the same force of argument. The parties to the late war are striking illustratrations of the law. "The rebels," men, women, and children seemed to have the same spirit and to ring the changes upon the same shibboleth. The same was true also of the North. Every shoddy army contractor and well-paid chaplain was " wiser than seven men that could render a reason ;" and knew the end and object that " God intended to accomplish by the war." But this is not all. By the processes of assimilation, the *nations* conform to a generalized standard. It is a marvellous susceptibility of human nature—a mighty power for good or for evil. Forty-nine fiftieths of mankind are, through life, just what they are taught to be ; and their qualities become inheritable from age to age. The fiftieth one is, in a sense, the reformer, through whom progress is possible. In this way, Penn, Fox, and Barclay, still speak to the heart of the Quaker, and give tone to his life. Wesley still holds class-meetings and love feasts, though he wears not the round-breasted coat. Calvin also imparts his spirit to the whole Presbyterian family ; and so on without limit. The man of science, the medical man, the lawyer, the professor, the scholar, the orator, the legislator—all men but the reformer—and he is only partially an exception, have admired leaders, whose spirit, thoughts, and feelings they inhale and exhale : only there is this modification—the leaders and reformers *feel* and *realize* what others are apt to imitate or at most approximate.

Hence, there is no reason to assume, in the face of examples so numerous and striking, *that the nations of the earth may not be brought under, and made to conform to, the spirit and practice of peace.* To contradict the idea, is to contradict the demands of the word of God, to defeat the teaching of prophecy, to overthrow the inferences of experience, and to thwart the highest hopes of mankind. And that the achievement of such a result is practical, can only be doubted by denying that man is rational. For the practicability is based on his rationality—is based on the idea that man may be brought into conformity, *rationally*, with the law revealed by Him who made him rational. And so surely as man is moved by interest and reason to form government, so surely may he be induced to support it by appealing to interest and reason ; while the support which is coerced has the natural tendency to destroy rather than to sustain it. For coercion is inseparable from tyranny—is tyranny ; and the natural tendency of all tyranny is to explosion and destruction. This is the voice of reason, and the lesson of experience—human nature will revolt and explode under the pressure of coercion or tyranny.

Still further. Beginning at the infantile nursery, the principle of assimilation may be carried into the detail of society. The whole spirit of war is a high moral and political crime. Let it be so regarded and taught from the cradle. Look at the condition of society in this country. How frequent the crimes which shock the moral sense of men! How revolting they are ! Whence do they proceed ? Whether men will acknowledge the fact or not, it is none the less true, *that war includes all crimes.* *The code of war formally justifies all crimes :* all crimes are included in war, as the whole includes all its parts. Carrying pistols, knives, or other deadly weapons, to be prepared for the murderous attack ; then quarreling to give occasion for their use, are included in the criminal spirit of war. War is, in short, the license for the commission of all the crimes specifically forbidden by the word of God, and for those known to, or conceivable by, the human mind. War is the climax in the rhetoric of crimes. And yet its fell spirit is inculcated, in various ways, upon the infant mind from its earliest activities.

Now, we contend that if this parent of crime was extirpated from the mind and execrated as a crime ; and the conception that it is a crime studiously impressed on the young mind through every period of its education ; the spirit of hatred would be caught and would do its work of assimilation, till a large portion of the revolting crimes would disappear from amongst men. The shocking and revolting crimes are only committed by those who allow that the spirit of war consists with Christianity. No one ever heard of a *real* Quaker's committing murder. Such things as murder are done by those only who think that war, and the elements of which it is composed, are right. Truly peaceable people never kill and are rarely killed excepting by persecutors, religious or political. Yet it is common for those who prize the heroic " right of self-defense," and wear pistols and knives to make it good, to purge the sin of murder in the dungeon, or in that other heroic right of " dangling upon the gallows." Personal courage and animal bravery are ranked in this age among the Christian virtues ; and it is not very uncommon for professors of religion to engage in personal fights with ruffians. There was a doctor of divinity in one of our cities, an ardent war-man, who was prominently marked on the face by a ruffian in a rencounter on the street.

Now, how must we interpret such facts in an argument against war? They have a logical significance. What is it? They show, as all observation and experience show, that the force of the common mind is formed by education ; show that the masses of mankind think and act as they do in accordance with their mental and moral training. They therefore demonstrate that society has the capability of being governed by rational and moral considerations as well as by the opposite, or warlike ones. Perhaps no custom ever practised by men was so irrational and unsuited to an end as war and the act of taking life for crime. And the history of criminal jurisprudence proves that crimes diminish in the ratio of the diminution of the offenses for which capital punishment is inflicted. Our unnatural ancestors made some two hundred and fifty offenses punishable by death. Some of them were most trivial in their character. To shoot a hare without the King's license—to cut through the mound of a fish-pond—to cut down a cherry-tree in an orchard, and to keep company for a month with those who were called Egyptians, were crimes legally punishable by death. Others were of the like general character. And, on war-principles, it is amazing that, in the face of these barbarous laws, the crime of killing a hare was more frequent in those times, than that of murder was, in the better portions of our country anterior to our late war.

And what, again, is the natural and legitimate influence? It is that severe penalties are unnatural, and therefore, do not tend to diminish crime. Man can be governed only according to the laws of his nature; and it is a consideration deserving the candid and patient examination of thoughtful men, whether any punishment, as such, is not cruel, contrary to nature, and unsuited to any desirable end. If the lessons of experience are suited to instruct us in wisdom, they seem sufficient to teach us that the mere fear of punishment has but little tendency in the aggregate to prevent the commission of crime. Secret crimes are always committed with the idea of escaping detection; those easy of proof, under the blinding impulses of overbearing passion. In either case, superficial reflection is sufficient to show that the fear of punishment has little relation to the crimes. It is certain that the only successful method of preventing crime is by such education as will regulate the passions and take from the mind and heart the disposition to commit it; that is, let the mind be so trained that it will perceive that the commission of crime is irrational and contrary to men's best interests. We contend that men can be made to see and appreciate this idea without supposing that they are real Christians; and so the world may be induced to embrace peace-principles without supposing the era of the millennium.

If we could but forget the traditions of the past—blot out the history which has been written in blood and tears—remove from our Statute books the relics of heathenish laws—reject the false standards of virtue obtained from a military spirit and practice—spurn the seductions of ambition and avarice—exorcise our hearts of the demons of malignity and revenge—and imbue our minds with the teachings of reason and morality—the work of assimilation to the standard of peace would easily and naturally begin and be carried on till society should become conformed to the requirements of peace and reason. Yet let the heroic and military spirit prevail; let reason and thought be ignored, and force be employed in their stead; let the interests of men be disregarded under government, and fierce and unnatural penalties be inflicted; and to the end of time humanity will continue to witness the re-enactments of the scenes of the late war, and the immorality and crime which now pervade and corrupt society, destroy its peace, and fill the jails and penitentiaries with criminals. As society is now organized, it is its own greatest corrupter.

§ 5.—*Some of the means that might be used to sustain government.*

When we studiously contemplate the means employed by the most civilized nations with the view of sustaining government and of suppressing crime, we are overwhelmed with astonishment; but when we learn that these means have ever failed to secure the desired end, we are appalled and dumb in horror. And for dreary centuries the means have been employed, and for dreary centuries they have proved a failure. The governments and the criminal codes of all the ages bear testimony to the failure. And the pertinent inquiry thence arises, *Why is this long continued failure?* Cannot humanity be governed by a more rational, humane system? Must the revolting system of butchering men upon the field and of murdering them upon the gallows ever be employed? Is not the reason of the signal failure to govern in the past evident upon reflection? And is it not because the whole scheme of penal sanctions employed is hostile to the mental and moral constitution of men? God manifestly intended that man should be governed by human law; and so He has laid a foundation for it in his nature. But the attempt has never been made to govern him on the manifest foundation of his nature. The schemes for governing him have ever regarded him rather as an animal being subject to physical penalties, than as a rational and moral being subject to reason and motives. As a material being, he is capable of pain and suffering;

and for the security of peace and order, the schemes have chiefly attached their sanctions to the material nature. But little comparative attention has been given to him as a rational and moral being, subject to those numerous wants intended by God as the basis of his government. His rational and moral qualities, being greatly superior to his material nature, create a greatly superior basis for his government. As all the schemes in the past have nearly ignored these higher rational and moral qualities, so they have proved as nearly failures. If such schemes should not prove failures, they would throw distrust on the moral administration of God, by evincing in Him indifference as to the obedience of man to the laws of His moral government. And upon the supposition that the schemes of men have been in violation of the scheme of God, as moral governor of the world,—as upon careful consideration of it in both nature and revelation, must appear—the only mode of saving them from failure would be by continually introducing miracles into the moral scheme, so as to suit its laws to the incessant violations of it by the human schemes. For the latter schemes, ignoring the action of man's rational and moral nature in relation to his wants and interests, could not do otherwise than fail, unless the divine scheme should be constantly adapted to the exigencies of the human schemes by the introduction of miracles, or the essential nature of man should be changed constantly to fit him to the exigencies of the human schemes. But since the human schemes, ignoring man's rational and moral nature as related to his wants and interests, have chiefly been founded on the idea, *that man is a mere physical being*, the miraculous interference to save the human schemes, would have degraded God's moral government from being a scheme addressed to reason and motives, to one addressed to mere material rewards and punishments. And careful reflection upon the nature of proper schemes of government, will satisfy the mind that the sanctions must, if successful, be generally addressed to the rational and moral nature; for otherwise they will not be responsive to the constitution which God has appointed in and around him; and so must certainly prove a failure. But, because man has a rational and moral nature, it does not follow that the schemes of human government may meddle with matters of religion and conscience, or append sanctions to the *violation of mere moral obligation.* For God allows His creatures to allure each other to virtue, without allowing them to punish for the refusal to follow it. It belongs to us to do good; to God to punish for not doing it.

While, therefore, it is the duty of government to put itself in harmony with the moral government of God, government may never punish for failure to perform mere moral obligations. And without forming government upon the idea that the wants and interests of man are those of a rational and moral being, it cannot be in harmony with the scheme of God's moral government; and to base it on principles in conflict with that scheme, is simply to provide for its failure. To preserve our minds from poisonous error, we must always distinguish between the means which may be used to secure obedience to law, and the penalties which may be inflicted in case of disobedience. They are not commensurate. The highest motives to obedience may be presented, but the highest penalties for disobedience may not be inflicted. Man may virtuously develop all man's mental and moral capacities, and even his spiritual capacities, in harmony with God's moral government; for the more perfectly these are developed, the easier will be his government. But man may not impose physical punishments, *because* he may develop rational, moral, and even spiritual qualities. God reserves to Himself the prerogative of punishing. Hence, man may preserve government and the order of society by appealing to interest, reason, and moral obligation; but, should these fail, it does not follow that he may hang and inflict the desolations of war.

In accordance with this reasoning, the difficulty arises out of man's self-agency: He appoints schemes of government and of social order in violation of God's moral scheme. But God's moral scheme is in harmony with man's rational and moral nature. Hence, man's scheme will not govern God's creature. And so, in the further exercise of his self-agency, man proposes to kill man, because he can not govern him according to a scheme which is at once contrary to the laws of his own nature and the laws of God. And this is the method of all governments founded in force. In them reason is passed by, moral principle is disregarded, and man is treated as a brute-being to be governed by fear of physical punishments. Whereas, if we would conform to the scheme of God's appointment, and thereby secure at once the best government and man's best obedience, the schemes of government and of social order must be reversed, and *primary* regard must be given to man as a *rational* and *moral* being. This would require the reversal of all the parts of the human schemes, reducing them to harmony with man's rational and moral nature, and into subordination to God's scheme of moral government. Were human governments so constituted, with so much experience under them as to show to men their advantage, brute-force would rarely be required to secure obedience—as rarely as it is now employed for discipline under church organizations. Is such a scheme of government practicable? Why should it be thought not so? Has not man all the elements to fit him to it? Let us consider the question briefly.

Successful government is a desideratum to our race. Our earthly interests sustain close relations to it. A sense of quiet and safety in pursuit of happiness, is indispensable to the well-being of society; while the reflex action may largely contribute to the spread of even spiritual and saving truth. Nothing of a mere secular nature can compare with well-regulated government, based on the laws of nature and reason, as the means of promoting and securing men's real interests. Yet it is not that government has in itself a religious or moral element. It has neither. But founded on its true basis, it would afford scope for the development of the rational and moral nature, in connection with interested natural developments. It would unmanacle humanity; and, emancipating *man* from a debasing bondage in the grasp of animalism, it would set him upon the plane of reason and morality. Both man's rational nature and the teaching of Scripture contemplate such a scheme of government. The visions of the Hebrew prophets contemplate just such a scheme; and they are to be worked out through the teachings of the New Testament.

They must be worked out in connection with a scheme of government appointed in harmony with the scheme of God's moral government over the world. They must be wrought out through the rational and moral nature of man. Government must be based on laws in harmony with man's rational and moral nature. Hence, the scheme for which we contend must sometime be inaugurated by men. Morality will oblige them to do it. But whatever morality will ever oblige them to do, it now obliges them to do, unless moral laws do not now morally oblige men.

But how is such a scheme of government to be introduced? Where ought it to begin? It ought to begin at the head of the government. The chief officers of the nation are responsible for the war which so lately desolated the land and so perverted the moral feelings of the people. With no ungodly ambition in both North and South, and with no foul party ends to serve, there would have been no war. On both sides, passion and hatred, avarice and ambition, had much to do in inducing bloodshed. A dare was given and accepted, making the moral guilt equal with both sides. The fountains of power must therefore be purified. The people should put no moral prostitutes into office,—and no man because skilled in the science of human butchery. This would indicate the beginning. Then every military institution in the land should at once and finally be abandoned. For what are military institutions but hot-beds of war? And they are not reliable for the end for which they are instituted. Whence came the "rebel" commanders in the late war? Came they not from West Point? There they were nurtured. And what is our history will, under the like circumstances, be the history of all people: men will take sides according to prejudice, fancy, and caprice, and will not be held to the truth by the morals of a military education.

And let a man but soberly think of a *military* institution—think of an institution whose object is to train men to kill each other!! Yes, to kill each other!—about what? *Why, about the different notions they have of an idea.* Professors—grave men—men calling themselves Christians— are hired at large salaries, and give their time and their talents to instruct rational, thinking beings in the arts and barbarities of human butchery!! Revolting idea! Rational beings subsist on the price of blood. They eat the price of blood; they dress upon what cost tears—upon the anguish of widowhood and the wails of orphanage? The thought is dreadful! At it the heart sickens and the sensibilities faint! It is hard enough to eat the bread of slave-labor; but to eat that of tears and blood, must require a stout heart and a rigid nerve!

But with such institutions in a country, it is no wonder the people have war. Such is human nature, that men will regard with thoughtless indifference the business of their ordinary calling; and will labor to bring their work to public attention. And think of the idea of training men for the business of war! War comes of the lustful passions. It is a part of the schooling, therefore, to instruct the passions to be alive to insult and as quick to resent—quick by physical force to vindicate insulted honor or national fame. Tried by the virtues of such schooling, he who fears the least to appear disembodied before God, he who can be steadiest in nerve with the ghost of death before him, and he who can take the deadliest aim at him who has the misfortune of holding a different notion, is in honor the most unblemished. And this is at once the *war-code* and the *code of honor.* For the two are identical in principle, the former being the latter generalized, and both being in antagonism with the dictates of reason and the teaching of Christianity. And we all know that military schools are by no means nurseries of piety. How could it be otherwise? Christ came into the world not to destroy but to save men's lives; and how utterly unlike Him is the profesional business of teaching the science and art of destroying life!—of destroying by the wholesale.

The next step, therefore, towards the removal of the great crime of war, should be the abandonment of every military institution in the land; while the expenditures attending them should be devoted to the development of the rational and moral nature, by impressing on it the unmingled criminality of war. The true nature of human government might be taught, with the real grounds of the well-being of society. And there can be no doubt that a distinct and impressive conception of the nature of God's moral government over the world, with the idea of the soul's undying nature, together with an accurate notion of the nature of human government, would be of more service to prevent war and preserve government than the mastery of the science of human butchery.

Then but let the cost on one protracted war be expended in instructing the masses in the principles of a scheme of government answering to the moral laws of God, and what would be the result? That we may have some just appreciation of this thought, we may dwell upon it a little. Let us take the United States and the late war. The people of the United States were four years killing the people of the United States. Let us strive to grasp the idea somewhat of what that killing cost; and then so to what extent it would have instructed the people. In estimating the cost, the money actually paid by the government is but a small fraction of the entire cost. We must consider the time of the soldiers on both sides—the time lost by men not in arms—the war-equipage on land and sea—the cost of feeding both

armies at disadvantage—the pay of officers and soldiers
—the value of property destroyed by both parties—hospital
expenses—the cost of enrolling and drafting men—the
expenses of travel and time lost in the whole country,
caused by the war—the millions, if not billions, spent in
luxuries and drunkenness, lechery and revelry, chargeable
to the war—the interest on the mortgage given on the
nation's bone and muscle for generations to come—the
oppressive taxes and exorbitant prices we have to pay—
the loss by idleness engendered by war-habits—the moneyed
value of the slain and crippled in the war, as the means of
gain to the nation—with the thousand other modes of loss
and destruction resulting directly and indirectly from the
war—and it is not extravagant to estimate the cost at fifty
billion dollars.

Suppose this sum, which is, by reason of its amount,
inappreciable by our minds, had been properly expended
in educating the moral and rational natures of the people,
instead of being devoted to their slaughter, would the war
have taken place? Let it have been divided into fifty equal
parts, and one part have been employed each year during
the fifty which next preceded the war—employed in teaching
the people better things than the horrid butcheries of
each other; and would we have had the late war? As has
elsewhere been said, forty-nine fiftieths of men are just
what they are educated to be. The fiftieth one is the
genius for good or ill, rising above or sinking below the
level on which he is trained—rising to think independently
and thence becoming in a sense the reformer, or sinking
into the depths of a deeper iniquity. And think of a
billion, yearly, for fifty years, expended in forming the
human mind! It will pay 300,000 persons more than three
thousand dollars each; and 3,000,000 more than three
hundred dollars, annually, to instruct the young. Three
thousand dollars would have commanded the best talent on
the globe to teach; and fifty years preceding the war would
have carried us to about the year 1810. The influence of

such men, with their hearts set to avoid the horrors of war, would have prevented the war of 1812, which was a political, party war, and have added its cost to the educational fund. If, during that period, we average the States at thirty ; and then divide each State into one hundred counties, and we would have one hundred teachers to each county in the United States. Then the money expended at military schools ; the pay of soldiers, seamen, and the regular army ; the cost of the implements and enginery of war and for all military purposes, during the fifty years, would doubtless have built suitable edifices in every school-district in the whole country.

In this way, the people in each district of the whole land, for the cost that caused them to utter a low deep wail for the slain of the first born in war, might have had a teacher as learned as the Presidents and Professors in our colleges and universities. To form an adequate conception of what must have been the result of such a state of things, transcends the powers of the mind. A large proportion of the people educated to an extent equal to graduation, and educated to believe that God rules over the world in a scheme of moral law, replete with justice and purity, whose final ends cannot be thwarted, and whose laws may not be innocently violated,—and what must have been the result ? Military schools and heroic notions abandoned, and lust and ambition given to barbarians, —what must have been our condition now, compared with the wasted, exhausted, and fainting state of the country, depleted of morals, of Christian charity, by the lancet of war, and reeling, staggering, and swaggering under the intoxication of mad passion ?

Had this rational system begun in 1810, its influence would have been exerted on all the youth of that time, and on all born since. Therefore, in 1861, it would have impressed on the minds of all, under the age of sixty, that men are born to a heritage more noble than dying on the altar before the Image of Horrid War ; and hence the people would have rejected the essentially heathenish idea that, "it is glorious to die for one's country," fighting, at the moment of death, like a wild beast of the forest. And thus taught for only fifty years, the national mind would be lifted far above the irrational animalism of war, and introduced into the elevated regions of reason and morality,—placing it quite beyond the reach of the lusts, schemes, intrigues, and passions which generate all wars.

As just intimated, the intellect of man could form no adequate conception of the results of such a system at the end of fifty years. These results would exert their benign influence in thousands of ways, baffling human foresight to anticipate; and each result would be ennobling to human nature, and constitute a new bond to good government and social order. The beneficent talent and genius of the nation would be developed; and, under the mild sway of peace-principles, these would multiply blessings, in modes now unimagined—searching out the curious and useful laws of nature, and causing them to bow and drop blessings on mankind—alleviating the natural sorrows of the race, instead of whetting the sword of vengeance to add thereto—elevating the race above the passion and animalism wherein all wars find existence, into the nobler spheres of the rational, the moral, and the intellectual—and lifting the souls of men from the shrines of Moloch, to the apprehension and appreciation of the grand and sublime scheme of God's moral government over the world, subordinate to which all human governments must be made before they can either be permanent or extensively bless mankind. In such a condition, instead of the horrors of war, mind would sharpen mind, the benevolent would rule the malevolent affections, and our country would exhibit such civilization, prosperity, intellectual and moral excellence, as would have captivated the nations and set them to emulate us. The national magnanimity would produce an astonishing bond of national unity, which would have taken the place of that bitterness, alienation, and moral prostration now paralyzing the nation. It is urged that *slavery* was the immediate occasion of the late war; and, linked with the corruption of party and of ambition, it was the leading occasion. But if it was the occasion, it would long since have disappeared; for it can exist only where the people are semi-barbarians, its basis being wholly in animal power, and of the exact nature of the use of the sword. Besides, the cost of the late war would have paid more than ten thousand dollars a piece for all the slaves in the country. And slavery never stood upon reason, but always on mere force. Hence, the passions schooled into subordination to reason, and the murderous ones extirpated, public interests would stand on reason and right; and hence, slavery, being a natural evil, and the legitimate offspring of war itself, would long since have been removed from the land, thereby removing the occasion for the war. But the unity of the nation alone, produced by such a system of education, would have preserved the nation from the devastations of war which half a century can hardly repair. A little reflection will satisfy the mind that local pride did much to produce the late war. It was pride, and not moral virtue, that gave slavery the power to bring on the collision. Pride and a love of luxury operated locally on the slave states; while pride produced by contrasting the prosperity of the two sections of the country, operated locally upon the free states. Their combined action brought on bloodshed. That neither party was actuated by moral principle, is evident from the conduct of each. The South wanted the ease and luxury of slavery. The North wanted the material thrift of freedom. And about these they slew each other, demonstrating that neither was controlled by *moral principle.*

Where the pride began, it is not our business to inquire. But when it began to exist, we know it found that wakeful response which, in a few years, threw the nation into the paroxysms of an insane conflict. More dispassionate minds marked the progress of it from bad to worse, till the very worst was reached. For our repose we may begin to consider the subject at a period within fifty years. And alas! how cruel pride exhibited itself! Pride, vanity, ambition—bad trinity!—united! How, in the South, in the North, they vapored! O the swellings of human vanity! How statesmen (?) ventilated in the halls of the National Legislature! The states which, respectively, *they* had the honor to represent, how great! How great the ancestors of each statesman! The chivalry! how it swelled! how it vapored! What a brilliant history had each inherited! What intrepid Quixotes had been the ancestors of all! How grand the proportions produced by the military swellings of the brilliant States of South Carolina and Massachusetts, as, issuing letters of marque and reprisal, they career about and capture each other on the high seas of revengeful debate; or press the enemy in some logical or historical channel wherein he had been driven by astute dialectic chivalry! Then, upon that fact, each little state vapors of the singular excellence of its civilization!—boasts of "the irrepressible conflict" and of the glory of the field whereon his grandsire tried to kill some other one's grandsire! And how great was the glory of the day! when some one cut off some one's head! Pride swelled, and vanity puffed up! What giants in those days!—Yet had pride and vanity attained their climax in empty wind, little harm would have been done. But they did not. There was contagion. Each party denounced the other. Each took its own position as the *measure* of truth and rectitude. Each anathematized the other as an evildoer, in departing from its standard. Local pride lay at the foundation. Neither party *knew* that it was right, nor could know it. For there was no certain standard. Pride, vanity, and ambition, wrought the mischief.

Slavery is a *peculiar interest*, and well suited to inflame local pride in those who oppose it. It fosters bigotry at home, and engages popular prejudice abroad. Pride set slavery on fire. Bad men fed the flames. They spread.

The nation became a vast furnace—an engulfing conflagration, burning, hissing, crackling, and flinging aloft its red forked spires for four long and terrible years, till, exhausted on the one side and nearly so on the other, it lies a smouldering heap of charred ruins, now depleting the people by taxes to rebuild the fabric which folly and wickedness destroyed.

The people had been so little instructed touching the sin of murdering each other, that they rushed fiercely to the conflict. Thousands on each side had no *intelligent* idea of the real principles involved in the war. Each party rang the changes on its shibboleths, and each summoned its hosts to the bloody orgies. Patriotism was screamed, but *bounties* and *monthly pay* were more cogent in their energy. It is a burlesque on human nature and a sad commentary on Christian purity, to witness what ·motives will induce men to plunge into war. One can hardly avoid the belief that the majority of men will little hesitate to commit any crime, if they can be screened from punishment and contempt by the mantle of public opinion. Now it is needless to say that fifty years' training of the national mind under a system such as we have mentioned, would have been a safeguard against the causes which led to the late war in this country. Three hundred thousand men of culture and moral worth, having educated the national mind for fifty years, could have averted the fearful work of bad men, in operating on the vanity and pride of state; while the fomenters of the war might themselves, trained in a better school, have been amongst the efficient educators. And, thus, the identical persons, who, under the influence of pernicious training, became the instruments of our national humiliation, might, under different training, have been the instruments of the national elevation and dignity.

Under such training, it is easy to see that the disappearance of war-feelings would be attended by the disappearance of all the varieties and species of feeling, which, united, constitute war-feelings. Disease located in a vital part, poisons the whole vital economy; and, upon removing the deadly distemper, a general salubriousness ensues. It would be analogous with the health of nations, were they cured of the distemper of war. For war has ever been the malignant disease, which, located in the vital part, has destroyed and consumed the proud nations of the earth. And the removal of war, by some rational method such as has been suggested, would remove from the body politic a vast complication of moral and deadly distempers, which exist in untold forms and degrees of malignity. And the spirit of war is the life of all manner of crimes. War, as a whole, includes all the crimes men commit. It is the generic crime—the most generalized term in any language expressive of crime. Founded on a blasphemous assumption of power from God, and being a usurpation of His prerogatives, its career is but a career of crime; and its spirit is the prolific parent of most of the crimes that afflict society. As a whole includes *all* its parts; so war includes nearly all crimes: It includes murder, robbery, theft, arson, and spoliation; fraud, falsehood, hypocrisy, and deceit; malignity, cruelty, avarice, ambition, and heartlessness; lust, quarrelling, brawling, and duelling; tyranny, oppression, and slavery; the suppression of free speech and the spirit of persecution; the right to kill for opinion's sake, and so the right to make opinions a crime; chicanery, letchery, drunkenness, debauchery, carnality, with all the species of evil and wrong-doing that afflict and disturb organized society.* Nay, it is the very spirit of war that be-

* Many men that are inclined to embrace peace-principles have great trouble in deciding how, on peace-principles, the officers of the law can enforce the sanctions of the law? how they are to arrest offenders who offer resistance? It cannot be denied that the question does involve difficulty. But much of the difficulty is obviated in the idea that the disposition to commit flagrant offenses against the peace of society, is developed from war-principles. It is certain that criminal dispositions do not come from peace-principles; nor does the disposition to resist officers of the law. To violate law, in the first instance, and

gets the state of things which is supposed to create the necessity for war. War is the legion of evil spirits which, inhabiting the body of society, torments it. Exorcise the world of the demon of war, and peace and order will prevail in society. Extirpate the foul spirit of war as brought into action by intemperance, and criminal codes and criminal courts will be much less needed; for crime, as inflamed by strong drink, and as punished in criminal courts, is but a mode of acting out the spirit of war. And, in this form, war costs the state thousands of millions annually. Let the people be educated up to the idea of their rationality and above their animalism, and four-fifths of the criminal courts might be abolished; when the able expounders of the law, at the same salaries, might, as public lecturers, become the able expounders of a scheme of government agreeing with the moral government of God. And with the reduction of criminal courts, there would be a reduction of civil courts; for a large amount of the business of civil courts grows out of the malevolent passions of men and the chicanery

then to resist the officer of the law who may seek to arrest the violator, are the developments of war, and not those of peace. Let the full fruit of peace-teachings become practical over a nation, and there will be few, if any enormous and revolting, crimes committed against society. Let a potent public opinion, firmly and constantly enforce the doctrines of peace; and, first, there will be few persons to be arrested; and, secondly, such arrests as may be necessary, will be more easily made without force *then* than they are with force *now*. The order of society is by no means well preserved by the use of force; and should it not be wholly preserved and become angelic for a generation or even a century, by the use of peace, there would still be a gain in the use of peace, because lives would not be taken. Moreover, we have the right to expect that God would vouchsafe His aid to preserve order, on the supposition that a government based on principles of peace, would be in harmony with His laws and government, and so would secure His approbation. In any view, if peace-principles are right, their reduction to practice will work better than the principles of war; and so the fact that we may not be able to remove rationally every objection that may be brought against them, can be no reason, in the minds of rational men, for refusing to reduce them to practice.

of barristers which are countenanced by the low morals of public opinion. And, slightly trained in the principles of moral integrity, the people would scorn what they now allow in themselves and others, in settling their differences by the uncertain and unsatisfactory processes of litigation. For nothing is more uncertain than a lawsuit; and often nothing is more uncertain than the law itself.

But it is impossible to portray the happiness that might have resulted and the misery that might have been spared, if, fifty years ago, it had been arranged to expend, in the education of the people, the money which, during the late war, was expended in killing them, the expenditure to have ended at the time the work of killing began. That with the education we should not have had war, is as certain as that, without the education, we did have war. And without the war we should have had great advantages: The expenditure would have covered fifty years instead of four, greatly relieving the burden of taxation. Then we should have had the great gain of homes undesolated; lovely districts of country undevastated; the national morals uncorrupted; the body of Christ less divided and less in contempt; the national unity unbroken; the condition of the unhappy and starving blacks much less distressing; manifold blessings added, with peace and plenty where gaunt want and ghastly poverty threaten starvation; more than half a million lives worse than thrown away; and the tears of millions of hearts wrung with anguish unconsolable this side of the grave. Alas! the whole war was a mad and insane adventure—as unwise as it was wicked—as impolitic as it was cruel—as unnecessary as the result is unsatisfactory. Reason set aside, passion revelled in the orgies of murderous hatred and destructive cruelty. As one recalls the whirlwinds of passion, reason reels, and he wonders if the beings whom he meets and with whom he converses, can be the same ones whom he saw driven hither and thither by the wild storms as he has seen the sheaves of fodder on the prairies by the surging tornado. As distance dims the memory of the past, he wonders if all is not the fancy of an incoherent dream, the fancy-paintings of the brain under the ravings of burning fever. And one is loth to believe that a nation of creatures endowed with reason, could be thrown into such spasms and contortions of wild passion. As he thinks, he would that the records of memory were the subjects of his volition, that he might obliterate some of them forever.

But these are rather the negative results which would have flowed from a half century's education. There would have come positive ones. In the way of truth and duty, God would have superadded " good and perfect gifts." We can neither nationally nor Scripturally doubt, that the people who, by earnest and persevering efforts, seek to know and do the will of God, and to bring the scheme of human government into harmony with that of the divine, will be both temporally and spiritually blessed in a high degree. Reason and Scripture unite in teaching us that God blesses signally those who put and keep themselves in harmony with His laws and appointments. Indeed, His laws themselves, appointed in wisdom and beneficence, naturally drop blessings on those who are in tune with them, and curses on those who are out of harmony with them. Blessings and curses are therefore the natural as well as supernatural bestowments of God. If men appoint government out of harmony with the government of God, tyranny and oppression will result; the people will be governed contrary to their interests; their passions will be aroused; they will rise up; and, if the sword is used to subjugate them, war will be produced. War, which is in violation of the laws of God, will be employed to perpetuate a government which is in violation of the laws of God.

Were society organized according to the moral government of God, and government according to society, there could be neither slavery nor war; for both slavery and war result from those departures from the laws of God which produce oppression, avarice, or ambition; and thence call for the sword to maintain them. And men may reason as they please, and start such plausible theories as they please, but no form of society or of government can accord with the laws of God or be permanent, unless based on the principles of peace, which are the principles of thought and reason.

§ 6.—*Objections to the preceding section noticed, with other incidental thoughts.*

Rash and impetuous men tell us that, as human nature *is*, government can be maintained, only by appealing to the sword. But we utterly reject that idea, because it utterly rejects the idea that man is a rational being. We admit that man is incapable, without Divine aid, of rising to a *saving* knowledge of God, but reject, as cruel and barbarous, the notion that a scheme of government cannot be appointed which will secure his approbation and support;—deny that, with proper instructions, he cannot be attached to his political rights and material interests so as to be rationally governed by them. In the preceding section, we endeavored to suggest some considerations showing how this can be done, and to illustrate the principle by the calamities of our late war, exhibiting the wisdom and economy of governing men as rational rather than as animal beings; and our late war proves that it would be better, more economical and successful, to use millions to educate rather than dollars to kill; while history demonstrates the failure of war to support government, and that of judicial murder to preserve the peace and order of society. And we argue that the pecuniary cost of war, which has failed to secure the desired end, would succeed in accomplishing it, if expended in the proper education of the people—would sustain government on the basis of reason and interest, and remove, in addition, a large proportion of the crime committed against society.

But our mode of dealing with the question will be assailed by all manner of objections showing mental imbecility, moral stupidity, logical obtuseness, and scornful infidelity.

With some it will be criminally novel. With others, it will suffice that our fathers did not adopt it. Others, still, will quote Greece and Rome. But the great and supposed conclusive objection will be, that it is directly in the face of the late war waged in the North against the South. The truth of the objection is admitted; but we deny that a theory and principle are false because opposed to the acts and practice of any nation or all the nations of the earth. Our concern shall not be great about what rashness, thoughtlessness, or even malice, may say, if, as the nation emerges from the sea of blood in which it has been baptized, Christian people and true statesmen will devise some human method of saving future generations from the horrors of war. And though men may rail against our reasoning because it condemns their late horrible conduct, we may still ask them in dispassionate reason, whether it would not be better to yield the barbarous custom of war, and make the attempt to govern reasonable beings by reasonable considerations? And we put to the objector the question and urge him to answer, CAN RATIONAL MAN BE GOVERNED AS RATIONAL MAN? If he cannot, then we ask the second question, *Shall men be destroyed by the sword because they cannot be governed by reason?* If men cannot be governed by reason, is it reasonable to destroy them for what they cannot help? But if they can be governed by reason, shall they be destroyed by the sword, without making an adequate effort to govern by reason? We ask reasonable men to consider these questions. Force has been employed during the period of sixty centuries, and at a cost variously computed from fourteen to thirty-five billions of lives, without any very marked success. Would it therefore be utopian for the nations to make an honest effort for ten or fifteen centuries, to govern rational beings upon reason and principle,—spending in their education the amount which, upon war-principles, would be spent in killing them? Such would be a fair and humane experiment at least. And if the business of slaughtering them by thousands of millions has been thought worthy to engage genius and learning, what shall be thought of the business of training them so that there shall be no need of slaughtering them? If the business of training them in the art of stepping, marching, and countermarching, so as to facilitate the work of killing, is worthy in men of learning and genius; what shall be thought of the business of employing that learning and genius so as to obviate the need of marching, countermarching or killing? Men are far gone in utopian dreams and farther gone in worse than utopian morals, to prefer the former business to the latter; especially with the teaching of history as to military failure, and that of Christianity as to military morality.

And will even rash men affirm that a few thousand earnest men, filling high positions, North and South, could not have saved our nation from the calamities of the late war? No candid and intelligent man will deny that up to the very hour of hostilities, a few earnest souls might have spared the country the horrors of fratricidal war? The number of righteous men that would have saved Sodom, if they had been found at Washington and Richmond, could have saved our country. But they were not found; and so fire and brimstone, iron and lead, rained upon the doomed cities and plains of the United States. And thus it cannot, with a decent pretext, be said that our land might not have been saved the horrors of being drenched with fraternal blood, if the people had been properly trained, or if the church and ministry had done half their duty without such training.

Let one consider carefully the scheme we have suggested, carry it out in detail; and he will no longer deny that rational beings may be governed by rational considerations; nor will he contend that they must be coerced to pursue their own interests.

We shall be asked, What would you have done when the Southern people seceded? We answer, we would simply have let them go. They had that inalienable right.

But then, we shall be told, they would have made slavery more perpetual; and is not slavery a great wrong and crime? We admit both branches of the proposition: slavery is both a wrong and a crime, and it might have been made more perpetual. What then? May one part of a nation kill another part for seceding and establishing slavery? This nation did the same thing less than a century ago. Had England the right to slay us for it? She had the same right the North had to slay the South. A wrong and a crime in one people do not confer on other people the right to kill them. The South had the right to set up another government, but had not the right to establish slavery under it. But if it abused its right, in establishing a wrong, the act could not confer on the North the right to slaughter the people. All nations have wrongs established by their governments. If, therefore, that fact gives the right to others to destroy them, there is the right for mutual and universal wars among the nations. We shall have occasion to allude to this branch of the question again.

It will be urged, as it has a thousand times, that other nations are rapacious and draw the sword; and hence that we must draw it or take the risk of being invaded and destroyed. But such objection is founded in bad morals and shallow philosophy. For when scrutinized in morals, it forms that miserable system which inculcates the doctrine of "counter crimes." And stripped of that deceptive appearance of right which addresses itself to the selfishness of the heart,—suited the better to mislead, because there is the appearance of right—it leads to the logical conclusion, that no one nation is morally obliged to act otherwise than the surrounding nations; and that is the same thing as to say, There is no rule of moral obligation higher than the morals of nations. This is simply a form of that atheism, adopted by Hobbes and others, which teaches that the law of the land is the highest rule of morality, and the will of the prince is the measure of duty. But, since the rule of moral obligation is the same for nations as for individuals,—the morals of a nation being composed of the aggregate morals of the individuals of the nation—it would logically follow from such reasoning, that no individual is morally obliged by any law different from the customs which prevail around him ; and hence that one may protect himself by using whatever means custom sanctions. Logically and practically, the principle will take this general expression : Surrounded by piratical and plundering nations, any nation may, by the rules of morality, practise piracy and plundering : and surrounded by a lying, thieving, and adulterous people, any individual may, by the rules of morality, practise lying, stealing, and adultery.

And this is the boasted war-argument. It is used by men whose intelligence would be insulted, to hint that its dignity is scarcely above the stupid. Nay, grave men, would-be statesmen and theologians ycleped, assure us solemnly, that the prevalence of the barbarous customs of war justifies the use of the barbarous customs of war. The *argument* is the same as to say, The heathenish customs of idolatry justify the heathenish customs of idolatry. And this is one of war's strongest arguments. The pulpit has thundered it, and called those who oppose it " dreamers " sleeping in the light ; and their own thundering they called " Christian patriotism.

Cousin-german to the foregoing, and employed by pulpit performers, is that other objection to abandoning the sword, which may be thus expressed : *If all men would observe the precepts of Christianity, there would be no need of war; but while they refuse to do this, war is a necessity.* But here is the culmination of both folly and wickedness. It is simply the arraignment of the wisdom of God ;— simply condemns Christianity as the standard of right and wrong, and as the rule of practice in life. It is virtually saying, The moral laws of Christianity would oblige *us*, were we not wise enough to see that they are wholly impracticable ! It is logically saying, We war-men would be glad to obey the precepts of Christianity and heed the voice of

God, were we not satisfied, if we should, that the best interests of society would go to ruin. If *all men* would only obey the requirements of God, they would *then* be wise, and *we* would obey them ; but, since bad men will not obey them, it is not wise for us to do it, and we must preserve the right by disobeying God. If all men were truly Christians and would keep Christ's precepts, war and judicial murder would not be needed ; but since they are not, the requirements of God are unwise, cannot be obeyed, and war and judicial murder are necessary to preserve the state and protect society.

And such is the logic, nay, morality too, of the war men. Miserable is the business of war ; and miserable, the logic, reasons, and morality urged in its support. For the best reasons and the purest morality that can be assigned to justify it, can as plausibly be assigned to justify the worst crimes men commit.

But Christians, at least, should turn away from the wretched logic and morality of the war-advocate. To them all such reasoning should be regarded as moral poison. Yet, who has not heard professed Christians pray for the time to come when the nations should learn war no more, and before the words had cooled upon their lips urge that war is consistent with the precepts of Christ? But if it is consistent with them, we might pertinently ask, why pray that the nations should cease to fight ? If war is consistent with Christianity, why pray that it may cease ? If it is not consistent, how can Christians engage in it ? One is sometimes tempted to fear, that *fighting* Christians are not marked for their candor. They reason and act very much as slaveholders used to do. And no genius can show a point of harmony between the precepts of Christianity and those cruel and murderous usages necessary to war. The precepts of Christianity regard man as a rational being belonging less to time than to eternity. But those of war regard him as a material being belonging alone to time. The precepts of Christianity would exalt him in the scale of existence, and make him the friend of angels and of God—would inspire him with lofty conceptions and endless hopes. But those of war degrade him in the scale of being, and make him the equal of the bear and the bulldog—would inspire him with neither conceptions nor hopes beyond a seared conscience and a bloody grave.

By what casuistry can Christians urge the continuance of war on the ground that bad men violate Christian precepts and reject Christian morality? In any cause but war, such logic would be esteemed as not less dishonorable to the head, than as corrupting to the heart. Think of such an argument in the mouth of Jesus and the Apostles. It would run thus: If all men would only be Christians, idolatry *should not* be practised. But as all men are not Christians, men may use the customs of idolatry, till all men do become Christians. We must deal with men as they are, and not deal with them as if they were as they should be. So professed Christians reason about war: We cannot stay the tide of sin which produces war, and so we may use the wicked customs of war, till the wicked customs of war make all men Christians, and then there will be no more need of war. If men will do wrong, we have the right to do wrong and kill them for it. But if all men would only do right, then we, too, could do right. Luther might also have employed the Christian war-logic thus: The commentators, fathers, and saints of the Church, have interpreted the Bible to teach Popery, and all people practise Popery. Therefore, I may continue to practise Popery till it issues into Christianity. But so soon as all men become Christians, it will be a grand thing, and I shall not be slow to practise it.

But it may be urged that we could not foresee fifty years ago that the nation would be wasted by distressing war, and why should so much be spent in educating the public mind so as to avoid it. True, this identical war might not have been anticipated. But all history lifted to our ears the voice of warning, and showed us our liability to be wasted by war, unless we abandoned its maxims, and trained the people to be governed by reason instead of the sword. And there are indications that this nation shall have another bloody baptism in less than fifty years, unless it shall abandon the miserable maxims of war and the more miserable morals in which war finds its support. For it demands no remarkable prescience to discover the elements which are likely to develope into another fraticidal struggle. It is only necessary that the selfishness which produced the late conflict should be allied with newly developing interests to bring it about. We may see in a general way, how it may be done. And, first, the nation has adopted an *axiom* and a *principle*, which are mutual destructives. The *axiom* is that of liberty and of self-government; the *principle* is that of coercion. Now, secondly, these mutual destructives will endlessly keep a *large* nation in strifes, feuds, and civil wars, unless, first, men cease to have those wants which are relieved by means of government; or, secondly, they grant the right to men to pursue the interests that are responsive to their wants, free from the terrors of the sword.

If the late war has not besotted the national mind by inuring it to the tyranny of the sword, a new sense of personal liberty will spring up in the hearts of the thinking,— and they will become more deeply imbued with the practical spirit of the Declaration of Independence. Thence they will see more and more clearly, the true objects of government, and will not hesitate to make it subserve their interests. As the undeveloped resources of the Territories lying towards the Pacific come to be settled, there are likely to arise interests which will conflict sharply with those of the Eastern States. These conflicting interests will demand different schemes of policy and call for different legislative action. For some years, the East may be numerically stronger than the West; and will naturally, though, perhaps, not always justly, give character to the legislative action of the country. And such policy being adverse to the interests of the West, it is easy to foresee that the West will become restive, as the South did when it saw its slave interests imperilled. Rasped for a time under what it will regard as unjust because not promotive of its interests, it will complain, scold, storm ; and finally meditate the practical adoption of the self-evident truth, that the people of the West are endowed by their Creator with the inalienable right of "rising up and shaking off the existing government, and forming another one that suits them better." And when that hour shall come, will a wronged people be deterred from asserting their rights, by those sterile dogmas of that purblind theology, which declare that "traitors to the government are rebels against God," for seeking such government as is suited to promote their interests? Such theological nonsense is available to promote the objects of the selfish and ambitious ; but, preached to a suffering people, it will be impotent as it is contemptible. It might impress the conscience of a New England manufacturer and bring a *silvery* tear to his eye ; but it would fall as harmless on the ear of the Arizonian as a rain-drop on his parched meadow. And reason as we may, and build a cob-web of sophistry mountain-high about us, unless all history is a lie, men will scorn and trample under foot the government that fails to secure or promote their interests. And that is strictly right. But let the East retain the idea that it may call to its aid the fanaticism of the pulpit, the passions of the interested, the hopes of the ambitious, and the power of the government ; and the natural result will be another bloody war. For the West will do as the South did, though two swords to one should gleam over their heads to deter them. Because, with the false right to make war assumed, men adopt other false and superstitious notions which delude them with the hope of success in spite of inferior numbers and resources. They arrogate to themselves *right* and *bravery;* and thence become infatuated by the idea, that *God* favors the right, and will give it the victory. The idolatry and heathenism of the infatuation are forgotten in the absorbing notions of self-complacency.

War must thus be the inheritance of the people who hold at once the right of self-government and the right to kill men for attempting to maintain it. One or the other of the principles is a lie and a delusion, and must be rejected. And the great question for this nation to decide is, which shall be rejected. Reject the right of self-government,—the manifest tendency of the age—and we go into despotism. Reject the other, and we must lay aside the sword as the bond between the subject and the government. It has been the effort to show in the foregoing pages that it is better to put away the sword. Men would then have in fact what they now have only in theory. *Actually* grant them the right of self-government, based on a scheme which is in harmony with the laws of reason and nature, employing, to educate them up to the demands of such a scheme, the money which would be used in slaughtering them under the present system of government, and the whole general notion we have of a free government will be attained. Men will then sustain government because government sustains their interests. Such will be free government. Nothing else is.

But fanatical and superficial people persuade themselves that, slavery being the cause of the late war and now being out of the way, hereafter the nation will be in no danger of being torn by civil strifes and desolated by the ravages of war. But such a conception is as delusive as it is shallow. The real cause of the war was the danger of supposed interests, which chanced to be in the form of negro slavery. Any other interests of the same magnitude, in whatever form arising in the future, will equally lash the passions into fury, induce a rebellion, and precipitate war. The amount of interest involved in slavery would induce either the East or the West to revolt in solid phalanx, in any future time. Touch deeply the manufacturing interests of the East, and all the cant theology of the world would be insufficient to induce the belief, that the act of rebellion would be sin against God. And a vast deal of *our* theology is a new coinage made to suit the exigencies of war. Like the postal currency, should such a rebellion take place, the old stamp of theology would be valueless, and a new issue would be forthcoming to meet the new demand.

Whence slavery was but the occasioning cause of the late war; and he who thinks the nation illiable to war because slavery is gone, but shows his puerility and ignorance of political philosophy. Unless all history and experience are false, our nation can be exempt from war, only by abandoning the maxims which lead to it. To be exempt, it must build the political fabric on man's rational and moral nature. It must educate instead of slaughtering the people. Self-destructive principles must be disunited, and those containing the poison of war must be rejected. And if these things are not done, in the fitful history of extinct nations, we may sadly read our own. Proud as we are of our national inheritance, and dismal as the picture may be, we must destroy the sword or the sword will destroy us. We may continue to fight and die, or we may cease to fight and live. Which would we rather do?

And here a very serious question is presented to the thoughtful mind: As the people of this country are now educated, are they capable of self-government, as founded in the laws of nature and reason? * Let us endeavor to

---

* Our hope of safety lies in the agitation of some novel political questions, which may enlarge and purify natural rights, and thereby cleanse the Augean Stables. The abolition of Negro Slavery presents a novel and difficult question. Should the freed African have the elective franchise? All rational men must admit that he is a human creature. And if so, he has *wants* just as other human creatures. The color of his skin cannot afect his wants; and in the estimation of God there may be no difference in a black or a white skin. We are told that God is the common Father, and that all are made of one blood. And a rational mind could scarcely affirm, that a little more intelligence in the white race gives more assurance of its favor with God. If *more* intelligence secures more favor with God, devils might stand before the

make the idea intelligible. We do it in this way: Let two men, equal in ability, come before the people for office, say for Congress. One may be a man of incorruptible integrity; and the other a smooth, plausible, heartless dema-

white race. But God gives *charity* as the standard of excellence; and therein, all things considered, the African race is hardly inferior to the white race. That the Negro does not so readily receive *our* civilization, may be nothing against him; since it is not easy to say upon the whole, whether it is a curse or a blessing to men. It is certain that it is a patchwork of Heathenism, Judaism, Popery, Barbarity, and Atheism, mixed with a modicum of practical Christianity. And it is essentially a materialistic civilization. There is little real pure spirituality about it. Our people, as a whole, dwell in materialism; and war is the natural outgrowth of a selfish materialist idolatry—outgrowth of the selfish worship of the things which are seen, in forgetfulness of the things unseen.—And upon supposition that the right to vote determines the means of securing worldly interests, *on principle*, it is impossible to say that the manumitted slave should not have the elective franchise. He is in this country without his choice; and his ignorance is the result of a system of wrong and outrage forced upon him. And to urge that such disadvantages, forced upon him, should be employed still, to his injury, is to add cruelty to injustice. In principle, it maintains the justice of one wrong by the infliction of another. If our reasoning heretofore is correct, that God ordains the *exousia* or *authority for government*, all men have the right to enjoy the benefits of any government where they may choose to live; and in justice have the right, the instant they come under it, to help decide all questions connected with its working. For the *exousia*, existing by the *creative act of God*, men have no right to restrict it to one class of human creatures. Created by the act of God, the *exousia* is a trust to be used for the benefit of all the rational creatures of God. "The earth is the Lord's and the fulness thereof; the world, and they that dwell therein;" and man's rights upon the earth do not permit him to limit the trust of government to any classes or colors. By the laws of nature women have the same right to the elective franchise as men—the black races the same right to it as the white races. And all human creatures have the right to migrate to any part of the earth, and carrying with them their wants, they have the right to enjoy the blessings of the government, with the additional right in common with others of saying how the government shall be managed; while their views of religion, of philosophy, or of politics, may in no respect be called in question so long as they are orderly citizens. The negro, *not even woman*, is an exception to the

gogue. Which will be elected to office? In the great majority of instances, will not the artful demagogue? And is not such the history of politics in this country? The late war was precipitated by the intrigues of such demagogues. For years, few of the great or honest men of the nation have been in office. Such men have been in obscurity, unwilling to sacrifice probity and conscience, and become the objects of odium and slander for the sake of office. And hereafter things will in this respect be worse, unless some of the agitated reforms redeem us. With the national con-

rule. He belongs to the human race; and that entitles him to all *natural* rights. The vulgar prejudices against rights and justice on account of color, or former condition, or anything peculiar to his person are below contempt. Yet the principle exhibited herein may, in charity, sometimes be modified: 1. Charity might allow the natural right to be restrained for the general good, as the waywardness of youth may be held in check for its good. Long down-trodden and wronged, the condition of the freedman is a delicate one. The manner of his manumission is far from challenging the approbation of reason. And while negro slavery is bad enough, it is not the worst of evils. Compared with war, it nearly ceases to be an evil. It is true that it grinds life out slowly, but it does not destroy so suddenly, both soul and body, but affords a ground of repentance and a ray of hope for the future. The difference is the difference between imprisonment for life and suddenly breaking the neck on the savage gibbet. Still, upon the whole, as the best thing that can be done, the freedmen should have the elective franchise as the means of educating themselves, as well as securing their worldly interests. But, 2d, if bestowing the franchise will reduce the races to a marriageable equality, it would be cheap to give the black race half the territory for a nationality of their own, rather than amalgamate the two races.

But neither the right nor the expediency of giving our females the full prerogatives of the elective franchise can be questioned. Masculine arrogance has long usurped despotic mastery over the best portion of humanity; and, in the effects of breaking that tyranny, we may find our future safety. But things continued as they now are, the hope of this nation is not cheering. It might not be an unwise experiment to break all the manacles of slavery and brute-force, and allow all that have the characteristics of rational manhood, unlimited by sex or color, to say how they prefer to pursue their own happiness, as the opposite method does not solicit, in its results, our special approbation.

science blunted by the corruptions of war, *military titles* are to be the evidence of competency to official position hereafter. Without merit or grave reflection, this and that hero is to be thrust into office; and, in a free country, of all men military men should most warily be chosen to office. Inured to arbitrary power and the disregard of forms of law, generally self-willed and imperious, familiar with suffering in others, with little sympathy, it involves no little hazard to commit the destinies of a free people to their hands. Yet as this nation is educated, the people look to and confide in military men. With *both political parties*, demagoguery is the staple. And in nominating candidates they vie with each other to see which can have the greater number of military men on the ticket, that they may play the demagogue with the people; while, as trained, the people are not unfit subjects of the imposition. Knowing no better, they are satisfied with what they think the best they can get. In this country it is difficult to find a man who will not tell you that it is your duty to vote for the best men offered for your suffrage, and that those of his party are the best. For the political morality of this country stands continually at neap-tide, while, without a radical change, ruin as certainly hangs over free institutions, in this country, as the flow of time is certain. For our government is but an immense business-partnership, of which all the people compose the firm. The officers of the nation are the clerks, salesmen, book-keepers, etc. And the durability of the concern will depend on the integrity of those who conduct the business. If they are dishonest the concern will end in bankruptcy; and that end is only a question of time. As educated, are the people competent to select honest managers of the concern? Dishonest employées, looking to their own and not to the firm's interests, will bring failure. The war recently brought us to the verge of failure and bankruptcy; and our peril is still great. About our future, dangers lie thick. We have launched our all on the treacherous sea of passion. Storms menace our burial beneath them. The ship of state needs new managers; and she is not a war-ship. Our safety lies in escaping from the sea of passion, and being deeply-based on the shores of reason and morality. Wherefore, our only security against final and fatal wreck, lies in educating the people so as to cause reason to take the place of passion.

As *men* have made such fatal and deadly blunders, and, as from their side of the question, the rapid tendency of this nation is to a centralized and imperial despotism, it might be wise in us to extend the rights of suffrage to our wives, mothers, and sisters, to see whether the refinements of their more impressionable natures would not outweigh in its elevating conservatism, he belligerent ferocity of woman's lordly tyrant during the ages of the past. Sometimes, experiments ought to be carefully guarded against as fraught with perils. But there is little to risk in breaking the shackles from the hands of women. Hitherto the *philosophic* sex has so signally aborted, after rivers of blood have been shed, that heroism may hopefully be exchanged, for a thousand years or two at least, for " the more unreasoning and certain guidance of refined female instinct." Give her a voice, at least in saying how her soul shall be taken out of her body, when she errs; and, if fight, we must still let her bear an equal part in the *honors of the bloody field.* If she sins against the majesty of a barbarous law, let her be tried by twelve women because the Saviour had twelve apostles, and not by twelve of her oppressors. And let *her* peers act as *her* counsel, define the law for her; and let her say a word, not that she shall not die, only *how* she shall die. Let not her lordly persecutor persecute her by saying that she shall die with a rope around her neck, if her delicacy should suggest to her a method that to her should seem preferable.

CHAPTER IV.

VARIOUS OBJECTIONS NOTICED.—INDEFINITE SECESSION.

VARIOUS objections have been urged against the idea of sustaining government and preserving order on peace-principles. Some persons have contended that those principles are impracticable; some, that they are visionary; some, that life must be taken by the sword and capitally that justice may be vindicated; while one has urged one objection and another has urged another. Some of the objections urged have been anticipated and answered, and others demand a more formal consideration; while some that have been alluded to may again be mentioned.

Now, if it is true as we have contended, that God nowhere, in either nature or revelation, authorizes life to be taken; and if at the same time it is true, that He ordains the existence of government, requiring men to live orderly and peaceably under it; then, all possible objections that can be urged to our mode of arguing are at once and completely answered. For if our train of argument is correct, it embraces within its scope, the answer to every objection that it is possible to urge against peace-principles; because, saying that God ordains government and order, and disallows the use of the sword, is saying either that government can be sustained on peace-principles, or that God is unwise in ordaining the existence of a thing while He disallows the use of the means necessary to sustain it. And there can be no mistake about this reasoning. If God disallows war, it is never necessary to the well-being of men; and if God disallows life to be taken, it is never necessary to take it. Therefore, the whole question of peace and war depends on the single question, *Do s God authorize man to engage in war or to take life?* If He does, it is right; if not, it is wrong. If the reasoning in PART FIRST of this work is correct, this question must be answered in the negative. And if it is answered in the negative, men have never derived benefit from war or the infliction of capital punishment; because no benefit can be derived from disobeying the laws of God. For the whole principle of our reasoning lies just here: *It is never necessary nor expedient to disobey or violate the laws of God.* This is the hinge of all our reasoning. The necessity for government is conceded, and also the necessity of obedience. But if God disallows war, it is not necessary: and the same thing is true of capital punishment. But there is another phase of the question: There are those who think war and capital punishment wrong, but contend that self-defence to the extent of taking life is right. But the three supposed rights stand on the same ground of reason; and they are all equally unwise and unnecessary if God disallows them.

God has made duty and interest coincident; and, therefore, it is always both wise and pious to obey His laws. Whence, if God disallows war, it is unwise and impious for men to engage in it; if He disallows capital punishment, it is unwise and impious to inflict it; and if He disallows taking life in self-defence, it is unwise and impious so to take it. Acts which are impious are sinful, and so have the disapprobation of God; but those which are unwise will fail to secure the end for which they are used. Now, our argument is, that *Revelation* shows these acts to be *impious;* while *history* and *experience* show them to be *unwise.* A thing is unwise when it fails in the end for which it is designed; and if war, capital punishment, and self-defence in taking life, have failed in accomplishing their end, they are unwise; and if they are unwise, then God did not design that they should be used. This unavoidable inference grows out of the fact that the divine constitution has that fitness which always makes God's appointments attain their designed ends. If men can prove a thing to be *immoral,* they prove it to be unwise at the same time; and it follows thence that it will not produce a beneficial natural result. To apply the principle: If the sword is not the means which God intended for supporting government, its use will not succeed. But all experience proves that war has not succeeded in supporting it: hence, the inference arises as strong as all experience, that war is not the means which God appointed to secure that end. We do not argue indeed that *all* seeming success proves the approbation of God. That is not the basis of our argument. Our argument is based upon *natural suitability to attain a result;* and not on accidental, occasional, or partial success. And *real* success implies the attainment of the desired end through moral means or through means allowed by God's laws. Thus, the government of England was never a *real* success, because it never conformed to natural law and right. Nor would the success of the British arms in holding the allegiance of our ancestors to the English Crown, have been a real success, since coerced allegiance is violative of natural right. The dominion of Great Britain over Ireland is not a success. Nor is the subjugation of the South by the North any more a real success than the perpetuation of slavery by the South would have been a success had not the North prevented it by the ravages of war. True, the North *prevailed* over the South by *might;* but that is precisely what the South *intended* to do with the slave, in order to perpetuate his bondage.

Mere might and coercion are rather badges of failure than those of success, because they imply the absence of reason and assent of will. Divine wisdom accords with this sentiment: "If a man also strive for masteries, yet is he not crowned, except he strive lawfully." Thus, is a *crown* properly worn, only when *lawful* means are used to attain it. Hence, no end attained by *unlawful* means, is properly a success. It is for this reason that we can no more regard the subjugation of the South a success, than we would regard the continued enslavement of the Negro race, by the South, as a success. And, generally, nothing is a success that implies wrong in obtaining or continuing it. In harmony herewith, Bishop Butler says, "The whole analogy of nature shows that we are not to expect any benefits, without making use of the *appointed* means for obtaining and enjoying them." "Now," he continues, "reason shows us nothing of the particular immediate means of obtaining either temporal or spiritual benefits. This therefore we must learn either from experience or revelation." "*Benefits*" come only by "the *appointed* means." This law pervades the whole economy of nature. If therefore the means employed generally fail to secure *benefits*, we may know that they are not "the appointed means," and hence they *are* unwise, and *may be* sinful. And since revelation teaches that the time *will be when men shall learn war no more*, it follows by rational induction, that war is excluded from the fitness of the Divine Constitution. And since revelation teaches that the type of government shall be much higher when men cease to fight about it, it follows that war is not "the appointed means of obtaining and enjoying" the "temporal benefits" which it is naturally suited to bestow. And this is also a complete answer to all possible objections that can be urged against peace-principles as "the appointed means for obtaining and enjoying" the ends of civil government. And since "reason shows us nothing of the particular immediate means of obtaining" the ends of government, and since "experience" shows that the use of the sword has failed to secure the "benefits," reason suggests that the sword is not the appointed means to that end. And the teaching of revelation showing that civil government will ultimately and more fully be sustained without the use of the sword, it inevitably follows, that the use of the sword violates the fitness of things, or the laws of God in the Constitution of Nature ; and therefore its use fails to sustain government and to secure its benefits, by failing to use the appointed means to that end. And herein is contained a demonstrable refutation of every objection against abandoning the use of the sword. Yet, as there may be those who will not grasp this succinct, though demonstrable, answer to all possible objections to abandoning the use of the sword in the interests of government, it seems proper to turn attention more particularly to some of them.

During the late war, an analogy was instituted between the life of a nation and that of an individual; and then the act of waging war was put on the ground of self-defence. And thus, appealing to the selfishness of human nature there never was found a popular argument at once more plausible and captivating, or more hollow and sophistical. And it is plausible and delusive in both branches; for it is founded at once on a false principle and a false analogy. It is so plausible, so false, and was employed with such fatal effect, that we shall devote a section hereafter to its exposure.

Another plausible but false process used to urge on the late war may be thus stated: "If the South may secede without coercion, then every State in the Union may secede; and if every State in the Union may secede, every County in the State may secede; and so we shall cease to have *any* government." Millions of people regarded this sophism as conclusive. Upon its strength, millions of armed men invaded the territories and desolated the homes of the South, and subjugated the Southern people. We admit that those who were satisfied by this argument were honest so far as men can be, while they are led by passion and false principles. But the Southern people were honest under the same limitations. Paul was honest, too, when he persecuted the infant church; and so were the opponents and persecutors of Luther, and the Puritans who hung Quakers. They were all honest under control of the "lusts that war in the members." *Mere wantonness* has rarely actuated the conduct of the most cruel of mankind. The cruelty which is manifested under some plausible but perverting hallucination, is that which has most affected and wronged our race. Crusaders, persecutors, witch-hangers, and warriors, all come under the same general laws of morality, and in their belief and conduct are alike honest and mistaken in thinking they "do God service." And there is no shadow of doubt that coercion by the sword may as properly be used to prevent secession in the church as in the State. Popery has ever regarded "it as just; and it *has* all the cogency of argument that the State can use for it in its interests. We have seen how the Papal bulls hurled anathemas at Luther, because secession uncoerced would open the door to indefinite division of the church, and its consequent ruin. But no such ruin followed, though secession did largely take place. Instead of ruin, enlarged liberty of conscience resulted; and from that liberty of conscience came the civil liberty which the people of the United States enjoy. Luther's secession was the principle which ultimately gave men whatever relief they have from spiritual thraldom; and political secession is the principle which is ultimately to give all men political freedom. And Mr. Lincoln was right in theory, when he said, "*This is a most valuable, a most sacred right—a right which, we hope and believe, is to liberate the world.*" Had Mr. Lincoln practiced his theory, posterity would have regarded him as the apostle of political freedom. But he did not; and thereby he lost the golden opportunity of the century, to place humanity on the exalted plane of civilization above the barbarism of the sword. And had he met boldly the exigencies of the hour, no other civil war would ever have occurred among the nations professing Christianity. But he employed not "the appointed means for obtaining and enjoying" the "benefits" of civil liberty; and in consequence starvation came on the one hand, and oppresive taxation on the other. *To prevent imagined* evils the sword was used and *brought actual* evils. Hence, we have two distinct and conclusive answers to the argument of *indefinite* secession." The one is drawn from the principles of reason; the other, from those of revelation. We shall notice the one from revelation first.

All sane men must admit that war is an evil; and that it is employed because it is thought that it will produce good. If any should be so lost to all reason as to contend that war is *not* an evil, we should regard it useless to reason with them; and so we assume it as undeniable that war is always an evil. If it is an evil, then sane men must use it because they think it will do good. Now, with these premises, let Paul decide the question. See Romans, 3:8. In substance, he asks, "Shall men do evil that good may come?" He then indignantly replies, "The damnation of those who should so contend would be just." And reason concurs in the decision of Paul. Meeting *imagined* wrong, or evil by *actual* evil, is a flagrant violation of the laws of our reason, meriting the indignant scorn of all right-thinking men. So says inspiration, and so says right reason. Let men *plunge* into the horrible sins and crimes of war, to prevent the imaginary evils of secession, and their condemnation therefor will be just. This brings the matter to an issue. Inspiration affirms, the war-man denies. Let thinking men judge between them.

But, apart from the indignant reprobation of Paul, reason furnishes a conclusive answer to the argument of "indefinite secession." It lies in this principle: Society is composed of individuals who have the same nature *in* society, that they have as individuals. Hence men are in no more danger from that "indefinite secession" which will work harm to them, than they are from engaging in other enterprises which will work harm. States and nations love, in the aggregate, the same interests that individuals love. The same laws that induce individual enterprise, will induce State and national enterprise. And the same laws that induce individuals to seek co-partnerships, that means and talent may avail to accomplish what individual enterprise cannot accomplish, will induce the millions which are necessary to form government that its ends may be accomplished. And as the motives which induce the formation of a partnership are sufficient to continue it as long as it ought to continue, so are the motives which induce the formation of government sufficient to continue it so long as it ought to continue. The moment either the partnership or the government ceases to attain the end for which it was formed, is the moment at which the injured party may justly put an end to its existence. Any other principle consists not with reason or justice, and cannot inure to the benefits of mankind. Nor is there danger that the principle will be much abused. Like all principles applicable to men, it will occasionally be abused. But the principle itself, like all the laws of God, involves its own corrective. The abuse of it will fail to bring the desired benefits, and thereby will secure the proper punishment, and suggest the proper remedy. The principle is as obvious and constant as the laws of agriculture. And so certainly as the sluggard fails to reap, so certainly will *improper secession* receive its adequate punishment. So surely as the man who violates the laws of nature by putting his hand in the fire, is punished for it; so surely would the men who should violate the laws of nature by irrational secession, receive a just and proper punishment for it. All the twaddle about *indefinite secession* is as ridiculous as it is absurd.

This is in accordance with the conception of Jefferson, as an inference from the history and experience of men. He says: " Prudence indeed will dictate that governments long established should not be changed for light and transient causes ; and accordingly all experience hath shown that mankind are more disposed to suffer while evils are sufferable, than to right themselves by abolishing the forms to which they are accustomed." No doubt *all* experience does establish this conclusion; and, in establishing it, it also establishes that there is nothing in the ghost of secession to frighten sensible men. That *prudence* which is the perfect safeguard against *indefinite secession*, results from the constitution of the human mind, as is shown by *all experience*, if Jefferson is right in his conclusion.

Prudence, then, dictates the conclusion, which is confirmed by all experience—*that government* is in no danger from *indefinite secession*. And it may be observed, too, that the experience of the church accords with that of the State. Luther's secession was far from being what Popery charged upon it. On the contrary, it brought religious liberty.

A little experience, with the application of reason, will infer the same conclusion in respect to the State. Sober reflection presents the whole objection in a light both ludicrous and absurd. But think of a country's undertaking to bear the expenses of the whole machinery of government! And it is only less absurd to suppose that an enlightened state would undertake such an enterprise, thereby foregoing the benefits which reason suggests would result from the numbers, means, talents, and experience, implied in the notion of a more extended and rational government. But, in the language of Mr. Lincoln, suppose some *State* should conceive the idea of "rising up and shaking off the existing government, and forming another one that" the people thought "would suit them better," what harm would result, *if the use of the sword was abandoned ?* Let us look at the matter for a moment. Put away the sword, and what harm would even the division of a government do? No lives would be lost; the country would not be desolated; there would be no burning, stealing, ravaging; there would be no "suspension of all the laws of morality," as Robert Hall expresses it; there would be no blasphemy, no drunkenness, no swaying to and fro of invading and retreating armies. None of the nameless sins, crimes and horrors of war, where would be the great wrong in dividing one nation into two? Agriculture, trade, and commerce, could go on as before. Friendly relations would not need to be disturbed. Imaginary lines between different friendly states could not affect the laws of production. Let the nations, then, cease the absurd and savage acts of going to war, and where will be the harm in dividing nations so as to promote the interests of the different parts of them—dividing them upon the principles of peace, suggested by interest, and controlled by the dictates of reason and justice? And let it not be said that men will not thus *act* on the principles of *peace* and *reason*. We are not arguing about what men *will* do. We are only arguing about what they *ought* to do. *Reason* is our guide; and it is only for us to show what would be the result of conduct under the control of reason. Whether men will follow the course of conduct dictated by reason, is another question. The course of behavior is left with men themselves. If they will fight and make war, *peace*-principles are not chargeable with such behavior; and it is only for us to point out the result to which they would lead if they were reduced to their full practice. And it is manifestly unjust to charge on peace-doctrines results which justly flow only from war-principles. Yet this is the manner in which war-men nearly universally reason. Now, let us try the division of a nation on peace-principles and note the result. Half a nation thinks its interests demand a separate government; and, accordingly, the nation is divided. There is no war, no raging passion, no burning and revengeful feelings. Each part of the nation or each new nation pursues its ordinary pursuits without molestation. Friendly relations continue, trade goes on, and no harm is thought of the seceding party's doing as it had the inalienable right to do. In a government like ours, a single State secedes. There is no war, no anger, and there are no invading armies. Where then will be the crime, the sin, the wrong in the division? If the seceded State prospers, if the people are happy and contented, and all the ends for which governments are instituted are attained, the act of separation would prove to be founded in wisdom. The smiles of Providence would be on the people. On the contrary, should the people of the seceded State fail in attaining prosperity and happiness under the new regimen, themselves would be the sufferers, and all the weight of their folly would lie on their own shoulders. Would not the *remedy* for their evil be readily suggested to their minds? And would not the punishment incident to their condition be ample for their folly, not their crime?

Upon this principle can any man say, rationally, that the interests of the people in this country, as a whole, would *necessarily* have suffered by the separation of the South from the North, and the establishment of two friendly governments? Or can any man say, rationally, that even the appalling horrors of the late war, would, upon war-principles, deter the South from repeating the attempt at secession, should its future interests prompt it strongly, the moment it has the persuasion that its power and resources give assurance of success by violence? On the contrary, is it not evident to the dispassionate mind, that two just and friendly governments would be infinitely better than the discord and hatred which the different sections of the nation now have, without considering the bloodshed we have had, and the burdensome taxation we must have for generations to come? We are therefore constrained to reach the conclusion, that a more specious and shallow sophism and delusion than that of "indefinite secession," was never successfully practised upon a people. And, surely, a more fatal one has rarely been practised.

To the abandonment of the sword, there is another specious but sophistical objection, which is held by a class of persons who are very different from those who cry the alarm at the idea of *indefinite secession.* This class of persons hold that the sword—holding it as the symbol of all forms of legally taking life—was put by God into the hands of the *magistrate*, to secure order and justice among men. And this class has two subdivisions; one holding that Christians may never engage in war or call for protection or aid from human law; and the other holding that Christians may seek both and engage in war. But reason stands against both of these classes. Both these parties, it may be observed, agree that *unregenerate* men may, by the laws of God, wage war in vindication of justice. Whence it inferentially follows that the sword may be used by non-Christians for the ends of *justice*, either individual, social, or national, involving self-defence, war, and capital punishment.

But since man has no absolute ideas, he has no absolute knowledge of right and wrong. Hence, he does not possess within himself a positive measure of justice and injustice, right and wrong. Therefore, in considering this objection, the first step is to find a *rule* of justice and right, whose opposites are injustice and wrong. And since man cannot find the rule within himself,—if it exists at all, it must be outside of him. There are two possible sources whence he may find such a rule external to himself—they are, first in the laws of nature; second, in those of revelation. These two sources of law may differ but never conflict. Nor, do they differ, only as the laws of the Gospel are added to those of nature. But, darkened by sin, the human mind is not able to know that its conceptions of the laws of nature are coincident with the laws themselves; and so it is unable to draw thence an unquestioned rule, or standard of justice. Hence, the mind cannot affirm with certainty that what it *conceives* to be justice, is justice. And since the human conception of justice may not be actual justice or even an approximation to it, too much uncertainty attaches to take human life to satisfy such demands of justice; because the *rule* of justice may differ as widely from *real* justice as the mind now differs from what it would have been if it had never been tainted by sin. And after what we of this generation have witnessed, in taking life in order to appease the exactions of justice, one could fain hope that all rational men would be content to let such justice go forever hereafter unsatisfied.

We have then the laws of revelation left as the alternative source of justice whence to derive the right to take human life; and hence is presented the old inquiry, Does God in His revealed will authorize the taking of human life ? This general branch of the question has already been considered. Yet it may be necessary to turn attention for a moment to that class of persons who believe that the sword is placed in the hands of the Magistrate for the vindication of justice. This aspect of the question presents the following consideration: Does the Gospel forbid in the Christian as sin, what it allows in the sinner as right? That is, Does the Gospel allow *unconverted* men to engage in war, while it forbids *converted* ones to do the same thing? The affirmative of this question must be unsound. For all men are obliged by the same law, though all may not be able to keep it in the same sense. How is this made evident?

The moral laws of the Gospel do not differ from those of nature. The Gospel, as such, is a remedial system appended to the moral laws of nature, leaving them wholly unchanged in their provisions and obligations. First, the laws of Moses, so far as they oblige all men, are but a more distinct statement of those laws which would have been intuitively perceived by all men and always observed by them, had not their minds been darkened and their hearts hardened by the fall from God's favor. The moral laws of God are eternally immutable, because founded in infinite wisdom. Hence, the lapse of man from the favor of God could not change God's law, nor man's obligation to it. But the law under which man was created, was the law of *love ;* and so all men are still *obliged* by that law, though sin has disabled them to keep it in a state of nature. And, secondly, as the moral laws of Moses are only a republication of those of nature made more distinct than they could be perceived by the depraved human mind ; so the moral laws of the Gospel are, also, a republication of those of nature more clearly and emphatically exhibited than they were by Moses. Both laws are the same in substance. For if Jesus said, Thou shalt love thy neighbor as thyself, Moses enjoined the same duty in the same words. Love was the rule of duty before the fall ; and love is still the rule. Indeed, love is the rule everywhere, obliging devils no less than angels, and sinners no less than saints. It is the law, because it was the law of the universe before the introduction of sin: while the introduction of sin cannot change the obligations of immutable law upon the sinner, whether man or devil. Whence, the greatest sinner, just as the greatest saint, is bound to love his neighbor as himself, though rankling hatred fester in his heart. Paul, the malignant persecutor, was obliged by the same law of love as Paul, the aged, feeling that he could be *accursed* for the sake of his kinsmen in the flesh. The law did not change to suit his different states. Its obligations continued the same. It obliged him when blind the same as when he was made to see—obliged him the same when a sinner as when a saint. Love obliged him in all mortal and moral conditions. And Moses declares love to be the law of nature; while Christ enjoins the same law, declaring it to be the sum of the law and the prophets. In keeping the original laws of nature man would have lived, as in violating them, he died. Hence, Moses says, "Cursed be he that confirmeth not all the words of *this* law to do them;" or as Paul renders it, "Cursed is every one that continueth not in all things which are written in the book of the law to do them." The law is the same still. Could men keep, in its true intent and spirit, the real significance "all things written in the book of the law," they would still be entitled to endless life. But the introduction of sin has rendered it impossible to live by the terms of the law, because no man liveth and sinneth not; and so it comes to pass, that a man is not justified by works of law, but by faith in Jesus Christ. And it is evident that no man is justified by law in the sight of God; for we are assured that, The just by faith shall live. Neither by the law of Moses, nor by that of nature, can a man live because "the law is not of faith;" while it is only "the just by faith that shall live." But it is evident that the exercise of faith cannot repeal the obligations of the law, nor release the *converted* from those obligations. They remain constrained by its requirements as before their conversion. Their relations to the laws of nature are unchanged by the exercise of faith. The effect of their conversion is not to change their relations to moral law, but it is to bring them into harmony with moral law: the change is in the mind of the person, and not in the laws of nature. The principle of love is created or revived in the heart; though no change is made in moral or natural law. The converted man is obliged to love his neighbor as much before conversion as after, though before conversion he cannot do it. The measure of one's *ability* is not the measure of his obligations. On the contrary, the unconverted man is obliged by the same law of the converted man to love his neighbor. In short, the condition of the man affects not the obligation of the law. The Christian and the non-Christian are obliged alike by those changeless laws which are established in the constitution of things, and neither can, by any possibility, keep them perfectly while in the body. Hence both, if judged by the laws of nature, must finally be lost. However, the exercise of faith brings the Christian under the provisions of the gospel, where, for the sake of Christ, all his failures in "confirming all the words of the law," are pardoned, and the benefits of the gospel, growing out of the relation he sustains to Christ, are so given to him as to stand instead of his "confirming all of the words of the law." But the sinner, having refused to exercise faith, and failed to "confirm the words of the law," will be judged by the immutable moral laws, without any benefit from the *remedial* provisions of the gospel, and hence must be condemned. But it will be observed that the remedial provisions of the gospel, in no respect change or suspend the obligations of natural or moral law. They only provide a way of salvation through Christ, without a perfect obedience rendered to moral law: they save men by the obedience of faith. The gospel, therefore, differs from the moral laws, by adding to them a great system of remedies, which confirms their excellence, at the same time presenting a scheme of aids and curatives, by which those who accept them may be saved by favor, without a literal compliance with the obligations of moral law. Yet these remedial provisions, in no respect change the obligations of moral law. Whence, the moral law continuing wholly unchanged under the gospel, it is not true that *unregenerate* men may engage in war any more than regenerate ones; and it is not true that wicked men may inflict the death-penalty more than righteous ones. There is one moral law to all intelligent beings, the wicked as well as the righteous, the fallen as well as the unfallen angels. Whence, it is wholly untrue, also, that the gospel allows the indulgence of a single passion by the vicious, forbidden to the virtuous. Hatred, malice, revenge; ambition, avarice, and lust, with all the elements which form the compound sin of war, are forbidden by the laws of nature as by those of the gospel; and hence are forbidden alike to the wicked and the righteous.

Our argument did not logically demand the special refutation of this error, as it is shown in the *first part* of this work that God has nowhere granted the right to take life. Still, it seemed proper not to omit a point to which some might attach importance. It is not an answer to this reasoning to say, The law is made for the disobedient, and that Christians are not of this world. Make the sanctions of law accord with moral law, and Christians may enforce them. We are not opposed to legal sanctions; we are only opposed to appending to laws immoral sanctions.

CHAPTER V.

PECUNIARY ASPECTS OF THE WAR-QUESTION.

IF there is any force in what is said in the foregoing pages, or if reliance can be placed in the teachings of reason, it is evident that governments are instituted by men for the security and promotion of their various interests;—that property may be protected, life rendered safe, and the people made happy in the enjoyment of both property and life, with all their incidents. Connected with the life in the flesh, is that higher spiritual life, which, gazing beyond the veil, dawns on the soul the glimmerings of the mysterious and endless future. And as that awful future has rational and moral relations to the present, involving freedom of thought and action, it is the duty of government to secure its subjects with it to the largest extent. Because we have material bodies, whose happiness depends on the acquisition and enjoyment of property, it should ever be the care and solicitude of government to render the citizen secure in its acquisition and enjoyment, levying upon him the smallest amount of taxes consistent with the absolute necessities. And all experience shows that property is acquired by the masses in the ratio commensurate with the security the subject has in the enjoyment of it. Hence whatever disturbs that security, becomes the enemy of the general weal and the destroyer of the public happiness. But the fell demon of war is the deadly foe and destroyer of all these. He breathes by turns his disease engendering breath upon them all; when, seized by contagion, with contortions and paroxysms, surrounded by gloom and confusion, they all expire together. And so intensely noxious is the foul breath of this demon of perdition, that it destroys whatever is lovely and of good report, coming within the reach of its deadly contagion. Breathing on governments, they disappear; monuments, and they crumble to dust; laws, and they are lost; cities, and they are not; institutions, and they are no more; nations, and they vanish; wealth, and it is consumed by flames; happiness, and it becomes tears and sighs; homes, and they are desolated; national morality, and it becomes a sepulchre of uncleanness; religion, and it becomes a by-word and hissing. All over this fair country, it has breathed its malarious breath, producing physical contagion and moral leprosy; while God alone has a just conception of the tears, and suffering, and anguish it has caused. The thoughtful contemplation of its horrors, appalls the heart in gloom and the soul in deepest sorrows.

But turning aside from a picture so touching and revolting, we may properly bestow more special attention upon the *pecuniary* aspects of the foul demon of war. Yet nothing like a tabular exhibition of its destructions shall be attempted. Like its sorrows and anguish, the all-seeing Eye alone can know the extent of its destroying influence. Yet manifold are the injurious effects, which we may recount, upon the material interests of a people. The mere moneyed expenditure of the government is a small fraction of the cost of war. Still, this is inconceivably great. But the mind will better comprehend the injuries of war, by looking at the subject in departments. Even then the aid of the imagination is necessary adequately to grasp the subject.

First, then, consider the cost of the mere implements of war, nearly worthless in themselves. It is said that, during our late war, more than three million men were called by the North alone to take up arms; and supposing the South called two millions, we would have, in round numbers, five million rational beings, called by two earthly potsherds, to slaughter each other about their notions and prejudices of a worldly good. Now, compute the cost of the rifles, muskets, pistols, swords, bayonets, and knives necessary from time to time, for these five million men, amidst the captures, destructions, and reverses of war! Hundreds of millions—sufficient to send Bibles and peace-missionaries to the uttermost parts of the earth—were wasted here alone. But to these must be added ammunitions—powder, lead, cartridges, and the numerous things, too ingeniously invented, for the purpose of desolating and destroying. Then put to the account the artillery, and its varied, complex and costly machinery—cannon iron and brass, in all sizes, calibres, shapes, and varieties—and with them, carriages, wagons, horses, mules, equipage, powder, balls, shells, etc., etc., as the necessary attendants. After these come army-wagons of all kinds and in immense numbers, with ambulances, carriages, and vehicles, for transporting baggage, luggage, and provisions, the sick, the disabled, the wounded. Then must be added the cost of horses, mules, cattle, drivers, managers, suttlers, attendants, with hangers-on various and diverse—thieves, pilferers, bawds, loafers, vagabonds, characters hard to enumerate and impossible to describe—filling highway, by-way, hedge, ditch, and field for dreary miles together. And in the first engagement, the men are shot, wounded, killed, mangled, or taken prisoners; while the long array of costly implements is captured and carried off, consumed, wasted, or given to the flames; and are consequently a wreck and loss to everybody. But should the implements escape destruction and survive the horrors of war, they are valueless for any desirable purpose. If we turn to the navy, we behold a similar condition of things. But think of the cost of a single gunboat, all bristling with guards and cannon, finished up in a style of magnificence worthy a better end than to be spattered with blood and brains, and be cumbered with broken limbs and dead bodies, and the dying, groaning, and mangled in all the hideous forms of shrieking, suffering, and expiring humanity! Yet, contemplate the hundreds of these "floating palaces," these lazar houses of moral leprosy, hot-beds of physical contagion and hideous death, which belong to the *civilized and Christianized nations* of the earth;—costing more than the intellectual, moral, and spiritual culture of the people! And they are all nearly useless aside from the ends of destroying bodies and souls.

And as, in the proper sense, the enginery of war is useless to a people, so the skill, labor, and material, are a loss to those who construct and own it. Therefore, the loss is treble—the things produced are a loss, the time of producing them is a loss, the material is a loss; and it may be added that the purpose of the things produced, is to cause destruction.

Then consider that instrumentality of war known as the Regular Army—that morbid, painful tumor upon the body politic—a dangerous, incurable cancer, unless extirpated root and branch, ever keeping the nation in a state of feverish excitability, while it is ever gnawing at its substance and eating out the vitals of its prosperity. It acts in the double ruin of national wealth—it produces nothing, and consumes much; and causes incurable moral pestilences amongst the nations. Heathenish in its origin, barbarous in its nature, destructive in its object, immoral only in its influence, it is the bane of the people's peace, their corrupter and oppressor, the invader and destroyer of their liberties. And it is truly the cancer which gnaws away the vitals of the nations.

It is worthy to be noted how war penetrates and disturbs all the wealth channels of a nation, destroying positively and preventing negatively, the accumulation of *interests*. Let us illustrate by reference to our recent war. As has been said, the Federal Government called for three millions of men, while the Confederate States probably called for two millions. Suppose that, during the whole war, one half the number called for was in actual service. We then have the spectacle of two and a half million men suddenly called from the various departments of active and productive industry to be put into the army. Suddenly leaving their old pursuits, they necessarily leave them under great disadvantages to the national wealth. And they not only cease to be productive operatives under circumstances of disadvantage, they also become active and profligate consumers of the existing national wealth. They are consumers in the ordinary way of living, and destroyers in the extraordinary way of war. Let us elaborate a little. A call is made on a people to pass from the condition of peace to that of war. The call itself or the supposed necessity for it, inflicts upon them the terrors of a panic, unfitting them for the presence and coolness of mind which are the requisites of all safe business transactions. While under such panics, all acts performed are liable to be prejudicial to the general economy. Acting under a panic, men always act unwisely and foolishly. Everything is done without reflection and by impulse, and so is done badly: present interests are sacrificed, neglected, and disregarded; present callings are unadvisedly forsaken—new ones are unadvisedly assumed; the community is thrown into feverish excitement, bringing on the body politic that kind of general stampede in which men run pell-mell, flinging away guns, coats, blankets, hats, and even side-arms, and make haste to take care of themselves by rushing into danger. And as such a panic soon pervades a whole army, imparting to it a wild and unguided impulse; so may a whole nation be brought under the impulse of a wild and unguided impulse, by the pervasive presence of a war-spirit.

Hence, in the very elements essential to war, we have those most unfavorable to national economy. All the regular conditions and on-goings of society are disturbed, and great detriment is done to the interests of the country. In this respect the late war in this country must have cost billions. Suddenly leaving all channels of industry to take care of themselves, thousands entered on new and untried experiments, suffering great losses, and sacrificing moral integrity. A few made princely fortunes, it is true, but they generally cost the honor and the honesty of the makers.

Two and a half million men, taken from the classes whence our soldiers came, ought to add to the national wealth from two to five times what they received for their services as common soldiers ; but, during the continuance of the war, they produced nothing, either valuable or desirable to the nation, and consumed and destroyed billions. Hence, here alone was a loss of from two to five times the sum paid the soldiery for their services. But what was paid to them was a total loss, because the war itself was at once a curse and calamity to the people. To the loss of their time and to the payment for their service, must be added the expense of feeding and clothing two and a half million men during four years, together with the gamblers, thieves, cutthroats, swindlers, bawds, and other straggling and loose characters which are the deformed births produced by the throes of war. For they all had to be fed and clothed, and that under circumstances detrimental to economy. At a heavy expense, the provisions had to be carried from where they were produced. And then, by the act of carrying, they were subject to loss and damage ; and were, also, on the arrival at their destination, inferior in quality and healthfulness. Then, by reason of other consequences of war, they cost twice or thrice what they ought, in their production or purchase. Finally, upon reaching their destination, all parties handling them, reckless by the very training of war, are wasteful, careless, and indifferent in their management. And these conditions combined are fearfully destructive of the interests of the people.

And we must never forget that the whole end of all these expenses is to destroy things already in existence. The cannon, the sword, the bayonet, the standing army, the navy, the military schools,—all the implements of war, and all its objects, *are to destroy.* War means destruction. Vandalism and outrage are its essential attributes. Victorious or not victorious, a moving army lays waste, destroys by fire, by sword, and by ravaging the country;—amidst friends or foes, an army steals, burns, and destroys. Millions and billions are lost by greed, by flame, by avarice, by vandalism, and by the wantonness of barbarism;— houses, barns, and fences are needlessly burned; timber is recklessly destroyed; valuable property is consumed for fuel; districts of country are overrun and laid waste; fields of golden harvest, inviting the reaper, are trodden under foot; and marching or encamped, the business of an army is to destroy.

Then, the uncertainties created by war deter men from sowing and render them indifferent to the productions of the fruits of the earth, not knowing who shall gather them. And the cautious and careful refuse, also, to invest or use their capital, unable to apprehend whether the income shall be for the benefit of friend or foe.

In war-times turn our eyes where we may, and we behold the channels of wealth clogged or destroyed. For real wealth comes from the producing classes; and in all civilized countries, they compose the large body of the people. Hence, upon the sudden eruption of war, much the larger moiety of those who fill the ranks of the army must come from the producing classes. Instead of being producers, in the army they become consumers, really producing nothing and profligately destroying much. And the producing classes being suddenly diminished, and the consuming classes suddenly increased, the laws of demand and supply are disturbed, and the whole economical policy of the State becomes diseased and deranged. And the necessary principles of war, being violative of the natural economy of things, the longer the war continues, the greater must be the diseased and deranged condition of the functions of the nation. Like the diseased and deranged condition of our animal economy, a nation may survive the shock of a severe paroxysm, but the disease continued beyond a given point, national dissolution becomes inevitable. The late war in this country would have produced anarchy in the Northern States, if it had continued a year or so longer. Disease was seizing hold of those vital ligaments which render society cohesive, and was rapidly destroying them. Eruptions on the body are the outward evidence of inward disease. And so eruptions in the body politic are evidence of disease in the bonds which tie the social fabric. The New York riots and the extensive secret societies formed throughout the Western States, during the late war, were the symptoms of fatal disease in organized society, produced by the malaria of war; and had the cause continued a little longer, a wild chaos must have commenced its dissolute reign. We-were rapidly approaching a horrible abyss of atheism, war, and terror such as that in which France was once engulfed, and from the same general cause. Open, revolting atheism engulfed France; but the atheism of the heart, forgetting God, engulfed us. France threw off even the forms of religion, embracing atheism in its amplitude and logical sequences. We retained the forms of it; but, rejecting its spirit and power over the life, embraced a real atheism only less intense than that of France, because the paroxysm of war was of shorter duration.

When by dissolute thoughts, the passions and lusts become stronger than the love of real interest, the preliminaries of war are settled. A people thus situated but awaits the occasion which they can themselves soon create, to plunge into the depths of war. And the financial condition of such a people will conform to the violence of the belligerent paroxysm. But when events portend a war-storm, men look about for some sort of shelter against its violence; and find it in withdrawing from circulation all the gold and silver they can command. And the gold and silver thus withdrawn, the representative of value is diminished, and a stringency is felt in money-matters. But war begun, its exigencies become imperative, though gold and silver have diminished, so that the urgency cannot be met. Thence moneyed expedients are devised, violative at once of morality and economy. In our late conflict, the expedient was to issue "greenbacks," and *call* them money. By a national law which was alike unjust and contrary to the spirit of the government, these were made *legal tender*, forcing the people to accept promises for money. Having no intrinsic value, these promises soon depreciated, and gave a fictitious and uncertain basis to all the interests of society. The increasing exigencies of the war and the diminished value of the national promises, created a necessity for throwing into circulation a vast number of these promises, the increased quantity having to compensate for the diminished value.

The effect of throwing vast quantities of depreciated promises into the veins of commerce, with great uncertainty attaching to their ultimate value, was to create feverish excitement in the national mind. In violent fevers, the pulse quickens, the brain is wild, the mind is irrational and wanders; and the man has hallucinations, dreams, fancies, and reveries. The condition is dangerous, because, against nature, it indicates disease. It is so with nations. The national money-veins may be full of the unhealthy blood of unnatural currency. Then one dollar may become three, and rush with feverish rapidity through the veins of commerce. The national mind becomes feverish, wild, and irrational. The people dream, have fancies, and reveries. In their illusions, they talk of national prosperity—speak of their increased riches, when they only have depreciated promises, which, by the fiction of a dream, they call money. But the whole process is simply depletive of the national wealth, as fever wastes the natural body. The influences of thrift are but the illusions of the disease. The inflated currency proves a healthy national condition, as feverish blood proves a healthy bodily condition. It proves the exact opposite. For it shows that the nation enters the market at a disadvantage exactly measured by its depreciated promises. When, therefore, its promises will buy gold in the ratio of three dollars to one, the nation enters the contest of trade with three to one against the interests of economy. Hence, the immoral and dishonest trick of the national legislature in compelling the people to accept one dollar instead of three. Such dishonest legislation does not tend to redeem the national credit, but it reduces the credit of the citizen to a level with that of the nation.

War creates high prices in two ways, each prejudicial to national prosperity. First, it draws productive operations from the business of creating, and puts them upon the business of destroying. The consequence must be to reduce the supply and increase the price. Then, secondly, it induces government to trade on a scale too large for its capital; when, menaced by failure in a true business sense, it tenders promises to pay instead of payment. Then, fearing competition, it interposes legislative action, *compelling* the people to accept promises as cash. But legislators cannot change things; though they may call promises payment. However, the people, true to their instinct of interest, will exact as many promises as will be an equivalent for what they give in return. In war the government must have money, but persists in calling, it may be, its *promises* money; while the seller practically neutralizes the trick, by saying he will part with what the government must have, when the latter delivers to him three dollars in promises, when he would accept one in coin. Thence, to meet the necessity it complies, flooding the country with promises, which, in this country, are contained in "greenbacks." The country thus flooded with depreciated promises made legal tender by law, gives to everything a fictitious value, and sets all things in a whirl of uncertainty.

Grave consequences grow out of such a condition of things. No real value is added to anything. Yet all the natural avenues of trade are disturbed, the currency, being mere promises, is inflated and uncertain, and a spirit of excess and extravagance is created—extravagance in living, in speculation, with a general recklessness extremely inimical to political economy. And the laws of economy not only are violated; those of honesty, justice, and morality, are trampled under foot. High living, extravagant dressing, hard drinking, extravagance, revelry, take the place of moderation, plainness, candor and sobriety of thought and behavior. The spirit of war is necessarily the spirit of atheism—is a want of confidence in God as a moral governor of the world; and hence it necessarily disturbs, deranges, and demoralizes the whole conditions of society.

War—a thing so unnatural—prevailing for a time, the laws of demand and supply become deranged upon a larger scale. Labor becomes scarce. Material for manufacturing becomes scarce; and hence manufactured articles become scarce. But the madness of war continuing, supplies must diminish till the natural consequences work suspension or ruin to manufacturing interests. Upon suspension, innumerable evils arise, all violative of economical interests—the manufacturers are driven out of business and all their hands out of employment, and the former are rendered unable to pay their liabilities. Their failure to pay will disable many more, producing severe loss and widespread confusion. The operatives thrown out of employment, adds to the confusion, subtracts more from the limited supplies, increases the prices, and aggravates the evils. Everywhere evils come to prevail, and exorbitant prices arise, while everywhere the horrors and feverish excitements of war increase the evils. It is possible for a wild delirium of deadly excitement to prevail all over a great nation called Christian. Recently, it did prevail all over this nation.

As the starting-point of war is wrong and criminal, so every result that it legitimately involves is wrong and criminal; hence the detrimental results to a nation. We cannot rationally expect that war will bring to a people anything but multiplied evils. Accordingly, it is impossible to contemplate an aspect of it which is not productive of evil and only evil.

In our recent sanguinary struggle, no one can be ignorant of the general and fearful panic, which, at the beginning, seized the people and paralyzed the economical interests of the nation. Property depreciated. Commerce stagnated. All the material interests of the nation were congested and threatened with ruin. And things thus continued paralyzed, till the terrors of bloody war formed new channels and produced unhealthy, spasmodic, and feverish activity in other directions—the activity itself being destructive of the real interests of the nation. And who can compute the loss which must occur to thirty millions of people, who are prostrated and paralyzed, for some two years smitten with helpless impotence by the fell terrors of war? The aggregate loss must have been billions.

Then the business of volunteering began in earnest. And what business it was! Speakers scoured the whole country; called public meetings, and brought millions from their business avocations, to hear tissues of bitterness, malice, mendacity and party hatred, at once corrupting the public conscience and injuring the public interests. All the time thus lost was money lost; and, North and South, millions were thus lost to the nation. To this, other millions must be added for waste of time by the volunteers and their relatives in preparing to start to their rendezvous. Then from the moment the idea of volunteering entered the mind of the soldier, he added little to the economical interests, but became destructive of them. He was restless, feverish, and inattentive; and, in too many instances, upon reaching the rendezvous, he became not only a nuisance but a curse—visiting dairies, orchards, and hen-roosts, demoralizing himself and annoying others by petty larcenies. From the moment the soldier volunteers till months after his discharge, he is a pauper on the national charities, on private charities, or lives by means less honorable. After his discharge, he may be either a curse or a blessing to society, and is frequently the former. Flattered by a false and corrupting public sentiment, he returns home intoxicated with exalted notions of personal importance, and filled with the idea that, hereafter, he is to be regarded as a benefactor of the race. Upon this illusive fame he lives, spending his time and money if he has any, in tippling, gambling, and lechery, till, penniless, he finds that the people care as little for him as for any other implement which they use to accomplish their purpose and then cast aside. And thus living till necessity impels to some kind of business, honest or dishonest, the number that choose the latter may be inferred by the shocking crimes they commit all over the country. Thousands are thus the predatory pests of society, prowling a living from others. Pause, reader, and contemplate the time and money lost to this nation by the mental and moral habits engendered by the late war! Sobriety, morality, and virtue, are elements of positive wealth to a nation. They will compensate for sterile soil, unfavorable climate, and absence of mineral resources. In this respect alone, the people of this country will suffer loss for half a century, and will lose sufficient to educate the children of the whole nation.

In counting the cost of our late war, we should not forget what the people spent in time and money, by visiting battle-fields and their children or relatives far distant in the army. And millions must be added in time and money spent in seeking sons, brothers, fathers, husbands, relatives slain on the hostile field, or dying in hospitals, that their remains might be interred in the family cemetery. To this must be added too the losses occasioned by friends sorrowing for those absent in the army, for those who fall on the bloody field, or expire in the damp and dismal hospital. But where shall the cost of war begin or stop? Who shall catalogue the losses of war? It corrupts the people. It drags men from useful avocations. It deranges the channels of commerce. It collapses the energies of the people by panic. It draws wealth-producers from their employments, and puts them as leeches on the public treasury. It deranges manufacturing and agricultural interests, reversing the economical laws of both. It deranges the laws of demand and supply, and aggravates the derangement by depleting the coffers of money and flooding the people with depreciated promises. It congests the national energies by investing all interests with uncertainty. It renders the products of the soil scarce, enhances their value, and oppresses the poor. It creates false conditions in society, and tempts the poor to imitate the opulent in prodigality. It draws the laboring classes from the production of things promotive of human comfort, and puts them upon the production of war-implements, used only to destroy both human life and comforts. It calls millions from their quiet homes and from peaceful industry, to butcher and be butchered on bloody fields. It pays billions, by bounties and monthly pay, to hire men with immortal souls to slaughter each other about different notions. It slaughters millions who might add thousands of millions to the national wealth. It destroys at once the lives and the usefulness of the citizens of the State. It deranges the whole machinery of society. It delights in destroying roads, bridges, houses, and districts of country. So it has done in this country. It has laid its foul and godless hand upon every human interest, and upon nearly every human heart. It touched the people, and they were seized by moral contagion. It touched the material interests of the nation, and they lay prostrate of paralysis. It touched the exchequer, and the gold and silver disappeared, and paper promises swarmed amongst the people like the flies and locusts of Egypt. It touched the church, and its spirituality departing, it prostrated itself in piteous idolatry before the blind image of political power. It touched the essential principles of freedom, and liberty lay prostrate in the dust. It touched the press, and the freedom of speech and of manhood fled from the land. It touched the people, and bound on them the galling yoke of slavery from taxation. It touched and broke the manacles of slavery on the black race, but fixed a burden only less intolerable on ten times the number of the white race. Whatever it touched, it blighted ; and wherever it looked, it breathed pestilence and disease. Properly, it conserved nothing, but desolated everything. To say that it cost the nation fifty billions, is to make a low estimate. Then we must add six hundred thousand lives lost by the sword, the young men of the nation, half as many more blacks and whites lost by starvation and the consequences of the war ; and what a dismal work it has been ! Yet, what is the benefit?—what to the black race, what to the white ? Not prepared for freedom as reason and Christianity suggest, the poor black race are infinitely cursed. The whites are also cursed—cursed politically and pecuniarily, morally and religiously. The integrity of the nation, too, has been tarnished—the spirit of the Constitution despised—the letter of it frequently violated ;—while itself has been used as a cheat and a fraud, to advance the dishonest ends of parties and politicians. To one half the nation it has been for years a lie and a deception, holding over them the terrors of coercion and the oppression of military despotism; while the people as heartily despise it, as Ireland does the British rule over them, or the Cubans the Spanish rule over them. The Constitution itself is hardly longer an aegis or a buckler. The stars and stripes, unfurled, scarcely symbolize protection or freedom, security to life or liberty ; they are rather the degraded badges of partisan ends, the symbols of terror and dismay, military despotism to one half the nation and oppressive taxation to the other. And all is the natural ripe fruit of war.

And now we shall be placed under obligations of gratitude to the advocate of war, if he will render *one* rational, Scriptural, or humane consideration for war. But this he cannot do. Instead of *reason*, he must employ *passion*. Throwing fanciful sanctities around government, he invokes some shibboleth of passion,—it may be some such heathenish saying as, " My country, right or wrong," or those other words of folly and impiety, " My God and my country "—the former really rejected and the latter idolized—when the hue and cry are raised; reason is drowned; humanity is ignored; Christianity is hushed to silence; while the wild storm of passion prostrates all things before it. Cool discussion is suppressed; free speech is overthrown; the press, daring to lift a warning voice, is destroyed; Churches are sundered; brethren in Christ are alienated; the cause of Christ, a victim torn and bleeding, is sacrificed on the altar of burning passion; and while humanity sends up a wild shriek of stifled woe and despair to the fainting heart of reason, war sends down thousands of millions of torn and bleeding victims to the embrace of bloody graves. But the fierce storm of war passed, the smoke of its desolation blown by, deadly passion a little abated, deranged reason returns partially to its abandoned and dishonored throne—to discover what? A wild and tumultuous wreck, the sorrowful work of malignant passion;—a country laid waste; property destroyed; ruins smoking; proud edifices smouldering amid the desolations; homes and homesteads alike in utter ruins; fair fields desolate and wild; large districts, once fragrant with flowers and beauty, and rich with golden sheaves, converted into noxious burial places for the slaughtered victims of war, and all the while helpless widows shriek a wild and unsubdued wail, and homeless infants cry for bread; cripples drag out a miserable and besotted existence; and the whole country groans and staggers under the enormity of the debt incurred in producing these direful results. O wretched, *rational* man! Thou art more savage than the wild beast! Why thus desolate the earth? Why plant the world in thorns? Thy remedy is a million billion times worse than the disease thou seekest to cure. Earthquakes, famine, and pestilence, are not to be compared with the remedy. Thou sheddest rivers of blood and causest oceans of tears to flow; and yet what dost thou gain? When thou hangest one man, thou causest two crimes thereby to be committed, so that thou mayest hang two more. And it is so with war. War does not tend to prevent war. By making wars thou renderest wars popular, and men will freely engage in whatever public opinion will justify. And thou dost not gain what thou fightest for. War can decide nothing, save that one people have more brute force than another. It can not decide between right and wrong. Why, then, O *rational* man, fight? — why tear human hearts and rend human hopes? O man, cease to fight and learn to think! Lay aside the sword, and take up the mind. Save money, tears, and anguish—save souls, and use reason. Thereby thou wilt have true liberty and durable government. Think, therefore, O man—think, and thou will not need to fight.

PART THIRD.

THE MORAL ASPECTS OF THE SUBJECT.

CHAPTER I.

THE REVEALED LAW OF GOD THE ULTIMATE RULE OF RIGHT.

IF we mistake not, it is shown in PART FIRST of this work, that man has no authority to take life, either as derived from the laws of nature or from those of revelation ; whence is drawn the evident inference that all war and all capital punishment violate the laws of God, natural and revealed, and fail to attain the ends for which the one is waged and the other is inflicted. But we have both admitted and argued that human government is an ordinance of God established by men in their natural or worldly interests ; and that it is designed to be permanent amongst men. Thence it became necessary to show how government could be maintained in the interests of the governed, without appealing to the sword. This general subject is considered in PART SECOND. In treating of this part of the subject, we assumed a free government as the basis of our reasoning, and the *theory* of our own as the best form of a free government. In attaining the conclusion that man has no right to take life, admitting at the same time that it is the design of God for government to be a permanent institution, we seemed forced to the end of showing how government could be sustained without violence. This task constrained us to question and repudiate war as a moral means of sustaining government or securing order in society ; and reflection led to the conclusion that a coerced allegiance is a species of heathenism still retained amongst Christian nations. In PART FIRST we inquired whether the right to wage war is derived from the laws of nature or revelation, and attained the conclusion that such right could not be found in either. Then, in PART SECOND, we compared the idea of a coerced allegiance with the *principles* and *axioms* of free government, where it is shown to be impossible to reconcile the use of the sword with those principles and axioms. We are thence brought to PART THIRD, wherein it is proposed to compare the necessary principles of war with the rules of MORALITY, in order to show that the theory and principles on which we have reasoned, are at once consistent with themselves, with the laws of nature and revelation, with the axioms of free government, and with the laws of the purest morality.

In prosecuting this part of the argument, it is necessary to ascertain the *true standard of morality*, with which to compare the principles employed in our reasoning. For man has no absolute truth, because he has no absolute knowledge. Hence, he must judge of truth relatively or by comparison, and, so, must have a *standard*. And, unhappily, there is a great diversity of opinion amongst thinking men respecting the *true standard of morality;* that is, there is great diversity of opinion among men as to the difference between right and wrong. This is very unhappy.

We shall not enter largely into the field of controversy, but shall present what we conceive to be the true measure of moral obligation. And it is obvious to remark, that there must be a *standard*, fixed, certain, and immutable, established, in some manner, by the will and ordination of God. For it does not follow that the standard of truth is variable, because men's notions of it have been. Their notions and disputations relate rather to their *conceptions* of the standard, and cannot affect the standard itself. And it is the evident conclusion of reason, that men's differences of opinion cannot change the laws and relations of things, so as to alter the basis of moral obligation ; while our moral intuitions teach us, that the rules of moral obligations are unchangeable, like the perfections of Him who appointed them. Whence men's differences of opinion have had relation, properly, only to the *imperfections* of their own minds: they have had controversies because their dark and sinful minds could not apprehend truth in its own perfection and excellence. One has taken one view of truth, and another has had another view; while each has chosen, as the standard of moral rectitude, the aspect of the subject which most impressed himself, without *knowing* that his view of the matter is the correct view. And all the disputations and differences conduce to the conclusion, that men's minds are so imperfect, that they do not certainly seize the truth as it is in its own nature; while they all show that there is a necessity for their minds to be aided, in order to attain a standard of morality which may be trusted. Mere deductions of reason cannot be confidently relied upon. And the best inferences of the best minds of other ages, were doubted by those who made them. Such men as Plato, Socrates, Zeno, Aristotle, Thales, Pythagoras, Seneca, Epictetus, Antonius Pius, and others, the founders of great systems of thought, could not confide in the conclusions obtained by their profoundest reflections; and, feeling the need of a surer word of prophecy, some of them hoped that *God* would make known to our race a more certain measure of truth, than could be elaborated from human consciousness. Like all who attempt to derive a standard of moral obligation from the human mind, they failed to find one that satisfied themselves or others. And so long as men look within themselves for a standard, so long will they fail to find one that will meet the demands of their own reason. Hence, if men have a standard of moral obligation, it must be derived outside of themselves. Whence is it? It is in the Revealed Law of God, contained in the Scriptures. The moral laws of God are as unchangeable as the perfections of God. And just what they were before Adam sinned, is what they are still, and what they will be during eternity. And as the moral laws are eternally the same, so are the moral obligations which they impose. Hence, the *standard* of moral obligations must possess the characteristics of the obligations; that is, the standard must be as changeless as the obligations which the standard measures. Therefore, the standard of moral obligation is as unchangeable as the perfections of God. Whence, then, is that standard to be derived? Can a standard of changeless perfection come from imperfect man? And is it true, as Hickock expresses it, that, "There is an awful sanctuary in every immortal spirit, and man needs nothing more than to exclude all else, and stand alone before himself, to be made conscious of an authority he can neither dethrone nor elude?" Is it true, too, that, "He is a law to himself, and has both the judge and the executioners within him and inseparable from him." As a *standard of right and wrong,* there is no such "judge and executioner within" man. Such philosophy is unsound. For, if it was true, the judge and executioner" would be the same "within" all men, and Hickock would not labor through many pages, to contradict what that "judge" has said to all the philosophical moralists that have preceded him. There may be "an awful sanctuary in every immortal spirit," but it is not true, that "man needs nothing more than to exclude all else,"—if that were possible—" and stand alone before himself, to be made conscious" of the distinctions between right and wrong, so as to derive the standard of moral obligation. Nor is it true that, "A stern behest is ever upon him, that he do nothing to degrade the real dignity of his spiritual being." Both the facts of experience and the teachings of revelation contradict these statements. The whole heathen world and the nominally Christian world teach a different doctrine. If man is "a law to himself," with "a stern behest ever upon him, that he degrade not the dignity of his spiritual being," all experience proves the "stern behest" to be impotent, when the moral standard comes from himself.

It may be replied, that the trouble is, so "to exclude all else" as to allow the "immortal spirit" to stand before the "awful sanctuary" of itself, so as to become the "law, the judge, and the executioner." It matters not whence the difficulty arises so it is insurmountable; since it then overturns the reasoning of Dr. Hickock. Dr. Hickock's reasoning, in this part of his work, appears to overlook man's depravity, which must forever preclude the idea that he can derive from himself a true standard of morality. Dr. Hickock makes *spiritual worthiness* the test of morality. But, as elaborated from the human mind, how is that *worthiness* to be ascertained? The worthiness itself needs a test. And every moralist who presents a test different from that of others, proves that a *certain* test cannot be found in the mind. How, then, may we know wherein spiritual worthiness consists, unless we have a standard by which *to try* it? Human creatures do not understand things *in themselves;* and the mind can derive, neither from the laws of its own thought, from the laws of nature external to itself, nor from both in any possible combination, *a certain and unerring rule*, by which other thoughts, feelings, and actions, can be decided as right or wrong. Such an idea would involve the ability of the fallible to produce the infallible. Wayland would extract the ultimate rule of right from the *relations subsisting in the nature of things*, made known to us by our intuitions. But it is impossible to repose confidence in this rule, because, darkened and perverted by sin, the mind can neither certainly apprehend these relations, nor appreciate the obligations springing from them. Yet, the ultimate rule of right may lie in the relations of things, not as apprehended in the human mind, but as appointed by God, and as would be apprehended in the human mind, were it not tainted by sin. And it is precisely in the relations of things that we are to find the ultimate rule of right, or the standard of moral obligation. The rule may formally be thus stated: The ultimate rule of right, or the standard of moral obligation lies in the relations of things as God appointed them in the original constitution of nature.

In his primeval integrity, man would, by intuition, have apprehended all these relations, so as to have discharged perfectly the obligations springing from them. But having sinned, he lost the mental ability to discover them and the moral ability to perform the obligations arising therefrom. The whole head became sick, and the whole heart, faint. The mental powers became sick, and the moral powers, faint; so that the *ultimate rule* could not be discovered; and hence the moral obligations could not be discharged.

Now, in compassion, God has been pleased to reveal to man *anew* the *relations* of things as they existed in their original constitution. This new discovery of the relations of things forms the *moral* law of the Old and New Testament. And the moral laws revealed in the Bible, are but the republication of the same laws as God appointed them in the primitive formation of things. Therefore, the ultimate rule of right grows out of the relations of these laws to one another; and so the ultimate rule of right is to be derived from the REVEALED WILL of God, which, as moral law, is identical with the moral laws of nature. Whence, we have, for the ultimate rule of right, not a deduction of reason, and not a conception of the laws of nature, but the INFALLIBLE UTTERANCES OF GOD IN REVELATION. If the teaching of the Bible is inspired of God, why should Christians want or ask for any other rule of duty, or any other standard of moral obligation? If inspired, it is invariable, infallible, and sufficient. Its inspiration we take for granted, and its sufficiency as the standard of moral obligation follows. One is puzzled to imagine how it has come that men have set up other standards! For take any of the tests of right which men have established, and one immediately asks, How is it known that the alleged *test* is true? To illustrate, take "the intrinsic excellency of spiritual being," as the ultimate rule of right. How can Dr. Hickock elaborate the rule of that intrinsic excellency, and say wherein it consists? Has the mind a test of its own test? Has it one law by which it determines that another law is the measure of intrinsic excellency? If two laws are the measures of each other, which one is the ultimate rule? and how can the mind choose between them? Can spiritual worthiness be measured by a law in the mind in which it resides? And what is spiritual worthiness? where is its criterion? Is it a law of the mind? And if so, is the *law* or the *worthiness* the moral standard? How shall we know wherein spiritual worthiness consists? We can know it only by finding a measure outside of the mind; and that measure must be a moral law of nature. Here the mind could find it, if the mind itself was not depraved and liable to mistake its conception of the law for the law itself. And since spiritual worthiness is conformity to moral law, its measure is found in moral law, and we can, without mistake, find moral law only in the revealed will of God; for outside of the revealed will, what we suppose to be moral law, may not be moral law, but our conception of it. Dr. Hickock's notion of spiritual worthiness may be wholly different from Dr. Paley's; and so his measure of it might be—might be as different as any two things well could be.

If any standard of right and wrong aside from the revealed will of God be taken, the inquiry must arise, How is it known that the standard is right? and the difficulty is not obviated by saying that the ultimate standard is apprehended by an ultimate power of perception in the mental constitution; for that constitution is poisoned by sin, and we cannot trust its processes. No elaboration, either from its purely subjective consciousness or from the laws of nature outside of itself, can be fully trusted. All experience proves this. If, again, we take the ultimate rule of Dr. S. Clarke, *as something inherent in the nature of things*, producing a *fitness*, the question still arises, How can we surely know wherein that fitness consists? We must have some *criterion* for determining that the fitness, in any given case, is the fitness inherent in the nature of things. Our impaired faculties may mistake the *conception* of the fitness for the fitness itself. The fitness of things may form the standard of right, but wherein does the fitness consist?

And when Wollaston says there is *truth* in all things, the statement must be accepted. But how shall we know when we find *truth*, unless we have a reliable test to which we can appeal? But an unerring test is not found in an erring mind; because the test, as conceived by Wollaston, differs from that of Hickock, Wayland, Clarke, and Paley.

Assume that what produces the Highest Happiness is the test of ultimate right, and the same difficulty arises: We must have a final arbiter to decide wherein the Highest Happiness consists, since one man will think it consists in one thing and another in another. Under this rule, one would be a Stoic, another an Epicurean, a third a bloody captain, the fourth an ambitious politician.—Say with Aristotle, that *moderation* is the measure of right, and then who shall decide what constitutes *moderation*? Or extend the rule of *highest happiness* with Paley, till it embraces religion and includes the future life, thus denying present gratification for future good; wherein, in that case, shall we find the test outside the revealed will of God? Or take the view of President Dwight and Dr. Taylor, and constitute *benevolence* the test, it still remains to be decided by some unerring standard, what constitutes real benevolence; and Dwight and Taylor might have differed about it.—And thus take all the human tests of right, and not one of them will stand a human test. The mind cannot trust the conclusions of the mind in which there is depravity. Doubt and hesitancy will come to us in spite of all efforts to believe. The soul craves a "more sure word of prophecy," and rests surely only when it has a "thus saith the Lord."

When we argue that God's revealed will is the measure of right to man, the idea that God has fitted him, with mind and conscience, to receive it as such, is included. And another just remark is, that the rule of right and wrong as presented by many moralists, may be true, though not so as the ultimate test. Duty springs from the *rela-*

tions of things, as Wayland argues; and there is *fitness in the nature of things*, as Clarke argues. So *truth resides in all things*, as Wollaston contends; and the *highest happiness*, as argued in its modified forms by Aristotle, Paley, Bentham, Dwight, and Taylor, must somewhere involve the rule of right, if the *highest happiness* can be brought to the test of a perfect standard; for the *principle* is involved in the general idea that God is a Benevolent Moral Governor of the world. So the rules of Adam Smith, Brown, Schlegel, Cudworth, Coleridge, Kant, and others, may be true, as aspects of the rule, but the difficulty is, we cannot trust them. They are human. They themselves must be *tested*. And one human rule cannot be tested by another. The *test* can be nothing but the law of God, in nature or revelation. But since the depraved mind cannot *know* what the laws of nature are, we can have left only those of revelation as our measure of both truth and duty.

The Scriptures teach the same doctrine. They teach the whole duty of man. They contain two distinct classes of laws: The one is the republication of the moral laws, or the laws of nature, now binding on men and angels. The other class includes that complex system of gracious laws, revealed for the salvation of sinners. Between these two systems there is no conflict; nor do the provisions of the latter suspend or relax those of the former. And every obligation that is incumbent on man, and every temper that he is bound to exercise, is revealed in the Scriptures. Herein are the laws which oblige all rational beings. To perform the obligations and discharge the duties therein required, will acquit man of sin and save him in heaven. If man had not sinned, he would naturally have kept all these obligations. But the requirements of moral law and the gracious aids of the gospel, are two quite distinct things. It is with the former we have to deal; for in them lies the ultimate rule of right; since meeting these requirements would be performing all the duties imposed on man. But right, duty, and obligation, are co-related ideas. With no right there is no duty, and hence no obligation. And if the rule of ultimate right is not contained in the Scriptures, neither is that of ultimate duty and obligation; and hence men would be obliged to do some things not enjoined therein. Where should we learn what those things are? and who may prescribe what shall oblige conscience? What mortal shall become even the expounder of the laws of conscience, and say that "spiritual worthiness" can be measured by any law or inference of reason outside of the Scriptures? And if the ultimate rule of right, or the standard of moral obligation lies without the Scriptures, men are obliged to do some acts which they do not require, and God requires them to do those acts. If men are required and obliged to do some acts to which they are obliged by an ultimate rule of right lying without the revealed laws of God, the Apostle was mistaken in saying, "All Scripture is given by inspiration of God, and is profitable for doctrine, for reproof, for correction, for instruction in righteousness; that the man of God may be perfect, thoroughly furnished unto all good works;" because, by the supposition, there would be "good works" required, whose moral test could not be found in the revealed will of God.

The ultimate rule of right, then, is found in the Scriptures. If we need doctrine, reproof, correction, or instruction, even to the point of making us perfect in "all good works," we are to go to the Scriptures. Every thought, every feeling, temper, and conception of the soul, and consequently every act of the life, must be tried, measured, and tested by the teaching of Scripture. In all cases and conditions of life, the revealed law of God is the criterion of moral right—is the ultimate test of what man should think, feel, or do. What that law teaches is right and obliges conscience; and what it does not teach, does not oblige conscience. If we perform what it requires, with the temper it requires, we perform our whole duty, and are "spiritually worthy." To do what it requires, as it requires, is moral virtue ; to fall short of that, is to fall short of moral virtue ; and to go beyond its requirement, is not virtuous. It is not morally wrong to do anything the Scriptures do not forbid. It is not morally right to do anything they do not require. What they define to be virtuous is virtuous, and what they do not define to be virtuous is not virtuous. And their obligations apply to all conditions of life—individuals, states, and nations, are subject to them. In them we may confide, because they are from God. And our final appeal herein shall be to them. *What they determine to be sin is sin, and what they do not determine to be sin is not sin.* We shall endeavor to test the moral aspect of the war-question by this ultimate rule of right. This is our axiom and first-truth. By it we shall stand or fall, unmoved by the opinions or maxims of men—satisfied that what God forbids is not necessary to the best interests of society, nor to the permanency or well-being of civil government.

CHAPTER II.

ELEMENTARY PRINCIPLES OF CHRISTIAN MORALITY.

IF we open the New Testament and look intelligently into the instructions of the Great Teacher, we discover a peculiarity which distinguishes His Code from all mere human codes. Other codes are composed of rules, injunctions, and prohibitions, minutely and elaborately drawn out, or developed by custom, usage, and judicial decision, with rewards and sanctions appended. These codes fill volumes and compose libraries, demanding a lifetime of study to become acquainted with them. And our best lawyers and ablest statesmen and judges, are often in great doubt as to what the law is in a given case; while the rules of law frequently conflict with each other. *These rules* chiefly relate to the *acts* of men, and the acts being nearly without limit, so must the rules be. Hence they must become numerous, and will conflict. But it is not so with the Great Law-Giver. Few and simple, His laws never conflict. Going straight to the source of thought, and gazing on the motives which give it the qualities of right and wrong, a few simple injunctions and prohibitions cover all the possible field of law; for it is evident that the outward act takes its character from the motives of the interior thought. And the moral quality of an action dwelling in the motive, the action is right or wrong as the motive is—the motive as tested by the laws of Jesus Christ, the only law-giver for conscience.

We did not create ourselves, nor the relations which oblige us. God made both. He made us and He placed us in relations to Himself and to others of our race; and out of these relations spring human obligations. So the Law-Giver teaches: "Thou shalt love the Lord thy God with all thy heart, with all thy soul, and with all thy mind. This is the first and great commandment. And the second is like unto it, Thou shalt love thy neighbor as thyself. On these two commandments hang all the law and the prophets." In this teaching, plain, simple, succinct, is contained man's duty—his relations to God and to man. Herein are found the duties of life, and hence the ultimate rule of right. Herein we learn the rule of right, and wherein virtue and vice consist, as connected with motives and conduct. Having the revealed law as the rule of right, and remembering that our fellow-man sustains to God the same relation we do, actuated by an ardent feeling of love in our treatment of him, we shall not go astray.

Even in critical cases, when the interests of self-love carry their urgencies with solicitude home to the heart, there is no fixed necessity of doing wrong. For even then the clamors of self-love may be so far repressed that the voice of reason may be heard and heeded; and, actuated by a conscious sense of love, honest duty may be performed. And *love* is ever the virtuous touch-stone. The rule of right resides in the relation of things; duty springs from that relation; while love tempers all and works no ill to a neighbor. Love is therefore the virtuous motive. Let us behold the practical use the Divine Law-Giver makes of the motive which alone is virtuous. He says, Thou shalt love thy neighbor as thyself. Love your enemies. Bless them that curse you. Pray for them that despitefully use you and persecute you. If ye love them which love you, what reward have ye? do not even the publicans the same? this is my commandment, That ye love one another as I have loved you. Owe no man anything but to love one another, for he that loveth another hath fulfilled the law. For this, thou shalt not commit adultery, Thou shalt not kill, Thou shalt not steal, Thou shalt not covet; and if there be any other commandment, it is briefly comprehended in this saying, namely, Thou shalt love thy neighbor as thyself. Love worketh no ill to his neighbor; therefore love is the fulfilling of the law. For this is the message that ye heard from the beginning, that we should love one another. Beloved let us love one another, for love is of God; and every one that loveth, is born of God, and knoweth God. He that loveth not, knoweth not God; for God is love. And this commandment have we from Him, That he who loveth God loves his brother also. These laws, enjoined by Christ on all men, are but the republication of the original laws of nature, and oblige all people and nations of the earth; while their import cannot be mistaken. Without condition or limitation, they declare at once the measure and the effect of love as a moral duty. Love must temper all virtuous actions, and, tempering them, it fulfils the law. Such is the law of the Great and Wise Teacher.

These are the positive principles of an Ethical System based on the revealed laws. We may also look at the negative side of the question; and may therefore quote the Great Teacher in that respect also, that we may have before the mind both the positive and negative elements of Scriptural Morality. We will quote by classes, beginning

1. With MALICE. Brethren, be not children in understanding: howbeit in malice be ye children. Let all bitterness, wrath, anger, clamor, and evil speaking, be put away from you, with all malice. But now ye also put off all these; anger, wrath, malice, blasphemy, filthy communication, out of your mouth. Wherefore laying aside all malice, and all guile, and hypocrisies, and envies, and all evil speakings.

2. MALIGNITY. Being filled with all unrighteousness, fornication, covetousness, maliciousness; full of envy, murder, debate, deceit, malignity; whisperers, backbiters, haters of God, despiteful, proud, boasters, inventors of evil things, without understanding, covenant breakers, implacable, unmerciful.

3. HATRED. He that saith he is in the light and hateth his brother, is in darkness even until now. Whosoever hateth his brother is a murderer; and we know that

no murderer hath eternal life abiding in him. If a man say, I love God, and hateth his brother, he is a liar. Now the works of the flesh are manifest, which are these : Adultery, fornication, uncleanness, lasciviousness, idolatry, witchcraft, hatred, variance, wrath, strife, seditions, envyings, murders, and such like.

4. ENVY. Full of envy, murder, debate, deceit, malignity. Some indeed preach Christ of envy and strife. For we ourselves also were sometimes foolish, disobedient, deceived, serving diverse lusts and pleasures, living in malice and envy, hateful and hating one another. The spirit that dwelleth in us lusteth to envy.

5. COVETOUSNESS. For from within, out of the heart of men, proceed evil thoughts, murders, thefts, covetousness, wickedness, deceit, &c. Take heed and beware of covetousness. Being filled with all unrighteousness, fornication, covetousness. But fornication, and all uncleanness, or covetousness, let it not once be named among you. Let your conversation be without covetousness. And through covetousness shall they with feigned words make merchandise of you.

6. EVIL FOR EVIL, REVENGE, VENGEANCE. Thou shalt not hate thy brother in thine heart. Thou shalt not avenge, nor bear any grudge against the children of the people. Bless them that persecute you ; bless and curse not. Recompense to no man evil for evil. Dearly beloved, avenge not yourselves. Vengeance is mine. If thine enemy hunger, feed him ; if he thirst, give him drink. But I say unto you that ye resist not evil. See that none render evil for evil to any man.

7. IDOLATRY. Mortify inordinate affection, evil concupiscence, and covetousness, which is Idolatry. Now the works of the flesh are idolatry, hatred, wrath, strife, envyings, murders.

And thus might we indefinitely extend and classify the hateful passions of the human heart, as forbidden by the law of Christ, and included in the idea of loving one's neighbor; and yet all these passions are absolutely necessary for war. For consider the matter. Without malice, malignity, hatred, envy, covetousness, revenge, returning evil for evil, idolatry, deceit, ambition, cruelty, hypocrisy, lust, and a host of other sinful and forbidden passions, war would be an impossibility. To speak of a war's originating *with men*, without a score of the most hateful passions of the human heart mingling, is simply absurd. We shall have something to say about the malevolent and forbidden passions hereafter. It is our purpose now, to exhibit a very brief outline of an Ethical System built on the teachings of Jesus Christ.

Let us, then, contemplate, in the briefest manner, an Ethical System, whose central and controlling conception is the second command, *Thou shalt love thy neighbor as thyself.*

We may consider it, first, in its relation and application to individuals. And what a paradise upon earth its full application would create! Love residing in each soul, would purify the fountains of moral action; would extirpate from the soul every foul and bitter root; would sweeten every malevolent passion; would render pure and pellucid the flow of every affection. The whole family of hateful passions, forbidden by the laws of Christ, and injurious to the peace of society, would cease to enslave the soul with imperious and painful insolence. The soul's amiability would gently flow out towards others. The heart, calm, gentle, thoughtful, the manners would be soft, the brow benevolent, the tones soothing, the smile earnest and attractive. No revenge in the heart, no slander on the tongue, the intercourse of friends and neighbors would be delightful. Vast would be the change from the existing state of things, the result of the teaching and practice of the Ethical Systems based on human-made morality. Enter any village, neighborhood, or church in the land. Alas! what a spectacle! All is uproar. The idle tale, the whispered gossip, the mysterious insinuation; the surmises, the whisperings, the evil imaginings; the envyings, the petty jealousies; how they destroy the peace of families, towns, neighborhoods, churches! Then the malignant slanders— the outpouring of base natures and the offering of murderous hearts; what piercing arrows, barbed of inflammable poison and set on fire of hell! And how they are sent hissing into fainting hearts, whose first information of the foul slander is communicated as the hissing arrow tears through and rends the bleeding soul! And how painful to record that this devilish malignity is not confined to the world. It deeply penetrates the church. Persons separate from the same house of worship, to whisper about each other, tales which are disgraceful and sinful, and which, if true, would rank them amongst the basest of mankind. Yet, these persons will meet with apparent affection, visit each other, continue together the forms of worship, and commune at the same table. Appalling inconsistency! Still, this passes currently for Christian morality; and the people compliment each other in public as disciples of Christ. But is this Christian morality? Is it not rather the morality of the camp, the morality which reconciles Christian ethics with war? Are not such vicious tempers in the soul, war in its very inception? Surely, it is war comminuted, and apportioned residences in individual hearts. Let these vile tempers be gathered together and concentrated by some cause sufficiently potent, and we will have another four years of deadly war, as the natural outward expression. The whole present condition of society is the logical result and expression of that war-morality, forbidden of Christ but taught by men—by men, saints and sinners alike.

But, secondly, we may consider such an Ethical System as applied to States and nations. These, as composed of individuals, are under the same obligations. Love must also control their conduct by the laws of Christian morality. The State, as such, is obliged by the same law that obliges the individual. And abominable and abhorrent was the doctrine taught during the late war in this country, and anon by the pulpit, that God allowed men *as citizens* to engage in war, though he disallowed it *as Christians.* Decorous language cannot sufficiently reprobate such abuse of the rational mind, and such perversion of Christian morality. Such perversion of things would send the same man to the devil *as a citizen*, and to the Saviour *as a Christian;* and so we should have the same man at the same time, in heaven and in hell. But such is about the consistency of the moral reasoning which reconciles war with Christianity.

But did the nations act on the law of love, the result would be analogous to that produced by individuals and neighborhoods: the happy effect would be generalized. Without national jealousies, avarice, hatred, and ambition, the bloody sword would be sheathed, and the warrior's career would end forever. Peace would reign amongst the nations, the visions of prophecy would be realized, and Christian morality would become a real fact and a living energy in the hearts of professing Christians.

If it is admitted that Jesus Christ does teach the moral system for which we contend, but is urged that, in the existing state of civilization, such teaching is impracticable, the admission contains all our argument requires; for we are not disputing about what men *will* do; we only seek to show what they *ought* to do. Our position is that war, with the tempers and passions on which it necessarily depends, is endlessly violative of the moral laws of God;—we contend that the Lord Jesus Christ utterly forbids the existence and indulgence of the feelings without which war is a natural and moral impossibility; and that, consequently, He utterly forbids war itself. "Keep thy heart with all diligence, for out of it are the issues of life," is the Christian morality: and that "wars and fightings come of the lusts," is the divine teaching. Therefore, this and this only, is Christian morality. If men cannot reconcile this teaching with war, and cannot reconcile keeping the heart with all diligence, with murderous lust, they cannot reconcile war with Christian morality. If they admit that the necessary principles and practices of war are contrary to those of Christian morality; and that, under the full development of the latter, the former will disappear, the admission is sufficient. For, if the necessary principles and practices of war are contrary to those of Christianity, the true follower of Christ cannot engage in war. The proposition is self-evident. Jesus says, "He that hath my commandments, and *keepeth* them, is he that loveth me." Men must observe the moral precepts of Jesus Christ, or they cannot be *His* followers. And to acknowledge that the principles of war are contrary to those of Christianity, and yet to act upon them, is to renounce reason, or Christianity, or both.

Were men frank and consistent, they would avow that Christian morality forbids all war; and that to engage in war, is to renounce Christianity. Intelligent war-men frequently declare that war, is subsersive of Christian teaching, yet continue to practise war; thereby arguing deplorable moral delinquency. And this is the position of the *pulpit* in this country, generally: and because this is the position of the pulpit in the country, we had the late war. No thoughtful and observant mind can rid itself of the conviction, that the late war came upon the country on account of the sad delinquencies of the pulpit, in not teaching what is acknowledged to be so by the pulpit itself.

CHAPTER III.

THE PRINCIPLES AND MORALITY OF WAR.

IN these pages we have sought to show that the principles and customs of war are contrary to the laws of God, natural and revealed; and that, consequently, war is violative of the principles of morality and the teachings of reason. Whence we contend that war must be destructive of the best interests of our race. Upon the suposition that God is the Natural and Moral Governor of the world; and hence that He has prescribed a fixed, unalterable, and wise system of laws for the government of His intelligent creatures; it accords with the influences of reason to expect that the necessary consequences of their conduct, under such a system of laws, would intimate to them when their conduct did or did not agree with the requirements of the laws of that system. And upon the further supposition, that the Author of such a system is benevolent, as well as wise, we should be supplied with certain tests, by which, in the diligent use of their faculties, they should be able to determine the agreement or disagreement of their conduct, with the demands of the appointed system. Under such a system, the consequences of their conduct must clearly and infallibly intimate the conformity or non-conformity of their behavior to its moral principles contained in it. The whole system being founded in benevolence, when their conduct conforms to its laws, happiness and prosperity must result, both as a natural consequence and a natural reward. But when their conduct violates its laws, unhappiness and want of prosperity must follow, as a natural punishment, and as an intimation that violence has been done to the demands of the benevolent system.

Now, we know, from experience and from revelation, that God has appointed such a system over His intelligent creatures on the earth—know that He has appointed such a system in unchangeable wisdom and benevolence, and that He has made His creatures intelligent and with moral natures, forming that kind of counterpart which responds to the outward benevolent system appointed in the natural constitution of things. And it is through the action of intelligence, reason, and conscience, in agreement with the laws of that wise and benevolent system, appointed by God, that God intends men to work out in their behavior a course of moral obedience before Him. To this end he has *fitted* the system of laws outside of man and the system of laws inside of Him; and the laws written on his heart is the counterpart of the laws of nature. And it is through this *intelligent counterpart of nature*, that earnest and candid men, seeking to learn truth and duty, are able to ascertain any considerable departure from the requirements of God's laws, as appointed in the Constitution of His Moral Government over the world. These two systems of law exist wherever humanity exists, and constitute man everywhere the subject of *moral law;* and fix in him a sense of moral guilt or innocence; while it is from the principles involved in them, that we have the *certain means* of knowing the nature of causes, by carefully attending to their effects. The union of the system of laws written in the heart and the outward system written in nature, constitute a *cause*, which is represented to us in Scripture under the symbol of a "*tree*," and the result of this union expressed in the life and practice of men is *effect;* and is presented in Scripture under the image of "*fruit.*" Between these two systems, God has appointed immutable relations; so that if we *know* the nature of the *tree*, we may as certainly *judge* the nature of the *fruit;* and if we *know* the nature of the *fruit*, we may as certainly *infer* the nature of the *tree.* And this law of cause and effect, or the tree and fruit, pervading God's whole moral system, we have a test for trying alike principles, conduct, beliefs, and mental affections. " Wherefore by their fruits ye shall know them," is the most extensive and perfect rule of judgment in possession of our race. By this infallible rule, we are willing forever to test the legality of all wars that have had their origin with men since the history of humanity began; and if *one* can be found whose fruit is that love which Jesus requires to be produced in the life and conduct of His disciples, we will no longer contend that its fruit is always barbarous and fiendish, but will agree that Christ authorizes "rebellion against the best government on earth" to be crushed out "by means suitable to make devils blanch."

But in this land, which is far from being truly Christian, we are not left for our knowledge to the two natural systems of law to which we have alluded. In mercy, God has revealed His law to us, and we may know the kind of fruits He accepts as good. Still, even the heathen may know and be obliged by the moral law which so clearly forbids war. For Paul argues that the Gentiles, not having the revealed law, should still perish for violating the law written upon their hearts; since their thoughts, or reasonings upon subjects of moral obligation, showed that they might have understood and obeyed the law inscribed on the heart, had their hearts not been set in them to do evil. But the revealed law saves us the task of elaborating the processes which exhibit the fruits that are acceptable to God. Paul graphically presents these fruits when he says, "The fruit of the Spirit is *love, joy, peace, long-suffering, gentleness, goodness, faith, meekness, temperance;* against these there is no law." Where such fruit is found, the tree is good. It will not be hewn down and cast into the fire; nor can it be readily mistaken by honest men.

Compared with this "fruit of the spirit," what is the fruit of the late war in this country? Was it *love, peace, joy, and long-suffering?* Were the delusion of war dispelled from their minds, would the thousands of widows over the land, now bowed in grief and sorrow because their husbands sleep in bloody graves, think the *fruit* had been *love, joy, peace, gentleness, and goodness to them*? Ah! no. But another inspired author tells us the origin of war, which agrees better with the feelings of anguish-smitten widows, when he inquires, "Whence come wars and fightings among you? come they not of the lusts which war in your members?" Whence, if we may believe inspiration, war is *born of lust;* and "when lust conceiveth, it bringeth forth sin; and sin, when it is finished, bringeth forth death." And thus we have the climax. And, indeed, what does war bring forth but sin ending in death? Could there be a truer account of it? War is born of lust; lust conceives and brings forth sin, and sin, finished, brings forth death. Fearful climax!—fearful, because true. And how shall Christian men avoid the conclusion, without rejecting the Bible? The very rack of criticism cannot make such language speak the feelings and desires of warmen. Perversion alone, winding through the dark labyrinths of the heart, can turn aside the force of the words of inspiration, so as to make them countenance the morality of "horrid war." It may be feared that he who destroys the word of life so as to make it utter the language of war, may destroy his part in the book of life; or adding to the words of the book, he may add to himself the plagues written in it. It is a fearful thing to trifle with divine utterances.

If it is thought hard to imply that a whole nation may perversely disregard the laws of God, in both nature and revelation, and plunge into the horrors of war, it is admitted that the implication is hard. O that it had no foundation! But still the doleful voices of more than half a million Abels cry to us from the ground; while the testimony of God is, that there are those who, knowing the judgment of God, not only violate His laws, but have pleasure in the conduct of those who violate them. And there is no shadow of doubt that a whole nation, as such, may, by some blind impulse, wilfully and perversely violate the plainest and most indubitable teachings of God's natural and revealed laws. Such was the case with the Jews, who, having been the signal recipients of God's special and repeated favors, not only rejected but crucified their own King and Saviour. Equally perverse was the conduct of the Carthaginians in waging, against the surrounding nations, those wars which ultimately brought their total and irretrievable ruin. No less perverse was the conduct of France in attaching her destinies to the wild and ambitious schemes of Napoleon, allured by the specious sophism of public liberty. Nor was the late joint act of the South and the North in this country, a much less perverse violation of the moral laws of God, when they madly and blindly plunged into the horrors of a fratricidal and needless war. And there is no mistake that whole nations do wilfully reject the counsels of God to their own overthrow.

For a time it shall be our business to look at some of the "fruits" of war, in order to infer the nature of the tree on which it grows; and to infer, also, from its intense bitterness, whether the people who "take pleasure" in it, do not justly rest under the charge of perversely rejecting the counsels of God.

We have already repeatedly alluded to the revolting qualities of war as incidental suggestions connected with the trains of thought at the moment; but the importance of this branch of an argument against *all war* as immoral and sinful, is such that it deserves a fuller consideration, though it may occasionally involve the repetition of a thought already suggested in another connection.

It shall be our endeavor to trace the consequences of war—its bitter, bitter fruits—in various and diverse directions, always expressly or impliedly founding the argument on the relations appointed by God between the two systems of law to which we have alluded,—judging and determining the character of the tree by the qualities of the fruit; or holding that, from the conduct of men, we may infer the agreement or disagreement of their behavior with the benevolent laws which God has appointed for the regulation of the lives of His rational creatures; and basing the argument on the idea, that when a *principle is correct*, all its legitimate consequences will be right—that when the tree is good, the fruit will be good.

From the converse of the proposition we shall also argue, that when the *consequences*, as admitted by all right-thinking men are wrong, the *principle* from which they result, must be wrong;—that if the fruit is intensely poisonous and deadly, spreading around blight and disease, contagion and death, the tree *must* be bad. And here the anti-war advocate might safely rest his cause, testing it by the divinely appointed relation between correct moral principles and the moral conduct that will logically and naturally result from them.

Now, the utterly immoral tendencies of war are, lamentably, too generally admitted to demand formal proof at our hands. The mind is naturally so formed as to recognize war as the generalized formula of every species of known crime—it is the synonym of all the wrongs and outrages that man inflicts on man. It is from this principle it results, that when the mind *intelligently* yields itself to the services of war, it scruples at the commission of no act which lies within the power of a human creature to perform. And it is hence that military men often perpetrate acts of treachery and barbarity, which shock the sensibilities and defy mortal power to excel. We read the acts of Herod, Nero, Antiochus, Cæsar, Tamerlane, Alexander, Genghis Khan, Napoleon, and others, with undisguised abhorrence and disgust; yet our recent and horrid war scarcely finds a parallel in the history of barbarism. Witness the affair at Fort Pillow and Andersonville Prison, on the one side; and the burning of houses with Southern women and children in them, too ill to escape, on the other side, when all burned together,—with the burning of a Confederate colonel, a prisoner unarmed, because he refused to surrender his money, as the writer was informed by Federal soldiers who witnessed the horrid acts. Truly has it been said by a man, at once eminent in ability and eminent in his inconsistency on the subject of war, that "war is a temporary repeal of all the principles of virtue." And it is true that war is the repeal by man of all the laws of God. It is the direct invasion of the divine prerogatives, and the practical suspension of the laws of virtue. And men so esteem it; for they no sooner become soldiers than they cast aside the obligations of uprightness and moral integrity. Accordingly, it is not uncommon to see young men who have led blameless lives at home, upon volunteering as soldiers, become profane swearers, reckless inebriates, and miserable debauchees; at the same time exchanging manners civil and debonair, for those which are coarse, boorish, and impudent. And in our late war-experience, cases are not wanting, where men of mature minds, scholarly attainment, and social and religious position, upon becoming volunteers and officers in the army, also speedily became meretricious profligates and shameless blasphemers.

The very constitution of the mind seems to be such, that men cannot cordially and intelligently embrace the generic crime of war, without bringing contamination to all the moral elements of the soul. For when the fountain is bitter, how can the waters be sweet? When war is born in the throes of sinful and murderous lust, how can its principles, when intelligently embraced, do otherwise than poison all the powers of the soul? In its own essential nature, war is an outrage upon human reason, and so reason suggests that every thought, every act, and every instrumentality necessary to carry it on, must also be an essential outrage upon humanity. And all experience so shows. Like the thoughts of the wicked, war is evil and only evil, continually. Itself is the monster-birth of lust, and is, in turn, the prostitute parent of mendacity, treachery, theft, robbery, murder, and other hosts of monster crimes and sins which degrade and dishonor humanity; while each of these lecherous and meretricious children, reflecting the lineaments of the parent, becomes the progenitor of a prolific offspring, till, like the direct and collateral lives of a natural progeny, the foul offspring of war spreads out and settles over all a nation. It is thus in the United States to-day. There is no nook or corner where the poisonous breath of war has not engendered moral pestilence and revolting death—in the state, in the church—all over and everywhere, the malarious breath of war has produced boils and chilblains—engendered pestilence and produced famine—caused moral leprosy and incurable maladies, till, as a nation, we tremble of feebleness and shame, and quake over the abyss of our degradation.

Assumed to be right,—surely never so proved,—war has, in the course of time, built about itself a kind of Ethical System. Being the primal and regulative idea, it has shaped the thoughts, feelings, passions, acts, and conduct to its own generic conception. And, like all ethical systems, it has its virtues and vices, the acts enjoined and those prohibited; —has its criterion and touchstone, by which the worthiness or unworthiness of its adherents and devotees are tried and proven. For our purpose, the system may be called war-ethics. Happily for us, we have an inspired insight into its axioms and seed-principles, into its origin, nature, and characteristics. Having its *origin* in the "lusts which war in the members," the strength of its principles is found in the irregular and furious passions of the depraved heart; while its *nature* and *characteristics* denominate those in whom they are found, *intelligently*, to be signally sinners.

These seed-principles, with the vast list of offshoots from them, wrought by the efficacy of the regulative conception into a harmonious system, constitute the Ethics of War. And whatever else may be said of the system, it is singularly consistent with itself, in all its parts. Its practices naturally and logically spring from its principles; and the component parts of the whole gracefully harmonize: its precepts and injunctions arise forcibly from its theory. Its vices and faults must be sought outside of its theory and practices, by the assumption of different axioms and a different regulative conception. Successfully to attack it, we must repudiate as virtuous the congeries of insolent, sinful, and detestable passions, whence it derives its elementary ideas and practices.

The practical object of war, the generator of the ethical system, is *to take* and *to destroy*. *Lust* is its generative principle, and to take and to destroy, is its primary object. Its process of development is in the following order: First, it takes the moral virtues of the people. Secondly, it takes the hard-earned money and property of the people. Thirdly, by fire and sword it burns and lays waste a country. Fourthly, it destroys the souls and bodies of thousands and millions. And, fifthly, it caps the climax, by giving tears, sighs, and taxes to those whom its *tender* mercies allow to live. But God alone can know the extent of the *virtues* of war in this direction. Humanity cannot grasp them.

That we may have a better basis of judgment, let us contrast a little the ethics of war with those of Christianity. We have seen that the teachings of God disclose to us the elementary ideas of the two systems. In this we are very happy; for we are thereby supplied with the means of prosecuting the contrast to a more satisfactory conclusion —have the opportunity of looking at the systems in their incipiency and before they are suited to mislead by being interwoven with delusive mental processes. Let us again glance at the elements of war-ethics and those of Christian-ethics. Whence, then, have we the elements of the former? We are told that they are engendered in those lusts of the soul which clamor for gratification. *War* itself gives them birth—war amongst the passions of the carnal mind. It is right that like should beget like. The malign passions burn with lust, and thence conceiving in sin, they bring forth the iniquity of war. Or, to change the figure, in the malign and diabolic passions of the soul are found the *axioms, first truths*, and *primal virtues* of war-ethics. They are suitable material from which worthy genius has, in the progress of the ages, constructed a consistent system. *Lust* is therefore the first and great element out of which the superstructure of war-ethics is built. On the contrary, *love*, acting in two directions, is the generative axiom of Christian-ethics. First, it expresses itself towards God, with all the heart, mind, and soul; and, secondly, it acts towards neighbors as it does towards self. On *love* hang the law and the prophets; and on *lust* hang the horrors of war. And from *lust* and *love*, as generative agencies, are created, respectively, war-ethics and Christian-ethics. Lust is the tree whose fruit is war; and love is the tree whose fruit is Christian ethics.

We have, then, in their elemental state the two ethical systems—lust and love. They are wide apart in their conceptions. We can scarcely imagine two things more intrinsically unlike than *lust* and *love;* nor can we imagine two things more unlike than the two ethical systems which have been constructed from them. Totally unlike in their elemental conceptions, they are totally unlike in every thought and feeling they impart, and in every habit and custom they require. Consistently followed out, the one brings men into harmony with the laws of God,—demands love and gives love. But consistently followed out, the other leads men to collision with the laws of God, and into the wholesale murder of each other. Love works no ill to its neighbor, and fulfils the demands of the law. But lust delights in doing ill to its neighbors, and violates all the demands of the law. Love is of God. Lust is of Satan. The one delights in acts of benevolence; the other, in acts of malevolence. The one secures life. The other insures death. The one brings forth fruit unto holiness, having, in the end, everlasting life. The other brings forth sin, and when sin is finished, it brings forth death. No two conceptions are more unlike than *lust* and *love;* and no two practices than those of *war* and *Christianity*. Like parallel lines, if extended endlessly, they will approach each other at no single point.

It has been attempted to avoid the force of such reasoning as this, by alleging that the apostle alluded to the *certain* wars which he rebuked. But that will not do. For the *force* of the rebuke lies in the *principle;* and that is necessarily the same in all wars. For it is naturally impossible for war to originate with men, without having its origin in rampant lust—as naturally impossible as for an effect to exist without a cause. We *know* that *lust, hatred, malice, revenge,* are inseparable from the *existence* of war. Apart from them, war is an impossibility. They are as necessary to the origin and continuance of it, as the lungs and the air, to human life. *They* are war's vital energy. Separate them from war, and that instant it expires. And it logically follows that if war is right, lust, hatred, malice, and revenge, are right ; and, indeed these *are commendable virtues* in the ethics of war. But not these alone,—a " legion " of kindred passions prevail and find full play, and demand generous commendation in war and military morality. And it is because reason and conscience must be subjected to the dominion of the vile lusts, that war-speeches, nay, and war-sermons, too, are always tissues of mendacity, hatred, malice and revenge. And professed Christians, infuriated by the delusions of war, have uttered sentiments vile and blasphemous enough to pale the midnight of perdition. Without experience, it would seem impossible that rational beings, possessed of undying souls, could be wrought up to the point which we have witnessed in *Christian* people. Nor could they be brought to such height, were they not completely reduced to the bondage of debased and execrable passion. It is hence that the more perfect the fitness there is for the services of war, the more perfect is the subjugation of the rational and the moral man to the ferocious impulses of the base passions. And since the various offices of the mind and heart are intimately related, the imperious insolence of the base ·passions may soon invade the dominion of the soul, and throwing it into chains, may lead it captive at the chariot wheels of the conquering tyrant. And, thus, all that is noble and generous, may lie the victim of lust, pinioned and manacled, without reason or conscience. The rational man is then in chains and the moral man in utter subjection. *Lust* becomes the tyrant-conqueror, and holds complete and unquestioned dominion; and thence leads, not its brave moral warriors to victory, but its abject slaves to the horrors of bloody war. It is thus, as Robert Hall says, that "War is the temporary repeal of all the principles of virtue." For in order to war, the obligations of God's laws must be disregarded; the monitions of conscience scorned; the dictates of reason hushed; the generous feelings of humanity stifled; and every throb of sympathy for our suffering kind, must be silenced and drowned by the uproars and tumultuous clamors of the unfeeling and vicious passions. And since vice in all its forms is very contagious, war-men, acting upon that law of our depraved humanity, appeal to the lower passions, and excite and combine their action so as to accomplish their lustful and ambitious purposes. The nature of the means they employ induces them to resort to any instrumentalities that will enable them to attain their objects; which in the nature of things they cannot be actuated by motives higher than those of avarice, ambition, or some mere partisan purpose. The *real* motive, too, is always carefully concealed. They go before the people, who are incapable of seeing the bottom of any great scheme, with some plausible and delusive pretext, by which they operate on their prejudices and self-love, or on some form of their diversified lusts, and thereby they deceive and impose on them, leading them into the vortex of engulfing war. The principles of virtue are neither clear nor deep in the minds of the masses; and with war-men conscience is laid aside as both useless and injurious, as no tender-hearted scruples are necessary in the minds of warriors. With them the end to be gained is, so to excite the lower passions as to render their victims oblivious to the claims of the soul. Hence, it is one of the first duties of the great captain to sear the conscience and reduce to silence the voice of the generous impulses of the heart; so that his instruments may revel, without remorse, in scenes of blood, and smile at the keenest anguish and sorrow. And it is thus true, that a people must lose their martial integrity and high-toned Christian character *before* they can engage in war. Before war is a possibility, the whole people must lose their moral virtue; but the people and the leaders lose it by processes very different. The love of dominion, ambition, avarice, and lust, destroy virtue in the leaders; while the people lose their moral tone, partly in the same way, but mostly by the sway of the brutal passions. Yet, bribes by monthly pay, by bounties, and by pensions, are offered to the people. But their ignorance, credulity, and superstitions, are largely made auxiliaries to war. Still, the great achievement is to bring the fighting soldier under the complete control of the brute-passions, so as to smother out rational thought and humane feeling, and to beget oblivion to the idea of the soul. And this feeling is the prerequisite to the attainment of that murdering point implied in war. For upon the whole earth there surely could not be found a man, who, with a distinct apprehension of the human soul, would take a life and imperil a soul, or send it unprepared to eternity, to save all the governments on the globe from being divided into as many distinct ones as there are square inches on it.

So war implies complete forgetfulness of the soul. The fires of passion and lust must kindle enthusiasm and fanaticism into a consuming conflagration, before the work of war can begin. The ethics of Christianity must be totally suspended. Reason must be dethroned. Passion must be enthroned. The lusts must wail their wild and murderous shrieks, till conscience, alarmed and terrified, no longer holds dominion in the soul. Then, and not before, the unique ethics of war, constructed from the wreck of all the noble powers of the human soul,—from wild and lustful passions,—come into play. On humanity broken, prostituted, and ruined, is built the foul and noisome institution of war. For in all the passions made auxiliary to war, not an amiable one can be found. But only the revolting and sinful ones are summoned to activity. Revengeful, malignant, murderous hatred—the tumult and furious storm of passion—the depraved and diabolic elements of humanity in a tornado of deadly destruction—these are the *necessary* conditions and virtues of war. *War's* virtues pluck up mercy by the roots; tear human sympathy into shreds and scatter it to the winds; and, overpowering, crush out from the soul every noble, amiable, and lovely emotion. The pen can paint but a feeble picture of the *theory* of war, the *facts* and *practices* of it eclipse imagination and fancy, and render language impotent to describe them. Still, the facts and practices legitimately grow out of the theory, and accord perfectly with war-ethics. War's practices accord with its theory; its precepts and principles harmonize. Born in the agonizing throes of vehement lust, we could naturally and logically expect from it nothing but unbaptized sins, nameless crimes, and heartless cruelties.

Accordingly, the facts of history show that the great majority of the wars that have desolated the earth, have originated in the avarice, intrigues, and ambitious cabals of those who hold power. Frequently, they have originated in causes both trivial and contemptible. Plutarch informs us that Pericles, instigated by the resentment of a courtesan, engaged in a war, which, after costing much blood and treasure, resulted in the destruction of the city of the Samnians. The same wretch, actuated by private hatred, to avoid being prosecuted for theft, or for official malfeasance, was the instigator of that famous and fatal war, known in the annals of Greece as the Peloponnesian, which, after intermissions, renewals, and vicissitudes of fortune, resulted in destroying the Commonwealth of Athens. The prime minister of Henry VIII., actuated by schemes of ambition and personal vanity, in defiance of the clearest dictates of State policy, precipitated England into war with France, at the peril of the kingdom over whose counsels he presided. Lust and ambition were the motives which actuated the minds of both Cromwell and Napoleon. But, divine revelation telling us that wars come of lusts, we find that all history is a witness to the truth of that revelation. And no genius can show, that, since the birth of Christ, there has existed a war, which did not originate in motives and for ends concealed by its authors, but in motives violative of Christian morality and for ends personal and vicious. And not an exception can be found. Tried by the standard of Christian morality, all wars, *offensive* and *defensive*, are violative of the laws of God; and hence destructive of the people's best interests.

And originating in lust and vehement passion, war is, from its mental conception to its actual expression in using swords, powder and lead, but a mass of sins and a series of ruthless and inexorable outrages, defiant towards God and barbarous towards men. And dispassionately considered in the light of Christianity, the proclamation of *any earthly* ruler calling on *men* to slaughter *men* for any cause imaginable or possible, short of the will of God made known by miracle, is an outrage to our common humanity, as it is a wanton and flagrant violation of the laws of God and the dictates of reason. Then to offer moneyed bounties to induce men to obey such a proclamation, is to add insult to outrage;—it is a proclaimed solicitation to sin and crime, which, anticipating refusal, is accompanied by a tendered bribe. In any business but war, such conduct would challenge only the scorn and indignation of all upright men. As has been said, all wars originate in the sinful lusts; and for a ruler to solicit his subjects to the slaughter of men, because he has some pique to gratify or some scheme of ambition to attain, is to insult our rational humanity, and should invite only our derision and scorn. And should rulers become infatuated by some such senseless generality as, "It is our duty to maintain our nationality;" and to that end, call on a part of the nation to destroy another part, they would act about as rationally and morally as the father who should slay an unruly member of his family in order to preserve the family unbroken. And the son who, in obedience to the call of a father, should slay another son, would exhibit the same morality as subjects who, in obedience to such a proclamation, should slay brother subjects.

For we must not reject alone, we must indignantly scorn, the heathenish idea generally accepted in our day, that the *citizen* is bound to obey the *government*, even when it calls him to arms; and that, in obeying, the responsibility rests on the government. That is a thought as detestable as it is false. Each individual is to obey God, and not man ; because each individual is *personally* responsible to God. In the final day, each is judged for himself, and each receives according to the deeds done in *his* body. There will be no shifting of responsibility upon ambitious presidents or cruel heroes. Each stands or falls for himself. And when, lately, the rival political potsherds of this country called men to do the work of death, the people should have set their faces like flints against them, resolving that, at no peril, would they obey them and disobey God. The people had the matter in their hands—the Christian people had—the pulpit had. The pulpit could have kept the people out of the slaughter-pens of the war. The pulpit could have saved more than half a million lives, billions of money, and the moral integrity of the nation. But it joined in the insane clamor, adopted the senseless shibboleths, and abetted the murderous work. And that work is before us. The fool may say, There is no God, and the fool may say, Our country was benefitted by the late war. But wise men will be little impressed by either saying. All know that the South is ruined ; its country is laid waste ; its citizens are destroyed ; its morals corrupted ; and its hopes blasted. If the South went to war for slavery, it lost it ; if for liberty, it lost it ; while the people of the South are themselves slaves under the iron heels of military despotism—their own slavery, the logical sequence of war, though none the less barbarous because chosen by themselves. But the North is also ruined. True, she smote the South; but it was a fatal smite. In the imagery of the man who did it, "the hope of our race," received the blow. The South had sinned,—had cruelly sinned,—but *liberty* had not. The South had enslaved the blacks, but that gave the North no right to enslave the South. By the war, the South and liberty lie bleeding together. The sword pierced the hearts of both, and side by side they lie in the dust. The right of self-government is gone; and those who insanely sought it for themselves, that they might take it perpetually from others, awaked from their dreamy delusions, find themselves the slaves and vassals of the sword which they employed. Instead of that self-government which reason and right have secured to them, they have the government of fear and liberty which the sword gives.

Official position suspends not moral obligations; and the President and the humblest subject, are equally obliged by the laws of God. Nor, in calling a people to the horrid business of war, can the President take refuge in the Constitution; for the Constitution can give no authority for wholesale murder, and war is nothing else. And as the Constitution can confer no authority to make war, the President can have no authority to call men to the work of slaughter. And so, to send out a proclamation for the people to engage in the business of war, is a flagrant wrong and outrage, without right or authority, and having the moral qualities of the lusts in which war originates; for no act of war can be more virtuous than the lusts in which it originates.

In passing, if it is not belittling the subject, it may be named as a task of no small difficulty, to conceive how an intelligent and well-balanced mind can witness the training of men for the work of slaughtering rational creatures, without a sense of disgust and profound humiliation. The evolutions, the marching and counter-marching in a certain manner and with a given step, the diligent training of *rational* beings to slaughter and to be slaughtered—their complete subjection to the capricious will of other men, rendered solemn and binding by the obligations of an oath—these all impart to the reflective mind feelings complex and mingled, composed of pity, astonishment, and humiliation. But the feelings are intensified almost to mental paralysis, as one reflects that mortals made rational and responsible, will completely abjure their personal individuality and put themselves under the arbitrary dictation of others, first to be trained and prepared, and then led into hardships, privations, and death, without themselves having a volition that dares to question the caprices of the superior to whom their manhood has been foresworn ; and all this without themselves having an intelligent idea of the acts for which their fellow-mortals or themselves are to be butchered on the battle-field, and without knowing that they or others shall ever reap the least benefit from their conduct.

Nor is it easy to drive from the mind the conviction, that the complete surrender of the soldier's manhood and responsibility, made perfect by the imprecation of an oath, is an act very offensive to the Christian morality; nor is it considered as its solemn nature demands. For the limit to the authority of the superior may be his own arbitrary will, the soldier having foresworn his own ; and so the superior may order the inferior to do what must be infinitely offensive to a tender conscience, with no alternative in the latter. Obey he must, or suffer such punishment as the same arbitrary will may choose to inflict. Such is indeed voluntary slavery, but it is also abject—is the slavery of the soul, of conscience, of rational manhood ; and such slavery as no man should allow to be exercised over him—such as God disallows, and such as is nowhere required or deemed necessary but by the demands of war.

The training being sufficient so that the slaughtering

can be done according to "the science of human butchery," the trained victims are hastened "to the front," to await the service of slaughtering or being slaughtered. But the trained victim may now be in "the enemy's country," and it becomes necessary to observe the ethics of the new situation. Observe, then, that the situation is voluntarily taken, through the lusts and ambitions of rulers, who, in violation of the moral laws of God, have called for the citizen, whom they train and fatten for the slaughter, and now place in the new situation. And we must notice what constitutes an *enemy* in the ethics of war, bearing in mind that the causes of enmity are as various as the phases of the sky for the fancies of dreaming; but they are generally and substantially composed of royal whims, presidential caprices, or statesmen-like fancies, whose substantial existence lies in burning lusts, distempered imaginations, ungodly avarice, the scheming of politicians to hold or get power, the infatuation of a political party by some ambitious delusion; or it is possible that bloodthirstiness in the masses, under some system of false education, may precipitate a country into the horrors of war, and give the people doomed to the merciless fate of the sword the name of "the enemy." This part of the definition of a war-enemy belongs to the one side. There is another side. Who compose this side? They are frequently those who commit the crime of refusing to submit tamely to wrong and oppression. Or they are those who do not yield graciously to be plundered by the avarice of a profligate tyrant. Or they may be those who wish to limit the tyrant's arbitrary will. Both England and France have afforded illustrations of the definition; and the former is still illustrating it in holding and pressing Ireland by the iron heel of the despot. Then, again, enemies have been made by abandoned politicians, who, actuated by love of power, have, by a series of mutual and galling insults, been successful in geographically dividing a country into angry factions, and then plunging them into the horrors of civil war, each faction calling the opposite one "the enemy." Such was our own recent condition ; for all intelligent and unprejudiced men *know* that there was no real cause for " the enemies," no cause on either side, or by any party. The South had no cause, for it flew to arms anticipating wrongs which *might* be done. The North had no cause, for however *insanely* the South might act, in a *free* government there is no other mode of deciding when or how it might withdraw from the dominion of the government, than by its voluntary act ; while there is no doubt, that had ninety-nine hundredths of the people occupied different geographical positions in the country, they would have occupied opposite positions in the war,—Federal officers would have been Confederate officers, and Confederate officers would have been Federal officers, and the position of the whole soldiery would have been equally reversed: nay, it is neither unreasonable nor absurd to believe the Presidents of the rival parties would have been exchanged, and that the occupant of Washington would have been the occupant of Richmond, and the occupant of Richmond would have been the occupant of Washington, had the one that went from Kentucky to Illinois gone to Mississippi, and the one that went from Kentucky to Mississippi gone to Illinois. And such is the uncertainty of the facts of life in view of which men slaughter each other. Nor is this all. Thousands who fought for the Federals would have preferred to fight with the Confederates, and thousands who fought for the Confederates would have preferred to fight with the Federals. So that friends slew friends on each side. This consideration alone shows that there is absolutely no justice in any war.

Let us pass now, with an army duly trained as it takes its position in " the enemy's country." The army and the enemy may be of the same blood, language, and religion. All that matters nothing. The army is in the enemy's country. That suffices. Without distinction of age or sex, all are ranged in the same category—palsied years, delicate womanhood, helpless infancy, can work no exemption from the horrors of being an enemy. The standard determining who are enemies is fixed by caprice. The war-order of some military upstart, waked from the potations of the previous night, may constitute a State or community enemies; and thence the work may begin. A methodical system of theft and robbery is initiated, which, in the language of war-ethics, is called *foraging;* and foraging is justified by customs which are heathenish in their origin and barbarous in their nature, but which have been introduced into Christian States under the less offensive name of the Laws of Nations, founded in the necessities of war. The necessities arise from the fact, that an army is *voluntarily* in the enemy's country, and is there because the invader could not resist the thirst for blood, and because even invaders must live—*must* live, though like the Crusaders, they have carried with them nothing to live on, and so are reduced to the necessity of foraging. Dire necessity! It is not unlike the necessity which impels a man to break into a neighbor's house at midnight, in order to get five or ten eagles, lest, being too lazy to work and too stupid to gain by gambling, he should suffer from cold or perish of hunger. It would be a strange system of morals that would justify such an individual necessity; and equally strange is the system that justifies *such* a necessity in a hundred thousand soldiers! But this is the alleged necessity for foraging. What is the morality of that avarice which allows an army to take and carry away what it can neither eat nor wear? Is this, too, a necessity? It is a necessity exactly as justifiable as the other; and both are justifiable by the precise logic of the criminal, who, to excuse his crime, alleges that his propensity to steal is so imperious that he cannot avoid it. The necessity in both cases is that of criminal lust.

What shall be said of the burning and destroying of an army, when the property can be neither eaten, worn, nor carried away? Is that, too, a necessity; and will Christian people tell us that the Laws of Nations allow it? The Goths and Vandals spread devastation and ruin wherever, in their wild fury they swept—sparing neither age, sex, nor property; and civilized nations, so-called, have adopted their customs, making them a part of the Laws of Nations: and are these to be the laws for Christians?

It is well known that, in our recent war, a celebrated general made a raid that elicited the applause of the "*more civilized*" (?) portion of the nation. A subordinate officer who took part in it told the writer, that he saw the *last* morsel of food taken from women and children, leaving them nothing on which to subsist; and saw the work completed by giving princely mansions and their furniture to the devouring flames; while "the enemies," being helpless women and children, were turned out to subsist on the bleak winds by day and to repose on the chilly earth by night. Another soldier said he was in another campaign made by the same officer, when the last degree of inhuman barbarity was perpetrated. Sweeping over territory many miles wide, the army laid waste everything before it;—destroyed crops, burned fences, drove off stock, foraged everything on which man or beast could subsist, turned women and children out of doors when able to be turned out, and when not, the frail domicils and the frailer inmates were consumed together. Some helpless females, robbed of their all by the process of foraging, and then burned out of house and home, pursued the army by the necessity of subsistence, till unable to bear their feeble bodies further, they lay down to the dreams of death from starvation and exhaustion—a vast army having voluntarily put itself where its necessities compelled it first to rob these helpless creatures, then to burn their homes and leave them to live on the wind or to die of starvation, their Christian robbers, plunderers, and burners, neither feeling nor caring for their sad and touching fate.

And all this constitutes the "glory of war,"—is done by the sanction of war-ethics because the people are "enemies," and those who do it call themselves Christians;

while Christians and Christian ministers ask the blessings of God to be on these robbers and plunderers! And the whole is called *Christian* patriotism. And it is true *war*-ethics. *Revenge* and *retaliation* are primary virtues in war-morality. They form its key-stone. Though totally disallowed by Christian-ethics, they are of wide application in war, and are employed in a manner singular and extraordinary. They extend far beyond the Jewish laws of retaliation. *They* permitted only like for like. But the retaliation of war-ethics allows a kind of seven-fold vengeance, being limited only by the will of some upstart, whose mind is made zealous by large potations of whisky.

War-morality has another phase. Each belligerent allows in itself what it condemns and pursues with infuriated vengeance when committed by the other. For instance, each loves to steal horses from the other, but each hurls hot bolts of vengeance at the other, when its own horses are stolen. Then the thief is a bandit and freebooter, deserving the halter. So, when some outlaws, inspired by the true spirit of war, surprise and murder a score or two, though the other side would have done the same thing, the Christian indignation of the party out-generaled, is greatly excited, and vengeance is sworn. It is declared that vengeance must be taken. Such acts of wanton barbarity, though they would have been feats of bravery if performed by the other side, must be visited by such condign punishment as will "deter the barbarians from repeating the infamous crimes." Therefore some war-general, burning with wrath and steaming with potations, orders double the number thus slaughtered in the heat of blood and the strife of glory, to be taken from the prisoners and murdered in cold blood, and with pure revenge; the poor murdered prisoners, it may be, detesting the crime for which *they die* as much as their murderers. Nay, the murdered men may themselves be in the war under protest in their secret hearts, driven there by the tornado of passion which they had not the courage to withstand.

And thus it is that war exercises itself. It creates the *feelings* and the *acts*, for which it murders the victims who have and do them. One belligerent justifies and lauds acts, for doing which by the other side, innocent men are coolly led out and shot down with as little feeling as if they were wild beasts. Yet men would persuade us that these revolting things are allowed by the precepts of the gospel, by the law of love. And when these cruel and revengeful acts are condemned, we are complacently informed that they are the *necessities* of war, allowed by the usages of civilized nations! And by such logic the masses of *Christians* are satisfied. But alas for the ethics of war! They may do for heroes and warriors, and for those whose consciences are hushed by the clamors of lust and passion.

But MALICE, as well as *revenge* and *retaliation*, is an essential ingredient in carrying on war; and is therefore a virtue in war-morality. Without *malice*, war would be an impossibility. It is *malice* that steels the heart and nerves the arm. It loves blood and sorrow, bitter tears and broken hearts;—takes delight in torture, agony, and death; rejoices in the groans of expiring victims; and makes merry at the tears of orphanage and the sighs of widowhood. When, therefore, war is fashionable, *malice* is virtuous. And because the lower classes have the most rampant passions and the most active malice, they are the first to volunteer upon the occurrence of war. Their poverty, too, is baited by the temptations of bounties. As these classes become exhausted, stronger appeals are made to the passions and larger temptations are offered to the cupidity of higher classes. And war-ethics, abolishing all moral distinctions, in war-morality, the malicious and revengeful are on an equality with the higher orders of society; and even the higher classes, coming under the sway of a war-feeling, cultivate the same malicious passions with the lower classes; tending thus to obliterate all moral distinctions in society, not by bringing the lower up to the level with the higher classes, but by reducing the higher classes to a level with the lower ones. Parents yielding to the exigencies of war-ethics—Christian-ethics being abrogated and extinguished—gradually fail to see and feel the distinctions between the benevolent and the malevolent affections, and so lose a high-toned sense of Christian obligation. And gradually failing to teach the duties of Christian morality to their children, their sons and daughters come to substitute the precepts and teachings of war-morality for those of the gospel of peace and love. The natural consequences then follow—the morality of the nation, thus acting, suffers a fearful deterioration. Crimes to name which would pollute, and which are not easily punishable by law, riot in exultant triumph; the whole tone of society is blunted; the standard of Christian morality is vastly lowered; while the virus of war, like a destroying contagion or swollen streams of death, runs through all the veins of human society. Houses which may not be named, the foul sink-holes of national purity, are full of wretched and fallen inmates. From these vile centres the malaria of moral death is borne on the breezes and carried to all the nooks and corners of the nation; and thus spreading the moral pestilence to the remotest and humblest districts and villas in the whole country. Other natural consequences follow: life becomes wretched beyond endurance, while the various forms of lust and passion take dominion of the mind and heart. And this condition has its natural consequences: suicides, in order to put an end to wretchedness which is intolerable, will be of frequent occurrence and of shocking character. Seductions and the murder or the abandonment of the victim of sated passion, will be of alarming and horrible frequency. Then daring robberies and bold and reckless acts of theft will startle those in whom a little moral virtue remains. And all these as naturally and necessarily flow from the feelings which are the necessary condition of war, as any logical consequence follows from its casual antecedent.

And such is the condition of things now over all our

land. Fearful is the moral condition of this nation; and not much better is the religious condition. The pall of impurity overspreads the nation, menacing its destruction. War has wrought the harm. The cardinal virtues of Christian morality have been set aside; while lust, fraud, revenge, malice, and brute-courage, the virtues of war-morality, have been substituted. In both church and state, the true spirit of Christianity has been dethroned, and the spirit of war has been enthroned: the scheme of God's moral laws has been suspended; and the scheme of war-morality has been inaugurated. The revolting crimes, the political corruption, the moral leprosy of the nation, are the natural result. War is the tree from which these are gathered as the ripe fruit.

CHAPTER IV.

BRAVERY, VALOR, COWARICE, TREASON, AND OTHER VICES AND VIRTUES OF WAR.

WE oppose *all war* because it is opposed to the laws of God and the best interests of the human race. In opposing it, we have argued the question in connection with cases where the right to wage it has been regarded as the freest from doubt, endeavoring to argue it on *principle*, not fearing to pursue the argument to every logical consequence. Satisfied that all war is at once an enormous crime and sin, and the direst calamity that ever afflicted or outraged the human race, we have scrutinized the axioms of all free governments, in order to ascertain, if possible, where, amidst the primal principles of government, is to be found that subtile and fatal error, which, up to this time, has proved at once the invader of men's rights and the destroyer of their governments. The whole subject we have treated with freedom, not highly valuing the laws, constitutions, or customs of men, however revered by them or sanctioned by time, when they violate reason or tolerate the crime of war or oppression. We have regarded the truth as lying in the nature of things, and as *certainly* made known to us only in the revelation of God; and so we have not studiously consulted human opinion. But when pertinent to the question, we have endeavored to adhere to the teaching of Revelation, as the only *reliable measure of truth to men.* By this free way of dealing with the subject, it is hoped that some rays of light may have been thrown on the question of government; and that it has appeared that men have hitherto been deprived by the sword of the right of maintaining free government. It has appeared, too, that the denial of the right of self-government, as in this country, has afforded the most plausible of occasions for using the sword. But the sword has been the destroyer of all—the people, governments, nations, morality, and social order: next to sin itself, the sword has been the worst, deadliest foe to the human race.

We shall still pursue the same course of considering the subject—shall pass by the notions of men, though announced to the world by tradition, judicial or ecclesiastic decision, and adhere to the revealed Will of God, as the unerring standard of truth and duty. The worship of government, the idolatry of ancestry, or the awful reverence of the past, the follies of heathens which largely mingle with the civilized nations of modern times, we disregard as having force in argument. But governments and constitutions we have found to be the institutions of men, made to conserve and promote their worldly interests. In this direction we traced the subject, as nearly as we were able, to its primal principles, endeavoring to show that the sword and coercion could not subsist with free government.

It is proposed to travel now in the opposite direction; to scrutinize some incidents which have been attached to governments as important and inseparable principles, and to show that they are neither *important* nor *inseparable* incidents, or if they *are* incidents, to show that they destroy the principles to which they adhere. What is said here may still be regarded as a part of the ethics of war, as of the virtues and vices of a war-morality. BRAVERY, COURAGE, VIRTUE, PATRIOTISM, with some of their incidents, antitheses and related ideas, together with TREASON, the unpardonable sin in the idolatry of government-worship, are the considerations which now invite attention.

These must be brought into comparison with the assumed standard of truth, that their *true* virtue may be tried; and that standard is nothing but the revealed word of God. What *that* says *is* sin, is sin; and what it says is virtue, is virtue; while what it does *not* say is sin, is not sin, and what it does not say is virtue, is not virtue. It defines all the duties and obligations of man, so that the man of God may be perfect, thoroughly furnished unto all good works. Therefore, the Scriptures are our sufficient guide in *all* the duties of life, in public or private, in the state, church, or family? Guided by them, a man may learn and do his whole duty everywhere. For they define virtue and vice— tell us what *is* and what is *not* sin. Obedience to their precepts, in their true significance, constitutes *real* virtue ; disobedience to anything, not enjoined by them, is not real vice. However, outside of the Scriptures, there are many vices and virtues, human-made, and " put up to order." It is these human-made virtues and vices, which we have disregarded in these pages, and which, under the name of war-morality, we propose still to disregard. Virtue, courage, valor, bravery, and patriotism, with every affection necessary to war, must necessarily belong to the man-made virtues; while the "crime of treason" belongs to the human-made vices; since, in the war-sense, they have no foundation in Scripture. But as they are familiar to us in the ethics of war, there is no doubt as to the real moral qualities of *virtue, courage, bravery,* and *patriotism :* they are heathenish both in their origin and nature. In popular language, virtue, valor, courage, and bravery, signify nearly the same thing; and indicate those qualities which enable men to encounter mere danger fearless of personal harm, and including these attributes which point to the hero and warrior. We shall mostly employ them interchangeably, noting the difference in them as it may seem proper to our purpose— observing that we do not use them in the higher, figurative sense, in which they have come to denote true moral excellence, because they enable the possessor to brave sin and wrong.

Now in all the qualities which these words represent, there is not one that Christianity either enjoins or commands. They are all mere natural animal qualities. A man may possess consummate *bravery*, without the lowest element of

Christian character. He may be *brave* and be an infidel, a scoffer, a lecher, a general debauchee; brave and be an atheist and blasphemer. And being a mere animal quality, it is possessed in a higher degree by some of the inferior animals than by the bravest warriors and heroes. Whence, if in the sense of Christian morality, there is virtue in that bravery which makes the soldier, some of the inferior animals are more virtuous than the most renowned soldier. And according to war-ethics, the lion, the bear, and the bull-dog, must indeed be commendably virtuous, since they are fearlessly brave. For it seems evident that the qualities which are virtuous in men, must be virtuous in the bull-dog; hence, the bull-dog, that has more bravery than the bravest warrior, must be more virtuous. And this is the logical conclusion of war-morality.

But it may be said that this is carrying the argument to its extreme consequences. So it is; yet it is perfectly legitimate. A *sound* principle will bear all its logical consequences; and if the principles of war-ethics are sound, they will bear their logical conclusions. But if the logical inferences of war-ethics are so preposterous as to shock common-sense, the real fault lies, not in drawing the inference, but in the absurd assumptions of war-morality. And it is, indeed, as preposterous to call *bravery* a Christian virtue, as it would be to call a bull-dog a Christian hero.

If it is said, however, that the *real* virtue consists not in the *animal bravery*, but in the principles which call it out, the ground of the controversy becomes changed. A new meaning is attached to the word, and bravery is made to consist in a new element. With that we may or may not have a controversy. If it is that kind of Christian bravery which encounters sin and wrong, we shall be at peace with it. We shall embrace and commend it. But if it be any form of the bravery that constitutes war-ethics, it is hard to find a principle to which it may be referred. However, we are not inquiring wherein true virtue consists. We are only contending that if there is *true* virtue in the bravery of war, some of the inferior animals are more virtuous than men. And if such a consequence is preposterous, the logical inference is, that the principle which would make bravery virtuous is equally preposterous. And, tested by Christianity, the virtues of war-ethics are as absurd, as the inference is, that the bull-dog is a Christian hero.

Boxing, fighting, duelling, and making war, have the same essential moral nature; and, in the popular sense, which is the war-sense, *bravery* refers to the act of exerting animal strength, fearless of the consequences which may befall the person exerting it. And this is clearly a mere animal attribute, having no element of Christian virtue.

That this is a true representation of the bravery of war-ethics, is shown by reference to *cowardice* as the opposite ethical quality. And by the war-code, *cowardice* is a high crime, and severely punishable. By it, he who shows himself a fleet pedestrian, when the deafening roar of cannon and the hissing screams of shells unsettles his nerves and dissipate his bravery, becomes the basest and wickedest of men; and for it, under the code, he may be arrested, disgraced, tried, cashiered, tortured, sentenced, and shot. Such relaxing of the nerves is a shocking crime—a sad perversion of the use of the feet and legs which God has given, deeply implicating the mind and heart in the outrage, and rendering the crime very shocking to humanity.

But what indeed *is* the revolting crime of cowardice? wherein does it consist? It, too, is nothing but an animal quality, and results from natural organization. It is no more under control of the will than the talents or the imagination. And he who is wanting in bravery can no more help it, than he who is wanting in poetic genius or in powers of eloquence can help it. Cowardice being the absence of bravery, the coward is subject to the same blame for it that the person is who has no imagination or power of eloquence.

The word *courage* comes from a Latin word which means *heart;* and it refers to the quality of the mind which is fearless of danger; while it has no moral quality, and is not under control of the will. It results simply from natural organization. So *virtue* is derived from the Latin, and it had reference, primarily, almost exclusively to mere *strength;* but in time it came to mean a *man*, vir— because *man* so constantly puts forth *strength*, a valued property amongst the heathenish Latins. *Valor*, too, is from the Latin, and originally indicated the qualities of the soldier with more accuracy than either *courage* or *virtue*. The term *bravery* also looks to a heathenish original, while its very idea is still essentially heathenish. It belongs signally to the chivalrous family. Indeed, they are all cousins-german, having descended from the same warlike ancestry. *Patriotism*, too, was begotten in the marriage-bonds of a pure heathenism. In them all we have no trouble in seeing the *physical* and the *moral* likeness of their ancestors, that lived in the midst of Roman idolatry; while they represent attributes about as well developed in the Goths and Vandals as in the people of the United States.

Now, if men act from the dictates of reason, how can they commend *bravery* or punish *cowardice?* It would be just as reasonable to punish for want of mathematical talent, or praise for physical strength; and the one is commended and the other punished, simply to suit the demands of war, both acts being wholly irrational and absurd. For both are more perfectly illustrated in the lower animals than in man. The bravery of war is illustrated in the dog, the bear, the tiger, etc.; while the ethical quality of cowardice, so intensely criminal in the war-code and the code of honor, is illustrated in the gazelle, the antelope, and the lamb. Whether the disposition of the tiger or the lamb most resembles that of the Perfect Man, each one can decide for himself.

However *men* may decide these questions, the Scriptures neither condemn *cowardice* as a crime, nor commend *bravery* as a virtue. Both are virtues and vices made by men to serve the interests of heathenish war. And a careful survey of the whole ground, will leave in the mind no doubt that there is not a spark of *Christian* virtue in *all* the bravery, valor, virtue, and courage of war; while in cowardice there is not the least criminality. And this conclusion is supported by both reason and revelation. For as *God* has made things, there can be no moral virtue in animal bravery, and no vice in the want of it. The virtue and vice exist only in war ethics. *Patriotism* also comes to us from heathenish parentage, unwashed and unbaptized, to take rank with the human-made virtues. For nowhere can it find a word of commendation from the Christian Scriptures. It is, therefore, not a Christian virtue; and so its non-exercise can take nothing from Christian character. That innominate entity, lately thrust into the family of real virtues, and christened *Christian* Patriotism, is wholly an earth-born virtue, unknown to Christ, the Apostles, and the early Fathers in the church. Nude of purity and unwashed, it came from Pagan and Papal Rome; and though unbaptized, it is in close communion with most of the churches in this country. As a concrete, the Christian patriot may be at once a patriot and a drunkard—a patriot and a wretch—a patriot and a lecher—a patriot and a plunderer of the public treasury—a patriot and a duelist—a patriot and a common liar—a patriot and a reprobate, an atheist, a contemner of Christ and His doctrines; and one can embrace the Christian patriotism of our day, and be in its full communion, while he despises both Christianity and all the virtues of it. Therefore, even Christian patriotism does not necessarily involve the idea of a God; much less the amiable virtues and tempers enjoined by Jesus Christ. Strictly heathenish in its origin and popular notion, both the most and the least that can be truly said of Patriotism, is, that it belongs to that class of human feelings which have in themselves no moral qualities.

Patriotism is defined as love of country. If one's

country does right, and seeks the good of the people, by such means as the laws of God allow, the patriotic feelings towards it will be neither morally virtuous nor vicious. At most, it is but *natural* benevolence—the wish of natural good to the citizen—the desire that he may prosper in the blessings of his world-life; and, in any strictness of words or thought, such *feelings* could not be regarded as having any qualities of moral virtue. But as generally understood and practised, *patriotism* is but the synonym of violence, fraud, and injustice: it is the disposition to aggrandize the nation by means fair or foul, by oppression, robbery, and wrong,—by agreement if the nation may, but by violence and the sword if it must. And the use of the sword, violence, laying waste a country by war and rapine, are all called patriotism; and are all virtuous by the war-code. The same sort of patriotism existed in Rome, Greece, Sparta, and amongst those Northmen who overran the Roman Empire. And as it is now in intimate communion with our Christianity, so it was with the religion of Rome, Greece, Sparta, and that of the Northmen; while it admits of a fair doubt whether their religion did not do as much to stay the horrors of war, as our so-called Christianity does. And true it is that the nations of to-day have nearly the same notions of patriotism, as the heathen people of Rome and Greece had. The *real* difference must lie in the idea, that modern civilization requires stealing, lying, robbing, and murdering to be done according to a *Christian* mode—since it is certain that they are all done. Modern civilization prescribes a *certain manner* of doing these several acts; and this may constitute that singular virtue called *Christian* patriotism. And that is the Christian patriotism which is peddled in the *religious* journals, hawked on the stump, and vociferated from the pulpit. Alas! the whole thing is but a bitter burlesque on true Christianity— is a hollow name—the morality of Alaric and Nero—is the spirit of barbarism in the costume of Christianity; and while it sings hymns and psalms, it kindles fires of torture for the weak and helpless ;—in a land of Bibles, it is sanctimonious self-righteousness, devouring the substance of unpitied widowhood, praying on the corners of the streets, wearing large phylactaries, and neglecting justice, mercy, and truth.

And such is the *Christian* patriotism of the United States, North and South. Most of us have seen it leer in self-righteousness; while it would fain torture and destroy about notions of worldly good. Would to God that the memories of the last few years of this nation's history were obliterated.

Still, there is a sort of patriotism different from this pseudo kind. It would bless the nations by the abandonment of the sword forever. It would give the sword to heathens and barbarians, where, with the idolatry of hero-worship and Vandalic civilization, it could be more consistently employed; while recognizing the catholic brotherhood of humanity, it would also recognize that governments are instituted in order to promote the temporal interests of men, rather than to destroy the people and lay waste the country. And it is incontrovertible that he loves his country most who most strongly urges the immediate abandonment of the sword forever. For all history, which is but the written experience of the past, proves that the sword has been the destroyer and not the conserver of the good of the nations. In all its forms, war conserves nothing but destroys everything; and those who resort to it are the worst enemies a country could have. In our own late bloody struggle, the worst patriots on both sides were the zealous war-men. If one side had the *glory* of conquering, it had twice the number of men and resources. If it humbled haughty pride, it aroused the wounded lion of uncaged passion. If the war set free four and a half millions of wretched blacks, it perhaps did little more than make them more wretched. For the heart aches and faints within one as he thinks of the wretched condition of these creatures in the year 1869. Wretched as was the condition of the slave under the lash, it has perhaps been made more wretched by the sword. And four millions have been made nominally free, to perish in their freedom; more than eight millions have been made military slaves, to suffer in their slavery. Yet, the latter are simply overpowered—conquerered by the sword, held down by the chains of military despotism. They cordially hate the government that conquered them; and would rise to-morrow, did a fair gleam of hope appear, and reënact the bloody tragedies which we lately witnessed. The result, therefore, of all the late exhibition of bloody patriotism, is the mere extension of power over the subjugated States; and singular indeed is such patriotism. The conquered portion of the country is a waste and a desolation, and the conquerors are themselves conquered; for a tear stands in every eye, and sadness presses every heart, while oppressive taxation bears like a nightmare on all the energies of the nation. To cap the climax, the infuriated beast of passion has been let loose, to prey upon and to devour the conqueror and the conquered. Yet men call this patriotism—the South calls what it did patriotic; and the North thinks its work patriotic. But is not the whole thing a misnomer? Is not such conduct, on both sides, *un*patriotic, actual hatred of country, the surest possible means of bringing it to moral ruin and moneyed bankruptcy? Such patriotism is mad ambition, gaining fame by mocking at tears and sorrows, and sporting with the lives and morals, the hopes and expectations, of its own subjects. It is the sword touching the life-blood of the nation on a hundred ensanguined fields,—the sword sending hundreds of thousands of beings into the other world, and millions of living ones into lifelong anguish and despair. And this, too, is called patriotism; but it is that furious kind of patriotism which reminds one of that furious Christianity which used to carry the prayer-book in one hand and the torch to light the funeral pile, in the other. Such patriotism as this is like that Christianity which, *professing* to be infallible, burns heretics. Real Christianity is a thing wholly unlike that, and so is real patriotism. Real patriotism would at once and forever abandon the sword, and pursue the nations' interests according to the precepts of Christianity. And yet, no form of patriotism can rise to the attainment of Christian virtues. In all its possible forms, it belongs to this world—is of the natural and can never attain to the supernatural,—it belongs to the carnal and may not aspire to the spiritual. Never was anything more unpatriotic than our late war. At once it has unsettled the policy of the country and imperiled the integrity of the nation. Loosend from its moorings in the sea of Peace, the nation has been hurled into the treacherous ocean of war, and the final result is not yet seen. Instead of settling a difference of political opinion by appealing to reason and justice, the nation appealed to the tribunal of the sword and the jostling conflict of contending armies; thereby unsettling all things and imperiling all things. And if we are to accept the precedent, hereafter political notions and differences are not to be decided by interest, reason, or right, but by the arm of blind power, uplifted and gleaming with the sole argument of coercive gladiatorship. Hence, hereafter, the important question for patriotism to ask, will be, *Can the logic of the sword succeed in establishing the phase of political ideas which is desired?* For war is based on just that mode of reasoning, and belligerent patriotism signifies the reason and justice which are found in the edge of the sword. And this is *our Christian* patriotism. By this sort of patriotism we must not expect this nation to be guided by the axioms of our rational intuition, regarded for four-score years as the basis of our political institutions; but, by the decision of the sword, these axioms are to be regarded as overruled and obsolete conceptions; and our axiom hereafter shall be, *The safety of this nation reposes, not in the suffrage of a free people, but in the logic of a sharp sword.* And another conception of a *fashionable* patriot may be added: "*Blood* is the cement of the United States." In these two mottoes resides the patriotism of this boastful nation.

That these are to form our national mottoes, is inferable from the practice of the government in annoying, during the late brute-force conflict, men who conscientiously opposed that kind of patriotism which expresses itself by killing those who have different political notions. But that kind of patriotism has one advantage at least—that of being cogent: it wholly disregards conscientious rights and constitutional guaranties. For as matter of fact, our Christian patriotism lately invaded the rights of conscience and the constitution, by compelling men to fight who thought fighting a crime against man and God. In truth, patriotism in this country, North and South, has become technical. By the *practice* of the governing power, it signifies willingness to abandon home, wives, and children ; then enlist and enter the army,—throw life away if the behests of war demand it ; but, if not, then to show a willingness to destroy and desolate the people of our own country, till they consent to embrace and reduce to practice certain political notions held by the conquerors, thereby producing a unity of political sentiments and feelings between the destroyers and the destroyed. And this, any one can see, is the exact basis of persecution. Indeed, all war about political ideas, as our late one was, must have the basis of persecution. War could not exist without that basis.

But patriotism sometimes assumes another phase. It seeks *gain* by acts patriotic. It becomes a wolf in the livery of a lamb. It volunteers, obtains good pay, and renders easy service without danger. Then it gains access to the national coffers, being provided with large pockets. And, thus prepared, it becomes blatant with the zeal of persecution, and makes thrift of fawning ; grows rich from the misfortunes of others, peculates from the government, commits thefts from the helpless victims of war, and fills the ample pockets prepared ; and then with velvet carpet, damask linen, and luxuriant upholstery, this pleasure and patriotism together cost only the tears, the sighs, and the life-long sorrows of anguished widowhood and portionless orphanage. And such is the fashionable *Christian* patriotism of the United States.

Now, to call *such* patriotism *moral* virtue, is grossly to pervert both thought and language. It is much more properly unmingled *im*morality and sin. Yet such is the practical working of patriotism in all the nations of the earth. Heathenish in its origin, it is barbarous in its practical working; while the whole influence of Christianity has only modified its extreme and savage barbarity. Still, *our* patriotism is a barbarian, whose accents are far from Christian.

Passing from our pseudo-patriotism, we come to notice the human-made crime of TREASON. And here the mind has a little doubt and trouble. For it is difficult to determine just what constitutes treason. In the history of the world up to this time, it has generally been the scape-goat for the malice and revenge of tyrants and capricious rulers; and it has been defined to consist in whatever stood in the way of attaining the end of imperious or ambitious schemes. Nearly the united political and Papal world agreed that Luther was a traitor and deserved death. The able chancellor of Baden said to Luther, " If we did not uphold the decrees of our fathers, there would be nothing but confusion in the church." And Charles the V., in his fulminations against him after the meeting of Worms, said, " For this reason, under pain of incurring the penalties due the crime of *high treason*, we forbid you to harbor the said Luther." When William Penn did some trifling act which displeased his ungrateful subjects, they maligned him as " a liar, a traitor, and a villain ; " and he was denounced as a *traitor* in England, because he was on terms of friendship with an unhappy and arbitrary sovereign who had long been the steadfast friend of himself and his father, after the former had fled to France, and the taciturn and ambitious William was surveying the British Crown. And the great Apostle to the Gentiles was charged with *treason* for preaching a *new religion* in the Roman Empire, though it was done in obedience to a divine command ; and it was probably for the crime of treason that he suffered death. There was never invented a greater convenience in the interests of tyranny than the man-made crime of *treason.*

But it is not needful that we inquire into the nature of the so-called crime of treason. If the revealed will of God is the measure of right and wrong, treason can be a crime only when so defined by that revealed will. It matters not what the nations may have held and practised on the subject. The nations cannot make or unmake right and wrong, guilt and innocence. God alone can do that. If God has defined treason to be a crime, it is a crime ; but if He has not, it is not, though all the nations should hold and teach otherwise. But no intelligent man, no thoughtful lawyer, and no judicial decision, ever taught that the revealed law of God defines the political crime of treason. A man would show himself to be an ignoramus, who should undertake to prove that the Scriptures define what treason against human government is, or that they teach that such treason is, in itself, a moral wrong. For if we separate the act of taking life from the conception of such treason, no moral wrong will remain. Everywhere, it is the war and murder which constitute the crime. The Constitution of the United States does not base the crime of treason on the laws of God. It says, " Treason against the United States shall consist only in levying war against them, or in adhering to their enemies, giving them aid and comfort." Now, careful inspection of this definition shows that it is a crime of purely earthly creation, having no shadow of basis in the Christian Scriptures. Nay, it is based rather upon atheism than Christianity ; for it clearly rejects the idea of God's providence as the Moral Governor of the world, and founds national safety in bullets and bayonets. Indeed, the very idea of war as the conserver of nationality, is atheistic in its essence. It ignores man's rational and moral nature, the rationality of God's scheme of laws over the world, as the counterpart of man's intelligence and the basis of all just government, and places the safety and permanence of government in the terrors of mere brute-force. It seeks, in short, to govern men, not by the laws of God, and not under God's Moral Government, but to govern them by mere power as if there was no God and no Moral Government. That is simply atheism.

War levied against the *people* of the United States must be criminal, since all war is criminal. But if a part of the people who compose the United States, actuated by the conviction that they could form a government that would suit them better, and for that purpose and apart from violence, should withdraw from their jurisdiction, the act would, in no sense, be a moral crime. In such an act, there is no levying of war, and no adhering to an enemy. The act is simply a withdrawal from jurisdiction—simply the resumption of the inalienable right of self-government. The act might be unwise, imprudent, impolitic, but could not be a sin against God, nor a crime against those who should prefer to remain under the jurisdiction of the United States. It would be no sin against God, for He forbids it neither in the laws of nature nor those of revelation. It would not be a wrong against the other people, because the right to withdraw is always reserved as a political axiom, founded in the nature of things as made by God ; and is, therefore, superior to the provisions of constitutional law. Nor could the act be *treason*, if treason is a *crime*, for it is not within the definition of the constitution and is nowhere forbidden by the law of God. But, in the case supposed, should the remaining people attempt by war, to conquer those who thus asserted peaceably a right with which they had never parted, the act would be a sin against God and a crime against the people ; for it would be making war against a people for asserting axiomatic and undeniable natural rights. Then, should those who assert these rights meet war with war, the act would be a crime just equal to that of the assailants; since God's laws disallow alike the *resistance* and the commission of evil. This conclusion is evident, because God disallows all war, defensive no less than offensive; and equally disallows wrongdoing in one party to justify it in another. The conclusion is evident, too, because defensive wars are prosecuted under the idea of expediency; while the idea of an expediency for violating the laws of God, is both irrational and impious. In the case supposed, God either does or does not allow war for coercing allegiance to the government. If He allows it, it is *right;* if not, it is *wrong;* and there is no *expediency* about it. As to *rights* and *wrongs*, there is no such thing as *expediency*. Expediency to *moral law*, is atheism.

That the makers of the constitution did not regard withdrawal from government as treason, is evident from the fact that itself took its existence in just that act; and we are hardly at liberty to suppose that they intended to define themselves traitors. Whence, treason must be something different from the act of withdrawing allegiance from one government in order to establish another. That act, done without war, violence, or other sinful tempers, is not, and cannot be, either wrong or a crime.

But we need not stay, to discuss the difficult and convenient laws of treason, through its intricate mazes and learned labyrinths. If not all, still much, of its criminality, apart from the sword, is merely *malum prohibitum*, made so to suit the exigencies of passion and despotism, without fitness in a free government. For the nations are still in chains of slavery to the traditions of the Past. And the cure of the national maladies does not lie in the enginery of war, the machinery of the gibbet, nor in uncaging the fierce beast of passion; but in laying aside the idolatry of government, and in pursuing worldly interests by the means which God allows: by ceasing to make and punish crimes, **not** crimes by the laws of God.

But should it be asked. " How is the most wicked crime of treason to be punished?" the answer is easy. First, apart from war, the *criminality* of *treason* has no existence. It is a purely ideal thing. The Scriptures define no such thing; and no such thing can be perceived in the laws of nature. It is one of those purely mythical creations, which has all its force from education and tradition. And having no existence in fact, it has ever been the convenience of tyrants. Paul died for treason, committed with the approbation and by the command of God. And in all ages, it has been employed to prevent innovations from being made upon the established condition of things—in science, in politics, and in religion. And all our notions of *bravery*, *patriotism*, and *treason*, are borrowed from heathenism. Not one of them is Christian. The dark and traditionary past holds the so-called Christian nations bound hand and foot: *we* are in the chains of slavery.

But, secondly, when men commit real crimes, *we* may not take vengeance on them. It is not for *us* to repay. We have no right to sport with the lives and hopes of men, and to slaughter them, though they may have committed "the wicked crime of treason." What right have men to usurp the prerogatives of God, set up standards of expediency, make crimes, and then slaughter men in view of what they have made criminal? Such things simply impeach the wisdom of God, urging, in effect, that our acts of horrid sin are necessary to preserve the peace of society. Such conduct involves at once atheism and the principles of persecution.

The most that can truthfully be said is, that *treason* is *political heresy;* and its trial and punishment by the sword are analagous to the *religious* fire and fagot. And political heresy, treason may be, but the connection between it and the sword is difficult to perceive—as difficult as that between theological heresy and the funeral pile. What *point* in the law of reason and right, connects the *sword* with political heresy? Why should the political heretic die? Can the state not be preserved without destroying the traitor? But has it been by destroying him? And since the effort has not been made, how can that question be decided? Once it was thought that the church could not be saved without the stake; but that has proved to be false. But were not persecutors as honest then as warriors are now? Were they not equally as honest and equally as mistaken? Yea, doubtless. For there is no doubt that God will preserve both the church and the state without the intervention of the sword or fire and fagot. Men need not usurp the prerogatives of God, and commit nearly omnipotent crimes under the idea that, if they do not, society and order will be abolished. For it is war itself, conceived in sin, and brought forth in iniquity, that does nearly the whole mischief. For it is the spirit of war that creates the supposed necessity for war. War is the destroyer, not the preserver, of the peace and order of society.

CHAPTER V.

WAR PUNISHES THE INNOCENT AND LETS THE WICKED GO FREE.

IN every sense in which it can be conceived, war is a calamity and an outrage upon human nature; while it is a shame and a disgrace to our responsible intelligence. The mere exertion of brute force, implying not a high but a low development of man's rational nature, it degrades humanity below the level of itself and below the level of the brute creation. It degrades it below itself, because man's rational and spiritual nature points to a nobler destiny than that of human butchery; and degrades it below the brute creation, because it mainly ignores reason, conscience, and the spiritual nature, by subordinating them to the mere brutish powers. And the more attentively we consider war as a means to an end, the more the rational mind revolts and the sensitive heart recoils; while the impression is more deeply fixed that it does debase humanity below the inferior animals. And the fiercest of the animals are less fierce than man with "high reason endowed." In all the creation of God, so far as we know, not excepting "angels fallen and spirits damned," man is the only being, who, "with instruments of fury and enginery of death," regularly organizes and drills, and then sallies forth in herds whose "tramp quakes the earth and the firmament fills with the echo," deliberately to engage in the work of mutual slaughter: yet, in all the realms of human thought, our intelligence can conceive of no means less suited to attain any desired end than the slaughter when accomplished. The lower animals, however impelled by rage or hunger, never seek to compass an end by means so unsuited to reach it. So that it is literally true, that the imagination can conceive of no sense in which war is not a calamity and a sin, a reproach and an insult to man's rational nature. Unsuited to the end, ferocious as a means, to say that war is barbarous, is telling only a part of the truth. Doing nothing that is good, what does it not do that is bad? What moral precept does it not violate; what right, not invade; what relations, not pollute; what innocence, not tarnish; what helplessness, not oppress? Yet what *justice* does it execute; what wrong, avenge; what oppression, remove; what right, restore; what homage from a just or generous heart, invite? And where do its cruelties fall? Do they fall on those whom *it* adjudges the ill-deserving? Does it drag the guilty to justice and to judgment? It is far from this. First it reverses all the laws of God—making that to be sin which is not sin, that to be virtue which is not virtue, and that to be crime which is not crime; when sallying forth, drunk with its own madness, it lays its bloody clutches, not on the few that may be guilty even by its own false tests, but on the helpless and the innocent, not dragging them to justice but inflicting on them sorrow, starvation and death. It seizes not the few who, by the laws of its own enunciation, have committed crime; but it lays hold of the many who have not committed it. War results from the intrigues, the selfishness, or the ambition of the few; while its inflictions fall on the many—the ignorant, the helpless, the old, women and children. And this consideration alone should deter *all good* men from lending war the least countenance. It is a maxim in civil law, That it is better that a hundred guilty should go unpunished rather than punish one that is innocent. But here, as elsewhere, war reverses the suggestions of humanity, and punishes the hundred who are innocent, and lets go the one that is guilty. And from the nature of war, this must always be the result; because, in the nature of things, of the multitude scourged by the curse of war, only a few can be guilty of the act for which the war is waged, which act itself, in the sight of God, may not have a criminal quality. If it is the dictate of reason that a hundred guilty should go unpunished rather than that one innocent should be punished, and if war punishes the hundred innocent and lets the guilty one go free, war stands against reason in the ratio of ten thousand to one. And, indeed, in the judgment of dispassionate reason, war does stand against such reason as ten thousand to one. Look at our own recent and useless war, brought about by a few demagogues on each side. The North is fierce towards the South as a whole, while the work was done by a very few plotting politicians. Still, the horrors of the war, fell on the *many*, not on the plotting *few*. Let us look at this question for a moment. At the beginning of the war, suppose the South had eight million whites. Then not less than five millions of these would be women and children irresponsible for the causes of war at all times. Of the remaining three millions, not above a twentieth part would have such general knowledge of politics as would enable them to form any intelligent opinions; while not one in five hundred ever read the Constitution of the United States, intelligently. And of the few who had some general notions of constitutional law, not one in a thousand could take an intelligible and comprehensive view of the whole scheme of government as related to the laws and moral government of God, because under the dominion and prejudices of the heathenish Past. Then of those who were driven into the war by the resistless whirlwind of passion, probably the very large majority went with those inward protestations which they had not the moral courage to express. And the division and subdivision may continue till it will be narrowed to a few hundreds who are the actually responsible agents of the late rebellion, as it is called. And of these few, how many had *intelligently* considered the *whole* question of human government as it related to the scheme of God's moral laws? Perhaps the number would not exceed half a score. And such is human nature as now educated. Custom does the thinking—a very few lead, the residue follow. It may safely be affirmed that not more than ten men were the *really* and *thoughtfully* responsible agents, in the South, in precipitating the war. And though thousands and scores of thousands engaged in it with all the passion of unthinking zeal, the *responsible agency* and *real guilt* lay with the handful of leaders. The bodies which passed the acts of secession, thus bringing on the conflict, were led by the fewest number of men; and one followed another in the secession, by a kind of mechanical imitation and furious zeal. And after the war began, in our *sui generis* Congress, a handful of men did what thinking was done, and the residue followed through party considerations. It has always been true, that the *guilty* responsibility of *national* crimes has attached to a *small* number of ambitious *schemers*, who, in the result, drag the masses down with them. In deliberative assemblies, so called, of all kinds, political, legislative, or ecclesiastic, the few do the thinking for all;—the few prescribe thought and feeling for the residue. To these few the intelligently guilty responsibility attaches; all the rest being common place followers by imitation. This idea agrees with the keen phillippic of Paul against the Roman leaders of his age, who spoiled the people through vain philosophy.

The same principle has been seen in our country. Compared with the masses, a *very few* leaders precipitated the nation into the dire conflict of arms and the cruel desolations of war—a few at the South and a few at the North are the guilty who brought on the *people* the sufferings which will only be fully realized in eternity. Yet it is frightful to retrospect the eight years which have just passed. How appalling the rage of fanaticism! How, like the ocean-waves in the storm, have ignorance, passion, and bigotry surged and tossed! A little leaven had leavened the whole lump—the spirit and temper of the few had been imparted to the whole. Fanaticism seemed supreme in dominion. Men and women alike in the North, though they had no intelligent idea of the national Constitution, could say *just how* the war should be carried on, wherein it had been carried on amiss; and seemed preternaturally endued with the exact views God held of the war. Ignorance and bigotry were so united as to produce just that compound which is the parent of persecution, and just that compound which must prevail before the people in a land of Bibles can be plunged into the vortex of insane war. Yet the whole was the deliberate work of the leaders. The *very few* did the work—wrought upon their dependants and satellites, who, in turn, operated upon theirs, till the whole nation—the South in its selfish interests, and the North in its—became wrought up to a point of true maniasm; the rule of a wild fanaticism was nearly complete. In the state, in the church, little was the difference.

And it is fearful to contemplate how human nature may be worked up and imposed on, and then misled to evil ends! A few deeply guilty spirits may set millions of men at the work of mutual butchery! And after the work is done, it is humiliating to observe the manner in which the wicked wretches reconcile their consciences to the deeds of iniquity. They draw their comfort from each other, and harden each other in iniquity. One imparts to the other a feeling, which he *returns* with increased intensity; when each will reason from the other to himself, seeking to deceive himself with the belief that the other *means* well, and so must be in the right; while himself, entertaining the same views and feelings, must also be in the right: deceived, they are yet deceivers: with hearts set in them to do evil, they are the deceivers of each other. Then, as evil men and seducers, they wax worse and worse, till they involve themselves and the whole country in the common ruin of desolating war. Now sporting themselves on their own deceivings, reveling in blood and cruelty, the multitude go hand in hand to do evil.

Thus moulded, those who are wrought for the purpose, are more fitted for the work than their moulders; for having a zeal untempered with knowledge, they are more yielding than clay in the hands of the potter. It is thence that the deluded soldiery so frequently exceed, in cruelty, the commands of their superior; while the *really great captain* sometimes shows a grain of magnanimity to his belligerent foes. But before God, those who generate the spirit of war, though they may be few, are responsible for all that follows. And the general who, in the late conflict in this country, led the raid wherein invalid women and children were consumed in the burning of their own dwellings, must meet a fearful responsibility in the day of inquisition; as likewise must those officials who take refuge from their cruelties behind the bulwarks of a paper constitution. All these earthly refuges calcined by the consuming fires of justice, when themselves and their peers in crime shall stand arraigned for the torture and murder of the helpless and the innocent, paper constitutions will be of little avail. Awful retribution!

How men who have wives and children and souls in their bodies, can be guilty of such omnipotent cruelties, it seems impossible to conceive! Knowing as all leaders do, that *a very few* are guilty of the crime which *they* allege has been committed, how can they, for such offence—which is often a mere difference in political opinion—inflict suffering so dreadful and fatal, on the helpless and defenceless—on young girls and feeble mothers, on tottering age and tearful infancy? Contemplate, for example, the facts after our late war closed, and gaunt famine stared in the faces of hundreds of thousands, for whom it reached out its cold and bony clutches! And this all came to pass at the instance of a few reckless, godless politicians, North and South, who, arraying themselves on opposite sides, struggled for power, through the medium of certain political notions, which they respectively alleged would promote the public worldly weal. As the eye glances back, the heart feels faint with sadness.

For the credit of human nature, it is hoped that some of the Southern people deplored the self-destructive war into which the nation was plunged; though some districts were criminally unanimous in bringing on themselves their wasting desolations. In other districts we know that leading individuals sought the aversion of the storm which swept over the country. In the North, too, there were several elements which opposed the war as unwise, needless, and criminal. It may be well to look at these for a few moments, as indicating the public mind.

The largest single element that opposed it was a political party one; and it was actuated by party considerations, having very little moral principle; just as the party which prosecuted it did so on party grounds, with little principle. However, there was a large Christian element which opposed *that* war, as all others, on Christian grounds, believing that all war is contrary to the teaching of Christ; but it was widely scattered throughout the country, and was alarmed and hushed into silence by the wild storms of passion which swept over the entire country.

Yet truth extorts the sad confession that many who had formally professed the peace doctrines, either openly renounced them, or, on account of their hatred of slavery, entered into very full sympathy with the Northern arms.

But could all the persons that opposed—those who opposed it on mere political, or party grounds—those who oppposed it on moral principle—and the many that secretly opposed it, yet went into the army because they had not the moral courage to stand against the beating storms of passion—have been united, they would probably have formed a majority during the whole war. In this, however, as in all other cases in life, the *right* was timid and faltering, while the *wrong* was bold and daring, the latter overbearing and terrifying the former into silence.*

* It cannot be denied that the Quakers quite generally sympathized with the success of the Northern arms, not always entertaining an enlightened faith on the subject of war. Their testimony had become traditional and shadowy, and existed rather as a dogma than as an active principle; but the question of slavery, constantly agitated, was vivid

The thoughts of these persons, terrified by the howling tornado of passion, were hushed into silence ; and thousands were forced into the army by outside pressure and there killed, for it required more true moral courage to

in their minds, and so led them very generally to sympathize with the work of the sword. They lacked the accurate primal principles on which alone the peace reform must be accomplished. These must be embraced, and then carried to all their practical consequences; and they will reverse many of the cherished notions of men, and destroy much of the present frame-work of society. And it seems impossible to discover any principle on which a true Quaker could vote with and sustain a war-party in politics. Unless he abandoned his peace principles, he could not without great inconsistency. Formerly Quakers who held closely to their doctrines, generally did not vote, but that cunning which plunged us into the late needless war, beguiled the Quakers to some extent, and seduced them to vote with one of the most marked political war-parties of modern times. And this thought is the subject of grief; especially as they were led to embrace, as the justification of voting, that false moral principle which teaches, " That of two evils, one must choose the less "—false, because morality disallows us *to choose* any evil, though if the alternative is so forced on us that we *must act*, we may *endure* but *not choose* the less of two evils. So, too, the Quakers were seduced into the common but erroneous belief that *the act of the South in seceding was in itself a wrong and sin*, apart from violence and war. But if peace-men would convince the world, they must take some rational ground on which they may stand, and all the practical consequences of which they are willing to accept. And that ground lies alone in the axiomatic principle, that the right of self-government in inalienable, and so may always be employed without violating the rights of others or disobeying the divine injunction of submitting to the instituted authorities. We may therefore hold with perfect consistency, that the South had the natural right to separate from the North with the view of instituting another government, while we intensely reprobate the use of the sword either to secure or to prohibit that end. And far be it from the writer to sympathize in the least with the rebellion just as it occurred. The rebellion was a fearful iniquity, with which I have no sympathy. But with the right of instituting and maintaining self-government without violence and on peace-principles, I cordially sympathize, whether Ireland, Canada, Cuba, Italy, or the Southern States, seek to employ it. In that right our nation took its self-governing existence ; and, with Mr. Lincoln before the war, by the use of that right and principle, I believe the world is to be liberated, while the sword is to be sheathed for-stand before the tornado of passion than to stand in the presence of an army. Yet, many as opposed the war or as did not properly exert influence in favor of it, *all* are made to suffer. The hearts of mothers, sisters, fathers, are wrung in anguish for sons and brothers, who, unable to withstand the whirlwind of passion, were engulphed in the vortex of war, and sank to rise no more. So oppressive taxes are wrung from all—even from the infant who derives its patrimony from the father slaughtered upon the hostile field. So that before prattling infancy can utter articulate sounds, it is *punished* by the loss of a father slaughtered, and perhaps by that of a mother destroyed of grief by loss of the father, while it is *fined* as a criminal for inheriting from a sacrificed father and a grief-fallen mother—*fined* in the form of oppressive taxation. What justice! what morality! what Christianity!

So, the man who honestly believes that God forbids all war, is drafted and compelled, willing or unwilling, to slay his fellow-mortals. Though he may feel that he cannot fight, that God forbids it, that he might as well be drafted to steal, blaspheme, or commit adultery, yet there is no relief, the imperious tyrant of war never relents: he must do what he regards as a crime or suffer harm, perhaps lose life or liberty himself. His conscience says to him, as God does, *Thou shalt not kill;* and he feels that men have as much right to suspend any other command as this; yet he is required against all this to engage in the work of slaughtering men. He is told that the Constitution requires him to fight. But he cares little for that, knowing that men make the Constitution, and that men have no right to set aside the laws of God. He regards the Constitution as an

ever. And the ground of the American Peace Society is as untenable as that of the war-man; for it simply leaves the right to engage in war in every case, to be decided by the people who may want to engage in it. The *substance* of its position is, It is best for a people not to engage in war, unless they think it best to engage in it. But we hope to see it take a higher Christian ground.

intricate and complex thing, as to the meaning of which men disagree. As for himself he never read it, and could not understand it if he had. But he has caught the spirit of Christ, and cannot imbrue his hand in his brother's blood. He *feels* the opposition to killing which he is unable to express, and what the wily conscience-seared politician could not appreciate; thus making literally true the statement of the late Secretary of War, when, in indignant and savage scorn, he said—" I cannot appreciate such consciences and such scruples." Had he appreciated such consciences, he could not have been party to the murder of hundreds of thousands; and a scrupulous appreciative conscience is a quality not much needed by a Secretary of War. What perversion and cruelty have rendered inappreciable to the war-man, is the most valued virtue in the conscientious mind; and to test such a mind by the moral standard of a Stanton, a Cæsar, or a Napoleon, is the greatest outrage.

But like Polycarp and the early Christians, the true peace-man cannot fight, though he is spoiled of his goods, thrown into noisome bastiles, or suffers death. Refusing to fight, lately the peace-man was called on to pay a heavy forfeiture instead of doing the work of slaughtering. And he understands this, as the cunning legislator did, to be only a quirk,—the same thing in principle, though a little different in form—and refuses to pay the forfeiture. What comes next? Simply the insolent officials, to enforce the forfeiture by distress and confiscation; thus, by fraud and by force, compelling the citizen, against conscience, natural right, and the laws of God, to slaughter men and lay waste their country. The mind can conceive of nothing more utterly without excuse, nothing more wanton and heartle s than a statute law, which, auxiliary to the demands of war, seeks to compel men, contrary to the teaching of God and against the dictates of conscience, to engage in the work of slaying their fellows, for whatever cause. And merciful Author of all good! must men be *compelled to kill* other *men*—dying mortals—when they regard the act as a most revolting crime? In all the acts of outrage and cruelty, what excels the statute laws of Congress on this subject? Are we still in the midst of barbarism? And are the rights of conscience to be disregarded, because unscrupulous politicians "cannot appreciate such scruples" as oppose the crime and sin of war?

A like question, in principle, arises under the burden of taxation. There may be involved no question of conscience, though it is a war-tax. But there is a question of outrage; for there are those who believe that war is not the legal means—under God's laws—to sustain even government; believe that it destroys everything, sustains nothing. Yet others, heedlessly and recklessly adopting it, regardless of the dictates of reason, the teaching of Christianity, or the lessons of experience, compel other men, by force of distress and confiscation, to pay, year after year, a heavy percentage of their earnings, to defray the cost of those crusades of slaughter which have their true foundation in godless lust. And to the reflective mind these are not trivial considerations. Yet they are not even to be compared to the *sufferings* and *sins* produced by war. And but think where the sufferings mostly fall! —on the helpless and the innocent. Think of the invasions, the marches and the counter-marches of an army through a country inhabited by civilized people! Hither and thither the armies stampede, as the fortunes of uncertain war veer, spreading terror and dismay *before* them ; and leaving tears and poverty, empty garners and charred dwellings *behind* them. As they sway to and fro, daughters are violated ; mothers give premature births ; fathers flee or are thrown into prison ; farms are despoiled ; houses burned ; property destroyed ; children doomed to poverty, rags, and starvation ; while the outraged and wretched persons are innocent of any crimes or wrongs ; and the leaders, the really guilty parties, not only go unpunished, but with large pay, they revel in luxury, debauchery, and ease ; and high officials sit at pleasure in dining-rooms and parlors, or attend theatres and places of amusement and sin at the great capitals. And such is war: the innocent suffer, and the guilty go free. And men are literally *driven* into the army from fear of conscription, and that in a *free* government! Men are *compelled* to fight for a *free* government! It is no less a burlesque on *true* freedom, than it is an outrage on human nature. It is not only a sin against moral law, it is no less one against natural right and the very name of freedom. Those who did nothing to bring on the war, who know nothing of the fraud and trickery which induced it, and who wish not to enter the army to slay others or to be slain, are yet goaded into it by sneers, jeers, scorn, and the terrors of conscription and confiscation. Upon sober reflection, few acts of mankind are better suited to fill the mind with a sense of outrageous injustice and cold intense barbarity. Let the reader think of it. An intelligent being, seeking to realize his responsibility to God, is coolly ordered to take a gun and load it with powder and ball; and then in cold blood to shoot down a dying mortal about some different notions—*he* knows not exactly what—which politicians have about the words of the Constitution; or it may be about something that *politicians* call *honor*, of which nobody has any definite idea. Yet about these *ideal* things men are conscripted and forced into the army, to suffer, to kill, it may be, or to be killed, leaving unprovided for a feeble wife and dependent children! What language can describe properly such acts of wanton cruelty? Think of it. A man does not want to kill, protests that he does not, urges that he knows not the ground of the war, names wife and children and his duty to them, suggests that God forbids the act which he is required to do; yet, with stolid indifference, as if he had neither affections nor soul, he is dragged forth, drilled for the work, forced to shoulder a musket, rush into the jaws of death, and every instant threatened himself with death, is ordered to fire on and seek the lives of others!! When we carefully reflect, such acts are an outrage upon humanity and a presumption against God, suited to make devils and infernal spirits turn pale and tremble.

Then the slain man, too, like the slayer, may have entered the opposing army under solemn protests, revolted at the idea of slaughtering a fellow-man—may have been conscripted and forced from home and family—may not have understood the object for which he is compelled to fight, or, understanding it, may have opposed it—may be the friend or relative of the man whose ball makes a hopeless widow or helpless orphans; yet barbarous war takes no heed. The insolent usurpers of God's prerogatives, who assume to wage war, care nothing for these things. If one has a soul to feel or eyes to weep for anguish-smitten humanity; if piteous tears could move, or heart-riven anguish could touch, the stony heart, he would be unfit for the leader of armies or the duties of war.

In the judgment of sober reason, the single fact that the sufferings of war fall mainly on those who are innocent in the judgment of war-men themselves, ought forever to deter humane men from engaging in it.

CHAPTER VI.

§ 1.—*Personal Self-Defence by Destroying Life.*

WARS, carried on in reference to government, are justified on the ground of false notions in regard to the nature of it. These false notions are based on a false assumption, touching man as an individual, which is carried, by a supposed analogy, from the individual to the nation, inducing a conclusion which, in our country, exerts a controlling influence on the popular mind, and constitutes nearly the first and chief argument to justify war. Whether the idea exerts much or little influence over those minds which are primarily responsible for the popular opinion and conscience, it is a fact that it has a controlling influence over the masses; and being specious in its character and permanent in its duration, it demands that careful attention which shows it to have no solid foundation.

We will state the argument much as it lies in the popular mind. When it is said that war is a great wrong, that it is revolting for rational beings destined soon to pass into the eternal world, to provide themselves with deadly weapons, and on deliberate purpose to begin the slaughter of each other, the reply is, "Yes, it is a terrible thing, and mostly wrong, but in the case of *our* war, it is right. Do not *you* think so?" Being answered in the negative, with surprise the response is made, "What! not defend the life of the nation? If an assassin should seek your life and that of your family, would you not kill him first if you could. And what is the difference in *that* case, and where rebels are seeking the life of the nation?"

Millions of honest people are deceived by this specious sophism, and people of respectable talent will urge it as if it had force in it. Yet the answer to it is as evident as demonstration, while one is astonished that sensible persons can be imposed on by it. For the very point in the supposed argument, is wanting. There is not the slightest analogy between the things compared. Indeed, what analogy can there be between my life and that which, by a bold figure, we call *the life of a nation ?* Has one out of every million deceived by it carefully reflected about what constitutes the life of a nation? And the vast parade made for the last few years about the nation's life in this country, has been as idle as it has been meaningless. For a nation is a corporate thing, having, in no proper or literal sense, either soul or body; and so it is wholly incapable of anything like death. The great objection to killing men is, that it sends their souls out of their bodies into eternity, and the souls of the wicked into a dreadful doom. Has a nation a soul to go before God in judgment? If it has not, what becomes of the great popular argument? The whole thing is a shallow delusive sophism, put into circulation to mislead the unthinking. What my life is we can readily understand; but who can form any conception of that which by a bold figure, is called *the life of a nation ?* Does not he who attempts to reason from one to the other, show that he has no ability at all to reason? And does not he who engages in war from the influence of such an argument, engage in it from imposition and delusion ?

But the supposed argument deserves to be analyzed and so presented to the mind that its real force may be estimated. We may divide what is called the argument. This we must do, and then scrutinize the several parts. And, first, there are some assumptions which demand careful attention. One of these is, *May I, by authority of moral law, mortally smite him who has a design upon my life ?* The principle involved in the question may be more briefly called, *The right of self-defence.* Most men simply take this right for granted. The basis of it is *feeling*, and not reason. The right is assumed, and never proved. No writer on the subject has reasoned it out by any legitimate processes; while no one can adduce an utterance of Jesus or any apostle in support of it. The whole spirit of the gospel—indeed the whole idea of God's moral government over the world, contradicts the assumption, that man should undertake to do for himself what God claims the right of doing for him. And the idea of self-defence, by violence, finally involves atheism; but we shall not pause at this point, to exhibit the proof of the proposition.

We are told that, *The right of self-defence is the first law of nature;* and it is called, *The instinct of self-preservation.* The *inferior animals* are also said to possess it; and thence it is thought to be established beyond controversy. And did the mind never go beyond these superficial suggestions and this infidel idea of safety in our own feeble arm, the reasoning might have an appearance of force. But even then the inference that the instincts of the lower animals are to stand as the law of God and the rule of duty to rational man, might not seem clear to the philosopher. This is a valued argument to the superficial thinker, and conclusive to the popular mind. But how far may the popular mind be trusted?

In some things, nothing is more reliable than the popular mind; but in other things nothing is less reliable. Matters of sense and the phenomena of things fall peculiarly within the popular apprehension; and so far it may be trusted. But the interpretation of what appears, the determination of the real which underlies the apparent, are offices too recondite for popular solution. The popular mind can confidently decide that the rising and setting of the sun produce the alternation of day and night. But how the sun rises and shines, how the appearance is to be interpreted, may not confidently be committed to the popular judgment. That is a severer task, and requires patient thought and reflection. In plain cases of duty, the judgment of the masses may be trusted, if not tampered with; but in any trying crisis of life, the masses cannot know what is right. They are subject to be grossly imposed upon and misled. What is very plain, they can see. But how to interpret an appearance, they do not know. It is here that they are constantly deceived and misled; while it is astonishing to see the extent to which the deception is carried. And it is more astonishing to see how the cultivated and educated are misled!

And in no respect, perhaps, have honest Christian people been more deluded than about the idea of self-defence. The depraved instinct they feel and know to exist. But how to interpret and understand it so as to learn their duty, is a task too severe for them. And hearing a plausible interpretation which *they* cannot answer, they accept it for truth, without further inquiry. For most people accept as true what *they* cannot see to be untrue; and whether credulity or infidelity has done more to degrade and curse the world, it would be difficult to say. All superstition and idolatry are but forms of credulity. Infidelity and credulity, the extremes united as they mostly are in the same mind, constitute the foe and destroyer of human happiness. And infidelity and credulity, in odious combination, are played on in the interpretation of the instinct of self-defence. Puny and infidel man has no faith in the promises and power of God to defend him; but is miraculously credulous in his ability to defend himself. Even professing Christians have little or no faith in the protective presence of God; and having little faith in Him as a defence, they arm themselves with knives and revolvers, that, refusing the defence of His name, they may defend themselves in their own. On their knees they confess that in Him they live and move, yet, practically they have no confidence in Him; and esteem a revolver more highly than the Almighty Power of God. Here, indeed, are infidelity and credulity combined, forming actual practical atheism.

But is it true that self-defence is the *first law of nature?* Is it true that the kind of self-defence intended is a law of nature at all? What is meant by a law of nature? If by it is meant the constitution of things as made by God, it is not true that the intended self-defence is a law of nature at all. For it is certain that as God made the laws of nature, there existed the right of neither attack nor defence. The law of nature is the law of love, and love works no ill to a neighbor. We must ever distinguish between the real laws of nature and our mere conceptions of them. These are frequently quite distinct things. And in interpreting nature, much depends on the rules adopted. How do we know what the utterance of nature is? Nature is polyglot; and unless we have a certain means of deciding what her utterance is, no reliance can be placed in what we make her say. But we repeat, What are we to understand by a law of nature? Are we to understand the law of brute nature or the law of human nature? and if the latter, are we to understand a law within or without the mind? But suppose we should learn the law of brute nature, that could hardly answer the ends of an argument in this connection, unless it is known that the law is the same in man and brute. Hence it is proper to inquire, Is it a law of human nature to slay him who attempts to slay us? For if the laws of brute nature are the same as those of human nature, what is the difference between men and brutes? And how do we learn the existence of the law of self-defence? Is it by analogy to the brute-creation? But animals rarely kill in self-defence. They mostly destroy for food or for the mere end of killing. Yet the inquiry, by analogy, simply reduces man to a level with the beasts. If man is but a brute creature, the reasoning would be plausible, at least. Still, even then, the law of the species might not be the same; for some species of animals will not defend their lives by fighting. But if man is known to possess reason and a moral nature, rendering him immortal, who will say that his *instincts* should not be subject to the dominion of reason and conscience? Grant, then, that he has the *instinct* of self-defence, how comes it that instinct is to govern him? Man possesses different natures.

To which of these does the instinct belong?—to his brute-nature, to his moral nature, to his intellectual nature, to his carnal nature, or to his regenerated spiritual nature? Did it belong to man before the fall, or is it one of the incidents of "that fatal fall that brought us all our woes?" With redeemed humanity, will *it* pass into the world of glory, or will it remain behind when the "carnal evil is unwound?"

All men with whom we reason admit that nature and revelation utter the same moral laws. Shall we, then, interpret Nature by Revelation, or Revelation by Nature? Shall we read the clear teachings by the mysterious ones, or the mysterious ones by the clear ones? It is acknowledged that nature is replete in secrets, demanding a medium of interpretation. And when it is supposed that nature is interpreted, no confidence can be placed in the interpretation. For the *supposed law* of to-day is the *known phenomenon* of to-morrow. Changeable as the aspects of a vernal sky, the supposed utterances of nature cannot be trusted. Nature truly utters a voice, but our dull ears may not correctly catch the sound of it.

The laws of revelation, however, we understand to be the true interpretation of those of nature. True, when the Infinite speaks to the finite, there must be mystery; and there is mystery in revelation. A large part of its impressiveness comes from its mysteriousness. Yet, as to the practical duties of life, its disclosures are so plain, that he who runs may read. Hence, in the duties of life and touching the question before us, our appeal must be, not to the dark and dubious utterances of nature, but to the clear teachings of revelation. The standard of truth is revelation, not the instincts of our animal natures. Whence, if we have the right of self-defence, we must derive it not from a brute instinct, nor from the first law of mysterious nature, obtained by some occult process of interpretation; but from the clear teaching of revelation. For if the revealed law disallows "the right of self-defence," the translation of an animal instinct into it, as a false rendering of nature is false, or God allows a law of the depraved instinct to be placed above the law of revelation. And Christians must decide for themselves whether tney prefer the word of God or an animal instinct as the guide to their duty.

Dr. Hickok disposes of this whole question in a manner far more brief than satisfactory. "But when a man attacks my person," he asks, "may I defend myself by assaulting and disabling him? I think the dictate of pure morality plain in the affirmative. If I only disable in self-defence, I may ever after regret that necessity as a misfortune; but if it has gone to the extent of taking life to shield my own, I shall not feel debased by it, as any invasion of the assailant's rights. He forfeited all his rights in the assault, at least to the extent of the injury he designed to inflict on me; and if I only defend myself at the expense of a like injury on him, he has no right to complain, nor I any reason to feel self-degradation. It would have been unworthy of me, to have passively assented to the injury, and allowed my own rights to have been wantonly and wickedly destroyed."

It would be difficult to imagine anything more unsatisfactory than such reasoning. The mere *ipse dixit* of a philosopher, it is supported by nothing but his feelings. The assailant "forfeited all his rights in the assault," and so may be disabled to "the extent of taking life," if the assailed should apprehend a design on his life. But where do we learn that an assault "forfeits all rights in the assailant?" The resentful feelings of a neoteric doctor are hardly a sufficient warrant to take life under a mere apprehension. Nor would the fact that he would not "feel degradation," prove his act to be right, unless we were satisfied that he was incapable of sin. But such loose dicta can convince those only who are already satisfied. For it would surely be better for the Christian to die by the hand of the assassin, and go to his reward, than to kill the wretch and send him to perdition. And if allowed to live, he might repent and both might dwell together in endless blessedness. And if Christianity is true, Dr. Hickok's reasoning is false, and so he might have good " reason to feel self-degradation " at the thought of slaying his assailant.

In part first of this work we think it is shown that death had no place in the original constitution of nature, and that it came into the world by sin. And as death had no place in the original constitution of nature, the right to inflict it could not be derived from that constitution ; and hence, under that constitution, there was no right to inflict it in self-defence. Before the fall, this was certainly the constitution of nature. And so, if the right of self-defence exists since the fall, it comes by the introduction of sin, since *all* death came by sin. In that case, we ask for the law giving the right since sin was introduced. Did the fall so change the constitution of nature as to make wrong right? Satan introduced sin, and sin introduced death; and so, if it exists, the right of self-defence must have come from Satan. But if God has given the right, we ask for the letter or spirit of the grant. Where shall we find it?

But if we cannot find the right in nature, where shall we find it in revelation? We demand the authority of Jesus Christ. We ask not the *ipse dixit* of some theological doctor. But we ask authority from the Great Master. Give us a positive precept or the necessary logical inference. Either will be satisfactory: less will not. The Scriptures instruct us as to every duty in life. If it is duty to kill in self-defence, we demand inspired authority for it. Yet we all know there is no such authority. There is no precept and no example—no " thus saith the Lord." In primitive Christianity, no apostle and no Christian interpreted an animal instinct, or a selfish " feeling " into the right of self-defence. When attacked and dragged to the stake, they " passively assented to the injury," and were not probably rendered so " unworthy " as Dr. Hickok thinks he would be by acting as they did. *But they lived* under a purer outside influence than we do. The spirit of chivalry amongst Christians had not attained that pre-eminence it now holds. But, like the Great Master, Christians were then true non-resistants. The Master did not disable assailants, and was not perhaps rendered "unworthy" thereby, though Dr. Hickok thinks himself would be. They adhered to peace-principles and refused to engage in war, though it cost them life; and we do not learn that they thereby gained the disapprobation of God. Is it not possible that we may do as they did and yet be "worthy?"

Did Christ or His apostles ever resort to this "first law of nature," "the instinct of self-preservation," or their "feelings" for authority "to disable an assailant?" If we know anything, we know He and they did not. All suffered the loss of property and life without it. And did they commit sin by violating the first law of nature, or act unworthily when they refused to disable an assailant? But it is urged that the cases of Christ and the apostles were singular. What then, about the Christians for the first three centuries, as they followed the example of Christ and the apostles, and refused to fight in self-defence? Was it unlawful for them to act singularly as their Master and the apostles did? To this age of heroic chivalry, such confidence in the Divine Teacher may appear singular. Still, we think Christians might continue to follow Christ's example and not thereby be "unworthy."

Rash and thoughtless men tell us that, when assailed, "not to defend one's self to the utmost of his power, would, if death should ensue, render the person accessory to self-murder." Be it so then. I would prefer to have my blood on guilty hands, rather than have guilty blood on my hands. And we prefer to follow the example of Christ, rather than an animal instinct or the imagined *first law of nature.*

But we are met here and assured that "the apostles did not defend themselves because they *knew* the attempt would be unsuccessful." Alas, for such a subterfuge! It is very weak; not more weak than wicked. Had they been heroes, honor would have attached to the attempt, though unsuccessful; and where duty commands, may good men pause to compute the chances of success or failure? How impotent and foolish is such a system of dialectics!

The example of the apostles and early Christians must remain for the instruction of the church in all ages, while it accords with the explicit teaching of Christ himself. It was foretold that persecution and slaughter awaited the Master's followers, as death had already befallen the Master. Then, when these followers should be assailed, should they be expected to act otherwise than as the Master and the disciples had? And in fact, how did they act? Just as the Master, the apostles, and the first followers did, till the heroic philosophy began to deal with *instincts, feelings*, and *first laws of nature.* And when the heroic philosophy began to imbue the church with its spirit, the spirit of Christ began to cease to imbue the church. The almighty protection of God was exchanged for the protection of an arm of flesh; when Christians laid aside the spiritual weapons which they were enjoined to use, and took up the carnal weapons which they were enjoined not to use. And Christians, rejecting the promises and protection of God, and seeking protection in the weapons of the flesh—the history of the church thenceforward is before us—is before us, written in tears and characters of blood. Thousands upon thousands have been torn asunder and tortured, slaughtered and mangled, with every circumstance of aggravation and cruelty; while no man can affirm that, speaking in a worldly aspect only, they were gainers by laying aside the Christian mode of defence and assuming the heroic mode; by rejecting the government of God over the world, and assuming the government themselves. But, by so doing, it is evident that they became *practical atheists;* and probably suffered a thousand fold more than they would, had they followed the example and teaching of Him who is the Moral Governor of the world, and who would have cared for them, had they put themselves under His care.

But as *they* became practical atheists in rejecting His care so does *he* who now rejects it for knives and pistols. And that is a sublime faith which seeks protection in the arm of the living God! Such faith is just that which God everywhere enjoins—is simply Christian faith. And what are knives, pistols, and swords, compared with the protection of Him who controls the minds and purposes which use knives, pistols, and swords? To the mad heart panting for blood, how easy for Him to say, "thus far and no further." And what is the harm of knives and bullets, unless directed by volitions and purposes? And which is the more consistent for Christians, to seek protection in Him who can control volitions and purposes, or in that arm of flesh which may use knives, swords, and bullets, because the ruffian and assassin use them? Which method is the more philosophical? and which, the more Christian?

But we hear professing Christians object that God interposes protection, only so far as we seek to protect ourselves with carnal weapons; thus quite ignoring the Scriptural idea of divine protection. And it is precisely here that Christian men, professedly, are atheists, practically: rejecting God's government over the world by His providence; casting away the protection of His mighty arm; and thereby falsifying their prayers in their cold and intellectual faith; while, actuated by a heroic and heathenish spirit, they essay to create a protective providence by the use of knives, guns, and pistols. If such conduct is not practical atheism, we know not where it could be found.

And what has been the success of this mode of self-defence? and what has been the success of fighting Christians, generally? Yet the success has been just what we might expect. Professed Christians but real infidels could not rationally have expected different results. For God blesses only the means of His own appointment; and we can learn His appointments best from His revealed will. And do the precepts of Christ authorize the use of violence in self-defence? Does His example? Anticipating that he may be shot, must the Christian make haste to shoot first? Must he ward off *possible* sin by *actual* sin? Apprehending that he *might be* slain, must he certainly slay? Such morality may be consistent in the duellist, the warrior, and the hero; but it is very inconsistent in the Christian, who professes that his life is hid with Christ in God.

Our view of the subject is established by both the letter and spirit of Christ's teachings. He uniformly taught that we should suffer wrong rather than to do wrong. The heroic, duelistic and resentful spirit belongs to this carnal sinful world: it is *its* mode of self-defence, because it knows no god but the one of might and power.

Actuated by this resentful spirit, it is no wonder that the churches over this land have hung their harps on the willow; while themselves, bowed as the bulrush, are prostrate in delusion and apostasy. And Christianity goes not forth conquering and to conquer, as it did during the two or three centuries of its purity. But, adopting the maxims of the world, plunging into wars, borrowing from idolators the heroic spirit, it lost its power to overcome the world, being itself overcome by the world. And so it remains to this day. In the right hand it has held the sword; in the left and feebly it has carried the *form* of the gospel. With it an animal instinct has been more potent than the law of Christ. The doctrines of the Prince of Peace have less controlled the inner life than the forces of the animal impulses. And what circle in society has not been poisoned by the heroic spirit? We have heroic historians, heroic orators, heroic poets; judges heroic, legislators heroic, and pulpits heroic. Nay, we have mothers heroic, sisters heroic, and heroic coquettes who make love to none but heroes.*
Indeed, is not this a heroic age? And yet it is all of *this* world. How soon it will perish! There is no Christ in it

---

* During the late war, the writer knew of a clump of belles who vowed *inter se* that they would bestow their gracious smiles on none but soldiers. Were they not worthy of hero-husbands?

all; none of His meek spirit; none of His gentle nature: in all the pomp and parade, *He* is not found. But it is all godless, vile, and intensely selfish.

Notwithstanding these considerations, which ought to satisfy Christians, the right of self-defence is pressed with no waning zeal. But it takes the form of an *argumentum ad hominem*. The imagination is invoked and excited to action. An ideal case is put. With knife and revolver in hand, the assassin is summoned to your door. In your own home, you, your wife, and children, are put into extreme peril by him. And then, amidst the trying and imploring appeals of wife, children, and self-love, you are made to judge what you would do in the fanciful case. All that is dear upon earth is made to appeal to your self-love. And indeed, this is astute special pleading, an admirably conceived supposition. A man must possess strange coolness if he does not at once decide in his own favor, and sentence the threatening wretch with the contents of a revolver. Yet if a man will consent to be judge in his own case, he must separate from himself all passion, and rule according to law. Let us put such a man in the second person, and then say to him, Your position is novel. You have consented to try not only your own case, but that of your wife and children, whose life is at stake. You should therefore suppress the clamors of self-love. Seated in the Hall of Judgment, justice must hold equal the scales of eternal right; and consenting to try your own case, cannot change the utterances of law. Therefore, guard diligently lest self-love choke the avenues of justice. For the heart is deceitful. Who can know it? And not only is the heart deceitful, it is desperately wicked. So beguiling is the siren voice of self-love, that it is a pity you consented to act as judge in such a trial. You may tarnish conscience and pervert justice. And would you not better refer the case, for trial, to the judge of all the earth? Or do you fear to trust him? He sits Supreme on the bench of the universe, and judges angels and men, swaying the scepter of Universal Empire. From Sinai's tempestuous summit. He has laid down the law, now unrepealed and unrepealable, THOU SHALT NOT KILL. In your pressing exigency, can you administer that law? If you cannot, does not your reputation for common honesty demand that you resign the place in which shrewdness has placed you for the purpose of blinding your judgment by the insinuations of self-love? Then where so much personal interest is involved, it would seem more proper to allow the Great Judge to prescribe the law, and even try the case. If the case is referred to that Judge, *He* may cause even the heart of an assassin to relent, so that you may all live. In ways that *you* cannot imagine, *He* can save you and yours. And the heart of an assassin is in His hands, and He turneth it whithersoever he will. And the life of the Christian is hid with Christ in God.

Or, since in all the long years of the past, history records no case at once so wicked and cunning as the one created by the supposition, it *may* be that you will never be required to act in circumstances so trying to your virtue. If you are a true Christian and peaceable citizen, it is hard to see why even an assassin should stand at the door of your domicile so thirsting for the blood of yourself, wife, and babes. It *may* be that a deed of such extreme atrocity, may never exist, save by the shrewd supposition which would render apparent the right to shed blood. And if you earnestly seek the protection of God, according to His requirements, He may save you the necessity of either smiting the foul assassin, or of sitting as judge in your own case. If you are homeless, have committed all your ways to God, and have renounced the bully's mode of self-defence, it is not easy to imagine the motive which would bring the assassin to your door, with knife and pistol in hand. Therefore, the whole thing is probably frightful only as a supposition, and as a creation of fancy, for the end of silencing conscience and perverting the mind to admit the right to kill men in the business of war. In the history of six thousand years, no case is recorded of an assassin who has acted *so* badly: and no one may do so for the same length of time to come, thereby sparing you the embarrassment of deciding in your own case. Hence, the shrewdly supposed case is not very practical in real life, and it may not be needful to torture the mind about the mythical assassin.

Yet, importuned in the hypothetical case, what shall be further said? Some one, it seems, has to be killed without authority from God. You must murder the assassin or he will murder you. If in this trying hour, you appeal to the writer for the law of the case as he understands it, and then for the application of the law to the facts, the following will be the finding and the judgment thereon: 1. The law which is to govern in the case, is God's law; and it being holy, wise, and suitable to the necessities of men, ought always to be observed. 2. By the teachings of that law, the desire and attempt of one to murder one do not justify me in actually murdering him. 3. The doctrine of counter-crime which justifies me in killing because the assassin desires to kill, finds no place in the laws of God, but finds basis only in the sinful passions, and authority only from laws which are anti-Christian and heathenish; and the argument founded on it is only specious at best, while it is clearly heathenish in spirit, and has manifestly been foisted into the codes of Christian nations, through the sophistries of Satan and the desires of a selfish heart, with which it so well comports and agrees. For, by virtue of its practical operation, a man may be released from all moral obligation; since its principle teaches, that, amongst thieves, one may defend himself by stealing; amongst liars, by lying; amongst robbers, by robbing; amongst adulterers, by committing adultery; amongst slanderers, by slandering in turn; amongst gamblers by gambling; amongst murderous warriors, by engaging in murderous war; amongst duellists, by duelling; amongst assassins, by slaying first the assassin: and, generally, amongst sinners, by sinning—releasing all men from all moral obligation. Now, as a judge obliged to render righteous judgment, we do not feel at liberty thus to rescind all the laws of God. 4. We hold that the assassin can only kill the body; and that *we* are still in the hands of God, after the frail outward tabernacle has been destroyed by wicked hands. 5. Therefore, we are forced to decide, though in our own case, that according to the law of God, it would be better for the assassin to commit murder by taking my life, than for me to commit it by taking his life; and that *his intended* crime cannot change the immutable laws of God, and suspend the obligation of the divine utterance. *Thou shalt not kill* —because *myself*, and *wife*, and *children*, are involved in the case. And as part of the judgment, we must hold that it is more consonant with *right* reason to suffer death passing into the joys of heaven, than to inflict it sending a soul to the torments of hell;—that it is better to do right and lose life than to do wrong in order to save it; that, having no lease of life from God, nor knowing the moment when *He* may require it, it is our duty to be prepared for death at every moment; and if not prepared, we may not do wrong *now* because we have not done right up to this time; and so may not prefer to take the life of a wicked man rather than let him take ours, alleging that we should be lost in the future by consenting to loss of life when we might save it by taking another's. But as this is a legal point and a little intricate, we may seek to render it more plain. Observe, then, that the *great* object of life is to be prepared for death; and that God has so appointed the moral laws, that we are bound to love our neighbor as ourself, because *his* soul is as priceless as our own. Nor does it matter that that neighbor is wicked; for his wickedness cannot change or repeal the law of love. By God's laws, we are still bound to him, and may not prefer *self* to him. Both are obliged alike to be prepared for death, and both are liable to be called at such an hour as they think not. Hence, if both are alike wicked, neither may, by the law of love, prefer his own life, to afford himself the opportunity to repent. Thus situated, should a neighbor be an assassin in heart, seeking our life, we may, not by the law of God, say that we are wicked, too, and unprepared to die ; and so would be lost if slain, and therefore hasten to slay the assassin on the ground that the soul of each is imperilled by the encounter. For, first, this is taking advantage of one's own wrong, by destroying another in order to save ourself ; and is casting contempt on that law of God which requires us to be always ready to depart this life. Secondly, no law, human or divine, will justify or allow such contempt, because the practical working of such violation of law would be to justify crime by alleging the wickedness of the criminal. Finally, we shall hold the law to be, that it is never wise to violate the laws of God, however passion may clamor or self-love may urge ; that at all times our surest safety lies in obedience to God, disregarding the blind and the depraved instincts of animal nature ; and that an unreasoning instinct of self-defence, found alike in man and beast, is not the criterion of duty to responsible man—is not superior to the law of God's revealed will ; and forms no ground of justification for slaughtering men with all the cruelties of war.

We have little more to say about this *first law and instinct of nature.* Tried by the revealed law of God, they cannot endure the test; while the practical effect of their ordinary interpretation is to dissolve all the obligations of moral law, making an animal instinct superior to them. And there being no reason for placing one instinct above another, there is no reason why all the instincts should not be held superior to the revealed law, and should not be gratified in opposition to its demands. And hence, on the same basis of reasoning, there is no reason why men should not be released from obligations imposed by God if they infringe the promptings of the instincts.

§ 2.—*Right to defend the life of a nation.*

Seeing that the right of personal self-defence, by taking life, is far from being an unquestioned right, it is now proper to show that that right is wholly unlike "the right to defend the life of a nation." And, first, has it not been established that there is no analogy between the life of a person and that which, by one of the boldest figures in language, has been called "the life of a nation?" But if one insists that there is an analogy, he would do well to attempt to represent it to himself intelligently; and he will soon be convinced of the folly of such idle fancy. Through our whole late war, it was but a *catchword*, employed to work upon the passions. And, noticing the play on words as one of the common tricks of political and military chicanery, the further discussion of the subject might properly be dismissed; but lest silence should be misunderstood and construed into defeat, it is proposed to pursue the matter a little further. And as the right to defend *the life* of a nation, by brute force, is esteemed as free from doubt, we shall find it, like all the pretexts for war, based on some specious and selfish sophism; and the assumed right is indeed so shallow and intrinsically offensive to reason, that the mind is embarrassed to know where to begin or how to exhibit the delusiveness. For, resuming the supposed argument from analogy, let it be observed how strangely loose and indefinite the expression is! And, indeed, what is *the life* of a nation? Wherein does it consist? Who can fix in the mind any definite sense to the expression? The life of a nation! Pause, reader, and consider. If one had not seen millions of human creatures transported for years through the fury of its magic echo, he would think it impossible that rational beings could be heated to the murderous point, by language so singularly vague. And striving to fix in the mind some precise idea and wholly failing; then observing the fierce wrath which it has produced, one cannot drive from the mind the remembrance of the Salem Witchcraft and the furious

Crusades. With no definite conception in the mind, nothing addressing the rational consciousness, yet millions transported with the wildest fury, there must be appalling delusion! And the *fury* of our late war must have been *witnessed*, to be believed; and when actually witnessed, one nearly doubts whether his own senses were not deceived, and he laboring under the hallucinations of some feverish dream. For could rational mortals act as he everywhere beheld men act? And if men are rational, is not he deluded,—are not his very senses under some strange hallucinations? But if he is not deluded, then men must have been the victims of some strange and infernal delusion. And were the Crusaders deluded? Were the victims of the Salem witchcraft deluded? Does history tell us of a whole people who have been deluded? And if so, were not the people of this Christian (?) land deluded during the late few years? Nay, can a reflecting mind believe that, with the teaching of Christ, any people ever plunged into war, under an influence other than some Satanic delusion? Is a war alleged to be waged in defence of a nation's life, an exception? Impossible to conceive a definite idea of such a reason,—yet the cause for slaughtering hundreds of thousands—is the reason less delusive than that for the Crusades? For we repeat the question, Wherein does the *life* of a nation consist? Is it in the *form* of the constitution? Is not this the same nation that rebelled against England?—the same nation that England once governed? Is it not the same nation that existed under the Articles of Confederation? Is England not the same nation that threw its haughty conquest over Scotland and placed its iron yoke on Ireland? Whether its dependencies are more or less, will the *life* of the nation be affected? If, then, the *life* of a nation does not consist in the *form* of its government, the extent of its domain, in the peculiar character of its laws, nor in the party or person who rules it, to talk about defending the *life* of a nation, is to talk nonsense; and to be thrown into spasms of murderous rage about it, is to be under the impulse of delusion.

But to inquire wherein the life of a nation does consist, if a nation can be said to have a life, is aside from our object. For our object it is enough to know that no proper analogy exists between the life of a nation and that of a person. We understand that the life of a person consists in the union of soul and body, and that death consists in separating soul and body. But wherein the *death of a nation* consists we frankly confess our inability to conceive. The term life cannot be literally used in respect to a nation; for a nation lives in no sense analogous to that in which an individual person lives; nor can its life be taken in any literal or proper sense. The nearest analogy we can find between the destruction of a nation and that of a person, would consist in the separation of the former from other nations by extermination; and that separation is most certainly done by the sword; while we do not know that the life of any nation has been saved by it.

There being then no analogy between the life of a person and that of a nation, every step in the process by which men have reached the conclusion that the defence of a nation and self-defence stand on the same ground, is both false and fallacious, leading the mind further and further into the labyrinths of error and delusion. As in an arithmetical involution, the first figure being wrong, every digit in the result is a digit of error and deception. But the process in hand leading to moral action, every action is a false digit, and leads only to error and deception—to falsehood, cruelty, and war.

Carefully examined, the boasted right of self-defence stands on a ground no firmer than a depraved feeling or an animal instinct; while the right of national defence by the sword is derived by analogy from that of self-defence. And we now perceive that the analogy on which the inferential process is based, has in fact no existence; and thence perceive that the inference itself has no existence; but if the inference is without existence, the people who act from its influence, act without a real cause, and so act from the impulse of a delusion. And these are the grounds on which our late war was waged.

But it is urged that the life of a nation is some way connected with an established form of government. And this seems to be the popular conception of it. In this conception, the radical alteration of the government would destroy national life; and if, in the popular idea, the alteration is made by the sword, the act constitutes national murder. Accordingly, Cromwell murdered the English nation; Napoleon, the French nation; and the people of the Revolution murdered this nation. And agreeably to this reasoning, should the English people establish for themselves a democracy, the act would be the murder of the English nation. So the attempt of any subjected people to loose the bands of despotism, would be an attempt upon the national life. In like manner a colony or dependency of a nation repudiating its allegiance with a view to self-government, would be guilty of a high crime. And, generally, the defence of the life of a nation is the same as that of personal self-defence.

With reflecting men, such a proposition needs not be argued. The facts which surround any given case completely expose the shallow sophistry. In the one case, the government simply changes its form; in the other, a colony withdraws from the shadow of a constitution. It is just as absurd to contend that a change in the *form* of a government is the death of a nation, as to contend that the change of a man's condition is his destruction. The change may be only outward in both cases, and may both be for the better. So the division of a nation is no more the necessary destruction of it, than the division of a family is the destruction of it. As a man may change the mode of his life, so may a nation. The state may change every law of its constitution, and be none the less the same state. And a man of tolerable intellect can readily see that to base an analogy on a mode of national life and a condition of personal life so as to reason from one to the other, is little less than the renunciation of reason itself. For such reasoning virtually declares that the form of political government is as sacred as the elements of human life; and alleges that the mere mode of government is identical with government itself. In the late war in this country, the North committed the error of saying in substance, that, unless the government should continue just as it was, it would cease altogether; and to support that position it drew the sword. "What!" exclaimed the abettors of the doctrine, "shall we stand still and see the life of the nation taken?" And did the life of the nation consist in a handful of slaveholders remaining subject to the constitution? If not, such sophistry only betrayed the morals of the North, and proved that ambition lay at the base of the Federal Government's coercive policy. The facts which have transpired since the South was *subjugated* for *freedom* (!) show that ambition was the true motive of the North in conquering the South.

If reliance can be placed in our rational inferences, we may feel sure that whatever may be the rights of personal self-defence by force, no right from analogy can be derived to defend the form of national life by the sword. For a total change in the *form* of national life does not, necessarily, imply destruction to the happiness of the nation. It is the sword that destroys. Put away the sword, let men cease to make wars about the *forms* of things, and people will be exempt from both tyranny and sudden revolution; while government will become the subject of rational discussion, and will exactly mark the progress of civilization.

And how absurd is the popular idea that personal and national life stands on the same ground! The difference between the two kinds of life is so great that one feels as if he was abusing men's intelligence in pointing out the difference. The attempt to reason from one to the other seems like offering incivilities to human intelligence—like the repetition of truisms—like announcing to intelligent people that there is a difference between right and wrong.

If the life of a nation lies in the *form* of the constitution, it is that which men make, and they make change or destroy it at pleasure, without committing sin or wrong. But if the life abides in the laws which God appoints, and from which men construct the *form*, men can no more destroy national life than they can destroy the elements of the air or the principle of animal existence. But if by national life is meant the lives of the individuals who compose the nation, we can understand both the force of the phrase and the value of the thing. In that sense nothing is more important than the life of a nation save the salvation of the souls of those who compose it; and nothing more likely to destroy both than the sword.

The means which may rightly be employed to preserve a nation, we are not now considering. We are only seeking the supposed analogies between the life of a nation and that of an individual, with their natural and logical consequences. But we perceive it to be quite impossible to find any appreciable analogies. And if we consider national life as consisting in the aggregate of personal life, the right to defend the life of the nation is not analogous to that of personal self-defence, but the identical principle, generalized, becomes involved. In this sense, it is quite impossible to imagine where national self-defence would be necessary; since we are unable to conceive the motive which would induce the desire to destroy the persons of a nation. Even savages rarely destroy life as the final end of war. Nor do *their* motives differ widely from those of so-called civilized nations. A people just and temperate in their intercourse with other people, are protected by the laws which God has appointed in the human soul. Penn and his followers were safe in the midst of savages, and that safety depended, not upon accidental but upon permanent laws of the human mind.

In civilized nations, wars are generally the product of long-fostered differences which spring from jealousy, ambition, or supposed collision of worldly interests. Ere the differences come to open hostilities, both parties always become involved in gross moral wrongs; and even with our modern civilization, a case could scarcely arise where the spirit of forbearance and candor would not, if earnestly pursued, avert the calamities of war. But nations usually have a morbid sense of honor. They quickly take and as quickly resent an insult. And the nations, too, as the duellist, have a code of honor; and are generally more sensitive to *its* laws than to the laws of Christ. A trifling violation of a treaty, the dismissal of a minister, or an imagined insult offered, and the belligerents fly to arms, and begin the insane horrors of war. Fighting a few bloody battles on land and sea, destroying thousands of lives,—neither party having signal success—and the foul blot is obliterated, both parties boasting and swaggering about the *bravery* of the men, when with great honor amicable relations are resumed. The whole thing is more puerile than the simpering follies of boyhood.

The candid mind cannot doubt that any nation, actuated by love of truth and justice, to say nothing of Christianity, could avert the calamities of war in all ordinary instances; while the notion that other nations would prowl upon such a nation, is too improbable for adoption as the basis of an argument. Contrary to the nature of man, such a notion is violative of all real human experience. It is a case similar to that of the mythical assassin at the door to kill women and children. It is the dreamy pretext of war-men for justifying themselves in a career of slaughter. In confirmation of this view let the colony of Pennsylvania be again a full testimony. Though the savages howled and yelled their war-whoops all round, the people not only escaped violence but secured the friendship and kind offices of the savages. And a Scriptural faith in God and His providence exacts the belief that the highest safety and well-being of a people would be secured in the abandonment of the sword forever, with the adoption of a full faith in the protective providence of God as the Moral Governor of the world. In this respect, whatever may be the professions, the nations *act* the part of atheists—act as if there was no God to govern.

But experience shows that individuals and nations alike more frequently fail than succeed in self-defence; and hence we may justly arraign the *wisdom* of employing it, as we have already arraigned the reasons on which the right to employ are supposed to stand. For the failure in success may be fairly urged as a negative argument supplied by the constitution of nature against the adoption of that mode of defence—an argument furnished from considering the benevolence of God displayed in appointing means to ends, and the fitness of the means actually appointed to obtain the justly desired ends. And the facts in the case cannot be mistaken. History teaches the same lesson as to both nations and individuals; and proves that more instances of defence by force fail than succeed. And on a broad basis of induction, it may be said that force has proved a signal failure. There have indeed been seeming partial successes; but we cannot say that the success would not have been more marked, if force had not been employed; and the nature and constitution of things as well as the positive precepts of God, argue against the use of deadly force, as the means of conserving anything true or of destroying anything bad. For those who take the sword shall perish by the sword.

And as there is no analogy between the life of a nation and that of an individual, so no inference from analogy arises, putting personal and national defence on the same ground. But considering the national life as consisting of the lives of the individuals who compose it, there arises no analogy but an identity of principle generalized from the individual to the nation; and thus generalized, personal and national self-defence stands in the same reason. But in that case, it is idle to argue the right of national defence by force, or by war. It is idle to argue it, because there is no kind of probability that the national life will be endangered. And it is idle, because, if endangered, experience proves that war not only fails as the means of defence but proves the unfailing means of final overthrow. Among the proud nations of the past,—and all appealed to the sword—none have survived the destroying ravages of the sword: in some cases only their elegant languages remain to indicate their culture and mark their folly; and the fact that they have ceased to exist is a melancholy and conclusive proof that they mistook the means which God intended for their preservation—is as conclusive proof as the destructive effects of alcoholic drinks are conclusive proof that God does not intend men to use them as the means of preserving life. For a time a man may live and use those drinks as for a time a nation may continue and use the sword, but ultimately both must be destroyed. The one may survive for years and the other for centuries, but the ruin of each is but a question of time, for God has so appointed in the nature of things. Whether the nations have or have not the revealed will of God, appealing to the sword, they perish by the sword. The effect follows as from a natural cause, independently of men's knowledge of the laws which produce it. And the prophetic declaration of the inseparable relation between the act of taking the sword and the fact of perishing by it, is but the authentic republication of a changeless law of the natural government of God over the world. The two things stand in the inseparable and fixed relation of antecedent and consequent. As the man who takes poison dies from it, so the nation which takes the sword perishes by the sword. And the act being done the consequence follows, whether men do or do not understand the connecting link between the two things. The act done, the sequence arises under the administration of God's government naturally, or providentially conducted.

The proof that such is the natural constitution of things, lies in the fact that He who made that constitution and administers it, has so declared, and the declaration is illustrated and confirmed by experience. Hence when the Incarnate Word announced, *That he who takes the sword shall perish by the sword,* He announced an immutable law of nature, true whether the sword is taken for offence or for defence ; while we should think it impossible to show that true morality sanctions defensive violence more than offensive violence. Hence, we must regard the parade and bluster about personal and national defence by deadly force, as having no foundation in moral principle, nor indeed anywhere but in the sinful *feelings* and *instincts*, which are manifest in the chivalry and bravado which have come to us from the warlike nations of heathenism. For *defensive* murder, stealing, lying, robbing, with all the ingredients of war, find no more justification in the gospel, than the same things done offensively. But it is true that one turns in vain to the morality of the gospel for many of the heathenish notions that have crept stealthily and unobserved into our practical and philosophical morality. And prominent amongst those heathenish notions stand the two valued but utterly vicious rights of personal and national defence by violence.

CHAPTER VII.

ENLIGHTENED REASON FORBIDS WAR AS THE MEANS OF PRESERVING CIVIL GOVERNMENT.

THE proof of this proposition is logically embraced in the general reasoning contained in the foregoing pages; but it merits consideration and illustration in more specific terms. The basis of our reasoning, it will be observed, lies in the idea, that the appointments of God make the duties and true interests of men harmonious and inseparable. Being infinitely wise and good, the scheme which God has appointed for the right government of the world, makes duty and interest coincident. And enlightened reason and Christian morality enjoin that created beings ought never to act in opposition to the provisions of that scheme. For while the laws of God constitute an invariable rule of duty, they also constitute an invariable rule of interest; so that it is no less impolitic than it is criminal to do wrong.

When war is waged for any cause within the terms of the foregoing proposition, it must be done to test some alleged right or to prevent some alleged wrong. And it is evident that a war so waged must have regard to ethical law; since it does, by its terms, involve questions of right and wrong. But does not enlightened reason teach that *war* cannot decide ethical questions? War is but the collision of mere power. And can the momentum of brute force decide questions of casuistry? Has it reason and conscience, so as to decide between right and wrong? Can numbers, greater material resources, more skilled chicanery and military generalship, alter the relations of things, inverse the appointments of God, and invest intrinsic wrong with the qualities of right? Can evil become good and good evil, with the changing aspects of a brute-force collision? As war sways hither and thither do the properties of right and wrong mutate with the victor? When one belligerent proves successful, does it follow that, as tested by moral law, his cause is right? And is it less absurd to attempt the settlement of a question by a war than by a duel? Nay, is it not more absurd in the ratio of the numbers involved and the dreadful consequences produced? Our ancestors were wont to settle legal questions by *wager* of battle. Bringing suit before the court, the parties invoked this mode of trial. The court granting it, the litigants repaired to the place chosen, where, from dawn to dawn, the parties or their substitutes fought like wild-beasts. The verdict—the true saying—was awarded to the victor in the brute-struggle.

This barbarous custom was based on the idea, that God espoused the cause of the right, and gave the victory thereto. And such is the exact principle on which war proceeds. For war proceeds on the ground that some right is assailed or withheld in violation of justice, and the appeal to arms is for the purpose of adjusting the matter of difference. Hence, the appeal is made to the *conscience of the sword*, and the trial proceeds on the assumption, that God favors the right, will direct the sword, and award the verdict to the righteous party. Upon the same principle, therefore, parties litigant formerly appealed to God in wager of battle, and parties belligerent now in wager of war. The one submitted to the test of personal combat; the other to that of a national combat. In both processes, the principle involved is the same. Both are equally uncertain, equally absurd, equally heathenish. Both are wicked appeals to God, involving the collision of brute-force, the one employing in the argument a *leather* target, the other powder and lead. And if it is absurd and brutal for *two* men to attempt to decide a moral question by brute power in the use of a leather target, is it less absurd for a hundred thousand or half a million to attempt the same thing in the use of powder and lead? Each is based on the ground that God is enamored with the idea of brute-bravery and physical strength; and such an idea is a pure heathenism. For can mere brute-power, whether used in the form of a leather target or in that of swords and bayonets, decide moral questions? If so, why not put the pugilist into the pulpit that he may entangle the nice questions of casuistry which have so long puzzled the world? And in reality, is it more absurd, that two doctors of divinity should thump each other's heads with their fists with the view of settling the Arminian and Calvinistic controversy in the church, than that two hundred thousand men on a side should shoot each other's heads off with the view of settling the controversy in the State about Secession and Negro Slavery? Is not the one as much more absurd than the other as two hundred thousand are more than two, added to the difference of having two heads thumped with fists and thousands shot off by cannon balls?

And were we not accustomed to the barbarities of war, we would be less shocked at seeing Heenan or Sayres in the pulpit with the style of D. D., than at seeing a *Rev. General* at the head of an army; while it would be immeasurably less absurd and anti-Christian to send some D. D. to accompany Heenan and Sayres as chaplain, from place to place, and doing the service implied in that office, than to send the same styled personage to accompany a hundred thousand men whose aim is to engage in work worse than that of Heenan and Sayres. For indeed it surpasses human genius to imagine anything more absurd than a hundred thousand men engaged in such a campaign of crime as war implies, attended by a chaplain whose duty is to pray that the blessings of God may accompany these perpetrators of all sorts of revolting deeds. In the very nature of things, all belligerent acts are criminal acts, and asking God to bless them is asking Him to become a party to crime—is unrobing God of His holy attributes and clothing Him with those of heathen divinities. Mere power cannot decide between right and wrong, nor can selfish passion finding vent in outbursts of carnal prayer, engage God to take part in a frenzied collision about worldly interests in men. And do military skill, expert trickery, heartless cruelty, and masterly chicanery, add Christian virtue to brute force, and engage God to espouse the cause and give aid where they most abound? What testimony is supplied by the Scriptures and the facts of history? Frenzied by infernal passion, nations have often plunged into war, and, having murdered hundreds of thousands of their own citizens, have fallen the easy prey to the rapacity by which they had rendered themselves insanely furious. We need not quote examples. History abounds in them, so as to furnish the induction that both reason and Christianity forbid the use of the sword as necessary to the well-being of society in any form. From the time jealous Cain slew his more righteous brother till now, maddened by their passions, men have engaged in the business of war, and have thoroughly tried that method of vindicating rights and punishing wrongs. And what is the result? Is it satisfactory? Perhaps not less than from forty to fifty thousand million human creatures have been sacrificed upon the altars of war. Contemplate the thought! The mind is stunned! Forty or fifty thousand million sensitive creatures, curiously organized by the benevolent hand of God! mangled, wounded, butchered, and sent into eternity by the hands of their fellow men! How vast, how appalling the number! The imagination cannot grasp it! The mental faculties are overpowered! It is several times the population of the whole earth! Let the mind attempt to conceive of fifty thousand million human creatures, exquisitely organized, endued with sensitive bodies, intelligent minds, and undying souls; and then think how they have been mangled, burned, tortured, torn asunder by every means that wicked ingenuity could invent, and cruel and diabolical hearts could execute. How fiendish and unfeeling beyond description must be the malignant passions which can urge rational beings to deeds of such infernal horror! Destined to dwell on the earth but a few days at most, how unnaturally cruel must be those brutal passions which can gloat over suffering and torture, and ask God to bless the perpetrators in their infliction. Wives, children, sisters, age-stricken parents, and condoling friends, have borne upon their hearts the badges of mourning through life. And a single battle has often caused nations to wail in anguish, deep and bitter, whose stifled moan only died away when another generation came on the stage of life, itself to wail over a new similar anguish. As the mind attempts to grasp the sorrows and desolations of war, its faculties are overpowered and it is rendered conscious of its insufficiency for the task. Angels may, but perhaps God alone can *fully*, comprehend the desolations and bitterness which war has brought upon our race. When the nefarious perpetrators shall meet the sufferers before the Judgment of God, how awful and appalling must be their doom! How tragic then will be the scene of warriors and heroes! Little will the idle homage which this world pays to successful crime then avail! Judge of all the earth! when the widow shall cast her eye on the hero, whose praises have been trumpet-tongued throughout the earth, but whose murderous hand made her a widow, it shall pierce him with ten thousand sorrows more acute than the dagger-point which made his accuser a widow, and intensify his anguish and doom in that world where heroism shall meet its just reward!

And at the bar of reason, has not the tale of woe sufficiently tested the competency of war to accomplish any desirable end? Yet how runs the story of history? What benefits have accrued to mankind from wars? Have they blessed the race and preserved the nations? Have the *lives* of the nations and the *forms* of their government been conserved by them? How different is the tale which history tells from the foolish question, recently asked, "What!

shall we stand still, and see the life of the nation taken?" For what means so sure to destroy a nation's life as war? All the facts of history confirm the declaration of Jesus, "That they who take the sword shall perish by the sword." In memory recall the great nations of antiquity. Where are they? They grasped the sword, and by the sword they were destroyed. They have been blotted from the face of the earth. Once where there were dense population and incredible art and wealth, now desolation and solitude alone are found. Babylon, Nineveh, Tyre, Jerusalem, Carthage, Athens, Rome,—where are they? And Egypt, Greece, Rome, Palestine, Phœnicia,—where may they be found? They are engulfed in the vortex of destruction—the evidence at once of their folly aud wickedness, and of the truth of the statement, that the sword shall destroy those who take it.

And we need not go to antiquity to learn that God forbids the use of the sword. Modern nations bear melancholy testimony to the same truth. Within a comparatively recent period, all the nations of Europe and of the East have been overrun and laid waste by the rapacity of heroes and warriors; while many of the nations have been exterminated or absorbed by other people. Nor have the desolating ravages been confined to the East. Heroes and warriors have breathed desolation on the Western side of the Atlantic. For there is no doubt that nations more or less advanced in the arts of civilized life, but extinct before Europeans discovered the Western hemisphere, inhabited portions of North America; while, in more Southern portions of the continent, the work of desolation has surpassed the wildest limnerings of the imagination. The nations have risen, by rotation have grasped the sword, have performed their work of savage barbarity; and, in turn, had the ploughshare of ruin pushed through them and the besom of destruction to lay them waste. The work goes on still, and the nations make haste to their appointed doom. And we have the awful apprehension that but too soon our own proud country will place the forbidden weapon at its own throat. It is always unsheathed and uplifted ready to be turned to inflict upon itself the fatal blow.

And what has resulted from this appalling destruction of human life? Have the terrors of the sword prevented the recurrence of war; or has the sword preserved the existence of nations? Does not history establish quite the contrary? And while there is no sufficient reason to believe that the sword has long preserved any nation, do we not know that it has destroyed many? In short, does not history prove that the appeal to physical force has ended in failure? By it the most renowned cities and nations have been blotted from the earth, millions and millions of human creatures have been cruelly slaughtered and wrung with sorrows wild and inconsolable, untold trillions of property has been worse than wasted, and yet what evidence is there that any real benefit has resulted to our race? And this long and dire tragedy ought to convince rational beings that God never intended the sword as the arbiter of differences of interest and opinion in this world.

But, laying aside prejudice and passion, a little sober reflection would teach us to expect just what history records as fact: war can neither make a good citizen, nor settle differences of interest or opinion amongst men; and can no more adjust questions of right and wrong between nations than force can between individuals. A battle and victory can no more expunge a blot from national character, than a duel or a murder can from individual character. And war and duelling stand on principles identical in force of reason. If enlightened reason and Christian morality justify war, they justify duelling. For if thousands may justly fight and slay each other about national interests, why may not two do the same thing about personal rights? If honor attaches to an army when it slays and vanquishes an antagonist, why does it not attach to the duellist when he slays and vanquishes his antagonist? If there is nothing barbarous in the duels of nations, why is there anything barbarous in duels between individuals? But if in the nature of things, the barbarous act of duelling can settle no differences between individuals ; in the nature of things, how can the barbarous act of war settle differences between nations? And as, according to the laws of of human nature, the occurrence of any number of duels does not tend to prevent the recurrence of them, so it is with wars. If the practice of duelling is prevalent and sustained by public opinion, the more duels there are fought, the more will be the occasions when men will think they must be fought. Like the laws of commerce, demand creates supply, and supply renders the article cheap, introducing it into many new channels. As the number of duels fought has no tendency to diminish the supposed occasions for them ; so the bad passions of men will supply sources for new challenges. The method of preventing their re-occurrence will be, not to restrict them to occasions falsely regarded as just, but forever to abandon the practice as barbarous in all forms and for all causes.

The same thing is true of war. When the barbarous practice prevails and is sustained by the public opinion of the nations, the more frequently wars occur, the more frequent will be the occasions when they are thought necessary. As in the case of duelling, demand creates supply. Look at the early history of England, when chivalry was esteemed the prime virtue. How trivial the cause that would call the lords and barons to the fatal conflict! and how revolting to read the barbarities of those times ! Peruse, too, the chronicles of the ill-fated Granada, Peru, and Mexico ; or those of any people whose moral sentiments sustained the practices of war, and behold what causes will throw the people into the horrors of belligerent conflict! And because war, as a remedy, has no fitness to cure the disease in which it originates ; so no number of them tends to remove the maladies for which they are prescribed. And neither duelling nor war has the least tendency to cure the distemper in which they originate. The contrary is true. In both cases, the remedy inflames the disease and ministers to its strength. Hence, the more duels and wars there are, the more are the occasions when they are thought necessary. The reason is found in the laws of human nature, applicable to nations and individuals—that repetition begets habit, habit begets relish, and continued, establishes itself, till that which shocked the sensibilities at first, can be done without revolting and with pleasure. To the mind unused to the battle-field, the horrors chill the soul at first, filling it with loathing indescribable; but familiarity removes the loathing, till, by and by, the same mind can witness scenes of blood with stolid indifference. Such a mind has lost the tone of moral integrity. We witnessed the full play of this principle in the late war in this country. The whole nation for the time became hardened.

On the contrary, let public opinion utterly condemn duelling, and how many challenges will be sent? And the fewer the duels fought, the fewer will be the occasions when duellists will think it necessary for them to be fought.

The principle would be the same with nations. A strong public opinion against war, would itself remedy the whole evil. As time would remove the nations from the bloody horrors, the sentiment of abhorrence would increase, and the moral sense of mankind would soon be as much shocked at the idea of war in the interest of government, as the moral sense of the people in England or America would be shocked to-day at the idea of war in the interests of an assumed orthodoxy. For there is just as much reason for waging war in the interests of religion as in those of politics. At no remote period England and America countenanced the use of the sword in the interests of religion, but they did it with misgiving. The next upward step in thought brought them a little, and only a little, beyond the stand-point of persecution. They trembled, for a moment, in the transition-period, when the scales inclined towards the higher civilization, and the sword, as an actual means of propagating religion, passed away. And the nations are now trembling in the transition-period between the barbarism of war and the liberty of political thought and action. Our own country went into the late war with misgiving—observed a thoughtful moment between the counterpoises of reason and barbarity. Unhappily for mankind, passion and ambition preponderated to barbarity, and the nation offered little less than a million more victims to the bloody Moloch. As we emerge from the revelries of these orgies, the eyes of many are opening, and we can but hope that another impulse will place the nation clearly within the plane of Christian civilization, and render war an impossibility with us.

The enlightened consciences of men are in harmony with the views given on this whole subject, but they have never found a practical expression. Even under the most democratic forms of government, the *many* have neither had the rule nor a large influence in determining it. The few have controlled the many, while the few have themselves been controlled by motives neither wise nor honest. The real public conscience has never found expression. A nation may be plunged into war, while the true national conscience is opposed to it. I think this was the case in our late war. Had the people on both sides had the war fairly laid before them, so that they could have grasped it in its nature and results, they would have declined the contest. Recall the effect produced by the firing upon Sumpter. The Northern heart was paralyzed. Dejection sat upon every countenance. Business stagnated. Property diminished in value. The national heart was faint. The generous impulses of that heart were opposed to war. The nation itself paused—thoughtfully paused. But party interrupted the thoughtful silence, and lifted its voice in words of flattery and cajolery. Ninety days, it said, with a few thousand men, would put down the rebellion and elevate the political morality. Speakers were sent over the land, making partisan appeals and creating a " war-feeling." Then the thoughtful pause was broken. Reason

18*

was dethroned. Passion was enthroned. Conscience was lost and hushed amidst the din and uproar. The nation plunged into war. All real freedom of speech was suppressed. Nobody took the proper ground before the people for the purpose of enlightening their consciences. Some took ground against *that* war, but not against *all* war. Instead of pouring oil on the troubled waters, by the amount of their influence, they troubled the waters the more.

When the system of flattery and cajolery became inefficient, and the people flagged in their zeal, their consciences were hushed by threats of conscription. When they reduced their indifference to practice, the goad of compulsion was applied and enforced by the strong arm of the nation's power. And when cajolery, flattery, and party influence failed to supply the ranks of the wasting armies, the deficit was made up by the terrors of conscription— conscience quite out of sight and hidden in alarm. And by and by, the enthusiasm, taking the form of a hurricane of passion, laid prostrate all things before it. Conscience was without a tongue. The masses, the middle classes, the educated, the churches, the pulpit, were hurled into the vortex of boiling passion. Thence one wild scream for war echoed in trumpet tones from one end of the land to the other. Old and young, saint and sinner, male and female, were seized by the dire contagion, and thrown into paroxysms of rage. Nay, the penitent utterances of prayer were suffused with explosions of wrathful passion. Even the Quakers were not exempt from the storm of contagion, and many of them were hurled into the ranks of the army. The Peace Societies of the land were laid prostrate before the first gust, and so continued during the beating of the whole wild storm.

And this was the condition of things in the philosophical North. In the "Sunny South" we know less. But effects infer causes. The child reflects the parent. We know what human nature is—and what the impetuous Southern nature is, rendered insane under the unnatural state of society which it fostered. It was anything but thoughtful or lovely. And alas! both parties had infinitely too much zeal to settle their differences by the horrors of the sword. And thus matters stand, the real differences unsettled, at the close of military hostilities; the country is threatened by a generation of strife, and the government by an overshadowing and centralized despotism.

Could the *people* have foreseen the consequences of the war, they must have decided unequivocally against it,—on every ground of reason, conscience, morality and Christianity, no less than policy. And there is no doubt that the real conscience of the Christian world is in harmony with the views we have presented herein of both civil government and of war. This is evinced by two considerations: 1. No form of civil government can be instituted that men will not demolish so soon as it fails to accomplish the end which they think it ought to accomplish. 2. When they have demolished it, no appeals to conscience can induce a sense of moral guilt. This is true because there is no deep and ineradicable feeling of the soul, fixing a sense of moral delinquency; while there is a deep and ineradicable feeling of the soul that war, with its unutterable horrors, is contrary to the teachings of reason and Christianity. And whatever theories men may espouse in relation to government, no intelligent man can be induced to believe that governments are so ordained of God, that men may not modify, abolish, or repudiate them, just as interest and convenience may suggest, without incurring moral taint or the displeasure of God. Then to sum up the whole matter in relation to this point: It is wicked as it is irrational to attempt to maintain any form of government, human or divine, by the terrors of the sword; and the attempt is founded on a misconception of man's nature; while it is violative of enlightened reason, repugnant to the teaching of revelation, and wholly unfitted to attain the end desired and intended. And all this might be inferred from reason because the moral laws of God forbid all wars, and what the moral laws of God forbid can never, in the proper sense, be attended by success.

CHAPTER VIII.

POLITICAL MORALITY.—WAR DELUSIONS.—CARE FOR NATIONAL DIVISIONS.

WHEN we read the teachings of philosophical moralists on the subject of war, and what they regard as justifiable occasions for it, we are bewildered in amazement, filled with perplexity and painful anxiety. Dr. Paley, usually so cautious a defender of Christian truth in most respects, thus loosely declaims on the subject before us: "The objects of *just* wars are precaution, defence or reparation. Every *just* war supposes an injury perpetrated, attempted, or feared."

When philosophers call such incoherent declamation as that Moral Philosophy, it is time to change the meaning of words, and disregard distinctions in ideas. If nations have the right to plunge into war because they *fear* they may sustain injury, *all* obligation to desist from it is removed; and if "just" wars may be waged for "reparation," the nations, under the two reasons for "just wars," may be always plunged into "just wars." In the form of an argument, we can devise nothing with which to encounter such morality. Dr. Hickok's authority for war is little more satisfactory; and the *principle* from which he derives authority is so volatile as quite to escape the wariest research. Indeed, the Doctor possesses the happy faculty of reaching conclusions without exhibiting any principle. He *assumes* his principles, and does not favor us by pointing either to the laws of nature or those of revelation as giving authority for war. But both he and Paley connect the right to engage in war *some how* with government. And this leads us to observe that few things, coming within the range of the mind's faculties to investigate, have challenged less proper investigation than the subject of human government. The views of men seem stereotyped from models drawn from the benighted Past. Dr. Hickok takes these views for granted, and then upon them bases his ethics. Dr. Paley took the current views of his age and country as established, and on them founded his morality. And upon such morality men act; and if one would escape persecution as a heretic, he must embrace as truth unquestioned, not only that the existing government is "the perfection of wisdom," but he must also accept the sword as the infallible and only means of continuing it.

And not only do Christian moralists thus reason about the ethics of war, but professed Christians employ subterfuges as a pretext to indulge in it. "To lay down the sword, is to return to barbarism," has been literally thrust down our throats by Christian hands; and impatience has been exhibited when we could not accept the *passionate* truism. But is that true, can it be? When men thus talk, are they not laboring under some kind of insanity?—are they not spell-bound under delusion? For is it possible that horrid, revolting war is the civilizer of mankind?!!! Reason, justice, conscience, the Bible, Christianity—are these nothing?—and before and over them all must we lift our hopes and thoughts to the altar of bloody Moloch, and regard that grim visage as the redeemer of our race from the horrors of barbarism? Yet *Christian* men urge that argument (?) for war—urge that society would dissolve without the conservation of the sword. Deluded, they surely are. They call evil good; and good evil. How fearful must be the moral perversion when men thus reason! The distinctions of right and wrong are nearly obliterated from the soul. The moral sun has nearly gone down, leaving the people in darkness that can be felt. "Woe unto them that call evil good and good evil; that put darkness for light, and light for darkness; that put bitter for sweet, and sweet for bitter." It is not a very strange thing in *this* world even for nations to become blinded by some strong delusion; and when so deluded, to reverse the nature of things. The whole moral taste may become contaminated; and then the moral sense, like certain optical glasses, reverses the objects of vision. And the perversion may become total. Thus situated, the mind may be unable to perceive moral distinctions. Moral day and night become undistinguishable. Wrong may be put for right. War may be regarded as the civilizer of mankind. It is a dreadful state of moral delusion. In this condition it cannot be otherwise than that the woe-trumpet of wrath shall sound in the ears of the people. And how like the condition of things in our country at this moment! War is called good—the "preserver of civilization!" The distinctions of right and wrong are not perceived. The horrid crimes of war pass unnoticed. Nay, the crimes are put for virtues. Not only is the bitterness of war not perceived; not only are the horrors of the battle-field disregarded; but lo! the delusion becomes so complete, that the deluded creatures assure us, "'Tis sweet to die for one's country!" They also tell us of the *glory* of the battle-field; the *brilliancy* of the charge; and the *noble* conduct of *brave* deeds. Bitter is put for sweet; the scourge of mankind is called a blessing; the very destroyer is called its preserver and civilizer. Great and terrible are the delusions of war!

We do not know that Christian men regard the deeds of war as things good in themselves. That would be too gross. Satan is more cunning than that. He does not deceive his victims in that way. He rather brings on them some delusi n; pe verts their moral discernment; causes them to mistake; brings before their minds *ulterior* good, inducing them to seek that unreal poetic thing called "nationality," or the preservation of "liberty alive," or the salvation of civilization and moral virtue. Now, Satan is delighted; for he has found indirection, a link out of the chain of reason. There is some remote indefinable good —the more potent because it invites the reveries of the imagination, and in those reveries lie hidden treasures of

good—good to civilization, to humanity, to religion. And
from imagination to war, the space is passed by flight. The
ideal abstractions of good rising like the exhalations of
a charm, the senses are lost in the trance of elysian blessings. Exalted into ecstasies and transported by the soothing delusion, such common-place maxim as, "That we may
not do evil that good may come," is disregarded. But under such rhapsodies, Christians have their perceptions of
the future supernaturally quickened, and determine, *by the
use of the sword*, to hasten the time when the nations shall
learn war no more. And, thus, by wrong, they conserve
the right. By doing evil, they hasten the good. By war,
and crime, and bloodshed they preserve and promote morality and religion; and when by war, and wrong, and
crime, the way is prepared and the knowledge of the Lord
shall fill the earth, war and crime, and bloodshed shall be
no more. Then war shall end in peace; crime, in virtue.
Blood shall beget love. War shall preserve the people
from barbarism. Light is put for darkness; darkness for
light. Bitter is called sweet; sweet is called bitter. Great
is the perversion of humanity. Hideous war is regarded
as the foster-mother of virtue and civilization. Statesmen
praise it; the press eulogize it; the church embrace it.
Thence the warrior is glorified; the journal pays him sick-
ly compliments; the undiscerning proclaim that he deserves the gratitude of the nation; and even the pulpit
flatters him with prayers, disgusting before men, if they
are not blasphemous before God. Then the private is rewarded by petty office; the major goes to the legislature;
the general to Congress; the general-in-chief is exalted to
the Presidency. As regimentals walk the streets they are
bowed to with deference: captains receive the charming
smiles of pale-faced beauty; while parlors are thrown open
invitingly to brave, self-denying privates. Valor takes the
place of moral virtue; chivalry stands before honesty;
daring equals religion; and blind devotion to a selfish
cause and death on the battle-field secure admittance into

heaven. Dreadful is the perversion. *God* is thought to be such a one as men are. His thoughts are regarded as *our* thoughts: and what *we* praise, we say he will not condemn; and so we identify Him with us in our moral perversion. But it is all idolatry—is putting the creature in the place of the Creator; is bowing the affections of the soul in worship before the God of this world. Against such people the woe-trumpet of God's disapprobation must sound in deep tones.

Could the best argument that ingenuity ever invented for war be brought within the rays of dawning truth, it would evaporate as the early dew before the rising sun;—at the touch of truth, it would disappear as evil spirits by the charms of the exorcist. Some of the arguments for war have been brought into the presence of truth in the foregoing pages, and their distortions have appeared. Others still await consideration. A peculiar one, negative in character, invites a passing notice. It may be brought before the mind in the interrogative dress which it mostly wears: "If we discard war, how shall those wicked wretches who seek to destroy the nation be punished for their wickedness?"—Now, this fervent and pathetic interrogatory would seem to be a grave one. But it wears, like some acting clown, several garments at once. When these are stripped off, there is little left. We readily see first a coat of passion; then there is one of malice; next a garment of revenge; and all are stained by a discoloration of falsehood. But most apparent of all lies outside of the other garments this gown of assumption, "Vengeance is mine; I will repay;"—perhaps a small matter with war-men, but should be a large one with Christians. And upon the whole, it may look as if the pathetic interrogatory is quite composed of those vehement passions "whence come wars and fightings" amongst men; and thus we might dispose of the whole difficulty. Yet we do not desire to dispose of it cavalierly. Let us, then, give it real life by supposition—if the paradox may be allowed: There is a country of large dimensions. The people are prosperous. They have wholly abandoned the sword. The blinding influence of passion is removed. Reason and justice rule in the minds of the people. Integrity and forbearance are the common virtues of the masses. Ambition, bravado and chivalric daring, are wholly abandoned. In short, the whole foul spirit of war is extirpated, so that a fair and charitable view of all differences of opinion and interest may be had.

Now, the spirit and fact of war abandoned, the passions have little material left out of which to fabricate a war. And now let us suppose a real collision of interest, in different parts of the nation, to arise,—such a collision as may produce division in the nation. Even this collision of interest can hardly create dissension. For lively affection, with an active sense of justice, delights in making sacrifices in behalf of those beloved; and the disposition to make sacrifices on one side, begets a disposition to complement them on the other side, as magnanimity always awakes corresponding and answering magnanimity. And a peaceable people must be magnanimous. The spirit of peace, as its natural fruit, produces magnanimity; while passion can magnify molehills into mountains, as magnanimity can reduce mountains into molehills. In an irascible people, justice and conscience act feebly, when the sword may take the place of the noble and amiable virtues. Then under the haughty rule of the sword, passion asks the heartless question: "If we discard war, how shall those who seek to destroy the nation be punished?" But, reader, will it not then be the sword and passion that destroy the nation— the sword and passion that divide the nation into angry factions? A tithe of the occasion that will divide a nation actuated by war-principles, would not affect it if actuated by peace-principles. Hence, ten divisions will occur in the State, governed by war-principles, for every one where peace-principles prevail. Nay, there will be a hundred divisions on war-principles for one on peace principles. For peace-men would seek no occasion for division, and would not be ready to accept one if offered. But suppose a real occasion for division should come, as we can readily see one might. Without bitterness, strife, or bloodshed, division would do no harm. But O what would be saved! There would be neither widow's wail nor orphan's cry; no mangled victims before the altars of Moloch; no country overrun and laid waste; no cities given to the flames; no terrified inhabitants fleeing before the invading army; none of the debauchery of army life; no prostitution of "war-widows;" and none of the general corruption produced by war. Bastiles and army hospitals, sanitary commissions and hospital chaplains, would become needless and unknown; and all would cease to exist. And the tens of thousands who now annually die from exposure to the hardships of war, apart from those who are butchered upon the battle-field, might be saved the horrible sufferings and deaths to which they are exposed. The Christian man who will seriously think of this matter, must admit, that, in these respects alone, the world would be infinitely blessed by the immediate and unconditional abandonment of the sword forever.

It is urged that serious ills may arise from the divisions of nations. So there may. All men are fallible, and nations may mistake their interest just as individuals may. What then? Suppose there should be a *disastrous* division in a nation? What ought to be done? What? but simply let the unwise people alone? For so sure as the laws of God are wise and just, so sure will the proper punishment follow. It will consist in losing the advantages of a better government. It will be just what it ought to be—right in kind and proper in degree—suited to suggest the remedy. Unattended by violence, the division would involve no crime—none against morality, religion, or humanity. It would involve only a mistake as to the best means of securing a worldly good, bringing exactly the proper remedy. What other *punishment* ought to be inflicted, or would be suitable to the case? If it is said that God ordains the government; may he not also ordain the division? How do we know that He ordains one more than another government?

Governments are to nations simply what enterprises are to individuals. The one is the more general, the other the more specific means, to interested ends. Both have the same *moral* character, and look to the same final object. If successful, they bring rewards of the same kind. If unsuccessful, they bring punishment of the same kind. Both have their bases in the same wants of human nature; and, tried by moral law, a mistake in each is *criminal* alike. Each brings its natural reward and natural punishment. Both have always been embarked in by men, and will be embarked in by them, so long as human nature continues as it is. In both there have been failures, and in both partial successes. Men have felt the same complacency in both, when they have had success; and in failure, it is impossible to make them feel *moral* guilt. And it is here that we find solution to the question which lately puzzled our pseudo-statesmen and purblind theologians during the last few years. They could not comprehend how it was that the men who were seeking to make a division in the nation permanent, exhibited no signs of conscious guilt. They had simply mistaken the laws of the human mind, and forgotten that the crime did not reside in the division, but lay in fighting about it. Neither Jefferson Davis nor any of his co-laborers can be made to feel moral guilt for the attempt to divide the nation. And to-day they are simply conquered. They are not cured. They are overwhelmed, but not convinced. They regard their defeat as ill luck, bad fate; but they are rebels still. And the sword can do no more than this. It does not reason, cannot convince, it can simply overpower. Hence, it makes neither a good subject nor a wise citizen.

But to dwell another moment on the consideration of the proper penalty for the unwise division of a nation, when the sword is abandoned. No maddened passions in the way, and no bravado to hinder, the discovery of the mistake in the division, would lay the foundation for a ready correction of it. The man who removes from a good country to one not so good, with the view of improving his worldly condition, on discovering his mistake, is neither disgraced nor humiliated by the retraction of his folly and the return to the former country. So giving up a profitable enterprise for one less profitable, a man is not, upon the discovery of the mistake and the attempt at reclamation, proven to be a bad man, nor a dishonored and humiliated one. The whole simply shows him to be a fallible man, and attached to his interests, though fallible. In both cases the act of abandoning a good thing for one less good, was unwise; but the want of wisdom in both, is sufficiently punished by loss of interest; while the natural punishment suggests the remedy, and shows the second act to be characterized by a commendable wisdom.

It would be the same with a divided nation. A part of the nation quitting the old government, and forming a bad new one, would sustain such a loss as would be ample punishment; and the loss sustained would afford ample punishment so long as the relation continued. And nations are composed of individuals; and the latter carry into the former all their natural attributes. And so men as states, are just as intent in the pursuit of interest, as men are as individuals; while one law is applicable to them in both conditions. The law of gain which holds them together in the various relations of trade, traffic and enterprise, is sufficient to hold them, so long as they should be held, under government. In principle, in morals, in devotion, these laws are one. God has made them so, and made them with sufficient potency to secure the desired end. And what God has made man cannot unmake, though he carry the sword and ruin to countless thousands of victims. *Interest* will continue the foundation of business and the basis of government, while man and the present economy of things continue. So long as men act in accordance with the laws appointed in the nature and constitution of things, they will receive the rewards which those laws naturally bestow ; and when they cease to act in accordance with them, they will incur the punishment which they naturally inflict. And where there really is no crime in the act, positive human punishment added to this natural punishment, is as unwise as it is cruel, tending neither to cure the evil, nor to reform the supposed evil-doer. Thus millions of men have been murdered in war, with no tendency to cure the distemper for which war is supposed to be the remedy. For centuries the remedy has been applied with no discernible mitigation in the disease. The reason is simply because the reputed remedy has no fitness to cure the supposed malady.

Had this nation regarded this obvious principle of human nature in the late secession of the South, it would have been measurably better for the whole country, in every conceivable respect. For we ought to foresee that the sword cannot remove the difficulty which caused secession ; and the peaceable separation of the nation into two would be infinitely better than the bloodshed and strife of war, and the generation of murder, agitation, and corruption that must follow the cessation of actual hostilities. A wiser philosophy and deeper insight into the nature of man will show the generations to come the great folly and wickedness of the late war. Wise men are now beginning to see them ; as time cools passion and develops the results, the folly and wickedness will become more and more obvious to everyone.

CHAPTER IX.

RELATION THE CHURCH AND MINISTRY ASSUMED TO THE WAR—
THE ASSASSINATION, ETC.

A FEW other matters, because in a general way they tend to illustrate the spirit of war, deserve a passing notice, though the matters themselves merit thoughtful consideration. Under this head, the first thing claiming attention is the policy the government used, to give the sanction of religion to the late war. For this purpose it conceived a scheme fraught with consummate skill, everything connected with the unnatural and sanguinary conflict favoring the scheme chosen. Slavery, which occasioned the war, is obnoxious to unanswerable objections. It violates all natural rights, and can be reduced to harmony with no principle of Christian morality. It is precisely such a question as, skilfully employed, could be used in the highest degree to play upon the passions of men. The government made of it both a Scylla and a Charybdis, and employed every fortuitous circumstance to give the war the sanction of religion. At first it proceeded slowly and cautiously, but firmly grasped every advantage gained. It took care not to anticipate popular sentiment, but every precaution was taken to hurry that sentiment onward to the proper climax. From the resources which the obnoxious institution of slavery afforded, the prejudices of the people were carefully but skilfully fed, and their passions were fanned and inflamed to the degree of intensity desired. And when all was wrought up to the requisite point, the whole was skilfully brought to bear upon the churches. The ministry was conciliated and given places of reward and profit in the army. Unusual days were appointed to be observed and unusual services of religion were required with direct reference to the war. The people were instructed to demand compliance with the services from the ministry. Even the general nature of the services was prescribed by the government, that they might take the form desired and give the war a religious sanction. The prescribed requirements were suited to mingle the elements of devotion with the passions suited to war; so prayer and hatred, devotion and revenge were thoroughly mingled, imparting to the mind, under its glow of excitement, an intense enthusiasm.

A twofold influence was brought to bear on the ministry : The government conciliated them, imparting to their minds false if not idolatrous notions of government; and then inflamed them with the idea that the occasion for the war was groundless, while the ground for it was a monstrous sin. Then, secondly, they were influenced indirectly through the people. Opinion is contagious. People can be made to breathe the sentiments and feelings of those who think for them. And, finally, the very spirit at Washington pulsated through the veins and arteries of those who drew their political breath from the leaders at the Capital. The same shibboleths, uttered in the same tone of voice, were used from one end of the land to the other. Each person seemed "wiser than seven men that could render a reason," and each seemed to understand just the view that God took of the war, and to comprehend the great problem that He was working out. And this presumptuous spirit was carried to the churches, and brought to bear upon the ministers. Thence the former tests of ministerial qualification were insufficient. It was not enough to preach Christ crucified. Cæsar idolized was added to ministerial duties, and the acceptance of the ministry was made contingent upon the new condition. The scheme was but too successful. The pulpit too faithfully echoed popular clamor, when the desired object was accomplished. Thence the purposes of avarice and ambition could be carried out boldly. Bearing the sanction of religion, the ministers employing their talents and position to mould the people and to consecrate them to the business of slaughter, the war attracted to itself all the energy of enthusiasm. The ministry were attached to the cause, first, by a misconception of the nature and office of civil government, arising from erroneous interpretations of Scripture; secondly, by false views of the sinful nature of slavery as compared with the sinful nature of war. And to any man who was in the country during the war, it is needless to say that the Church and the pulpit were amongst the most efficient aids the government had in the work of blood, and slaughter, and desolation. The pulpit preached, prayed, and exhorted, till the war did indeed seem to be conducted in the name and by the authority of religion. So, as might have been expected, the war had Rev. Privates, Rev. Captains, Rev. Majors, Rev. Colonels, and Rev. Generals. So far as possible everything wore the mien and aspect of religion. Churches were converted into recruiting offices, and the Sabbath was devoted to the services of war. Days of fasting and humiliation were appointed when the Federal arms met defeat, and days of thanksgiving when they had success; and with an ostentation of piety commanders were forbidden to *begin* a battle on Sunday, and to keep *that* day, as much as might be, from the irreverent desecrations of war. The whole scheme was an extraordinary one, and was accomplished with consummate skill, and amidst the shrieks and groans of the dying, and the sighs and sobs of anguished millions. Natural right, law and religion, were alike trampled in the dust; the sanctity of conscience was spurned, and the inoffensive and non-resistant were scorned, jeered, insulted, and outraged. The ministry carried their fiery zeal into ecclesiastic bodies, where their notions exploded in vapory speeches about their devotions to Cæsar, thereby outraging the tame determinations of the Apostle to know nothing but Christ crucified. They also converted ecclesiastic bodies into something kindred to political conventions, and in the name of Christ, construed the meaning of a secular constitution, announcing that the government was looking with anxious interest to the action the church should take in giving expression of encouragement to the government in conducting the war.—Then religious patriotism—a monster-birth—came into being, and culminated in the zenith of folly, by passing resolutions expressive of the fealty which the kingdom which is *not* of this world owed to the kingdom which *is* of this world. Alas! we forbear to put on paper the part the church acted, during the late war. The record of the church is sufficiently humiliating, and all true lovers of Christianity must deplore to the end of time the part the church acted. The consequences of that part are what might be expected—declension and moral prostration. The pulpit echoed the trumpet-tones of war; thousands would not attend upon the sanctuary; blood and slaughter took the place of the cross; and mistaking feelings of revenge as they mingled with those of worship, the worshipper could turn from the altar of prayer to butcher a brother upon the horrid battle-field without compunction. As a consequence the Church lost much of its spirituality, and the ministers much of their power for good, while both church and state lost moral tone and religious purity.

And a passing notice may be given to another ecclesiastic phase of the war, as it exhibits more strikingly the delusion under which men labored, and the extent to which they sought to give to war the sanction of religion. We allude to the custom of praying to God to give success to the sword. Ludicrous and irrational was the conduct of men, and hardly less wicked than irrational. By prayer and humiliation the respective parties sought to engage God in the horrid work to which they had committed themselves. They felt respectively great zeal in the cause in which they had engaged. And it is a law of the mind for great excitement to give vividness to the feelings and a glow to the emotions. To this generation the calamity of war was a new experience ; and imparted great vividness and tone to the intellectual activity, producing a reflex activity and intensity to the religious devotions, through animal sympathy. The plan of the war on both sides, assuming the properties of a religious persecution, the fiercest passions of the respective belligerents were mingled with their devotions, giving them fervor and intensity to their supplications, and misleading them to believe that their prayers were unusually effectual. But as God did not signally answer the fervent prayers, the supplicants were thrown into disappointment and confusion. The question was taken up and discussed in the religious journals, and one doctor of divinity ventilated it as he presided over a spiritual court. God promises to answer the fervent prayer of the righteous, yet He had not answered the war-prayers. There was mystery. Search was made for the cause. Finally, the Federal Constitution was examined. Fearful discovery! It was found to be *Atheistic*. The name of Deity is not in it. The mystery became plain. God was offended at the omission, and so would not engage in the war. Or it might be because there was fighting on Sunday. Ludicrous was the whole subject. Gnats were strained at, camels swallowed down.

Why God did not take part in the wholesale murder, *they* could not see, unless He was offended because His name was not in the Constitution, or because they violated the Sabbath by engaging in the ordinary business of butchering. At length, in his second inaugural, the Executive took up the question without signal success in solving it. Not remarkable for theological learning, mists and clouds obscured the mental vision. He could see that those who ought to be brethren were butchering each other ; and that those who were butchering each other possessed similar religious natures, and read the same Bible. He could see that God had given success to neither party. And precisely where he took up the mystery he laid it down. Pitiable was the confusion on the whole subject. The mote was seen, the beam escaped detection. To kill, rob, plunder, was right, but must not be done on Sunday. The name of God might be cursed and blasphemed, but He was sorely offended at His name's being omitted from the Constitution. Mocked with the outburst of passion, it was strange that He refused to hear these prayers. And thus ludicrous must be the attitude of all *fighting* Christians.

Kindred to the last mystery difficult of solution by fighting Christians, was another spectre called into being at the bidding of war. When the President was assassinated, half the nation was petrified in horror at the deed of revolting wickedness. And the horror was only equalled in astonishment at the iniquity of a rebellion which produced such results. " Now," it was said, " the people can begin to understand the wickedness of a cause producing such depths of depravity." And amazement and horror stood tiptoe. No one seemed to dream, much less think, that for four dreadful years, the whole nation, North and South, church and State, had been prayerfully cultivating the spirit whose climax is assassination. And the nation seemed as slow to discover that the spirit of war is the spirit of assassination, as to discover that God cannot take much interest in human butchery. And in the intensity of their impetuosity men neglected to reflect that, divided into two maddened parties by geographical lines, the whole country had for years been slaughtering each other on a scale nearly omnipotent, about the difference of an idea. Nor did they reflect that both parties had bad men, whose passions they were cultivating and whose moral sense they were weakening, till, becoming monsters, they would be capable of any deeds. Yet the fact is true. War always trains to the commission of most revolting crimes. War is itself a series of all revolting crimes. Assassination is but a branch of war in a form exquisitely disgusting and revolting, because we are less familiar with its savage accent and hideous deformity. Still, it is simply unbaptized war, uttering in the tongue of its native barbarity.

Put on it the dress of civilization; let it be baptized in the name of religion; come to us from the pulpit; be the foster-child of prayer, and come to the communion of the churches; and the language of its utterance will be quite as genteel as that of war. The taste of dealing so severely with the child while so fondly cherishing the parent, is questionable.

And assassination is the legitimate offspring of war. It is always the product of an exuberant growth of war-feelings. History assures us of the frequent births. And the steps from war to assassination are few and easy to trace. The mind only passes through a brief process of comparisons and analogies. If war is right for the purpose of settling a difference of opinion, how easy to believe it right to assassinate him who is in the way of attaining the end arising from the difference of opinion. And while the idea of the deed inspires the mind with emotions of disgusting horror, tested by any moral standard, it is as difficult to see how it is more abhorrent than war in its best estate. A man has no right to take his own life, nor can he innocently stake it in the chances of war. And the offer to risk it upon the stake, has the same moral guilt as to take it upon the risk. The purpose of war is to kill; and there being no right to kill, every act of killing must be an act of murder. The homicide of war is not reduced below murder because there is no special malice in the killing; because the general purpose to kill will constitute the murder. But this is the best phase of the case. It often occurs that the aim to kill is as deliberately taken in war, as the aim the assassin takes at his victim. We would not lessen the disgust of men at the crime of assassination, but we would intensify the abhorrence to war; and if from infancy, we were not familiar with the fiendish and infinite cruelties of war with little or no condemnation heard against it, the idea of slaying a man in war would fill the soul with that loathing and disgust which now possesses it at the idea of assassinating one. In both cases, it is hurrying a soul into the presence of God without right, and from motives unjustifiable and vicious. If the place, the manner and the circumstances of the assassination of President Lincoln, fill the sensitive mind with intense and unalleviated horror and disgust; the circumstances and death of General Lyon were suited to impress the soul with horror and humiliation no less intense and sorrowful.

In passing, another aspect of the question is not unworthy of notice. In the hostile conflict each belligerent accused the other of crimes infamous in the annals of war—crimes sufficiently revolting, were it not that each *justified* itself in doing what it denounced as barbarous in the other. But the tender mercies of a business whose so e purpose is to destroy and kill, are, at their best estate, sufficient to sicken the heart, and the difference in killing persons in war or by assassination, is too attenuated to be apprehended by any but those who fritter away the crimes of war by some accommodating casuistry. To me the whole business is cruel and unchristian war—the work of the carnal mind, inflamed into madness by the murderous passions; while the difference in destroying life in war and by assassination is rather a difference in the extent of the destruction than in the moral character of the act in itself. And the accusations of each party against the other, during the war, rende both fit subjects of the inspired invective exhibiting men's inconsistencies centuries ago: "Therefore thou art inexcusable, O man, whosoever thou art that judgest: for wherein thou judgest another, thou condemnest thyself for those that judgest doest the same things!" And the pungent application may be added: "And thinkest thou this, O man, that judgest them that do such things, and doest the same, that thou shalt escape the judgment of God?"

And ought we to pass the unique subject of war-ethics without calling before the attention of the really Christian public another matter impressive from the generous title by which it is introduced to our acquaintance at least. We allude to that entity bidden into existence at the nod of war, and called "The Christian Commission." But at this point we would be understood. Our profoundest sympathies are excited by the miseries of the common soldiers. They are hardly to blame for the existence of war. Imposed upon, deceived, and misled, they elicit only pity. The *blame* falls elsewhere, fixing the responsibility on those whose lusts induce the condition of war.

But let us consider the fact and office of "The Christian Commission." Called into being at the behest of war, what is it in its moral office? It is simply an elaborate and costly provision anticipative of appalling sin and suffering expected to attend a scheme of crime stupendous in its dimensions. And in all the realms of thought, we know not where to find a similitude of illustration. It is of its own kind. If we conceive of a person, who, while he forces and holds the hand of another in the blazing fire, calls loudly for a curative to assuage the pain, so soon as *he chooses* to release it from the consuming element, the instance would not be parallel; for we may *imagine* that *one* man might be so infatuated as to commit such an act. But in the real case, *million* o beings, by the force of that public opinion which s more powerful than physical force, hold *millions* of beings in the fiery flames of war, while they wildly shriek to themselves TO FLY with the Christian Commission to relieve the sins and sufferings produced by themselves. Or regarding the mere moral aspects of the question, it reminds one of a vast scheme projected for the purpose of alluring millions into some interminable seraglio, where, knowing that moral contagion must be produced, the scheme is accompanied by a vast preparation of remedies, in the form of tracts, sermons, Bibles, chaplains, and spiritual advisers, with the view of relieving or curing the contagion which all foresaw would result.

But all imagery fails adequately to portray the office of the Christian Commission. It must remain nondescript. Still, in the way of illustration, it reminds us of a sentim‿nt that found place in the war-journals of the day, taking the form of an argument for war after this style: War, causing destitution and want, crime and suffering, appeals to the feelings of benevolence and sympathy, awakening emotions of charity and influencing the people to give, that the evils of war might be mitigated. And that is the principle, perhaps, on which the Christian Commission stood, and the whole stands on the principle of doing evil that good may come.

Nor is it certain that the plan of army chaplaincies find support in principles which will endure the scrutiny of Scriptural and moral tests. Not coming to us by direct divine authority, their expediency is as questionable as their authority. In too many instances during our late war, the evidence is too free from doubt, that chaplains were not wholly free from considerations which are thought to influence men moved by carnal motives. While at home, some of them were shepherds without flocks; and so we should not be surprised, if such shepherds made into chaplains, should leave the mind in doubt whether they afforded much relief either to distressed consciences or suffering bodies. Indeed, careful reflection may leave the mind in serious doubt as to the propriety of chaplains at all, either in guiding the army to successful battle or the legislator to successful law-making. Christ authorized men to preach the cross. But the commission to the chaplain must be searched for aside from the authority of Christ. Compared with the age of Christianity, the institution of chaplaincies is a novel thing—the invention of human ingenuity, for the purpose of investing war with the mantle of religion, with the view of giving it the sanction of Christianity. Suppose a chaplain should pray and preach his regiment into the spirit of true Christianity, of what account would that regiment be in war? Could it lie, or steal, or kill? Could it burn and lay waste? Could it have feelings of revenge, hatred or malice? Such a regiment would pray for and forgive the enemy; and could it shoot him, run him through with a bayonet, or waste his property?

So during the late war much was said about Christians making the best of soldiers. This we can only believe by disbelieving the teaching of the Saviour. Men may call themselves Christians and others may call them Christians, and these may make good soldiers, even the best of soldiers. But such circumstances afford small evidence that they are *real Christians*. *Real* Christians must keep Christ's commands; and these demonstrably condemn as sinful every passion and feeling necessary to the existence of war. War is born of the sinful lusts, and cannot live apart from them; while a real Christian *cannot* be under the dominion of them. War and Christianity are moral contraries—as much contraries as right and wrong, sin and holiness. The spirit of Christianity is the exact antagonism of the spirit of war. If, therefore, Christians make the best of soldiers, the teaching of Christianity is not true, and Christianity itself is false. Wherefore it is not Christianity but the want of it that makes men the best of soldiers. And, surely, it requires but little reflection, if guided by the spirit and teaching of the Gospel, to show that the whole spirit, teachings, morality, machinery, and manipulations of war, are totally contrary to the teachings of Christ. No thought, or element, or principle, or feeling necessary to war, can be made to agree with the thoughts, elements, principles, feelings, and emotions necessary to Christianity.

CHAPTER X.

RELATION OF THE CHURCH AND MINISTRY TO WAR.

THE teaching and practice of the early Christians were unmistakably against all war; while the position of some acute and learned men, in after ages, is coincident with the teachings of the early Christians. Erasmus says, " Those who defend war, must defend the dispositions which lead to it; and these dispositions are absolutely forbidden by the gospel." The Bishop of Llandaff says, " War has practices and principles peculiar to itself, which ill quàdrate with the rules of moral rectitude, and are quite abhorrent from the benignity of Christianity. The prohibition of war by our Divine Master, is plain, literal and undeniable." The utterance of Dr. V. Knox is not less specific and pointed: " Morality and religion forbid war in its motives, conduct, and consequences." The language of Robert Hall is, " War is the temporary repeal of all the rules of morality."

Hence is derived the conclusion that, H. who defends war must, by the necessities of reason, defend the dispositions on which war depends. But war depends on lust, avarice, ambition, hatred, revenge, and other malevolent passions forbidden by Christianity. And so he who would consistently defend the practice of war, assumes to abrogate the injunctions of Christianity. And if we look to facts instead of professions, we find that those war men who grasp the whole subject of war, do nullify Christianity both in its conceptions and its practices; for it "is plain, literal, and undeniable," that " morality and religion forbid war in its motives, conduct, and consequences." In war, lying, fraud, robbery, stealing, treachery, and cruelty, are justifiable. Nay, by its authority, what may *not* men do? Indeed, there is a single boundary to the immoralities of war—the boundary that limits the capacity to commit wrong. And by the necessities of consistency, the advocate of war must defend all these immoralities; and, though he never saw a hostile field, nor heard a cannon roar, he is morally responsible for the consequences of the war which he advocates.

It is upon this moral principle that we hold the churches and the ministry responsible for the late terrific war in our country. For it is a well known fact that they made no persistent effort to stay the tide of war, but they did much to hasten it onward. The ministers of religion were generally the fiercest of war-men, and screamed and shrieked for the prosecution of the war. Claiming to be placed by the Lord Jesus upon the watch-towers of Zion, that they might sound the alarm at the approach of Zion's enemies, as the deadly enemy of war came within view, the watchers, instead of lifting up the voice and crying the alarm, opened the gates and bade war enter the sacred enclosures. And we must think that they were guilty of double deeds of unfaithfulness to Zion's King. They not only failed when it was their duty to warn, but they invited the enemy within th egates. Standing on the watch-tower, with the glass of God's word before their eyes, it was their duty to descry the enemy even afar off, and descrying, they should have sounded the clarion of alarm to those within Zion's city. For they were watchmen unto the house of Israel, but spake not to warn the wicked of his way, to save his life; and the wicked died in his iniquity; but his blood will God require at the hand of the watchman. Nevertheless, if they had warned the wicked of his way to turn from it; and the wicked would not turn from his way, he should have died in his iniquity; but Zion's watchmen should have delivered their souls. This is the spirit of God's laws. And under it are not the ministers of religion largely responsible for the lives destroyed in the late **war**, and for all the other consequences of it? They spake not to warn the people of the intense wickedness of war; but spake to hasten war; even by fiery words uttered from Zion's watch-towers, they added to the ferocity of the war. So that Zion's watchmen upon the towers of the house of Israel, became more wicked than the House of Israel. The high priests digged down the altars and committed sacrilege in the temple: the ministers of the Gospel of Peace became the minister of a gospel of war. At once they facilitated the onset of war, intensified its ferocity, and gave sanction to its iniquity. They are therefore responsible largely to God and humanity for the consequences of the war. Many already hold them responsible, and as reason is restored to her forsaken and dishonored throne, and the dreadful consequences of war stand in their appalling magnitude before the mind, reflecting men will more and more arraign the ministers of religion as being largely responsible for the fearful national calamities. The facts testifying the part the ministers of religion acted in the late tragedy of war in this country, stand recorded in the annals of men and among the archives of Heaven, against the ministers who, charged with the message of Peace, delivered such a message of bloodshed as conduced to plunge thirty or forty millions of people into the tragical horrors of an insane and fratricidal war.

And thus has nominal Christianity performed another horrid tragedy in the name of Christ—has, by the thunderbolts of war, forged another argument for the Jew, the Gentile, the infidel and the scoffer. And Christianity has thus become Her own worst enemy. Christ is wounded in the house of His friends. Christ's friends have crucified Him afresh, and put Him to open shame. Christ's friends have changed the truth of God into a lie, and have worshipped the creature (government) more than the Creator.

And now, watchmen, tell us of the night; what its signs of promise are? Your work is done. How has God blessed it? How has Zion prospered? In her have sons and daughters been born unto God? Have the bonds of love been strengthened, and has the commonwealth of Israel dwelt together in unity? Has it been a sight pleasant to the eye to behold how the Christians of this land have loved one another? Has the very God of *peace* that brought again from the dead our Lord Jesus, the great Shepherd of the sheep, through the blood of the everlasting covenant, made you perfect in every good work to do His will, working in you that which is well pleasing in his sight? Standing on the watch-towers of Zion, as they have extended into North and South, have you seen eye to eye, and walked hand in hand? Have you had love towards each other without dissimulation; and thanked God upon every remembrance of each other, always in every prayer making request with joy, for the fellowship of each other in the gospel, from the first day until now? Is God your record, how greatly you have each longed for the other in the bonds of Jesus Christ, that your love towards each other might abound yet more and more in the knowledge and love of Jesus Christ? Has every man not looked upon his own things, but every man also upon the things of others? Have you had the witness of the Spirit that you have passed from death unto life, because you, Northern and Southern brethren, have loved each other in the bonds of Christian affection? Have you endeavored to keep the unity of the Spirit in the bonds of *peace?* and with all lowliness and meekness, have you forborne with one another in *love?* Taking the Master's yoke, have you learned of Him; and been meek and lowly in heart? When reviled, have you not reviled again? When cursed, have you not cursed in turn; but have you returned good for evil? When smitten, have you turned the other cheek; and have you *loved* your *enemies*, and fervently prayed for them? Have you freely forgiven *them* as you hope God may forgive *you?* Have you freely allowed each other liberty of thought; and not sought the lives of each other about the treasures which moth may corrupt and thieves may steal? Forgetting the things of earth, has Zion been your chief joy, and her welfare dearer than the apple of your eye? That there might be no schism in the body of Christ, have you sought that the members should have the same care one for another? When one member has suffered, have all the members suffered with it; and when one member has been honored, have all the members rejoiced with it?

Alas! alas! for the watchmen of Zion and the house of Israel! Would to God that much of their behavior during the war were given to oblivion. Then would the millions of hearts they caused to bleed be mollified with ointment and assuaged of their suffering. Then would the body of Christ not have been rent in twain, and been now dismantled and lying prostrate in the dust. And would that the memory of their bitter words were wholly forgotten;—would that those whom their fierceness drove from Christ, were won back to Him;—and would to God that the hatred still in the church could be exchanged for love and fraternal fellowship. And O that the ministers before the Holy Altars, did not still show a war sp'rit little less than furious; and that their idolatrous love of Cæsar were much less intense in the watchmen of Zion and the house of Israel! But it is bitter—Oh! how bitter! to recall the conduct of Zion's watchmen and the house of Israel! Nothing but fidelity to truth could cause us to recount the mistakes they have made. But they have been many and great: They severed Zion, and tarnished her purity. They raved, blustered, execrated, and slaughtered. They persecuted and tore asunder. They were revengeful, malicious, and bloodthirsty. They assailed the innocent, and destroyed the helpless. They breathed out threatening and slaughter, and procuring letters of authority from their lusts and from the high priests of civil power, they arrested men and women and flung them into the noisome prison or brought them to the gallows. They offered not much less than a million victims on the idolatrous altar of government, and reduced hundreds of thousands from plenty to want, from wealth to poverty, and from pleasant homes to beggary. They invaded the sanctity of conjugal love, and deflowered the purity of connubial fidelity. They demoralized the national integrity, and caused the land to swarm with thieves, cutthroats, and assassins. They filled the nation with mourning, and houses not to be named with foul inmates. They put into every eye a tear, and upon millions of cheeks a stain. They caused men to be treacherous, and women to be corrupt. They made purity to mourn in solitude, and vice to riot openly. They caused religion to be feeble and timid, and crime to be daring and insolent. They opened wide the flood-gates of passion and sin, when crime and iniquity inundated the whole country. They practically for the time abolished the laws of morality, and substituted vice for virtue. They called bravery, valor and daring—the scorpions and hissing serpents that have stung mankind—by names inducing the weak and ignorant to regard them as Christian virtues, and perhaps to rely upon them for salvation. They substituted heathen for Christian morality; and made brute bravery on the battle-field take rank with the Christian bravery which seeks to conquer sin. They corrupted the youth, by teaching them the fell spirit of war, and thereby lowered the standard of morality. They destroyed the purity of the church and the *true* integrity of the state—abolished Christ's axioms of morality and the nation's axioms of freedom. They denied and smote with the sword the rights of free conscience and the fact of free government. They filled the nation with pensioners, and emptied the coffers from which they are to be fed. They hid more than half a million in bloody graves, put as many more on the nation's charity, disqualified hundreds of thousands to labor in the valuable pursuits of life, and heaped on the residue an oppressive national debt. They destroyed the people's means of acquiring wealth, and bound on them the iron yoke of taxation. They wrung from the people forty or fifty billions, and left them billions in debt. They brought on the nation appalling impurity, enshrouding it in gloom, and making the thoughtful tremble for the future. They have inured the nation to tyranny, and thereby may be preparing the way for despotism. They have inured the national mind to military rule, and thereby may be preparing the mind for other despotic measures. They have familiarized rulers to the use of usurped power, and the precedent may be employed for the nation's overthrow. They have imperilled many things dear to men, regarded both as citizens of the state and members of the church. They nearly turned the state and the church upside down ; while they cut loose and set adrift an avalanche of passion and fanaticism—destroying many valuable principles of belief and more pure rules of practice. They have,—it may be under the *delusive* guise of benevolence —struck the yoke of tolerable bondage from four millions of beings for whom Christ died, leaving them to a condition of horror even worse than their bondage. They have, to the full extent of their great influence, been the worst enemies the people, North or South, black or white, have had in the whole country. They have taken appearances for realities, names for things, sounds for sense. The superficial has been mistaken for the profound, zeal and fanaticism for thoughtful deliberation, and pseudo-benevolence and whining formality for statesmanship and Christian morality.

This may seem a severe philippic, but it is not more severe than true, and the conduct is just what enlightened reason would teach us to expect. Assuming to abrogate the laws of God, we could rationally look for nothing different. And that madness which could set free millions of mortal beings for whom Christ died, from centuries of unthinking bondage, without the preparation for their new condition suggested at once by Christian charity and the sheerest mercy, was only surpassed by the cruelty that put them in bondage, and eclipsed by the precipitancy that plunged the whole nation into the vortex of an insane and horrible war, in defiance of all the rules of morality, every principle of true policy, and every axiom of civil liberty. When the wicked rule, the people mourn. In tears and sorrow, clad in deep mourning, the people of this land mourn; how unnaturally wicked therefore have been those who have at once ruled and ruined this people. And North and South, we have been ruled and ruined—ruled by the influence of the watchmen of Zion and the house of Israel, and ruined by the sword in the hands of warriors against sin, under the Prince of Peace!

We charge all the desolation primarily on Zion's watchmen, because wielding mighty power, they made no effort to stay the tides of war. They sounded not the alarm, nor screamed in the ear of Israel. They could have seen the threatening tide, and should have stayed the advancing waves. They held their peace when they should have lifted up their voice. Nay, they lifted up their voice, not to stay but to hasten, the swelling tides of war. Therefore, as watchmen set over the house of Israel, the blood of those that died shall be upon them. Awful thought! But God pronounces the doom. Zion's watchmen must know, and knowing, they must do. They can save their own souls, only by warning others. But they were not only guilty in not warning, they positively went with the multitude to do evil. How sad to the lover of the true Israel!

And if in the headlong career of life, we pause and take a thoughtful survey of the transient and tragic scene around us, what language of men or angels can picture the emotions? More frequently than the watch ticks, a soul passes from time into eternity. Passed from time unprepared, millions of time-cycles, each exceeding the duration of the world's history, will find it suffering the unalleviated wrath of God, where the worm dieth not and the fire is not quenched. Nor can billions of earth's time-periods bring relief to the lost soul: it writhes still in anguish unmitigated, eats still the fruit of its own undoing. And upon the veracity of God, Christians profess to believe all this; while they mangle and slaughter each other about a *temporal* good—worse, about the *form* of a temporal good. Christians will slaughter wicked men, who might repent and be saved but for the sword in Christian hands. Christians will war and fight, slander and persecute each other, will divide the church, by their hatred and cruelty, will drive each other from the privileges of the sanctuary and the communion of the church—will harm their own and destroy the souls of others—will trample under foot the laws of the gospel and the precepts of Christ—will give ground for scoffing and occasion for sneering at Christ and His truth—will engage in all the sickening horrors of war, about the *form* of a governmental constitution, and its extension over a few miles more or less territory! Oh! we know not by what symbols of thought to portray the excess of such folly and madness. Words are beggared; imagery fails; the imagination is overpowered; the sensibilities faint; and humanity stands piteous and mute, transfixed with astonishment! When we enter the eternal world, how infinitely absurd must such things appear! Life itself but a *point* in the line of endless duration, infinitely drivelling must appear the scrambling, brawling, quarrelling, and fighting of men about the empty names of earth—glittering dust, undefinable honor, which is an *empty* name, a bubble in the air, the *ignis fatuis* which cannot be overtaken. Surely, surely, it is all madness.

In this connection let us again allude to the period in the history of the church, when the nations shall literally learn war no more, but when they shall exchange hostile implements for domestic ones. The church contemplates that as the period of triumph and glory to the King in Zion—the period when *His* scepter shall sway from sea to sea, and His Kingdom shall extend from the river to the ends of the earth; when the mountain of the Lord's House shall be established, that the nations of the earth shall flock to it, and the children of men shall seek refuge therein;

when the wolf shall dwell with the lamb; and the leopard shall lie down with the kid; and the calf, and the young lion, and the fatling together; and a child shall lead them; when the cow and the bear shall feed, while their young ones lie together, and the lion shall eat straw like the ox; and the sucking child shall play upon the hole of the asp, and the weaned child shall put his hand upon the cocatrice's den: then shall the people not hurt nor destroy each other in the Lord's holy mountain; for the earth shall be full of the knowledge of the Lord, as the waters cover the sea; and they shall beat their swords into plowshares and their spears into pruning-hooks, and nation shall not lift sword against nation, neither shall they learn war any more. The Christians of the world observe an evening of the Week of Prayer, calling upon God to hasten the realization of these sublime prophecies. The church exults in contemplation of this time; good men pray that it may be hastened; and the Christian world stretch forward in expectation, to catch the first thrilling and subduing note of that peaceful reign. In the sanctuary, the minister becomes as a flame of fire in the meteor flashes of eloquence, as he touches and is touched by the entrancing theme. The whole soul of the church leaps out in the fervors of prayer, that the Head of the church would ride upon the wings of the wind and make his triumphant chariot overturn, overturn, and overturn, going forth conquering and to conquer, till the Prince of Peace shall assume the throne of Universal Dominion: yet amazing, infinite inconsistency! Ere the subduing tones of eloquence cease to bathe the soul in the dew-drops of heavenly peace, or the words of pathos cease their echo between the walls of the sanctuary, or the incense of prayer reach the throne of God, those tones of melting pathos are turned into screams for blood and war; and the hand that was uplifted in tearful supplication, grasps the sword to begin the work of desolation and death. —And such is the consistency of the church of God. And how, O Christians! are the days of peace to come to Zion?

Are they to come in spite of Christian effort? Shall Christians fight and slay till fighting and slaying introduce triumphant peace? Might not wicked men as well curse and swear till cursing and swearing bear them through the pearly gates into the Holy City? Might not the minister as well curse and swear from the pulpit, expecting thereby to turn the wicked to a holy life? Ah! it is all flagrant inconsistency, reminding one of the ambassador of God, who, sent to the world alienated from the life of God, with the olive branch of peace, while the glories of the cross are streaming from the Throne, eternity blazing with overwhelming solemnity before his face, could turn with leisurely indifference and drag into the pulpit topics from the fetid pool of party-politics, while thousands of undying souls are trembling upon the verge of the abyss. Think of this, O minister of God! You profess to have a message from the Imperial Court of Heaven; and can you be a trifler, neglect to deliver that message, and turn aside to a war-message from a potsherd of earth? Commissioned to proclaim peace on earth, good will to men, and to aid in bringing about the era of peace, can you despise the sublime mission, and deal in words of burning taunt, to appease the malice of virulent passion, arising from the ambition of earthly rulers? It is verily a drivelling process which would eclipse all belief were it not pressed upon our attention by actual observation.

And during our late war, not a small act of guilt in the church lay in the fact that she set up a false standard of Christian morality. Ignoring the virtues of Christianity by overshadowing them with the ethics of war, she let loose upon society a den of foul critics, who, with impudence, assailed all those who would not comply with the demands of the heathenish standard set up by these miscreants, who, in some instances, wearing the sacerdotal gown, had less fidelity to Christ than to the horrors of the war. I know of no decorous language by which the meanness of political preachers can be adequately described. I say it boldly.

During the late war, though the character of a person might be as pure as it falls to the lot of erring mortals to possess, yet if he esteemed it his duty not to meddle with politics, he was assailed and persecuted as if he was a rogue and a criminal. North and South the same spirit prevailed. Neither conviction nor conscience formed a safeguard to the man who wished to stand aloof from and take no part in the horrors of the war. It makes the heart ache and feel sick to recall the conduct of Christian people during that reign and storm of terrible passion. And how true it is that wars come of the lusts which war in the members of men! Ah! the mind turns away from the contemplation of the frightful scenes through which the church lately passed. May such scenes be witnessed no more forever.

CHAPTER XI.

FINAL GENERAL REFLECTIONS ON THE SUBJECT OF WAR.

WE now appeal to the common-sense of mankind for confirmation of the views given of the whole subject treated herein. And tested by reason and Christian morality, can there be any doubt that these views are correct? And could not these views be made practical in real life? Suppose that a portion of the time and energy which are employed in exciting a war-spirit, were employed in explaining the true office of government and the social and moral obligations arising therefrom, would not the substantial views advocated herein command the approbation of mankind? But the wide difference in the views herein expressed and those generally entertained, is freely confessed. Why is it so? It is owing to the mistaken notions of men respecting human government. And did we suffer ourselves to derive our views of the nature and office of civil government from men's writings, from tradition, from the discourses and even the sermons of some—bidding adieu to reason and conscience and the lessons and teachings of the Word of God—we should be induced to regard civil government as the most important and sacred thing with which intelligent and responsible mortals are conversant. As we trace the words and observe the conduct of rational beings, we are overwhelmed with mingled astonishment and horror. And if the words and conduct were confined to *wicked* men, we might satisfy ourselves by regarding them as influenced by Satan. But this state of the case is far from being true. The *church of God*, the elect children of Zion, are as deeply implicated often as the most abandoned reprobates. And looking at the behavior of those professing to be the subjects of the Prince of Peace, the heart bleeds of anguish. How clearly their conduct shows that they love most *this* world ! Wistfully gazing on the things which are seen and perishable, they lose sight of the things which are unseen and imperishable. Attaching vague and undefined notions to civil government, there is excited in the mind an impetuous and deadly enthusiasm, which never pauses to reflect, nor scruples to employ such means as the frenzied mind may suggest to preserve the *form* of it. And a doubt often lingers in the mind, as to whether the zeal of Christians may not, in relation to this subject, be in the inverse ratio to the clearness of the views they entertain of the nature of civil government. It is certain that a very small portion of mankind entertain accurate and well defined views of the nature of government, and still, for the sake of saving the mere form of it, they will hazard health and life, with all that is dear in time or valuable in eternity. Yet this is not done for the sake of government itself ; because that is as indestructible as human nature, having its foundation in it ; but it is done on account of the merest unessential *form* of it. Nor do men only hazard their own all for two worlds ; they hesitate not to perpetrate every kind of crime known to depraved humanity, in the attempt to save the form, which, of course, by *that* means they must fail to do. Deception, lying, and cruelty ; burning, desolating, and laying waste ; the destruction of men, women, and children,—the helpless, the aged, the afflicted—these are the sport and pastime of war—the merriment and entertainment of a *brilliant* campaign or a *glorious* raid. And to crown this coterie of cruelties, committed by Christian men, Christian ministers become the generals and heroes who command such horrid deeds to be perpetrated upon Christian people. Contemplated seriously, the soul revolts with intense horror! It is the professed followers of the Prince of Peace murdering the professed followers of the Prince of Peace, with all imaginable indignities, about a form of attaining a worldly good? Abhorrent thought! Soul-sickening contemplation.

If the reasoning in these pages is correct, we would entreat Christian people to pause and think about this matter; and while they are pausing, we would ask them, *Where they find the warrant for plunging into a business whose necessary consequences eclipse in horror any picture the pen can paint or the imagination can conceive?* Good government, we trust, we do not undervalue. Yet it is only a a *worldly* good; and the *form* of it is simply the work of men—is the work of men as much as the erection of a house or the construction of a road. This is a subject which, in a pre-eminent degree, each man should, in view of his responsibility to God, consider for himself. He should employ the mind that God has given him, remembering that what men tell us is by no means always true. *We* should learn to employ our own faculties. *Men* have held and taught all manner of absurdities and superstitions. Even the learned, so-called, have been deluded and duped hardly less than the ignorant. For the most learned are ignorant about some things that are very simple. And while the hearts of men are wrong, it is hard for their heads to be right. Depart from the Word of God, and we launch upon an unknown sea. Apart from the Word of God, and a people dwell in the midst of confusion. Look at the nations of Rome and Greece. Their follies and superstitions nearly transcend belief. And look at the Jewish nation in the time of our Saviour. Nay, cast the eye upon the nations of the present time. Observe their conduct; note their follies; mark their superstitions—the blinding influence of selfishness and bigotry. See how, in the name of truth, they persecute it; how, in the name of liberty, they bring it to the stake; how, in the name of religion, every sentiment of charity is outraged, and every injunction of God is defied; and how God's children butcher each other about a worldly good! For centuries men have been scorned and persecuted, if they had the originality or the daring to snap the fetters which have bound both the souls and bodies in the traditions of the past. In this Christian land, within the last decade, men have been prosecuted and imprisoned for denying that God sanctions the horrors of war, as the means of establishing or sustaining government. And, Christian reader, will you consider these things, and then say whether you will follow men in the pursuit of truth? or, disregarding for a time the babel they have produced by their heathenish processes, will you endeavor to use the reason and conscience which God has given *you* ? Will you remember, too, that age added to error cannot convert it into truth? and that though millions believe falsehood, it will be falsehood still, though believed for thousands of years? For if the lie Satan uttered to the mother of mankind had been believed by mankind from that day to this, would it not still be a lie?

And now allowing the mind to do its own thinking, let us return to the moral character of war waged in the interests of the *form* of a government. Is it not the invincible conclusion of reason, that *men* make constitutions and the forms of government? And with the same moral character might not any form be made? For what *form* does *God* require men to make? Are not all forms matters of simple choice with men? Is religious or moral obligation at all involved? If a people were about to erect a government, might they not make a Democracy, a Republic, a Monarchy, with the same moral character? And would the *form* of government chosen any more affect their moral character than the form in which a man should construct his residence would effect his moral character? Each would be a simple act of preference, having no regard to moral qualities. Both are made for worldly comfort, and have the same moral qualities. Yea, both are made for the same *general purpose*, and are invested with the same essential *moral* attributes. The one differs from the other in being more general—in including the worldly good of a greater number. Upon reflection nothing is more evident than this. For where is the moral element in the *form* of civil government, not in the *form* of your domicil. And where is the element in the form of government that allows the sins and calamities of war to preserve it? Where can the justification be found but in the cruel usages of men? And whence come those usages?—whence but from the ages of heathenism? Can a real Christian find authority in his feelings or in the suggestions of reason?—in the teachings of Jesus or an Apostle, or even in the inferences of a large and philosophical view of self-interest? In none of these sources can authority be found for war. But startled by so novel and bold a declaration, the question may be asked, Whence did the nations have the authority to engage in war? The answer must be, The authority came from their lusts. They could, they did, have no other. All the customs of war are exotics to a Christian soil; they are indigenous to the soil of paganism. When these customs are mingled with the benign usages of Christian morality, no wonder that the belligerent lands of Christendom present so strange a mosaic of morality, and such a jargon of uncouth sounds as the following: "Christian wars," "Christian soldiers," "Christian generals," and "Christian heroes." Of course, as the corelates, we have *Christian hatred, Christian vengeance, Christian murder,* and *Christian patriotism.* And we have become possessed of a rigmarole of war-rhetoric, as indecent and shocking, when mingled with the language of Jesus, as the idolatry of the Goths or the bloody rites of Montezuma, would be in a temple dedicated to the worship of the Prince of Peace. For if any thought fills the mind with unutterable horror, it must be that of slaughtering a human being, and sending his soul unprepared before God. Thrilling and sickening is the contemplation of it. From it the soul recoils in utter abhorrence. The disgust is supreme. The slain is *now* full of life and hope. *Then*, in a twinkling, he is cut off, and sent into the dreadful unknown. Then, in the next twinkling, the slayer slain, his naked spirit is hurled into the abyss. And this is done by Christian hands, about the form of temporal good—is done under circumstances which exclude the possibility of the slayer's knowing whether he or the slain is right. Christians of the same household of faith—and whether so or not would make no difference—meet each other sword in hand, and, at the same instant, each plunges the reeking blade to the other's heart, when, falling face to face, their spirits hasten into the presence of God. Do those earth-enraged spirits fight on *after* each has sent the other out of the flesh? Clinched in burning hatred still, each exerting the utmost power to destroy the other, do they fly into the presence of the Prince of Peace? Are both saved or both lost? If saved, as the accursed blade of each touched the other's heart, remitting the soul from the body, do they clasp glad hands in love, rejoicing in the *riches* of grace, which impelled each to thirst for the other's blood about the *riches* which moth and rust may corrupt? Or if both are lost, with horrid curses and execrations and their earthly rage indefinitely increased, amid the hoarse jeers of the lost, are they hurled into outer darkness, each cursing the other for his *too* early doom in hell, by the malignant hatred created by earth's horrid wars? Have we any reason to believe that the spirit's leaving the body changes its temper beyond earthly scenes? Will not those who die rankling with hatred in the soul, hate on *in* eternity? and hate on *through* eternity? And would not hatred, malice, and all the infernal tempers necessary to war, kindled into flame, create, in the consciousness, the very fires of hell, whose smoke and torment could only cease with the change or annihilation of the soul itself?

We are sure that Christian people have not duly studied the horrible business of killing each other. Oh! unutterably revolting thought! Returning, for a moment, to the case where two kill, each the other: suppose one a Christian, the other not. From intimations of Scripture, we may infer that each will know the other's doom. What must be the thoughts of the saved spirit, as it beholds the doom of the lost, and hears its wails, sent to perdition by its own infernal instrumentality? And, to indulge the imagination, one can almost hear the sepulchral execrations of the lost soul, as they echo across "the river" and reverberate dolefully in the ears of him whose hated blade had done the fatal deed. And were the belief permitted, we could imagine the saved soul as wailing in heaven, during a billion of earth's time-periods, over the folly of human creatures in butchering and sending each other to the regions of the lost. For my own part, I am free to say, that if every government on the earth was, in value, a million fold what all the governments on the earth are, I would not kill a man, make his wife a widow, his children orphans, and send his soul into future torment, to save them from being divided into as many separate governments, as there are square miles embraced within their limits. Nay, I would not send a deathless soul to a dreadful doom, for the material universe, though I could be its sole monarch for a billion ages.

But pitiable is the consideration for which men will plunge into war. Frenzied by a catchword and prompted by an inconsiderable bribe in the form of a bounty, with a few paltry shillings a month, will induce them to slaughter each other by hundreds of thousands. Obliged by the law of Christ to love each other as they love themselves, yet, for a contemptible sum of money, they are hired to slaughter their fellows in countless numbers. Suppose a sum of money were offered to a man truly honorable, to buy him to the deed of slaying his own wife,—with what intemperate scorn would he reject it! —while each additional higher bid could only aggravate the indignant and scornful rejection; and so the greater the bid, the greater would be the insult to his sense of honor. The single idea that he could be bought to an atrocious deed, would ravish his soul with the loathing scorn for which language affords no expression. Yet every

Christian man must see that the law of Christ makes no difference in the obligation due to wife or a fellow-man. That law makes the wife as part of one's self, while it obliges to love a fellow as one loves himself. Hence the law of Christ obliges that one should as indignantly scorn a bribe to kill a fellow in war as to kill the wife at home. And the *form*, or *interest*, or *honor* of *government*, should no more bribe us to the commission of crime than any other form of bribe.

But we must inquire, Why are the souls of men, reeking in blood at a brother's hand, remitted thus into the presence of God? Is it through the wantonness of cruelty? The mind refuses to accept that solution. There must be some illusive view of duty. There is somewhere an overpowering imposition; there lurks somewhere a secret subtile poison of thought which induces the horrid sins. Nolitions and volitions precede powder and lead; and the former are poisoned before the latter are used. The poison consists in the views men entertain of worldly good. And then false views lead to false practices. An error in the head leads to error in life. One form of good men deify; and having made it a god, they worship it with human sacrifice. This god is civil government. The steps to this idolatry are not hard to trace. The first error is the depravity of the heart shown in the love of *this* world. The second is in the false notions of the head as to the means which may be used in gaining this world. The third includes the mode of carrying the notions of the head into practice. And deadly errors being in the fountains of the soul, the springs of thought and feeling being poisoned, the streams flowing out are only bitter waters,— oh! how intensely bitter wormwood and gall—rivers of blood—horrid war!

Charity constrains to this view of the subject; for we must think that, misled, deceived by false views of duty, some real Christians have been induced to engage in war; as some real Christians have been induced to engage in persecution. Yet, engaging in war is no less abhorent or to be reprobated because real Christians may engage in it. And the law of Christ affords as much authority for idolatry or persecution as for war. The repugnance of real Christian affection to war must be as great as its repugnance to idolatry or to persecution. The repugnance of real Christian affection to the horrid cruelties of war may be illustrated. In order to illustrate it, let us first glance at the affections on which war depends, although frequently referred to heretofore. How pertinently the Apostle James puts the argumentative interrogatory ;—" From whence come wars and fightings amongst you ? Come they not hence, even of your lusts that war in your members ?" And did *men* ever wage a war that did not come from their idolatrous lusts ? Without rampant passion, godless ambition, vehement lust, burning malice, hellish malignity, deadly revenge, war would be a natural and moral impossibility. And men act in view of these passions when they wish to engender a " war-feeling." For what is a *war-feeling ?* what but all these nefarious passions warring in the carnal members ? and so creating that heartlessness which can laugh at suffering, make merry at tears, and remorselessly butcher those who stand in the way of realizing the ends of godless lust ? Accordingly, the means used in producing a " war-feeling " are tissues of wormwood and gall, envenomed appeals to hellish passions ; shibboleths, surcharged with the foulest ribaldry ; and all set ablaze by the fires of hell. And it is by these foul means that conscience is dosed to sleep or frightened into silence, and reason is hurled from her throne amid the wild din and furious uproar. Nay, till proper reason, " Heaven's highest arbiter in man," is drowned in the deluge of passion ; till lust usurps nearly supreme dominion over the soul, a man is ill-fitted for the services of war, and is quite unsuited to be a great Captain or a successful Conqueror. And war being born of the lusts, the more completely the lusts domineer over the rational soul, the better is the warrior, the braver and more daring the hero. The great means of war is brute-force; and so the more nearly the noble man can be made like the ignoble brute, the more nearly perfect is the "war-feeling."

Now let us contrast this war-feeling with Christian feeling. To illustrate we may take the tender John, whom Jesus loved. Old, he has witnessed many of the follies of the world. His character rendering him offensive to human government, he is banished to Patmos. Nearly a hundred years old, his hair like the wool, he *realizes* that the time of his departure is at hand. His soul, calm as the light, mellowed by the power of grace, is soothed with delight as it approaches the pearly gates. The celestial Canaan is coming into view. An occasional glimpse is caught of things within the veil, while gentle sounds float from beyond "the river." Already are kindled in the bosom the flames of heavenly love, as a stream of light is thrown from beyond the separating veil.

And now, nearly conformed to the law of love,—the passions and lusts that give life to war destroyed,—how would the sainted John's feelings have comported with war-feelings? Standing on the confines of *the sea of-glass*, and about to bathe in it, what would have been *his* views of the ever-changing *forms* of human government? In the moment of such contemplation, what would have induced him to send a soul to wail eternally in the world of the lost? What would he have thought of *patriotism*, a *bounty*, and *monthly pay*? For these would he have felt like entering the army?—But the feeling formerly described is a war-feeling. John's feeling would be a Christian feeling. Is there no repugnance between them? The one is the lusts of this world in the ascendant. The other is reason restored—is the soul made meet for the kingdom. The one is humanity schooled in lust, with this world rampant. The other is humanity schooled by Christ, with this world overthrown. The one is the fruit of war. The other is the fruit of grace. No contrast is more perfect than that between a war-feeling and a Christian feeling.

But we are not left to imagination as the means of learning the feelings of the Christian, as standing on the shores of time, he contemplates the things of eternity. Doctor Timothy Dwight, the acute thinker, profound scholar, and mature Christian, was once brought to the verge of the grave, where, possessed of perfect consciousness, he lay, for days together, contemplating the things of time and those of eternity. His disease taking a change, he rose from that bed of death, and delivered to his students a sermon which was prepared in his mind, while lying and looking across into the eternal world. With the appearance of one who had returned wearing the drapery of the grave, the soul bathed in the dews of heaven, in eloquent and pathetic tones he uttered the following impressive strain: "To him,"—alluding to the true character of worldly good—" who stands on the brink of the grave and the verge of eternity, who retains the full possession of his reason, and who at the same time is disposed to serious contemplation, all these things become mightily changed in appearance. To the eye of such a man, their former alluring aspect vanishes, and they are seen in a new and far different light.

"Like others of our race, I have relished several of these things, with at least the common attachment. Particularly, I have coveted reputation and influence to a degree which I am unable to justify. Nor have I been insensible to other earthly gratifications; either to such as, when enjoyed to moderation, are innocent; or such as cannot be pursued without sin. But in the circumstances to which I have referred, all these things were vanishing from my sight. Had they been really valuable to any supposable degree, their value was gone. They could not relieve me from pain; they could not restore me to health; they could not prolong my life; they could promise me no good in the life to come. What were these things to me?

"A person circumstanced in the manner which has been specified, must necessarily regard these objects, however harmless or even useful they may be supposed in themselves, as having been hostile to his peace, and pernicious to his well-being. In all his attachment to them, in all his pursuits of them, it is impossible for him to fail of perceiving, that he forgot the interests of his soul and the commands of his Maker, became regardless of his duty and his salvation; and hazarded, for dross and dirt, the future enjoyment of a glorious immortality. It is impossible not to perceive that in the most unlimited possession of them, the soul would have been beggared and undone; that the gold of the world would not have made him rich; nor its esteem honorable; nor its favor happy. For this end, he will find that nothing will suffice but treasures laid up in heaven; the loving kindness of God; and the blessings of life eternal.

"Let me exhort you, my young friends, now engaged in the ardent pursuit of worldly enjoyments, to believe that you will one day see them in the very light in which they have been seen by me. The attachment to them which you so strongly feel, is unfounded, vain, full of danger and fraught with ruin. You will one day view them from a dying bed. There, should you retain your reason, they will appear as they really are. They will then be seen to have two totally different faces. Of these you have hitherto seen but one: that, gay, beautiful, and alluring, as it now appears, will then be hidden from your sight; and another, which you have not seen, deformed, odious, and dreadful, will stare you in the face, and fill you with amazement and bitterness. No longer pretended friends and real flatterers, they will unmask themselves, and appear only as tempters, deceivers, and enemies, who stood between you and heaven; persuaded you to forget God, and cheated you out of eternal life."

And just what the hero, reeking with the blood of slaughtered thousands, is in comparison with the heavenly

Dwight, speaking from the confines of the grave; so is the fierce and cruel spirit of war in comparison with the pure and gentle spirit of Christianity. But, reader, you will soon stand on the line dividing between time and eternity. If a true disciple of the Master, what will be your feelings at that awful moment? Lingering yet, on mortal shores, and catching a ray of celestial light, rapt in a transport of delight, how think you your feelings will comport with those of war? Could war-rhetoric *then* fill your mind with the lust of this world, and your heart with the fell revenge of war? Would you be racked with desire to bayonet a brother, whose notions of a worldly good differed from yours? Ah! no. At that awful hour, the Christian beholds things in a far different light—beholds them in their true light. Then the idolatry of this world disappears, and things appear as they are. And earthly things are truly tested only as they are seen in the light of the future world. In sober thoughtfulness, the things of this world have but little value. Yet how Christian men will butcher each other about them! In the light of higher reason, the act is at once infinitely absurd and infinitely wicked. It is the creatures of eternity slaughtering each other about the things of time! Creatures, destined to live during eternity, fight and kill each other about a bubble which disappears too quickly to be distinctly seen. Infinite folly, madness immeasurable!

Now the law of Christ requires the best feelings of the heart always to be in exercise, and such feelings are opposed to the necessary spirit and principles of war. And does not this consideration demonstrate that the necessary spirit and principles of war are violative of the teachings of Christianity? For by the laws of Christ, may the dying feel one way and the living another? Does that law exact one feeling for the loving John or the dying Dwight, and another for the ambitious hero and the bloody conqueror? Is the law of Christ not one for all ages and all men? Yea, it is one for all. It is always and everywhere the law of *love*. Its obligations are perpetual. At every moment of life, every rational human being is obliged to be under its influence—in life or in death—in sickness or in health—on the battle-field or on the death-bed—the obligation is the same. And he who preaches love in the pulpit, and out of it teaches that one may slay his neighbor, is as inconsistent as he who exhorts to temperance from the pulpit, but ceaselessly reels in intoxication upon the streets. So he who comes from the field of battle and says he is glad that he does not *know* that he has slain any one, admits to his own conscience that the war in which he has been engaged is wrong. For his heart condemns him. And is not God greater than his heart? Will not He too condemn him? And who can abide the day of God's wrath? It is fearful to fall into the hands of the living God! Alas! for heroism in the wrath-avenging day.

That Christian people should give the least sanction to the fell spirit of war is amazing. But just here is the trouble. If war was made to stand upon its cold naked principles of heathenism with its practices of barbarism, together with its revolting idolatry, it would speedily disappear from the earth. But that is not so. Christians give it the sanction of Christian morality. The church baptizes it with a Christian name. Christians reject the spirit, laws, and plain teaching of Christ, refuse His protection and seek their own protection in swords, powder, and bullets. They renounce promised divine protection, and *act* as if there was no God. We may properly elaborate this idea a little. God offers men the protection of His Providence. *In him we live and move and have our being.* He is the moral Governor of the world. To reject the protection of His providence, is to reject His moral government. Then to institute a providence formed of swords and bayonets, powder and bullets, is really and practically to abjure God from the universe. What more or less is such conduct than practical atheism? What is it but the renunciation of God and His government, and the adoption of another government established upon swords and bayonets, guns and bullets? It is logically and rationally declaring that we have no confidence in the moral government of God. And what is that but atheism? The use of bravery, chivalry and brute force, in defence either of our persons or of the nation, is but the use of atheism in different forms—are different forms of acting as if there was no moral Governor of the world—no God to care for us and protect us. Nor is it seen how this conclusion can be escaped. Nor can we avoid the profound conviction that the Christian churches in the United States act the part of practical atheists in rejecting the moral government of God as the protection of human government. It matters little what people profess. By their fruits ye shall know them. If they reject the idea that God will protect them against harm, and seek to protect themselves, by means which God has forbidden, they are virtually rejecters of Him—are virtually and practically atheists; since they believe and act as if there was no God. The principle is the same with nations and individuals. The individual who, complying with the requirements of God's laws, is unwilling to seek protection in the Providence of God, but seeks protection in the forbidden use of knives and pistols, acts as if there was no God—virtually and by his conduct says, that he has no confidence in God; and so rejects both His counsel and protection. The Christian idea is, We are earnestly to seek to know our duty, and faithfully to perform it; and then in so doing, God will lead us into real duty, and therein protect us by His providence, so far as best comports with his purposes concerning us. Anything else than this is, and can be, only practical atheism. And as it is with individuals, so it is with nations. For the nation that does not seek its protection in truth, justice, and probity, under the protection of God, but seeks protection in the terrors of the sword and the desolations of war, is a nation of practical atheists. Now, judging by this rule, what must be our conclusion about our own nation? As a people, are we not real atheists? It can hardly be doubted. What confidence have we in God's protective care? What confidence that, if we trust Him, He will work out the problems involved in our national existence, without our seeking their solution in the terrible enginery of war? The thinking mind must admit, that the employment of force, as the means of national protection, contrary to, and in defiance of, the teaching of the revealed will of God, is practical atheism. Nor can the thinking mind deny, if honest, that the great majority of the people in this land act, in this respect, as if there was no God. And the act of waging war—in the absence of a command from God—necessarily rejects the idea that God is a moral Governor of the world; and so the people who yield an intelligent and hearty assent to such a war, naturally act the part of atheists. But atheism practically and intelligently embraced, naturally, perhaps necessarily, produces all forms of sin and crime. It is thus, that, when theology becomes atheistic, the morals of the people become dissolute. It is thus that the reign of atheism in France was the reign of undisguised dissoluteness and bloody terror. And it is thus that vice and crime, and shameless prostitution, in all their revolting forms, revel and riot where the spirit of war possesses the minds of a people. We witnessed this state of things during our late war. The churches seemed impotent for good. Everywhere the practical atheism disseminated its immoral and deadly influences. In the family, in social life, in the church, the upas breath and baleful touch of war spread spiritual leprosy and moral disease.

But why should we not expect this consequence? It is the logical and natural sequence of the reasoning of war-men in Christian lands. The revealed will of God most surely forbids the spirit and practice of war; and so to construe it as to derive from it a sanction for the spirit and practice of war, necessarily amounts to practical atheism. It construes God out of the universe, dethrones Him from the government of the world, and substitutes in His stead a blind and bloody god of war—the besmeared Moloch—the horrid image of mere brute power. And still, as we have said elsewhere, it must be confessed that the whole *idea* and *practice* of war are entirely consistent with the *theory* of it. Its fundamental conception ignores the idea of a God of intelligence and beneficence, presiding in wisdom over intelligent beings fitted by Him to be governed through their rational natures. Its fundamental conception is therefore atheistic. It at once ignores the fact of God's existence, as a wise moral Governor of the world, and the fact of man's intelligent moral nature fitting him to be governed by the laws appointed by God for the very end of his government.

Because the idea of war is atheistic, we find, just as reason would teach us to expect, that the entire system and theory of war come into conflict with the whole teaching of God in revelation. It is hence that "war repeals all the moral laws of God," and gives license for the perpetration of all forms of crime. And it is hence that the principles of war are the principles of atheism; and that when the knowledge of the Lord shall cover the earth, swords shall be beaten into plowshares and spears into pruning hooks, and men shall learn war no more. That the teachings of the gospel are the teachings of peace, there can be no doubt in the mind of the really thoughtful Christian. Thence the simple question for Christians to consider is, Whether they will or will not put themselves into harmony with the teachings of the Great Master on this subject. If they will, they must become real peace-men. If they will not, they must take position with the practical atheist. Even Christians have been long serving other gods. Is it not so, Christian readers? Have you not long bowed before the image of the horrid Moloch?—long trusted more to the sword for protection than to the living God? And may we not fittingly say to you as was said to the people of God of old? And if it seem evil unto you to serve the Lord, choose you this day whom you will serve, whether the gods which your fathers served that were on the other side of the flood, or the gods of the Amorites, in whose land you dwell: But as for me and my house, we will serve the Lord.

THE END.